Philip Schaff, Samuel Macauley Jackson, Henry Codman Potter

The American Church History Series

Vol. 3

Philip Schaff, Samuel Macauley Jackson, Henry Codman Potter

The American Church History Series
Vol. 3

ISBN/EAN: 9783337766962

Printed in Europe, USA, Canada, Australia, Japan

Cover: Foto ©ninafisch / pixelio.de

More available books at **www.hansebooks.com**

A HISTORY

OF THE

CONGREGATIONAL CHURCHES

IN THE UNITED STATES

BY

WILLISTON WALKER

PROFESSOR IN HARTFORD THEOLOGICAL SEMINARY

(*Third Edition*)

The Pilgrim Press

Congregational Sunday-School and Publishing Society

BOSTON AND CHICAGO

CONTENTS.

A HISTORY OF THE CONGREGATIONAL CHURCHES IN THE UNITED STATES.

BY

WILLISTON WALKER,
PROFESSOR IN HARTFORD THEOLOGICAL SEMINARY.

BIBLIOGRAPHY.

Congregationalism has always inclined to publication, and the number of works really germane to the history of the denomination is enormous and constantly increasing. The connection of the body with the settlement of New England and the opening up of the West has led to some treatment of the features of this story by almost every writer on the beginnings of the northern United States, and the intimacy which marked the relationship of the Congregational churches to the civil governments during much of their American life renders town and colonial histories, legislative records, and even personal journals scarcely less sources of religious than of secular history. Fortunately for the student of Congregationalism, a bibliography of works in any way related to the theme was prepared by the late Rev. Dr. Henry M. Dexter, and published in his "Congregationalism of the last Three Hundred Years" (New York, Harper & Brothers, 1880). This magnificent list, the result of years of investigation, extends from 1546 to 1879, and embraces 7250 titles. Yet even this is not exhaustive, and a complete bibliography, brought down to 1894, would probably include at least 8000 works which might justly be claimed to illustrate the story of Congregationalism more or less directly. The present writer, in his "Creeds and Platforms of Congregationalism" (New York, Charles Scribner's Sons, 1893), has given extended bibliographies of the leading Congregational symbols and of the discussions out of which they have grown.

No one library includes all Congregational literature; but the student will find large collections in the possession of the Congregational Library at Boston, of Yale University (Dr. Dexter's own library), of the Massachusetts Historical Society or of the Public Library (Prince Library) at Boston, and of the American Antiquarian Society at Worcester. Smaller collections of value are those of the Connecticut Historical Society at Hartford, of Andover Theological Seminary, and of Union Theological Seminary.

The following list is presented merely as suggestive of works of special importance for Congregational History.

Declarations on Faith and Polity.

A Trve Description ovt of the Word of God, of the Visible Church. [Dort], 1589. (The first Declaration of the London-Amsterdam Church.)

A Trve Confession of the Faith, and Hvmble Acknovvledgment oe the Alegeance, vvhich vvee hir Maiesties Subjects, falsely called Brovvnists, doo hould tovvards God, and yeild to hir Majestie and all other that are ouer vs in the Lord. [Amsterdam], 1596. (The second Declaration of the London-Amsterdam Church.)

A Platform of Church Discipline gathered out of the Word of God: and agreed upon by the Elders and Messengers of the Churches assembled in the Synod at Cambridge in New England. Cambridge, 1649. (The Cambridge Platform.)

Propositions concerning the Subject of Baptism and Consociation of Churches, Collected and Confirmed out of the Word of God, by a Synod of Elders and Messengers of the Churches in Massachusets-Colony in New-England. Assembled at Boston . . . In the Year 1662. Cambridge, 1662. (The Half-Way Covenant Synod.)

A Confession of Faith Owned and Consented unto by the Elders and Messengers of the Churches Assembled at Boston in New-England, May 12, 1680. Boston, 1680. (The "Confession of 1680.")

A Confession of Faith Owned and Consented to by the Elders and Messengers of the Churches in the Colony of Connecticut. . . . The Heads of Agreement, Assented to by the United Ministers, formerly called Presbyterian and Congregational. And also Articles for the Administration of Church Discipline Unanimously agreed upon and consented to by the Elders and Messengers of the Churches in the Colony of Connecticut in New-England. Assembled by Delegation at Say-Brook September 9th, 1708. New London, 1710. (The Saybrook Platform.)

The "*Plan of Union.*" Minutes of the General Assembly of the Presbyterian Church, etc., 1789 to 1820, Philadelphia [1847], pp. 224, 225.

The "*Burial Hill Declaration.*" *Congregational Quarterly*, vol. x., pp. 377, 378.

Ecclesiastical Polity. The Government and Communion Practised by the Congregational Churches in the United States of America. Boston, Congregational Publishing Society, 1872. (The Boston Platform.)

The "*Commission Creed of 1883.*" *Congregationalist*, March 6, 1884.

All of the above, except the "Boston Platform," are reprinted in full in **Walker, Williston,** *The Creeds and Platforms of Congregationalism.* New York, Charles Scribner's Sons, 1893.

Besides these official declarations, the various state bodies publish *Minutes* of their meetings, and the following National Assemblies have published records, viz.: (1) *Proceedings of the General Convention of Cong. Ministers and Delegates in the United States, held at Albany, N.Y., on the 5th, 6th, 7th, and 8th of Oct., 1852.* New York, S. W. Benedict, 1852. (2) *Debates and Proceedings of the National Council of Congregational Churches, Held at Boston, Mass., June* 14–24, 1865. Boston, American Congregational Association, 1866. (3) *Minutes of the National Council of the Congregational Churches of the United States of America.* (Issued triennially since 1871 by the Congregational Publishing Society, Boston.) (4) A *Yearbook* of statistics, ministerial lists, etc., has been published in some form since 1854, and is now issued by the Publishing Committee of the National Council and printed by the Congregational Publishing Society, Boston.

Treatises on Congregational Polity.

Browne, Robert, *A Booke which Sheweth the life and manners of all true Christians,* etc. Middelburg, imprinted by Richarde Painter, 1582. (Extracts reprinted in Walker's "Creeds and Platforms.")

Barrowe, Henry, *A Brief Discouerie of the false Church.* [Dort], 1590.
Robinson, John, Various treatises written between 1610 and 1625, and collected by Robert Ashton, *Works of John Robinson.* 3 vols. London, John Snow, 1851.
[Mather, Richard], *Church-Government and Church-Covenant Discussed, in an Answer of the Elders of the severall Churches in New-England to two and thirty Questions.* London, printed by R. O. and G. D. for Benjamin Allen, 1643.
Cotton, John, *The Keyes of the Kingdom of Heaven.* London, 1644. Reprinted, Boston, Tappan & Dennet, 1843; and Boston, S. R. Whipple & Co., 1852.
Hooker, Thomas, *Survey of the Summe of Church-Discipline.* London, printed by A. M. for John Bellamy, 1648.
Wise, John, *The Churches Quarrel Espoused.* Boston, 1710.—*A Vindication of the Government of New England Churches.* Boston, 1717. Both reprinted in one volume. Boston, Congregational Board of Publication (now Congregational Sunday-School and Publishing Society), 1860.
Mather, Cotton, *Ratio Disciplinæ Fratrum Nov-Anglorum.* Boston, S. Gerrish, 1726.
Upham, Thomas C., *Ratio Disciplinæ; or, The Constitution of the Congregational Churches.* Portland [Me.], Shirley & Hyde, 1829.
Cummings, Preston, *A Dictionary of Congregational Usages and Principles.* Boston, 1852. Sixth edition, Boston, S. K. Whipple & Co., 1855.
Buck, Edward, *Massachusetts Ecclesiastical Law.* Boston, Congregational Publishing Society, [1865].
Davis, Woodbury, *Congregational Polity, Usages, and Law.* Boston, Proprietors of "Boston Review," 1865.
Dexter, Henry M., *Congregationalism: What it is; Whence it is; How it works.* Boston, Nichols & Noyes, 1865.
Roy, Joseph E., *A Manual of the Principles, Doctrines, and Usages of the Congregational Churches.* Chicago, 1869.
Dexter, Henry M., *A Hand-Book of Congregationalism.* Boston, Congregational Publishing Society, [1880].
Ross, A. Hastings, *A Pocket Manual of Congregationalism.* Chicago, E. J. Alden, 1883.
Boardman, George Nye, *Congregationalism.* Chicago, Advance Publishing Company, [1889].

SOURCES AND HISTORIES.

The *Colonial Records* of the several colonies of Plymouth, Massachusetts, Connecticut, and New Haven. Now largely printed, and to be found in any well-equipped historical or public library.
Bradford, William, *History of Plymouth Plantation* (Gov. Bradford's Journal). Boston, Little, Brown & Co., 1856.
Winthrop, John, *History of New England from 1630 to 1649* (Gov. Winthrop's Journal). Best edition that of James Savage, Boston, Little, Brown & Co., 1853.
Mather, Cotton, *Magnalia Christi Americana.* London, 1702. Other editions, Hartford, Silas Andrus, 1820; and Hartford, Silas Andrus & Son, 1853–55.

Young, Alexander, *Chronicles of the Pilgrim Fathers.* Boston, Little & Brown, 1841 and 1844.—*Chronicles of the First Planters of the Colony of Mass. Bay.* Boston, Little & Brown, 1846.

Hanbury, Benjamin, *Historical Memorials relating to the Independents, or Congregationalists: from their Rise to the Restoration of the Monarchy, A.D. MDCLX.* 3 vols. London, printed for the Congregational Union of England and Wales; Fisher, Son & Co., and Jackson & Walford, 1839–44. (An ill-arranged work, but filled with reprints and abstracts of great value.)

Felt, Joseph B., *The Ecclesiastical History of New England* [to 1678]. 2 vols. Boston, Cong. Board of Publication, 1855–62.

Sprague, William B., *Annals of the American Pulpit,* vols. i. and ii. New York, Robert Carter & Bros., 1857. (Biographies.)

Punchard, George, *History of Congregationalism.* 5 vols. in revised edition. New York and Boston, first by Hurd & Houghton, and then by the Congregational Publishing Society, 1865–81.

Waddington, John, *Congregational History.* 5 vols. London, Simmons & Botten, 1869–78. (Valuable, but not always accurate in quotations.)

Dexter, Henry M., *The Congregationalism of the last 300 Years, as seen in its Literature.* New York, Harper & Brothers, 1880. (An indispensable work.)

Huntington, George, *Outlines of Congregational History.* Boston, Cong. Pub. Soc., 1885.

The following Histories will also be found of great value:

Hutchinson, Thomas, *History of the Province of Massachusetts Bay.* 3 vols. Boston, Thomas and John Fleet, 1764–69.

Palfrey, John G., *History of New England.* 5 vols. Boston, Little, Brown & Co., 1859–90.

Doyle, J. A., *The English in America: The Puritan Colonies.* 2 vols. London, Longmans, Green & Co., 1887.

Fiske, John, *The Beginnings of New England.* Boston, Houghton, Mifflin & Co., 1889.

SPECIAL THEMES.

Adams, Charles Francis, *Three Episodes of Mass. History.* Boston, Houghton, Mifflin & Co., 1892.

Bacon, Leonard, *Thirteen Historical Discourses, on the Completion of 200 Years from the Beginning of the First Church in New Haven.* New Haven, Durrie & Peck, 1839.

Bacon, Leonard, *The Genesis of the New England Churches.* New York, Harper & Brothers, 1874.

Clark, Joseph S., *Historical Sketch of the Congregational Churches in Massachusetts.* Boston, Cong. Board of Publication, 1858.

Congregational Quarterly. 20 vols. Boston, 1859–78.

Contributions to the Ecclesiastical History of Connecticut; prepared under the Direction of the General Association. New Haven, William L. Kingsley, 1861. (Of great value.)

Contributions to the Ecclesiastical History of Essex County, Mass. Boston, Cong. Board of Publication, 1865.

Ellis, Arthur B., *History of the First Church in Boston.* Boston, Hall & Whiting, 1881.

Ellis, George E., *The Puritan Age and Rule in the Colony of Massachusetts Bay, 1629–1685.* Boston, Houghton, Mifflin & Co., 1888.

Goodwin, John A., *The Pilgrim Republic: An Historical Review of the Colony of New Plymouth.* Boston, Ticknor & Co., 1888.

Hill, Hamilton A., *History of the Old South Church, Boston.* 2 vols. Boston, Houghton, Mifflin & Co., 1890.

Lawrence, Robert F., *The New Hampshire Churches.* Claremont, published for the Author, 1856.

Ohio Church History Society, Papers. Oberlin, printed for the Society, 1889–93.

Parker, Edwin P., *History of the Second Church of Christ in Hartford.* Hartford, Belknap & Warfield, 1892.

Robbins, Chandler, *History of the Second Church in Boston.* Boston, John Wilson & Son, 1852.

Tracy, Joseph, *The Great Awakening: A History of the Revival of Religion in the Time of Edwards and Whitefield.* Boston, Tappan & Dennet, 1842.

Trumbull, Benjamin, *A Complete History of Connecticut, Civil and Ecclesiastical.* 2 vols. New Haven, Maltby, Goldsmith & Co., 1818.

Walker, George Leon, *History of the First Church in Hartford.* Hartford, Brown & Gross, 1884.

White, Daniel A., *New England Congregationalism.* Salem, no publisher given; printed at Salem Gazette Office, 1861.

THE CONGREGATIONALISTS.

CHAPTER I.

THE BEGINNINGS OF CONGREGATIONALISM.

IT has been said that the Bible is the religion of Protestantism. With even more truth it might be affirmed that the Word of God is the historic basis of Congregationalism. Yet neither of these statements is exclusive of similar claims for other branches of the Christian Church. In a real sense all are founded upon the Bible. But as Protestantism in general has made a peculiar use of the Scriptures and attached to them a unique authority in all matters of doctrine, so Congregationalism, at least in all its earlier history, has attributed a regulative importance to the directions of the New Testament writers regarding church administration, and has given a normal value even to their most incidental narratives of church usages, more fully than any other system of ecclesiastical polity. Whatever stress is now properly laid, in any estimate of the claims of Congregationalism to general recognition, on its democratic simplicity, on its independence of state control, its voluntariness of association, or its ready adaptation to new surroundings, is but incidental to the one merit which its modern founders claimed for it—that it represented the pattern of the primitive and apostolic church, as laid down in the New Testament. To understand how this claim came to be made, and how the Congregational system came to be what it is, it is necessary to glance at the attitude of the Reformation toward the Scriptures and toward church polity.

The great teacher of the medieval church had uniformly held that the Bible the ultimate source of religious authority. But it was not the Bible interpreted by the individual. No thought fundamental to the Roman Empire had been more impressed on the minds of men than that of visible, external unity—a unity finding expression in a uniform system of government, a uniform body of law, and a visible, earthly head. This great Roman imperial conception had produced the medieval papacy; it produced also in the political world the far less efficient, but no less assertive, Holy Roman Empire. For such a body, characterized by such external marks of unity, an authoritative exposition of that which it claimed as its fundamental law, the Bible, was imperatively necessary. That exposition was believed to be set forth by the church itself, speaking through tradition, the consensus of its fathers and doctors, the decrees of its popes, and especially through general councils. All these made a mass of authority which, though professedly subordinate to the Word of God and merely interpretative of it, really, if not theoretically, put it in the background; and substituted for a direct appeal to its prescriptions, a mass of exposition, the slow growth of centuries, which buttressed an elaborate system of doctrine, polity, and ceremonial, itself the result of gradual accretion through nearly a millennium and a half of years.

Naturally, with such a sense of the necessity of unity and such claims to continuity in its explanation of the divine message, the position of the medieval church was equally clear that for an ordinary uneducated layman to attempt the interpretation of the Scriptures was a matter of exceeding peril. The medieval church felt that it had some justification for this position. The sects with which it had struggled, sometimes with very carnal weapons, had claimed to base their departures fr m Roman obedience on the warrant of the Scriptures The Waldenses and the Cathari had been the source of infinite trouble to the medieval church, and the Roman leaders felt that much in their beliefs could be traced to erroneous interpretations of the Bible by ignorant laymen, a danger which they thought could only be avoided by a careful restriction of its use wherever such errors were prevalent. So it came about that when the great revolt against medieval authority which is called the Reformation took place, it found the Bible bound about with a web of authoritative interpretation which explained its meaning in conformity with the system against which the Reformation rebelled and asserted that any other interpretation was illegitimate. The explanation had grown to be more practically important than the Scripture itself.

The early Reformers broke with this theory of interpretation altogether. In throwing off the sacerdotal system of the Roman Church, they asserted the right of immediate access of every believing soul to God, and its capacity to comprehend the divine message. They attacked the whole medieval hierarchy as a growth of middle-men between the Divine Spirit and the human soul, where God intended there should be none. They rejected the whole fabric of tradition and conciliar definition by which the medieval polity had been supported as something man-made and fallible. But some final authority they felt there must be, some test of religious truth; and that they found where the church had always asserted that it lay, in the Word of God. Yet just as the medieval system, by emphasizing tradition and churchly authority in interpretation, had really, though not nominally, minified the Bible, so now the Reformers, by rejecting the testimony of the church and the traditional views of truth, and asserting the self-explanatory nature of the Scriptures, actually raised the Bible to an authority in the church, which, whatever the theory, it had never before possessed, not even in the earliest centuries. Whether this extreme assertion of biblical authority was undue or not is not here the question; but no one can understand the early history of Congregationalism without recognizing clearly the emphasis which the Reformers put upon the Scriptures as the infallible, complete, and self-interpretative expression of the will of God and the nature of his relations to men—a record to which no tradition could add anything, and which by its fullness excluded the necessity of any further revelation.

Two principles plainly flowed from these views of the Reformers, though not recognized in their fullness of application by the leaders in the reform movement. It is evident that if the Bible is a complete revelation, then all that is really essential, whether in belief or in practice, must be contained in it, and all that cannot be found there delineated is at best a matter of human judgment or convenience, that, however useful, is in no way essential to the faith, organization, or ordering of the church. The Bible must be the only final test of that which God designed his church to be or to know. It is no less clear, that, granting the correctness of the Reformers' principles, it is always right for a man, or a body of men, to apply this test to the actual condition of any organization claiming to be the church, and if it be found wanting, to attempt its alteration into conformity with the prescriptions of that divine standard.

But though these principles were involved in the assertions of the Reformers, their full logical sweep was not at first evident. No great movement is wholly radical. The past is not swept away in a moment. And tremendous as were the changes which the Reformers introduced, that which they left unchanged in the doctrine and organization of the church far exceeded that which was altered. In the field of Christian belief, while the battle raged with fierceness over the problems of the method of salvation and the nature of the sacraments, the Reformers as a whole accepted the faith of the ancient church regarding the nature of God, the person and work of Christ, and even the state of man, without serious discussion. Even more was this true regarding church polity. If the Reformers altered that which was chiefly political in the administration of the church, or those offices which seemed most intimately associated with the sacerdotal system against which they revolted, they left untouched the medieval theory that all baptized inhabitants of a Christian country were church-members unless formally excommunicate, and they preserved enough of the ancient conception of visible unity to hold that but one form of faith and worship was to be allowed within a given territory.

Other causes than these operated also to make the question of the proper polity of the church a subordinate one for the early Reformers. The brunt of the struggle was at first chiefly doctrinal, and naturally so, for purification of doctrine was more important even than the right organization of the church. Then, too, the early German and Swiss Reformers, Luther, Melanchthon, and Zwingli, were not organizers; and though Luther at least caught a glimpse of a system very like Congregationalism in the pages of the New Testament, they all felt the need of the aid of civil authority in their struggle with Rome; and, partly because they could in no other way enlist the services of princes and city magistrates, partly because they feared the fanatics whom the Reformation drew in its train and who threatened to bring the cause into discredit if they became dominant, these leaders in the struggle allowed their churches to be remodeled and ruled by the authority of the state. This condition of affairs, which they hoped would be temporary, became the universal rule in Europe, and has continued to the present day. Whatever may have been its merits or its seeming necessity in a time of transition, when tested by the standard of the New Testament it is at least as unwarranted as the system which it supplanted.

If the German and Swiss Reformers of the first generation failed thus to apply the same Scriptural test to the organization that they did, in part at least, to the doctrine of the church, this was even more the case in England. There the Reformation was undisguisedly political in its character at first, and even doctrinal reform had to win its way slowly. Under the reigns of successive sovereigns of the house of Tudor the Church of England became in turn Anglican, Protestant, Catholic, and again Anglican; and at each alteration of the constitution the transition to the new form was made as easy as possible for clergy and people by the retention of offices and much of ceremonial which had marked the organization of the English Church for a thousand years. At each transition, too, clergy and people were expected by the government to acquiesce in the new revolution at least outwardly; and that this acquiescence should be more easily obtained, little strenuous inquiry was made as to the spiritual character or actual beliefs of the ministers and members of the Establishment. In doctrines the English Church at last came to be fully Protestant, but its terms of membership were unchanged and its offices remained substantially and intentionally unaltered, save that their holders now looked with Erastian servility to the king as the sole source of ecclesiastical appointment with even greater dependence than they had before manifested toward the pope. Certainly no one could justly claim that Henry VIII., or the government that ruled in the name of Edward VI., or Elizabeth, in giving a constitution to the church, was moved by a consideration of any pattern which might be laid down in the Word of God. Yet if the Reformation principle that the Bible is the sole rule of faith and conduct was once admitted, there could be no logical halting-point either on the continent of Europe or in England before the inquiry had been diligently made whether the organization of the church and its forms of worship were not matters of divine revelation as truly as its doctrine. The Reformation could not be stopped at the point where political expediency tried to limit it.

This tendency of the Reformation to go further in the direction of a logical carrying out of its principles than the position taken by its first leaders was manifested in the guiding spirit of its second stage—Calvin; though he too failed to apply the Reformation test in its fullness to the organization and membership of the church. But Calvin went far beyond Luther and Zwingli. He was an organizer by nature; his personality dominated the small community, Geneva, in which his work was done, so that he had freer scope to carry his views into practice than Luther would have enjoyed had Luther possessed his organizing ability. And Calvin, too, felt strongly that the Bible should be regulative of the pattern and order of the church in a general way, even if he did not make it exclusively formative. His Genevan church thus approximated far more nearly to the New Testament conception than that of the English political reformers or of Luther, while it did not fully or exclusively submit itself to the biblical test. Thus Calvin went a long way toward the position of Congregationalism when he held that ministers were to be approved by the congregations whom they were to serve, instead of being appointed by spiritual superiors, sovereigns, or patrons; and when he committed the government of churches not to a clerical order but to elderships, composed of ministers and laymen. These were long steps in the direction of a more logical application of the Reformation test, and they were to be profoundly influential in the ecclesiastical development of English Puritanism, out of which most of the early Congregationalists were to come. But Calvin admitted that certain features of his system were based primarily on expediency, and he retained the conception of the church as an institution practically coterminous with the state, though independent in government, having all baptized citizens of respectable lives as its members, and whose discipline is to be enforced by state authority.

But while the chief of the early leaders of the Reformation thus only partially carried out their principles, and the churches which they founded thus took up into their organization, in greater or less degree, elements foreign to the New Testament, or at least not illustrated in the New Testament churches, some who were touched by the Reformation at its beginning were more radical and consistent. Whether it be true, as Ludwig Keller has asserted but hardly proved, that these completer Reformers were representatives of the more evangelical medieval sects, like the Waldenses, which had continuously opposed Roman claims, it is certain that the movements initiated in Germany and in Switzerland by Luther and Zwingli were speedily disturbed by the preaching of a class of teachers nicknamed the "Anabaptists," from their limitation of the baptismal rite to believers of adult years—a doctrine which seemed to the Lutherans and Zwinglians an insistence on "re-baptism," since they, in common with all others born under the rule of the medieval church, had been baptized in infancy. Doubtless the fanatical exhorters of Wittenberg and Zwickau, whose words and deeds induced Luther to leave the protection of the Wartburg castle in 1522 to preach against them, were representatives of the same radical tendency; but the "Anabaptist" tenets were more fully and more nobly developed in Zürich, the scene of the activities of the Swiss Reformer. Here, under the lead of Grebel, Blaurock, Hübmaier, and others, a party of considerable size developed, which insisted that the close connection of church and state encouraged by the leading Reformers was wholly wrong, and which attacked the reformations of Luther and Zwingli as but half-hearted and incomplete. These men were as obnoxious to the Protestant as to the Catholic civil authorities, and were at once objects of persecution in every quarter. Attacked by the government of Zürich in 1525, the effect of this attempt at their suppression was the rapid diffusion of their sentiments throughout Switzerland, Germany, and the Netherlands, while by 1535 they had extended to England and soon after appeared in Italy. By the Catholics and the Anglicans they were burned, by the continental Protestants they were drowned. There was indeed a degree of explanation, though not of excuse, for this universal severity of treatment in the fanaticism which characterized many of the Anabaptists, and which led them into wild and sometimes dangerous and immoral attempts to alter the foundations of society, of which the fantastic misrule so bloodily brought to an end at Münster in 1535 is the most notorious example. Like the radical party in all movements which profoundly stir men, the Anabaptists gathered to themselves extremists of all shades. To the Catholics they seemed odious as the most pronounced illustrations of the tendencies which were leading multitudes away from the ancient communion; to the moderate Protestants they appeared a peculiar menace as likely to bring into contempt the Reformation cause and forfeit the support of those worldly powers whose aid seemed to the leading Reformers well-nigh indispensable.

But though the fanatical Anabaptists caught the public eye, they were but a small proportion of the party. The vast majority were earnest, sober, God-fearing men and women, who came chiefly from the lower ranks of society, and whose prevailing ignorance led them to many diverse and fanciful interpretations of Scripture, and much over-confidence in direct illuminations of the Holy Spirit; but who sincerely sought to pattern life and worship upon the Word of God. Especially was this true of those of the Anabaptists who came under the influence of Menno Simons, and who bore from their discipleship the popular name of Mennonites—a body which was strongly represented in Holland, where it obtained from William the Silent in 1575–77 the first toleration granted to Anabaptists by any European government.

Though the Anabaptists, unlike the Lutherans, Anglicans, and Calvinists, had no creeds that were generally recognized as binding on all local congregations, and though there was necessarily great variety in opinion among them, their main principles are readily discernible. First of all they drew a broad line of distinction between those who were experimental Christians and those who were not. Instead of the general inclusiveness which swept all the inhabitants of a city or a state into the church—an inclusiveness which characterized the systems of the great

Reformers as well as that of Rome—they held that only Christian believers constitute the church. Of that church and of all religious life the Bible is the only ultimate law. Human enactments have their value for the maintenance of unregenerate civil society and the control of the vicious, but the supreme test of every man-made statute is its conformity to the Word of God. Only when his commands are not contrary to the precepts of Scripture is obedience due to the civil magistrate. That magistrate has no right to interfere with the church, for the rule of its spiritual communion is the Word of God, and not his law; nor should Christians hold civil office, since such worldly posts of power, though divinely permitted for the best good of a society still consisting in large measure of unregenerate persons, are not appointed as part of the government of the church, nor are the laws of their administration the statutes of Christ's kingdom. God alone, and not the civil ruler, appoints what the Christian is to believe and practice in all spiritual concerns.

This church, they affirmed, consists of the congregations of professed disciples of Christ scattered throughout the world. Admission to it is obtained by baptism, consequent upon repentance and faith; and hence the Anabaptists maintained, like their spiritual offspring, the modern Baptists, that this rite was designed exclusively for adults —a contention in which English and American Congregationalism, with a keener sense of the covenant relation of the Christian family in the kingdom of God, has been unable to follow them. Of this church the Lord Jesus is the only head; and its congregations enjoy the ministry, sacraments, doctrines, and discipline which he has appointed. Its officers are to be chosen by the congregation to whom they minister, and ordained at the hands of its elders, with confidence that the Holy Spirit will guide his people in the selection, if made with fasting and prayer. The offenses of its membership are to be redressed by admonition and excommunication by the congregation. An uncritical literalness of interpretation of the commands of Christ induced the Anabaptists in general to forbid judicial oaths, the bearing of arms, or recompense for ministerial services.

Here was a conception of the organization, duties, and ministry of the church very different from that entertained in the state establishments founded by the leading Reformers, and characterized, in spite of all oddities and local differences, by a sincere desire to pattern its organization and government on the Word of God. Furthermore, we find this attempt leading everywhere to the thought of the church as a collection of local bodies of Christian people in some sense separate from the world, ruled by divinely appointed laws, capable of choosing their own officers, and administering their own affairs without interference from the state. It was a conception naturally repugnant to the mass of men in the sixteenth century, for they had not outgrown the idea ingrained into thought by over a thousand years of teaching that the church is a body marked by external unity—if not the unity of an undivided Christendom which the Reformation had destroyed, at least by uniformity of creed and worship within a given territory—a uniformity maintained by the state, and binding on all its citizens as members of the state church. It was repugnant also to governments, since it denied to them a much-cherished prerogative and markedly limited their powers, while it encouraged democratic tendencies at variance with the prevailing spirit of sixteenth-century political theories. Hence, had the radical Reformers been less feared for their frequent doctrinal vagaries than they really were, their views would have been slow in winning favor during the Reformation period.

The influences and parties which have just been considered were continental, not English. But the same divergent tendencies were to be apparent in the English Reformation, and the influence of some of these continental parties was to be largely formative in that movement. Owing in part to the caution with which the English mind accepts changes, whether in religion or in politics; to its willingness to adopt compromise even if compromise is not wholly logical; and in part also to the political character of the early history of the English Reformation and the opposition of the sovereigns to its more radical aspects, the movement advanced far more slowly in England than on the Continent. It was in a true sense a period of religious education, as well as of change, for the English people. This slowness had its advantages both politically and religiously. The nation as a whole had hardly been removed from Catholicism under Henry VIII., save that it preferred English autonomy to submission to a foreign pope. It had learned something under the rule of the counselors of Edward VI., though the people in general regarded their violently Protestantizing measures with aversion. But it viewed the equally arbitrary Catholic rule of Mary with yet greater dislike, and by the accession of Elizabeth it was convinced that Protestantism was more desirable than Catholicism. The cautious and intentionally compromising policy of Elizabeth's early reign had one merit at least—it continued the development of the English people toward Protestantism without serious risk of violent Catholic reaction; it was not till the Protestantism of the nation had passed the half-way position of the queen that she became a drag on English religious growth. This slow development saved England the bitter civil conflicts which desolated some of the continental lands during the Reformation period, and it also had an effect upon the religious life of the nation which was ultimately, though not immediately, beneficial. A generation passed away before the transition of the land from the Roman obedience of the early years of Henry VIII. to the very moderate Protestantism of Elizabeth had been accomplished. All this time English religious institutions were in flux, doctrinal standards were being established looking first in one direction and then in the other, the thoughts of men were exercised with religious problems without long being cast in the mold of any one governmentally imposed system. At the same time no single leader, such as dominated the Reformation of Germany, Switzerland, or even Scotland, arose in the English Church. The result was that the people of England came—in a dim way, it is true—to think for themselves on religious problems more generally than the inhabitants of those countries of the Continent where the Reformation was more rapid in its introduction. Though the real spiritual awakening of the people was not manifest till Puritanism had carried its work well into the reign of Elizabeth, the hold which that movement took upon the English people was in no small measure due to the fact that for the first three decades of the English Reformation the Bible was studied by widening circles of thoughtful men, while the government spoke with changing voice.

But while this delay and change which marked the progress of the English Reformation doubtless worked good in the outcome in that it made a wider and deeper and freer religious life eventually possible than would have been the case had the people passed through a less tedious education, this slowness of development was a source of profound grief to the leaders in the Protestant movement in that land. From the first they labored to bring the Church of England to the degree of Protestantism illustrated in the state churches of the Continent. In the early days of the English Reformation the German theologians of the school of Luther had the sympathy of English Protestants, but by the time that the second prayer-book of Edward VI. was issued, in 1552, the influence of Calvin had become more powerful in the doctrinal thought of the English Reformers than that of the Lutherans. Thenceforward, till the incoming of Arminian theories in the reign of James I., all parties among English Protestants were Calvinists in theology. This desire to conform the Church of England to the Genevan model, which was already felt under the nominal rule of Edward VI., was greatly, though indirectly, stimulated by the persecutions of Mary. The more earnest Protestants fled from England to the Continent, preferring exile to conformity to Catholicism. There they found a welcome in Switzerland and in the Calvinistic portions of Germany, though not much favor from the Lutherans; and on the death of Mary they returned to England filled with admiration not only for the doctrine but for the polity and forms of worship of Calvinism, which they wished to introduce into their home land in Genevan fullness. Elizabeth had no sympathy with this aim; but she needed men for places of prominence in her ecclesiastical Establishment who could be trusted to oppose Catholic plots and strengthen Protestantism, and of such men the Marian exiles were the most conspicuous. So it came about that, in spite of her own preferences, Elizabeth was forced to give prominence in the English Church, at the beginning of her reign, to men who desired a much more radical Protestantizing of the ceremonials and liturgy of that body than found favor in her eyes.

To these Protestants of the more earnest type, the most

serious objection to the Church of England at the beginning of Elizabeth's reign was not any fault in doctrine; they agreed fully in its prevailing Calvinism. Nor did they at first oppose its retention of bishops. In fact, the Reformers as a whole had no dislike to an episcopal rank in the ministry, at least as administrators of church government, though circumstances prevented its retention in most of the churches which they founded on the Continent. Even Calvin advised the King of Poland to continue the episcopal office in that land. Melanchthon thought bishops desirable as a means of establishing good order in the church. But none of the Reformers conceived of bishops as possessed of spiritual powers superior to those of other ministers. It was as administrative posts that the Protestants of the early reign of Elizabeth were willing to see the episcopal office continued. Nor did these Protestants at first object to the control of the state over the church—they accepted office from the hand of government without reluctance. Their opposition was directed in the beginning against none of these things, but against the retention of certain vestments and ceremonies which seemed to them to savor of the Roman liturgy. Thus, the cap and surplice were reminders of the old priestly garb which had seemed to make broad the line of distinction between the clergyman and the layman. So, too, the use of the cross as a symbol, the employment of the ring in marriage, and kneeling at the reception of the sacrament, seemed to these Protestants acts fitted to perpetuate the misuse of the sign of the Saviour's passion, to encourage the thought of marriage as a sacrament, and the conception of the Supper as a transubstantiation of the elements into the very body and blood of Christ, against which all Protestants of the Calvinistic school set their faces. These were in themselves acts of little moment—the battle-flag is seldom of much intrinsic importance—but they symbolized much, and no one recognized their significance more clearly than Elizabeth. Their retention meant the continuance of that policy by which the admission of Catholics into the Church of England was rendered easy—a policy which had so much politically to commend it. Their abolition would signify the full Protestantizing of the Anglican body, as Protestantism was understood in the Calvinistic churches of the Continent, and the abandonment of the policy which made it a half-way house on the roadway of reform. As early as 1550, under the reign of Edward VI., Hooper, the bishop-elect of Gloucester, had denounced the prescribed vestments. The more earnest Protestants at the beginning of Elizabeth's reign, like Grindal, Sandys, and Jewel of the high clergy, and Burghley and Walsingham of the statesmen, were also their opponents. But Elizabeth was determined in her ecclesiastical policy; and on this point she had the sympathy of that large party in the kingdom whose affection for the abolished Catholic worship continued, and who wished to make as few departures from it as were consistent with obedience to the law. In opposition to the desires of the more earnest Protestants, she insisted on the enforcement of her ecclesiastical regulations. Thus there arose in the bosom of the Church of England, at the commencement of the reign of Elizabeth, two parties, one of which, from its desire to purify the church from remnants of Roman usage, was nicknamed "Puritan"; and the other of which, marked by a wish to maintain churchly usages in the compromise condition in which they were, and to support the royal supremacy in order to that end, may, for want of a more descriptive title, be styled "Anglican."

The problem with which the Church of England was confronted at this juncture was of the most serious character. A mass of clergy and people, swept five years before by government edict out of nominal Protestantism back to their original Catholicism, had now been carried over to Protestantism again. The incumbents of the higher offices of the church had been generally changed; but the overwhelming majority of the parish ministers of the new order of affairs were the same who had served under Mary; and they were generally ignorant, unable to preach, often incapable of setting a worthy example of Christian living to their congregations. In place of this inefficient body of clergy the Puritans were anxious to establish an educated, spiritually-minded, and zealous ministry. It is no unjust criticism of the Anglicans to say that they were not so alive to the spiritual necessities of the land; they were themselves very largely the ministry against whose inefficiency the Puritans protested. As far as a geographical division of England between the two parties may be made, the south and east, especially the vicinity of London and the counties along the North Sea from the Thames to the Humber, may be said to have favored Puritanism. This was the region of England which had most welcomed Wiclif and his laborers, and where the Reformation had found most ready lodgment at its beginning. It was the region also from which the strength of the opposition to the tyranny of the Stuarts was to come, and where no small share of the future settlers of New England had their home. It was no accident, therefore, that made the more eastern of the two English universities, that of Cambridge, the home of Puritanism almost from the beginning of Elizabeth's reign, and the training-school not only of the most strenuous Protestantism of the home land, but of most of the early New England divines.

The opposition of the authorities of the English Church, under the impulse of the queen, to the modifications desired by the Puritans, led to a second stage in Puritan development, and one much more radical in its departure from the polity of the Establishment than that just considered. The forcible retention of vestments and ceremonies which the growing Protestantism of the reform party increasingly condemned soon led to questionings as to whether the system itself which permitted their retention was that divinely intended as the normal polity of the church; some Puritans no longer criticised rites and garments, they began to examine the constitution of the English Establishment in its fundamental principles. Naturally, the test by which they judged it was largely borrowed from Geneva. The leader in this second stage of Puritanism was Thomas Cartwright. Born in 1535, he was identified with the University of Cambridge from the year 1547, and as student, fellow, and teacher contributed more than any other Englishman toward making that seminary a stronghold of Calvinism. His greatest prominence came in 1569, when he became Lady Margaret professor of divinity in his university; but this post of influence exposed him to the immediate attack of the Anglicans, of whom the most prominent was John Whitgift, the later Archbishop of Canterbury. By this opposition Cartwright was compelled to abandon his professorship in December, 1570, and in September, 1571, he was driven from his fellowship; thenceforward, till his death, in 1603, to be a sufferer for his belief.

This dispute, centering in the university which best represented the advancing Protestantism of the nation, made Cartwright the leader of the Puritan party, and impressed his views on his followers. He had gained from Calvin the conception of the church as independent of the state in administration—a theory toward which governmental opposition had been forcing the whole Puritan party. He had come to the conclusion that church polity is taught authoritatively in the Scriptures, and that no church could be truly reformed till its government was adjusted to the biblical model. He had learned from Geneva also a faith in the efficacy of discipline to remedy the spiritual imperfections with which the unquestioning retention of the whole Catholic population of England in Elizabeth's Establishment had filled the membership of the church. He had come to the belief that the system of diocesan episcopacy was no part of the divine model, and ought at least to be essentially modified. He was convinced that the people of each parish should have a share in the selection of its ministers. These principles were in radical contravention of the Elizabethan theory of the government of the church by officers of royal appointment and by laws imposed by the sovereign; no real compromise between them and the Anglican theory was possible. Elizabeth and the Anglican party generally saw their threatening character, and the power of the government was therefore set in yet more determined opposition to the Puritan cause.

But though Cartwright moved thus with firm tread in the direction in which Calvin had led the way, and perhaps went a little further than Calvin, he retained most of Calvin's limitations also, and in his merits and shortcomings alike he represented the whole Puritan movement in which he was so conspicuous a leader. From the time of his expulsion from Cambridge down to the civil war that party largely walked in his footsteps—the Presbyterian Puritans, always a majority of the body, did so always. Like Calvin, Cartwright held to the conception of a National Church, of which all baptized and non-excommunicate inhabitants of England were members. Like Calvin, he believed that this vast assemblage of the good and bad was to be trained and purified by the labors of ministers of the Scripture designation and the enforcement of an active, searching discipline by the officers of each congregation and district. Like Calvin, he believed it the duty of the magistrate to aid the church by repressing heresy and compelling uniformity, though it was only in the path designated in the Word of God that the magistrate could rightfully compel men to go.[1] That that path should not appear the same to all really good men was a thought which the Puritan did not readily entertain. The national Church of England seemed to Cartwright too sacred an institution for men to separate from without peril of schism, and he relied on the civil government, which had already carried it over from Catholicism to Anglicanism, to effect its alteration, as a whole, once again into Presbyterian Puritanism. Therefore, in Cartwright's view, the work of a Christian man desirous of bringing the English Church into conformity to the Scripture model was to agitate, labor, argue, and try to move the government to effect the change; to introduce, as far as he was able and the government would permit, the worship and discipline of Geneva, in order to raise the inert mass of the all-inclusive membership of the Establishment; to encourage earnest, educated, spiritual-minded ministers; but on no account to withdraw from the national religious body. It was a theory that required for its successful establishment the conversion of the dominant forces of England to its support, and though that conversion seemed in Cartwright's time exceedingly probable, and under the concurrent influence of opposition to the tyranny of the Stuart sovereigns was temporarily brought about during the parliamentary struggles of the seventeenth century, it was never permanently accomplished. Moreover, the views which Cartwright impressed on the Puritan party, like those of Calvin, had the two great defects of an unspiritual theory of church-membership and an unscriptural intimacy of relation to the state. As Elizabethan Anglicanism was a half-way house between Catholicism and full Protestantism, so Puritanism was a halting-place between Anglicanism and Congregationalism. It was to be the training-school of early English Congregationalists; but it could not be permanent, for it was intermingled with elements inconsistent with a logical application of its own principles.

The Puritan movement grew rapidly in strength as Elizabeth's reign advanced; especially after the death of Mary of Scotland, in 1587, and the defeat of the Spanish Armada, in 1588, relieved the fear of Catholic intervention, which had united, in a measure, all opponents of the papacy. The one great book of English reading became the Bible, and to hundreds and thousands of the more earnest Protestants the Bible taught the Puritan lesson. Men full of new enthusiasm for the unfettered Word of God cared little for the writings of the fathers, the opinions of the councils of the fourth, fifth, and sixth centuries, or what is now called the "historic continuity" of the church. To their thinking, God had made a plain revelation of his will, and all that did not evidently conform to that message, however ancient or of whatever generality of usage, was an insult to the divine Law-giver.

But as Puritanism advanced and became more dogmatic, Anglicanism advanced also. The Anglicans of the opening years of Elizabeth's reign had found the chief warrant for the existence of diocesan episcopacy in the preference of the sovereign for that form of church government. They were willing freely to admit the true churchly character of an ecclesiastical organization unprovided with bishops. But the growing Puritan criticism of prelacy led the Anglicans more and more into its defense. Whitgift, Cartwright's opponent at Cambridge, and from 1583 to 1604 Archbishop of Canterbury, and always one of the most violent of opponents of Puritanism, did not venture to assert more than that episcopacy was the most ancient and desirable type of organization. He used language that certainly allowed the inference that possibly other forms of government were more accordant with the New Testament intimations. But by 1589, in his sermon at Paul's Cross, Richard Bancroft, afterward to be Whitgift's successor in the see of Canterbury, declared—a little obscurely, it is true—that episcopacy is of divine authority. This theory was elaborated by Thomas Bilson, later Bishop of Worcester, in 1593, and episcopacy and apostolic succession were asserted to be essential to the existence of the church. The careful Richard Hooker, in his "Ecclesiasticall Politie" of 1593, did not indeed go further than to affirm the superior antiquity and scripturalness of episcopacy, while denying its absolute necessity; but the Anglican party as a whole moved in the direction pointed out by Bancroft and Bilson—a direction which found its complete exponent in William Laud, Archbishop of Canterbury from 1633 to 1645, and which was the radical antithesis of Puritanism, not only in the stress which it laid on episcopacy, but in its attitude toward those features of worship against which the Puritans protested. Puritanism thus stimulated its opposite tendency in the English Church. The hostility between the two parties thus became more pronounced, as their divergence became more extreme throughout Elizabeth's reign; and the queen's mighty influence, controlling appointments to high ecclesiastical office, and largely determining the strictness or laxity of the enforcement of uniformity, was thrown fully on the side of the Anglicans, a little, it may be, because their growing high-churchism appealed to her religious taste, but chiefly because the views of the Anglican party best comported with her theories of the royal supremacy.

This largely political character of Elizabeth's opposition to Puritan views marked the whole Anglican party. It was not merely religious opposition that embittered the discussion. It was also the perception, dim at first, but growing clearer all through Elizabeth's reign, of the fact which became so patent in the time of the Stuarts, that the differing principles of the two parties regarding church government led also to radically divergent conceptions of the relation of the ruler to the state. In the Anglican view the clergyman was either the representative of the sovereign in the religious administration of the kingdom, or, as with the high-churchmen who gradually arose in the Anglican party, a member of a divinely appointed order over which the sovereign had a regulative control. In neither phase of the Anglican theory was the clergyman in any way responsible to the people to whom he ministered. He looked to his sovereign, his ecclesiastical superior, or to God, as the only authority that could take cognizance of his acts. In actual practice the Anglican saw in the king the ultimate source of ecclesiastical power. Now this conception of clerical responsibility not only greatly aided that dependence on the sovereign of all the ecclesiastical interests of the land which was dear to the Tudors and Stuarts, it gave to the sovereign himself a station which accorded him a divine right to rule. A ruler who was the "supreme governor" of a church whose ministers owed no responsibility for their actions to their flocks, was not likely to be held answerable to his people for his deeds. If he rightfully appointed and controlled those who were members of a divinely constituted order, his own power must be of divine appointment. The tendency of men to think in political affairs as they do in questions of church polity—a tendency always illustrated in the history of the church—made the Anglican naturally a supporter of that Tudor and Stuart view of the royal authority, which held the king answerable to God but not to his people.

On the other hand, the Puritan learned from Calvinism that the minister should serve his congregation with their consent. The Puritan believed that to the people, in some measure at least, belonged the right to select their spiritual guides. Such right of choice implied responsibility to the choosing power. The preacher was not a royal agent or a member of a sacred order set over a parish whose inhabitants had no voice in his selection; he was a minister whose leadership had been sought by those whom he served. Such a relation implied responsibility to his people—a certain measure of control on their part over him, even if wholly undefined. Then, too, the statute-book which the Puritan insisted should be the ultimate rule of ecclesiastical administration was something other than the laws of the realm. No ceremony or office "by law established" was right till it accorded with the Word of God. And though the Puritan held that the Bible was so plain that all who sincerely read its teachings must understand them in the same way, what he really did was to subject the ecclesiastical statutes of the realm of England to revision in accordance with his individual understanding of the divine revelation. This habit of testing by the Word of God taught the Puritan, as no man of his time was taught, to think for himself. He might be slow in carrying his principles from the realm of the church to the field of politics; but the Puritan could no more avoid applying them equally in both directions than the Anglican. It was no accident that made the Puritan query whether a sovereign was not responsible to his subjects for his administration of their interests, or whether the royal acts and enactments should not be justified by some standard higher than the kingly will. It was a perception of this tendency that, quite as much as any religious antipathy, roused the hostility of the supporters of the royal authority against the Puritan.

The influence of continental Calvinism in developing one of the two great parties within the English Establishment has thus been seen to have been profound. But the degree in which the more radical movements which are now to be considered were dependent on impulses traceable to the Anabaptists of the Continent is far less certain. These movements, springing up on a soil made ready by Puritanism, were the source of modern Congregationalism. In many respects—in their abandonment of the State Church, in their direct appeal to the Word of God for every detail of administration, in their organization and officers—their likeness to those of the radical Reformers of the Continent is so striking that some affiliation seems almost certain. Nor is the geographical argument for probable connection with continental movements less weighty. These radical English efforts for a complete reformation had their chief support in the eastern counties, especially in the vicinity of Norwich and of London. These regions had long been the recipient of Dutch immigration; and the influx from the Netherlands had vastly increased during the early reign of Elizabeth, owing to the tyranny of Philip II. In 1562 the Dutch and Walloons settled in England numbered 30,000. By 1568 some 5225 of the people of London were of this immigration; and by 1587 they constituted more than half of the population of Norwich, while they were largely present in other coast towns. Now these immigrants were chiefly artisans, and among the workmen of Holland Anabaptist views were widely disseminated; and while it would be unjustifiable to claim that these exiles on English soil were chiefly, or largely, Anabaptists, there were Anabaptists among them, and an Anabaptist way of thinking may not improbably have been widely induced among those who may have been entirely unconscious of the source from which their impulse came. Certainly the resemblances between the Anabaptist movements of the Continent and English Congregationalism in theories of church polity, and the geographical possibilities of contact between the two, are sufficiently manifest to make a denial of relationship exceedingly difficult.

But the points of dissimilarity between these extreme English Protestants and the continental radicals are also conspicuous. They rejected doctrines much prized by the Anabaptists, like believers' baptism; they retained oaths; they recognized it as the duty of a Christian, if so required, to serve the state as a magistrate or a soldier. These diversities, combined with the absence from their writings of any sense of indebtedness to continental teachers, and the purely English character of their names as far as known, show that whatever they may have gained from the thought of the Continent was indirect and unconscious, and that their own work was in a large measure independent.

The first traces of a movement in England which insisted on a separation from the Establishment in order to a fuller reformation, and which thus went beyond Puritanism in the direction of early Congregationalism, are found in London in the year 1567. Attempts have indeed been made to demonstrate the existence of Separatist churches under the reign of Mary, but the secret congregations of her time seem to have been simply persecuted Protestants of the

Establishment as it had been in the days of Edward VI. On June 19, 1567, however, the authorities broke up an assembly of another character. A body of men and women had gathered at Plumbers' Hall in London on that day, ostensibly to celebrate a wedding, and really with the added purpose of holding worship in what they deemed a purer manner than that of the Church of England. The inruption of the officers of the law into their little meeting was followed by the arrest of some fifteen of those present, their committal to prison, and their examination by Edmund Grindal, then the bishop of the London diocese. By this examination it appeared that this little body regarded the ceremonies and canon law of the Establishment as evil, and had therefore organized for its own worship apart from the constituted parishes of the land. Other papers, especially a petition to Queen Elizabeth, prepared in 1571 after their pastor and deacon had died in prison, show their views and procedure more clearly. In this document they style themselves "a poor congregation whom God hath separated from the churches of England, and from the mingled and false worshiping therein used." As a church assembly, it furthermore appears that they had at least two officers of their own selection, "our minister, Richard Fitz, Thomas Bowland, deacon"; and that they "do serve the Lord every Sabbath-day in houses, and on the fourth day in the week we meet or come together weekly to use prayer and exercise discipline on them which do deserve it, by the strength and sure warrant of the Lord's good Word, as in Matt. xviii. 15–18."

Here was a very rudimentary type of Congregationalism; but its advance beyond Puritanism was decided. These men and women had evidently cut loose from the idea of a national church. They had come to the conclusion that they themselves could constitute a church on the

Scripture model. They had chosen their officers; and they had administered discipline apparently as the work of the whole congregation, though in regard to this most important particular the petition, as just quoted, is not as definite as could be wished. These acts, taken together, certainly show that this persecuted body at Plumbers' Hall was groping after the Congregational ideal. They were indeed far from its full realization. They were a company of poor, ignorant Christians, trying to carry out a complete reformation. They had seen only a little way on the road thither; but they had caught a glimpse, imperfect though it was, of the New Testament pattern of the church.

This little London church of which Fitz was minister had no lasting influence and arrived at no greater definiteness of view. The strong hand of government was heavy upon it, its worship was broken up, and after a period of suffering in the various prisons of London which cost its leaders their lives, it disappeared from human sight. Possibly its scattered members maintained worship for years in London—we get occasional glimpses of illegal assemblies, the nature of which is not very clear, meeting from time to time in and about London, and attracting the occasional notice of the government. Possibly it contributed to the formation of the London church which, twenty-one years after the petition that has been quoted, chose Francis Johnson for its pastor and John Greenwood for its teacher, and which had Henry Barrowe for its leading member. But though perhaps probable, this continued existence of Fitz's church is only conjectural. Had it been the sole witness to a completer reformation, Congregationalism would never have come into being. The work which the London church of 1567 apparently began to do was really accomplished, and the Congregational system really set forth so as first to claim any considerable degree of attention, through the labors and writings of Robert Browne—to whom this polity is so indebted, in spite of any beginnings made by Richard Fitz and his associates, that he deserves the title of the father of modern Congregationalism.

CHAPTER II.

EARLY ENGLISH CONGREGATIONALISM.

ROBERT BROWNE, whose writings contain the first definite statement of Congregational principles from an English pen, was neither in fixity of character nor in sagacity of method a man to win admiration or to command personal respect. His ultimate conformity to the Church of England caused early Congregationalists to resent the application of his name to their churches, and still leads occasional writers on Congregational history to disparage his services or discredit his leadership. Nor have historians of the Establishment forgotten, in spite of his reconciliation to the English Church, the fierceness of the attack which he made for a time upon that body. His personal qualifications were not those of a leader in an enterprise demanding patience. He had little capacity to give peace or permanency to the congregations which he founded, and small faculty for holding continuous fellowship with his associates. He was a man of rash impulsiveness of temperament always.

Yet when all detractions have been made from his personal worth, there can be no question that he was, at least during the portion of his career with which we have to do, a man of sincerity and of warm Christian faith; and the probability seems strong, as Dr. Dexter has pointed out, that the abandonment of his Congregational professions, which has cost him the respect due to a confessor, was the result of mental break-down consequent upon disappointments and imprisonments rather than any real denial of the beliefs for which he had proved himself ready to suffer. Whatever his defects may have been, he enjoys the distinction not only of being the first to formulate Congregational polity, but the earliest Englishman also to proclaim the doctrine that church and state should be mutually independent. A man of such clearness of insight, and who made such large contributions to Congregational development, cannot be denied a prominent place in the history of Congregational beginnings.

Browne came of a family of considerable local prominence in Rutlandshire, which had an estate at Tolethorpe, and was connected with that of Lord Burghley, who was from the neighboring county of Lincoln. Here at Tolethorpe Browne was born about the year 1550, though the exact date is still undiscovered. No details of his early life have been preserved; if we may judge by his early manhood, he must have been a youth of feeble health but of eager impulsiveness. By 1570 he was a student at Corpus Christi College in the University of Cambridge, and in 1572 he received there his degree of bachelor of arts. The university at the time was turmoiled by the great controversy between Cartwright and Whitgift—a contest which cost Cartwright his professorship in December, 1570, and his fellowship at Trinity College in September, 1571, but which made him more conspicuously than ever the champion of the Puritan cause. No atmosphere more adapted to excite an eager young student could well be imagined; and Browne was doubtless now awakened, if he had not been before, to the importance of a further reformation of the English Church. Evidences of his own pronounced attitude in sympathy with the radical party are soon apparent. Unless the historian Strype has confused him with a man of similar name, as is not impossibly the case, Browne was in 1571, a year before his graduation, a chaplain in the household of the Duke of Norfolk, and of opinions so obnoxious to his churchly superiors that the duke was moved to plead in his behalf that his position was a privileged station, in order to save him from citation. However this may have been, for some three years after his graduation he taught school, probably in Southwark; and during this period he preached occasionally, at considerable peril, to unlawful gatherings of Christian people met together for divine worship in gravel-pits about Islington. His teaching being interrupted by the plague, he was soon back in Cambridge; but more important for him than any course of study undertaken at the university was his entrance into the family and under the theological instruction of Rev. Richard Greenham of the neighboring village of Dry Drayton. Introduced into this strenuous Puritan home, Browne's good qualities won speedy recognition from its head, and though Greenham had little sympathy with Separatist ideas, Browne was encouraged by him to preach in Puritan pulpits, apparently without the license of a bishop. Nor were Browne's ministrations in any way unacceptable. An urgent request from a congregation in Cambridge, probably that of Benet Church, induced him to labor for half a year in that town, and his hearers would gladly have secured his ministrations more permanently had not a change in his own views rendered his continuance even in the Puritan wing of the Church of England impossible.

This momentous change, which transformed the zealous young preacher from a Puritan, waiting like thousands of others for the further reform of the English Establishment by the slow process of agitation and the hand of civil authority, into a Separatist, attacking the Church of England as an unchristian body and insisting on the segregation of religious men and women from its fellowship, occurred during this Cambridge ministry, and probably in 1579. As Browne looked upon the condition of the Establishment, with its all-inclusive membership and its too frequent toleration of unfit men in the ministry, he felt, as every Puritan did, a burning desire for its reformation. But he felt now, what the Puritan did not, that the only way that this reformation was to be brought about was by separation from a body where such unworthy persons were tolerated. Most of all he was convinced that any dependence upon the licensure of bishops for ministerial authority was a sin, since to the bishops more than to any other class of church officers it seemed to him that the hindrance of the necessary reformation of the church was due. They prevented the exercise of discipline desired by the Puritans, they silenced the preachers most eager for reform, they kept the church in much the state in which it had been when it came out of its papal subjection at the beginning of Elizabeth's reign. Browne therefore now proclaimed to his Cambridge hearers that their own reformation was incomplete; and, though it seems almost certain that he must already have received episcopal ordination, he now repudiated all dependence on the authorization of bishops, and denounced the whole order. The consequence was that he was speedily silenced.

The notification of his inhibition from preaching Browne received with scorn, and he seems to have been impelled by it to a yet firmer conviction that it was his duty to leave a church where episcopal authority could be, as he thought, so abused, and where full Christian life seemed to him so hedged about with hindrances. Having heard that in the adjacent county of Norfolk there were those who were seeking a purified church, he now determined to join them; but at this juncture a former acquaintance,

Robert Harrison, came to Cambridge from Norwich, the chief city of Norfolk, and it was to this friend's house at Norwich that Browne went when he took his departure from Cambridge, probably in 1580. Harrison, who for several years was to be the companion and associate of Browne, was of maturer age, though his seems to have been the less masterful mind. He had graduated at Corpus Christi College, Cambridge, in 1567, and had already had difficulties with the ecclesiastical authorities owing to pronounced Puritan scruples regarding certain portions of the service. A man less erratic in his tendencies than Browne, and less fruitful also in his reasoning, he added an element of stability for a time to the congregation which Browne gathered, and his pecuniary assistance apparently made possible the publication of Browne's books. But his connection with the Congregational movement was brief; by about 1585 he was no longer of the living.

It was in study and discussion with Harrison at Norwich that Browne fully worked out his theories of church polity. Evidently his investigation of the scattered hints contained in the pages of the New Testament was profound; and to his thinking the Scriptures were the direct source of his system. But it is not impossible that some indirect influence of Anabaptist thought may have aided in shaping Browne's views. He had been attracted to Norfolk by the presence there of persons desirous for a radical reformation of the Establishment as well as by his friendship for Harrison. Who these persons were it is hard to tell. But Norfolk was a county whose towns contained a large admixture of Dutch handicraftsmen, and the suggestion seems a probable one that Anabaptist modes of thought, imported with these Hollanders into their new English home, may have borne some fruitage, and may have unconsciously affected Browne himself in his conceptions of the church. Though no trace of a recognition of indebtedness to Anabaptist thought can be found in Browne's writings, and though we discover no Dutch names among the small number of his followers whom we know by name at all, the similarity of the system which he now worked out to that of the Anabaptists is so great in many respects that the conclusion is hard to avoid that the resemblance is more than accidental. At the same time, its unlikeness in other important features, as, for instance, the doctrine of baptism, is so marked that we may be sure that Browne did not borrow directly or consciously; and that if influenced by the Anabaptist movement at all, as it seems decidedly probable that he was, it must have been in consequence of an Anabaptist way of thinking in the regions of eastern England, where Dutch immigrants were numerous, rather than by contact with avowed Anabaptists.

Browne was, in early life at least, a man in whom belief was coupled with action; and the development of his system during the first months of his residence at Norwich was followed by the formation, on Congregational lines, of a church in that city some time in 1580 or 1581. But though Browne was the pastor of this little flock, his missionary efforts extended beyond the borders of Norfolk certainly as far as Bury St. Edmunds, where his preaching was received with much appreciation by the humbler classes, and where he possibly established a church, and certainly made disciples who ultimately suffered death for distributing his books. This activity brought upon Browne the hand of ecclesiastical restraint, though his relationship to Lord Burghley and that nobleman's interest in him—an interest which involved no sympathy with his views—prevented the degree of severity that would have been measured out to a less powerfully connected innovator. But the opposition of the Bishop of Norwich, and soon that also of the Archbishop of Canterbury, convinced the major part of the little Norwich church that it was useless to attempt to carry on its work in England; and therefore, after some debate in which Scotland and the Channel Islands were considered, it emigrated, probably late in 1581, to Middelburg, a little city in the Dutch province of Zeland, which had long had extensive trade relations with the eastern towns of England, and where resident English merchants maintained a congregation of strongly Puritan tendencies, now under the pastoral charge of the exiled Cartwright. A portion of the church, it seems certain, remained at Norwich and continued in some humble fashion its organization.

Arrived on Dutch soil, Browne and Harrison still continued their interest in their English home. The congregation under their care preserved its independence, it appears, as long as Browne remained. Indeed, Browne deemed that Puritanism, even of the strenuous type represented by Cartwright, was unworthy of fellowship, since it continued in the national church, from which he thought it the duty of a Christian to come out; and this feeling of dislike was repaid by the aversion of the Puritans to the whole Separatist movement. To influence the people of the land which he had left, Browne, with the aid of Harrison, sent forth from Middelburg three tracts during the year 1582, of which two are of the utmost importance in early Congregational literature. One, named "A Treatise of Reformation without Tarying for anie, and of the wickednesse of those Preachers, which will not reforme till the Magistrate commaunde or compell them," carries its burden on its title. It is a strenuous argument for instant separation from the Establishment, and a special attack upon the position of the Puritans who were waiting within the Church of England for its reform by civil authority.

The other, entitled "A Booke which Sheweth the life and manners of all true Christians, and howe vnlike they are vnto Turkes and Papistes, and Heathen folke," is the first systematic exposition of its principles which Congregationalism produced. In it, under an elaborate and somewhat mechanical form of questions, counter-questions, and definitions, Browne outlined his system as he read it in the Word of God. To his thinking a Christian church is a body of professed believers in Christ, united to one another and to their Lord by a voluntary covenant. This covenant is the constitutive element which transforms an assembly of Christians into a church. Its members are not all the baptized inhabitants of a kingdom, but only those possessed of Christian character. Such a church is under the immediate headship of Christ, and is to be ruled only by laws and officers of his appointment. To each church Christ has intrusted its own government, discipline, and choice of officers; and the abiding officers are those designated in the New Testament, the pastor, teacher, elders, deacons, and widows, whom the church is to select and set apart for their various duties. But the presence of these officers does not relieve the ordinary member of responsibility for the welfare of the church to which he belongs. On the contrary, Christ is the immediate Lord not only of the church but of every member of it, and each member is responsible to him for the stewardship of the graces with which he has been intrusted. This directness of connection between Christ and all the members of his church made Browne's polity practically democratic, and rendered it more prophetic of what Congregationalism has become in our century than were the more aristocratic theories of Barrowe and of the settlers of New England.

But while Browne thus asserted the full autonomy of the local church and the full responsibility of each member for its good order, he held also that churches have obligations one toward another which bind them to mutual watch and brotherly helpfulness. Here, then, in germ at least, Browne set forth that conception of mutual accountability which is one of the distinguishing features of Congregationalism, and which renders his system something more than bald Independency.

In one other matter also Browne's views were prophetic. To his thinking the civil authorities have no right to exercise lordship over spiritual concerns, or to enforce submission to any ecclesiastical system. It was an opinion already advanced by the Anabaptists of the Continent, but which no Englishman had yet proclaimed, and it found little echo even among his immediate disciples. Harrison did not share it, the London-Amsterdam church of Johnson and Ainsworth did not sympathize with it, and we shall find that early New England had no place for it. But in this, as in many other directions, Browne saw more clearly than men of his century of far greater stability and personal worth than he.

The opinions advanced in these tracts by Browne from his safe retreat in Holland were far too revolutionary to meet with toleration in England, and it was for circulation in England that the pamphlets were designed. Soon they were sent in considerable numbers, apparently in unbound sheets, to those places in his native island where Browne had labored, and on June 30, 1583, they called forth a proclamation in the name of Queen Elizabeth, in which they are described as "sundry seditious, scismaticall, and erronious printed Bookes and libelles, tending to the deprauing of the Ecclesiastical gouernment established within this Realme"; and all persons possessing them are ordered to give them up, while all who distribute them are threatened with the penalties of sedition. But even before this proclamation had been put forth, on June 4 and 5, 1583, two men, John Coppin and Elias Thacker, were hanged at Bury St. Edmunds on the dual charge of heresy and the circulation of the works of Browne and Harrison—some forty of the confiscated books being burned at the executions.

But by the time that these martyrs to Congregationalism were giving up their lives, Browne's flock in Middelburg were in serious division. His own disposition unfitted him to unite or conciliate discordant elements. He disagreed with his friend Harrison, he felt that his presence with the congregation which he had led into exile had become irksome; and therefore, late in 1583, Browne and four or five of his followers, with their families, went from Holland to Scotland. But in Scotland Browne met with nothing but opposition, extending even to imprisonment, from the ecclesiastical authorities of that Presbyterian land. Here he not only utterly failed to secure any following of importance, he came to the conclusion that the church government of Scotland was more overbearing and less tolerable than even the Episcopacy of England.

Browne's work as a reformer was now nearly over. By the summer of 1584 he was apparently once more in England, where he seems to have met with imprisonment, from which he was relieved by Lord Burghley. One more attempt to proclaim the truths for which he had witnessed—this time at Northampton, it is probable—led to his excommunication by the Bishop of Peterborough in 1586. He might well be discouraged over his successive failures, and there is reason to believe that his health, never robust, had been shattered by his trials. The conjecture advanced by Dr. Dexter, that he was worn out mentally and physically, seems probable. At all events, he became head of a grammar school at Southwark, in November, 1586, on terms which bound him to keep peace with the Establishment and submit to its rites. In September, 1591, he received the rectorship of Achurch-cum-Thorpe—no doubt as the gift of Lord Burghley—and as rector of that obscure village he lived for forty years, dying, however, some time between June, 1631, and November, 1633, in Northampton jail, where he was confined owing to his violent resistance to the collection of a debt or a tax by an officer of his parish.

The seed which Browne had sowed in so many places, and which he had not the qualities long to cultivate, bore a harvest that was better than the sower. At Norwich a portion of the church which Browne had gathered continued the organization after he and a majority of its fellowship had gone to Holland; and in other places, Congregational views, spread we know not how, took root and bore fruit. The preface to the Confession put forth by the London-Amsterdam church in 1596 speaks of witnesses to Congregational principles in Bury St. Edmunds, in Gloucester, and in London; while other hints are given us of Separatist associations in Chatham and in the west of England. But of all these obscure adherents to what they believed to be the polity taught by the Word of God, only those of London formed a church of any prominence or influenced the development of Congregational thought. Possibly some continuous religious organization had been maintained by the London Separatists from the time of Richard Fitz and his fellow-prisoners of 1567; but it is not till 1586 or 1587 that the existence of the Separatist gatherings from which the London church was to be developed is clearly manifest. The early history of that church is closely bound up with the stories of three men of high character—Henry Barrowe, John Greenwood, and John Penry—all of whom gave their lives for the cause which they advocated, and one of whom, Barrowe, turned Congregational thought in a direction considerably different from that imparted to it by Browne; so that his work constitutes a second stage in the growth of the system. Neither of these men can be affirmed to have been the founder of London Separatism, however, nor do they seem to have been the only proclaimers of Separatist doctrines in that city. On the contrary, hints of occasional meetings in private houses and in secluded spots in and near London, and of the ministrations of a dozen leaders of these petty assemblies, show that the Separatist leaven was considerably widespread during the four or five years previous to 1592. But the first event of importance in the history of London Congregationalism as now known to us is the arrest of Greenwood in the autumn of 1586.

John Greenwood was a young clergyman of the Establishment, who had studied from March, 1578, to his graduation in 1580-81 at Cambridge, where he had been a sizar, or pecuniarily assisted student, of Corpus Christi College. His graduation had been followed by his ordination; but Puritan scruples, possibly imbibed at Cambridge, led Greenwood to become a chaplain in the household of Lord Rich, a Puritan nobleman of Essex. By what further processes he advanced from Puritanism to Separatism we do not know—not improbably Browne's books may have awakened his thought—but certainly in the autumn of 1586 he was preaching to illegal assemblies in London, and at one of these gatherings, held at a house in that city, he was seized and thence transferred to the Clink prison.

On news of his arrest, Greenwood was visited in his prison by his friend and fellow-laborer, Henry Barrowe, a man of higher social rank, of maturer years, and far greater abilities. Barrowe's teaching had already incurred the displeasure of Archbishop Whitgift; and therefore the jailer, without legal warrant, but well knowing that his arrest would be gratifying to the ecclesiastical authorities, detained Greenwood's visitor as a prisoner. Thenceforward till their death on a common scaffold, Barrowe and Greenwood were imprisoned, save for brief periods of release on bail; and during most of this time they shared the same sufferings and labors.

Henry Barrowe was a man of much more than ordinary talents and advantages. He was of a Norfolk family of some prominence, and his education had been at Clare Hall, in the University of Cambridge, where he was a student from 1566 to 1569–70. Though brought thus into a Puritan atmosphere, no thought of personal religion, much less of ministerial service, was apparently entertained by him during his student days, or for some years thereafter. He came to London, becoming a lawyer of Gray's Inn in 1576, and was of sufficient prominence to have access to the royal presence; but he was a man of immoral life, and might have so continued to the end of his days had not a chance sermon been the means of his spiritual awakening. A man of impetuous temper always, he passed at once from his former profligacy to extreme Puritanism. And from Puritanism he was led onward—there is some reason to think through the agency of Greenwood—to a type of Congregational Separatism, which, if not quite so extreme as that of Browne, nevertheless viewed the English Establishment as unscriptural and therefore unchristian.

The two prisoners were speedily and repeatedly brought before Archbishop Whitgift, John Aylmer, Bishop of London, and other ecclesiastical dignitaries; and also examined by a commission, embracing, besides these high officials of the church, the chief-justices, Lord Burghley, and other prominent civilians. Before all these examiners they maintained firmly their conviction that the government, rites, and sacraments of the Establishment were not ordered as Christ designed; and that its all-inclusive membership made it no true church. They as firmly asserted their belief that the queen was sovereign in all civil affairs, but they denied to her any power over the church, of which Christ is the sufficient head. In these harassing interrogations Greenwood was the more self-controlled; the impetuous spirit of Barrowe met the browbeatings of the bishops more often with anger and invective. Lord Burghley, when he appeared on the scene, manifested much of his usual gravity; but the impression left on the mind is that the bishops in these examinations showed little charity and less courtesy. All attempts to shake the constancy of the prisoners were unavailing.

Having failed thus by judicial examination to bring the two Separatists to an acknowledgment that their teachings were erroneous, Whitgift and Aylmer, with the counsel of the two chief-justices of the realm, after Barrowe and Greenwood had been for more than two years in confinement, commissioned a number of the clergy of the vicinity of London to visit these and similar prisoners at least twice a week and attempt their recovery to conformity. The visits were useless; but they provoked a desire on the part of the chief prisoners to set their case before the reading public, which bore notable fruit. Under the most disadvantageous circumstances, unable, as Barrowe himself declared, to keep one sheet at hand while a second was written, compelled to smuggle their writings out of prison page by page, and to have them carried surreptitiously to Dort in Holland by friendly hands for printing, Barrowe and Greenwood produced no less than eight controversial and expository treatises, containing over nine hundred printed pages. Chief in importance perhaps is the "Trve

Description ovt of the Word of God, of the visible Church," of 1589, a brief sketch in which the writers set forth their conception of what God designed his church should be, and which, though somewhat ideal in tone, is evidently a document which the yet imperfectly organized congregation at London looked upon as in some sense its creed. But almost equally valuable, and far more voluminous, are Barrowe's "Brief Discouerie of the False Church," of 1590—a cogent criticism of the existing condition of the Establishment—and Barrowe and Greenwood's "Plaine Refutation of M. Giffards Booke, intituled, A short treatise gainst the Donatistes of England," printed in 1591, which was not only a vigorous reply to the censures of an able Puritan critic, but was to be in a most remarkable way the means of the conversion of Francis Johnson, the first regular pastor of this London church of which Barrowe and Greenwood were so conspicuous members. Here, then, was an activity which must greatly have annoyed the supporters of existing ecclesiastical institutions, while it aided much in the spread of Separatist views.

In these tracts Barrowe and Greenwood presented a theory of the church in most points identical with that of Browne. With him they hold that a true church is a company of "faithful and holie people," having as its officers pastors, teachers, elders, deacons, and widows, who obtain their office "by the holy & free election of the Lordes holie and free people." To this church, as a whole, the power of discipline has been intrusted, and of it Christ is the immediate head. But while the London prisoners thus agree for the most part with Browne, they were not as democratic as he. The execution of government they shut up, practically, in the hands of the church officers. It is the duty of the ordinary membership to be "a most humble, meek, obedient, faithfull, and loving people." And this semi-Presbyterian conception of the internal government of the church, instead of the democracy of Browne, dominated all early English and American Congregationalism. As Rev. Samuel Stone, of Hartford, epigrammatically expressed this theory two generations after Barrowe's death, it placed the officers as "a speaking aristocracy in the face of a silent democracy." That in modern Congregationalism this democracy is no longer silent is evidence that in this particular Browne saw more clearly than Barrowe; but, for a century after Barrowe wrote, his view was the generally accepted Congregational theory of the relations of officers and people.

These writings from the London prisons, and the efforts of humbler members of the Separatist company, gained converts. Barrowe and Greenwood, if the most prominent, were by no means the only Separatists now under confinement. At the time when certain of the London clergy were deputed to attempt the conversion of the Nonconformists in 1589 there were fifty-two persons under arrest, and though it is too much to affirm that all were Congregational Separatists, it is probable that most of them were of Barrowe's way of thinking. A petition preserved by Strype, and probably of the year 1592, has appended to it the names of fifty-nine surviving prisoners who besought the favor of Lord Burghley, and in this case there seems little doubt that all the signers were Separatists. Whether this petition had any influence on the government or not, it is certain that the treatment of these prisoners for a few months in 1592 was less severe than it had been, and that Greenwood, if not Barrowe, was occasionally allowed to go beyond his prison walls. This lull in the storm, if such it deserves to be called, was marked by two events of importance, the addition of John

Penry and of Francis Johnson to the Separatist company, and the completion of its organization by the London church.

John Penry, one of the martyrs of Congregationalism, and one to whom youth and purity of character lend a touch of romance, was of Welsh birth and Roman Catholic training. In 1580 he entered the college of Peterhouse, at Cambridge, when about twenty-one years old, and before his graduation in 1583–84 had abandoned Catholicism and embraced an ardent type of Puritanism. His ready pen was soon busied with tracts advocating the claims of Wales on missionary effort, and urging at the same time the Puritan cause. Besides a voluminous series of controversial tractates of which he was the acknowledged author, he appears to have been connected with the publication, though not probably with the composition, of the remarkable series of satirical attacks upon the Establishment issued in 1588 and 1589, and known as the Martin Marprelate pamphlets, the moral worth of which is still disputed in some quarters, but which are confessedly among the most effective pasquinades ever written in the English tongue.

Penry's acknowledged writings speedily called down upon him the censure of Archbishop Whitgift and the High Commission; but it was not till the pursuit after all suspected of connection with the Mar-prelate tracts had become keen that he fled from England to Scotland in 1589. Here he found so much sympathy for his Puritan views, that, in spite of an autograph letter of Elizabeth requesting his extradition, and a proclamation of James VI. against him, he enjoyed protection till 1592. He now came to London, and whether he had advanced from Puritanism to Separatism during his stay in Scotland, and was so attracted to the congregation of which Barrowe and Greenwood were members, or whether he was won to their principles after his return to English soil, Penry joined the Separatist communion in the autumn of the year of his arrival.

Like Greenwood and Penry, Francis Johnson, the second of the notable additions to the London Separatists, was a clergyman of the Church of England. Of Yorkshire birth, he had, like them, enjoyed the training of Cambridge, where he had graduated in 1581. It was while enjoying a fellowship in Christ's College that a sermon of strong Puritan flavor preached by him led to his imprisonment, and ultimately to his expulsion from the university in 1589 and his self-exile to Middelburg, where he became pastor of the English church which had enjoyed the services of Cartwright. Johnson had no more sympathy than other Puritans for the Separatists, and on learning that Barrowe and Greenwood's "Plaine Refutation" of his fellow-Puritan Gifford's attack upon Separatism was being printed in 1591 either at Dort or at Middelburg, he notified the English ambassador of the proposed publication, and was charged to see the books burned. This he did most thoroughly; but as a memento of his exploit Johnson preserved two copies from the flames. He had not yet read the works which he had condemned, and the perusal of this volume carried conviction to him. He resigned his position at Middelburg, sought out Barrowe in the London prison, and was soon one of the most prominent of the London Separatist church.

Thus strengthened in membership, and enjoying a little respite from the severer forms of persecution, the London church felt encouraged to perfect its organization by the appointment of the officers designated, as it believed, in the Bible. The church had, indeed, for several years exercised certain ecclesiastical acts. It had admitted members as early as 1588 by a formal covenant that they "wold walke with the rest; & y[t] so longe as they did walke in the way of the Lorde, & as farr as might be warranted by the word of God." It had also exercised the discipline of excommunication; though, owing to its want of officers, it does not appear to have administered the Lord's Supper. That it had so long remained unofficered was doubtless due to the hope that those who were the church's recognized leaders would be released from imprisonment; and now that Greenwood was allowed to go beyond his prison walls and Penry and Johnson had been added to the company, the time seemed ripe for action. Barrowe was ineligible, we may believe, by reason of his continued confinement, and Penry refused an election, since he still hoped to spend his life in Wales rather than in London; but in September, 1592, the London church, gathered in the house of a Mr. Fox, in Nicholas Lane, elected Johnson as its pastor and Greenwood as its teacher; and associated with them as elders Daniel Studley, who had helped to smuggle Barrowe's manuscripts out of the prison, and George Kniston or Knyveton. At the same time Christopher Bowman and Nicholas Lee were chosen deacons, and the sacraments of baptism and the eucharist were administered.

This evident growth of the Separatist Church in London renewed the alarm of the ecclesiastical authorities. In December following Johnson and Greenwood were both lodged in prison; Penry avoided arrest for a few weeks longer, but in March, 1593, he was captured, and the same month saw the arrest of fifty-six of the humbler members of the persecuted communion. It was determined to make an example of the leaders. Accordingly, after examination before Chief-Justice Popham, Barrowe and Greenwood were tried on March 23, 1593. Their accusation was based distinctly on the law of the twenty-third year of Elizabeth, making it a capital offense to write any book maliciously attacking the authority of the queen or inciting to rebellion. On this charge, in spite of their protests of loyalty in all civil matters, they were convicted; but it was not until an attempt had been made to induce them to recant by the labors of certain clergymen, and they had once been reprieved on the gallows itself, that they were hanged, on April 6, 1593. Their martyrdom was followed on May 21st by the condemnation of Penry—the conclusive evidence in his case being an unfinished draught of a petition to the queen, in which he complained that she and her government prevented the due service of God as enjoined in his Word. This private paper was held to be a seditious attack upon the sovereign, and on May 29th Penry joined that company who have not counted their lives dear unto themselves that they might testify to what they believed to be the gospel of the grace of God.

These executions had the warm approval of the bishops, but they were not regarded with satisfaction by many in England who were far enough from sharing Separatist opinions. While these witnesses for their faith had been under trial Parliament had been discussing a bill introduced by the bishops designed to strengthen the action of the courts in dealing with critics of the Establishment. In the discussion of this bill Sir Walter Raleigh had uttered his absurdly exaggerated estimate that the Brownists of England numbered more than twenty thousand. But the bishops had found the Commons unsubmissive, and the law as finally passed made the penalty for the denial of the queen's supremacy, or attendance on illegal meetings, forfeiture of goods and banishment, instead of death. It was under this new law that the government now began to treat its numerous Separatist prisoners in a manner well calculated to destroy their feeble organization. While their more prominent survivors, like Johnson, were kept in confinement, the less important prisoners were compelled to go into exile. These poor artisans, aided in part by a little property left for their use by Barrowe, made their way within the year of his execution to Holland; and there after a few months settled in Amsterdam, living in the direst poverty, and still looking to their officers in the London prisons for leadership and advice.

It was in the first year or two of this Dutch exile, however, that a young man of whose early history we know little joined himself to this company—Henry Ainsworth; a man who probably never enjoyed a university education, but who had few superiors as a Hebraist in his own day and whose expositions of the Old Testament are still held in esteem. The most learned of early Congregationalists, he was also one of the most deserving; and his sweet-tempered love of peace made him an excellent counselor for the struggling church in the years of internal turmoil which it passed through at Amsterdam. Ainsworth had been born in 1570 or 1571 at Swanton, probably a village of that name near Norwich, the city where Browne established his church; but of the means of his conversion to Separatist views or of the circumstances which brought him to Amsterdam we know nothing, save that he probably came by way of Ireland, and gained his livelihood after his arrival in the Dutch city as a porter in a bookseller's shop. And here, in some way unknown to us, these London Separatists found him, living, if Roger Williams was correctly informed, on boiled roots at ninepence a week, and eagerly pursuing every opportunity to increase his learning. This was the man whom the exiled church now chose, at some uncertain date, but clearly within two or three years of its coming to Amsterdam, to the teachership made vacant by the death of Greenwood.

Having thus in some measure made good their loss by martyrdom, this divided church, part of whose members were still in the London prisons and part in exile, put forth in 1596 a statement of its faith and polity and of the reasons which had led it to separation from the English Establishment, under the title of "A Trve Confession of the Faith, and Hvmble acknovvledgment oe the Alegeance, vvhich vvee hir Maiesties Subjects, falsely called Brovvnists, doo hould tovvards God, and yeild to hir Majestie and all other that are ouer vs in the Lord." Its execrable typography attested the poverty of its publishers, but its spirit was one of confident persuasion of the justice of its cause. In doctrine it did not differ from the current Calvinism of the age, while in polity it set forth the main principles of Congregationalism as already expounded by Barrowe. As was natural from men who had suffered so much for their beliefs as to the polity which the Bible enjoined, it was severe in its denunciations of the English Church, holding that "all that will bee saued, must vvith speed come forth of this Antichristian estate, leaving the suppression of it vnto the Magistrate to vvhom it belongeth." These poor prisoners and exiles were ready enough to affirm that the magistrate had no power to prescribe any other order than that established by our Lord, but they appealed to the same hand which had dealt out exile and death to them to abolish an ecclesiastical organization the unscripturalness of which they believed that they had demonstrated.

How long this division of the church between London and Amsterdam might have continued it is impossible to say, but it was brought to an end at last by the English Government itself, which, early in 1597, allowed the greater part of the still imprisoned members to join their associates in Holland, while it permitted Johnson and three others to join in an abortive enterprise for planting a colony on the Magdalen Islands in the Gulf of St. Lawrence, an expedition from which Johnson returned in time to join the waiting church at Amsterdam before the end of the year.

But unhappily the coming together of these separated elements was not altogether a union of peace. On no feature of church administration did Puritans and Separatists alike lay more stress than on discipline; and it must be confessed that those Congregationalists gathered by Browne at Norwich and these exiles from London carried the duties of brotherly watchfulness to a degree of minuteness that was captious and irritating in the extreme. The quarrel which was to turmoil the early Amsterdam life of this little communion had its beginnings in London in the objections of the pastor's brother to the fashion of the garments worn by the pastor's wife. It was protracted, dreary, personal; and it illustrated the fact, so often exemplified, that leadership in a great enterprise is no guarantee of exemption from pettiness and uncharitableness.

The story of this London church to its full gathering on alien soil has thus been followed with some minuteness; a glance at its later history will be sufficient. On the accession of James I. to the English throne in 1603, in common with reformers of all shades, its members cherished the hope of a change from the ecclesiastical policy of Elizabeth—a hope that was bitterly disappointed. A vain attempt to secure permission from the new sovereign to be allowed to worship God in England on the same terms as congregations of French and Dutch Protestants enjoyed in that island persuaded them that their only safety was in continued exile. But that exile was stormy. Johnson and others of the company were men of strong opinions. Divisions rent the church, especially after the arrival of the erratic John Smyth and his Gainsborough congregation in Amsterdam about 1606. Diversity of opinion as to the extent of the duties of church officers and the amount of power to be allowed to the ordinary members in church government separated Ainsworth and Johnson, and divided the flock under their charge into two congregations in 1610. Johnson died in Amsterdam in January, 1618, and Ainsworth followed him, not, as has sometimes been alleged, by poison, but by that plague of seventeenth-century scholars, the stone, in 1622 or 1623. With their departure from the scene the vitality of this much-divided organization seems to have been nearly spent, though there is reason to believe that it continued a feeble existence till 1701, when the remnant was received into the English Reformed Church of Amsterdam—a Puritan organization conformed in government to the Calvinistic Established Church of Holland, which had always enjoyed the approval of the Dutch authorities.

It is with mingled feelings that a modern Congregationalist looks back upon the attempts to establish the Congregational polity which have been narrated in this chapter. The story is one of strength and courage, of suffering willingly undergone, of heroism and martyrdom. But it is a story also of weakness and division and failure. The men whom it presents to our view had their full share of human infirmities; but they had a faith in God and a simple desire to do his will that is worthy of all praise. Yet had Browne and Barrowe and Greenwood and Johnson and Penry and Ainsworth been all the leaders that early Congregationalism produced, the system which they loved would scarcely have survived them. They did a noble and an indispensable work; but it was well that other workmen, more patient, more united, if less gifted, entered into their labors and reaped the harvest which they had sowed, but which they were not fitted to garner.

CHAPTER III.

CONGREGATIONALISM CARRIED TO AMERICA.

THE qualities of permanency, which were lacking in the Separatist churches thus far considered, were possessed by a Separatist congregation in the north of England, itself apparently the fruit of the labors of one of the most unstable men ever associated with the story of Congregationalism. John Smyth, the founder of this church, is first known to us as a student at Christ's College, Cambridge, where he graduated in 1575–76, and where he enjoyed a fellowship. What he did immediately after leaving Cambridge is not clear, but he seems after a time to have obtained a living as a clergyman of the Establishment at Gainsborough-on-Trent. How long his connection with the Church of England continued we do not know, but a period of nine months of mental struggle brought him to the Separatist position; he renounced the Establishment, and gathering a little flock of like-minded people, most probably in the year 1602, he became its pastor. Though this Congregational church had its origin and seat at Gainsborough, it soon gained adherents in the farming district outside the town, especially in the region where the borders of Nottinghamshire, Lincolnshire, and Yorkshire adjoin. Chief among these out-of-town converts to Separatism was William Brewster, the postmaster at Scrooby, on the main road from London to York. The ample, though dilapidated, "manor-house" which he occupied gave room for the gathering for worship of Separatist sympathizers like the youthful William Bradford of the neighboring hamlet of Austerfield, and others from other villages in the vicinity. Brewster was, at the time of the gathering of the Gainsborough church, a man nearly or quite forty years of age, of fair classical education, and of a good deal of knowledge of the world, gained in the employ of William Davison during that unfortunate statesman's embassy to Holland. A man of maturity, sound judgment, and stability, Brewster was a natural leader, though not in the pastoral office, for that section of the Gainsborough church that had its center at his house. But even more important for its development was the addition to the little company, apparently in 1604, though the exact time is a little uncertain, of John Robinson, on the whole the best-known minister connected with early Separatist Congregationalism. There seems some reason to believe that Robinson was by birth from the Gainsborough region, and that his union with Smyth and Brewster and their associates was in some sense a home-coming. However this may have been, he had entered Corpus Christi College, in Cambridge, in 1592, when about seventeen years of age; and after passing through the ordinary course of a student's life, became a minister of the Establishment and a fellow of his college. From about 1600 he labored, probably as a curate, either in Norwich or its vicinity. Here, in the neighborhood where Browne had taught, and where some traces of his work still continued, Robinson's thought advanced from Puritanism to Separatism, and his teachings became so marked as to lead to his suspension by the Bishop of Norwich; in consequence of which inhibition, and after a good deal of mental conflict, he now removed to the vicinity of Gainsborough and joined himself to the church there. It was at some uncertain date in 1605 or 1606, not long after his coming, that the Gainsborough church amicably divided, for safety and convenience, one portion continuing to meet under the guidance of Smyth for a little longer in its old home, and the other having its simple services at Scrooby and enjoying the ministry of Robinson and of the venerable Richard Clyfton, who had been rector at Babworth, a village near Scrooby.

The two branches of the original Gainsborough church were destined to experiences in some respects alike, but in other features singularly diverse. Both were speedily objects of governmental persecution. To escape this interference Smyth and the Gainsborough flock emigrated to Amsterdam, probably in 1606; while the Scrooby congregation was moved by similar reasons to try the same exiles' road in 1607 and 1608. But in Holland the differing qualities of the leaders of the two congregations had much to do in giving them different destinies. On their arrival in Amsterdam the impetuous Smyth and his associates settled as a second church side by side with the London-Amsterdam church of which Johnson and Ainsworth were the leaders, the stormy experiences of which have been mentioned in the preceding chapter. But with this older church Smyth soon quarreled. To his thinking the congregation of Johnson and Ainsworth was in error, since it used the English version of the Scriptures in public worship, instead of translating *viva voce*, and in 1608 he called on his church to have no fellowship with their neighbors until they should reform. The same prohibition of written or printed helps he extended to preaching and the singing of psalms. It was after this step had been taken, but probably in the next year, 1609, that Smyth, led thereto by contact with the Mennonites of Amsterdam, adopted Baptist views, and reorganizing his church, baptized himself and his associates. But even here Smyth did not rest. Doubt as to the rightfulness of the step which he had taken seems to have entered his mind, and some changes in other directions seem to have modified his theology, so that he and his sympathizers were next cast out, by his associates Helwys and Murton, from the congregation which he had led through so many changes. Smyth then made a vain attempt, in 1609, to enter the communion of the Amsterdam Mennonites; but failing in this, he remained outside of formal church fellowship till his death, in 1612. It was probably in the year of his death that his associates till the quarrel of 1609, Helwys and Murton, established in London the first of Baptist churches on English soil; and thus the Baptist fellowship of England and America traces its direct sources back to the same fountain at Gainsborough from which Plymouth Congregationalism flowed forth.

If Smyth thus gave to the exiles whom he led from Gainsborough a stormy experience at Amsterdam, the story of the Scrooby congregation under Robinson was healthful and peaceful. Their transfer to Amsterdam in 1607 and 1608 was effected in the face of much governmental opposition and many hardships, and, once arrived in the chief commercial city of Holland, they were debarred from permanent settlement by the well-grounded fear entertained by the leading members of the company that they would become involved in the disputes distracting the churches of Ainsworth and Johnson and of Smyth. Accordingly, in 1609, they took up their abode in Leyden, under the pastoral care of Robinson, and with Brewster as their ruling elder. Here they dwelt, working at such trades as they were able to learn, at peace with themselves, and earning the respect of their Dutch neighbors by their unswerving honesty. Here, too, Robinson and other prominent members purchased a large house, opposite St. Peter's church, for the use of the exiled congregation. Here Brewster printed books for such as desired to publish what was forbidden in England; and here, after a time, Robinson's unusual powers of debate won him recognition as a disputant against the Arminian champion Episcopius in one of the minor episodes of the great struggle over Calvinism then convulsing Holland.

But life was hard at the best for the exiles, though their church grew largely, and though some of their most valuable material, like young Edward Winslow, was added during this Leyden sojourn. It was difficult to keep the children free from the temptations of an alien city; it was above all distressing for those who were English in feeling and sympathy to see no prospect but that of gradual absorption in a foreign population; and for Christian men such as these not the least element of dissatisfaction with their lot was that it afforded so few opportunities to extend the knowledge of the gospel in its purity beyond their own circle. So it was, that, as time went on, the Scrooby-Leyden church began to debate more and more strenuously the possibility of emigration. Guiana, just then much talked of in English circles as a promising region for colonization, was discussed; but happily for the future of the United States, the decision finally reached was to apply to the London branch of the Virginia Company—a sub-organization having authority from King James I. to establish colonies on the American coast between the thirty-fourth and the forty-first degrees of latitude—for permission to emigrate under its auspices. There, on soil yet unbroken by the plowshares of civilization, but nevertheless in a real sense English, they hoped to plant the institutions of the gospel for which they had gone into the exile in Holland, and live as Englishmen, though free from the ecclesiastical Establishment which enforced uniformity in every hamlet of their native island. It was a momentous decision, far surpassing in its boldness any proposition of emigration in these days when the world is brought close together by steam; but the Leyden Christians had the example of the settlers of Virginia before them to show that it was not impossible of accomplishment. Yet it was not easy to carry the resolution into execution. The Virginia Company was willing enough to receive promising emigrants to open up its territories; but the Leyden congregation desired permission from the king, if possible, for the free exercise of their worship on the soil of the new settlement. That privilege was the real difficulty. In hope of securing it Robinson and Brewster provided their two commissioners to the English authorities in 1617 with a statement of the position of the Leyden church drawn up in seven remarkable articles, and intended to make the utmost possible concession to English prejudice. There is much reason to think that Robinson's type of Separatism was less strenuous and more tolerant than that of Browne or Barrowe, but in these articles the Leyden pastor and ruling elder declare their willingness to admit the authority of the king to appoint bishops, and his supremacy in all causes and over all persons, as well as the duty of yielding at least passive obedience to all his commands. They even were willing to admit the authority of the existing bishops as royal representatives, though they were careful not to ascribe any spiritual authority unto them. It was the utmost extreme of concession to which these exiles could go; and it is noteworthy in that while it preserved the most essential elements of the beliefs for which its writers had suffered, they were willing to give full toleration to the religious institutions established by law in England. Perhaps this readiness was the product merely of the strong desire to secure the privileges of toleration in return; but the London-Amsterdam church had shown itself wholly intolerant of the Establishment when in circumstances even more necessitous, and a large degree of toleration of others—when judged by Anglican or Puritan standards—was ever characteristic of the Plymouth colony, which had its germ in this Leyden church.

Conciliatory as this presentation was, the king, supported by the English ecclesiastical authorities, would give no guarantee of toleration to the suppliants. The utmost that could be obtained from James was a verbal understanding that as long as they behaved peaceably in their new home they would be unmolested. Encouraged by this promise, a patent was obtained from the company in June, 1619, in the name of an English friend of the struggling church—John Wincob—a patent of which they ultimately made no use. But in spite of the granting of the patent, the arrangements for the transfer of the exiles to America dragged; and at this juncture, early in 1620, negotiations were begun by merchants of Amsterdam looking for their settlement in New York, then the Dutch territory of the New Netherlands. It was while these new discussions were in progress that the London merchants, whom they had already approached, made definite terms with the Leyden emigrants. As finally agreed, the colonists and merchant-contributors were made into a stock company, in which the labor of each emigrant over sixteen years of age for seven years was considered equal to a contribution of £10 by the merchants. During the first seven years all profits and results of labor and trade as developed in the colony should go to the common stock, from which food, clothing, and tools for the colonists should come; and at the end of the period all should be divided among the stockholders. That the Leyden emigrants should be willing to enter into a bargain which valued their labor at so little in proportion to the financial contributions of the moneyed members of the partnership shows in the clearest light, as Palfrey has expressed it, "the slenderness of their means and the constancy of their purpose."

Yet even the conclusion of this hard bargain did not relieve the emigrants of their difficulties. Their scanty means, the uncertainty of the enterprise, and the inability or unwillingness of some of their number to undertake the journey even had their pecuniary resources been greater than was the case, had already made it evident that not quite half of the church could embark upon the expedition. With the majority Robinson was constrained to remain, though with a hope on his part to follow his friends later; and it may be that the wishes of the majority in this matter were aided by the opposition of the English contributing merchants, who probably were glad to avoid the notoriety of the presence in a colony, for the religious aspects of which they cared little, of so redoubtable an exponent of Separatism as Robinson. So it was agreed that the minority, who were to undertake the voyage, should be under the spiritual guidance of Elder William Brewster, and that while each body—those who went and those who remained—should be sufficiently independent ecclesiastically to administer its own affairs, yet they were to be still sufficiently one to receive members one from the other without question or testimonial. As a matter of fact, Brewster, who was an effective preacher, though retaining his position as elder, was practically pastor of the colonists, save in the administration of the sacraments, for nearly ten years after the settlement at Plymouth—the emigrant church looking upon the absent Robinson as in some sense their pastor as long as he lived, and finding no satisfactory successor for several years after his death.

In the smaller of the two vessels which had been obtained for the expedition—the "Speedwell"—the emigrants, or, as Bradford styles them, the Pilgrims, left Delftshaven, the port most convenient to Leyden, not far from the middle of July, 1620, encouraged on their way, either at the time of sailing or more probably at a fast just before leaving Leyden, by Robinson in a memorable and eloquent address urging upon them the duty of open-mindedness to the leadings of the Divine Spirit, and voicing the remarkable prediction that should English Puritans leave their island home and come to the New World no essential difference in church administration between them and the Pilgrims would be found. It detracts nothing from the sweetness and charity of this noble utterance that the "further light" from the "written Word" which Robinson exhorted his disciples to be ready to receive was, to his thinking, light on church polity rather than on doctrine. The declaration is in advance of the spirit of the speaker's age, and it shows the breadth of sympathy, that, combined as it was with firmness of conviction on those matters which he deemed fundamental, made him the best beloved and the most influential of the Separatist ministers.

From Delftshaven the "Speedwell" made her way to Southampton, England, where the "Mayflower" awaited them with some additions to the colony drawn directly from English sources. On August 5th–15th both vessels set sail, but soon put into Dartmouth for repairs; and the start was made afresh. But again the "Speedwell" proved unseaworthy, or, as the Pilgrims afterward believed, her captain and crew repented of the voyage; and back they turned, a hundred leagues beyond Land's End, for the English Plymouth. Here it was decided to abandon the misnamed "Speedwell," and here too the courage of some gave out, as well it might in view of all the difficulties of what must have seemed an almost hopeless enterprise. But at last, on September 6th–16th, the "Mayflower" sailed from Plymouth on her lonely voyage, freighted with one hundred and two colonists, of whom twenty-two were hired servants. Most of the independent members of the expedition had been of the Leyden congregation, though as the younger men naturally were more largely represented in the enterprise than the older, a considerable proportion of the Leyden emigrants had not been long of Robinson's fellowship. Brewster and Bradford had shared the fortunes of the church since its beginnings at Scrooby; John Carver, the first governor of the little colony, Deacon-Doctor Samuel Fuller, its physician and the man who was more than any other to be the means of transforming New England Puritanism into Congregationalism, Edward Winslow, its able man of affairs, Isaac Allerton, its unsatisfactory agent, had all been prominent in the congregation at Leyden; while John Alden, more famous in romance than conspicuous in the beginnings of the colony, had been engaged as a cooper at Southampton after the long journey had been begun. Quick-tempered and brave Myles Standish had come with the Leyden emigrants from Holland, but though he was to do much for the colony, he hardly sympathized with the religious aspirations which animated most of the company, for he was not a member of the church, and may have been by family inclined to Catholicism; but his heart was in the success of the enterprise for which his military ability had probably caused him to be chosen. This was the company, of somewhat diverse elements, but dominated by the men of Leyden training who constituted the majority of its adult membership, that sailed from the English Plymouth, and which, after a tedious voyage of no special eventfulness, found itself off the end of Cape Cod on November 9–19, 1620.

But here a serious embarrassment presented itself to the voyagers. The patent under which the company proposed to make its settlement was issued by the London branch of the Virginia Company—a body having no claim to jurisdiction north of forty-one degrees, a little northward of the present city of New York. They were clearly where they had no legal authority to be; and in this condition, finding it impossible to go to any place within the limits of their charter owing to the opposition of the sailors who had brought them over, they determined to settle in the region where Providence had cast them, and to provide for the good order of the little community by the organization of civil government. There is reason to believe that this step had been planned before leaving Leyden, but the form in which it was carried out must have been due to the unforeseen exigencies of the situation. It is strikingly illustrative of the indirect effects of Congregational training that these charterless exiles now proceeded, on November 11th–21st, to provide the basis of their state by a covenant, just as they would have organized a church. This document, drawn up and signed in the cabin of the "Mayflower," is as follows:

"In the name of God, Amen. We whose names are vnderwritten, the loyall Subiects of our dread soveraigne Lord King IAMES, by the grace of God of Great *Britaine*, *France*, and *Ireland* King, Defender of the Faith, &c.

"Having vnder-taken for the glory of God, and advancement of the Christian Faith, and honour of our King and Countrey, a Voyage to plant the first Colony in the Northerne parts of VIRGINIA, doe by these presents solemnly & mutually in the presence of *God* and one of another, covenant, and combine our selues together into a civill body politike, for our better ordering and preseruation, and furtherance of the ends aforesaid; and by vertue hereof to enact, constitute, and frame such iust and equall Lawes, Ordinances, acts, constitutions, offices from time to time, as shall be thought most meet and convenient for the generall good of the Colony: vnto which we promise all due submission and obedience. In witnesse whereof we haue here-vnder subscribed our names, *Cape Cod* 11. of *November* in the yeare of the raigne of our soveraigne Lord King IAMES, of *England, France*, and *Ireland* 18. and of Scotland 54. *Anno Domino* 1620."

Thus erected into a civil community, they chose a governor in the person of John Carver, and proceeded to look about for a place of settlement. After a month of exploration, on Monday, December 11th–21st, the investigating party landed at the place where Plymouth was afterward to stand, and finding it suitable for their purpose, the greater part of the ship's company were set to work within a few days preparing dwellings for shelter during the winter season already upon them. It is illustrative of their strong religious antipathy to what they deemed the improper observance of unscriptural festival days in the countries of their birth and exile that on their first Christmas in the New World "no man rested." They had kept "ye Sabath" with scrupulous care even in the most pressing season of their exploration, and they equally scrupulously endeavored to make Christmas as if it were not by going "on shore, some to fell timber, some to saw, some to rive, and some to carry."

Yet winter, even an exceedingly mild winter as this was, is a sober time at best to be house-building on the New England coast, and its exposures were rendered more destructive by the long use of ship's food; so that the settlement had hardly begun before its scanty numbers fell ill. By the 1st of April forty-four of the little company had died; but the few survivors were determined to push on, and when the "Mayflower" sailed for England on April 5, 1621, she took back with her only her own sailors. The prospect was indeed gloomy enough; scarcely had the "Mayflower" sailed when Governor Carver's name was added to the list of those no longer living, and with his death the little colony's tale of loss counted up twenty-eight of its forty-eight adult males. By the following autumn the attempt had cost the lives of exactly half of those who had come over in the "Mayflower" as settlers. Such a bare statement of facts shows better than any rhetorical picture, however brilliant, the sincerity and singleness of the attachment of the members of this little band to the principles of church government which they believed to be divinely appointed; and the intense satisfaction which they felt in being at last where they could combine freedom and self-government with life on English soil. However tolerable, as compared with a persecuted existence in their native island, their Holland sojourn may have been, the most eloquent testimony to the hardness of their lot in Leyden is the willingness of these Pilgrims to continue their adventure in New England.

These qualities of courage, patience, and steadfastness were general rather than exceptional in the company, but they have no better illustration than in the person of William Bradford, now chosen to succeed Carver in the governorship from which he had been removed by death. Thirty-one years of age, he was in the full vigor of manhood, but he had behind him certainly fifteen years of tried fidelity to the interests of the community of which he was now made the head, and before him till his honored death thirty-six years of continuous service as the leader of its affairs and for the greater part of that time its governor. A man of education for one who had not the privileges of a university, a natural leader, his modesty was as conspicuous as his devotion to the concerns of the colony was entire. No one can read the "History" in which he has recorded the chief events in which he was so conspicuous an actor without feeling that we have to do with a man who commanded affection as well as respect, a strong, sweet, self-forgetful Christian character; and it is the presence of such men as Bradford that best shows us why the enterprise at Plymouth did not die.

The enterprise thus inaugurated slowly grew. In November, 1621, just a year after the arrival of the first settlers, the "Fortune" brought thirty-five new colonists—a welcome addition—among them a son of Elder Brewster and a brother of Edward Winslow, but most of them apparently picked up by the merchant-partners in England, and, as Bradford describes them, "wild enough." In July, 1623, about sixty additions were brought to the colony by the "Anne," "some of them being very usefull persons, . . . and some were so bad, as they were faine to be at charge to send them home againe ye next year." That these less desirable elements came with the better was due to the somewhat discordant aims of the partners in the Plymouth undertaking. On the one hand, the Leyden Pilgrims desired first of all the maintenance of Congregational institutions and the preservation of the moral tone of the community; on the other hand, the merchants of London, who had furnished the chief part of the money for the adventure, cared little save for a flourishing trading colony which should yield satisfactory profits. A divergence of wishes speedily manifested itself. The Pilgrims desired to bring over their Leyden associates as speedily as possible, but bound as they were to their partners, they could not well raise the money for such an end. On the contrary, the merchant-partners preferred to send active young men, picked up where they could get them, who might make good hunters, fishers, and tillers of the soil. They looked askance at the Separatists still at Leyden, most of all at Robinson, whom the Pilgrims desired above all others should come to them. They felt that if something could be done to minimize the Separatist characteristics of the colony it would grow more rapidly. And so, in 1624, instead of Robinson, the merchant-partners sent over a certain John Lyford to minister to the church, which was led in its worship by Elder Brewster, and still regarded Robinson as its pastor.

Lyford was profuse in his expressions of admiration for the institutions of the colony on his arrival, and joined the church as if he had been at heart a Separatist instead of a very unworthy member of the Puritan party; but it was not long before his real character appeared. Certain elements of discontent, as has been seen, were to be found in the composition of the colony; and of the discontented faction perhaps the most conspicuous was John Oldham, a man of headstrong temper, who, as a late arrival come at his own charges and not bound by the general agreement for common labor under which the original settlers and most of their successors had made the journey, was displeased with the limitations placed on trade by the Plymouth government —limitations designed to secure as much as possible for the payment of the debt for which so many in the community were jointly liable. In company with Oldham and a few others, possibly among them Roger Conant, the future founder of Salem, Lyford now "set up a publick meeting aparte, on ye Lord's day," for worship as a Puritan minister of the Church of England. A rather high-handed seizure of letters from these malcontents to the merchant-partners in London by Governor Bradford showed that they were actively attempting the overthrow of the supremacy of the Leyden Pilgrims, and were anxious to prevent the arrival of those who had been left behind in Holland but who were looking eagerly across the sea. In view of these evident attempts to stir up trouble for the Pilgrims, and certain revelations as to Lyford's previous immoral life, both Lyford and Oldham were expelled from the little community.

The news of the rejection of the unworthy Lyford precipitated a quarrel among the merchant-partners, many of whom were disheartened over the comparatively meager financial prospects of the enterprise; and after some negotiation, to the great joy of the Pilgrims, the London merchants, with whom they had been so unsatisfactorily yoked, sold out in 1626 all interest in the colony to the colonial leaders for the onerous sum of £1800, to be paid in nine annual installments. Thus at last wholly their own masters, though still burdened with a large debt, the Plymouth Pilgrims determined to bring over to the colony their former associates who had remained at Leyden and whose coming had been so much desired. As a result, two companies were brought over, one in 1629, the other in 1630, in all about sixty persons, at the expense of those to whom they came.

But the man of all others whom they would have been glad to welcome was no longer of the living: John Robinson had died at Leyden on March 1, 1625 (N. S.). It was no feigned sorrow that the lonely Plymouth settlers felt for him, and it must have been with a feeling of almost filial bereavement that they thought of him as no longer a possible member of their earthly fellowship. For, taken all in all, Robinson was the greatest of the Separatists.

His originality as a thinker was not equal to that of Browne, but in every other respect he was the superior of that erratic leader. He was not called to the test of martyrdom as were Barrowe and Greenwood and Penry. But he was vastly better fitted than they to be a guide in a movement requiring patience, forbearance, and union. He was no mean controversialist, his writings made him looked upon as the representative Separatist of his generation; yet his chief power was his capacity to mold those who came under his personal influence. The Pilgrims who crossed the ocean and founded Plymouth were strong men, of marked individuality, yet they and their colony bore permanently the stamp of Robinson's forceful training. There was in him a quality of charity and tolerance in marked contrast to the Separatist leaders before him, which led him into kindly relations with the Dutch churches as far as they would permit, and which softened his antipathy to the Church of England every year that he lived. Nor was his conception of his own powers in his congregation autocratic, like that of Francis Johnson. Though he failed to reach the full democracy of Browne, his theory of church administration was more democratic than that of any early Congregational leader beside. And these qualities became in a measure the characteristics of the colony of which he was truly one of the founders, though he never set foot upon its soil.

From the coming of the Pilgrims in 1620 to the arrival of the last company of their Leyden associates not quite ten years later, the little colony grew to about three hundred members. It had taken firm root, it had maintained its institutions, it had passed through perils of famine, sickness, opposition in England, internal discords, the dangers of Indian hostility, and the worse peril of the lawless deeds of the rough traders and adventurers who settled about Massachusetts Bay under Weston, Gorges, and Morton at various times from 1622 onward. By 1630 the continuance of the colony seemed fairly assured, while the coming of the new forces from Leyden made it more certain than it had been during the early years of struggle that the religious element would permanently dominate the community. But already the great Puritan immigration into Massachusetts had begun which was to leave Plymouth, hampered by its sterile soil and slow-growing population, far behind in the material development of New England; but on which Plymouth was to do its best missionary work in fashioning Puritanism into Congregationalism.

Through these years of sacrifice and struggle till 1629, when a moderately gifted minister was procured in the person of Ralph Smith, the Pilgrim church had been ministered to by Elder Brewster. The merchant-partners had sent the unworthy Lyford in 1624, and the colonial agent, Isaac Allerton, had taken it upon himself to bring over the mentally distracted Rogers in 1628; but the church preferred to listen to Brewster, who, though refraining by Robinson's advice from administering the sacraments, "taught twise every Saboth, and y^t both powerfully and profitably, to ye great contentment of ye hearers, and their comfortable edification; yea, many were brought to God by his ministrie." A letter of De Rasières, the Dutch chief-merchant at Fort Amsterdam, the present New York, describing a visit made by him to Plymouth in 1627, gives us a glimpse of the meeting-house and congregation:

"Upon the hill they have a large square house, with a flat roof, made of thick-sawn planks, stayed with oak beams, upon the top of which they have six cannons, which shoot iron balls of four and five pounds, and command the surrounding country. The lower part they use for their church, where they preach on Sundays and the usual holidays. They assemble by beat of drum, each with his musket or firelock, in front of the captain's [Myles Standish's] door; they have their cloaks on, and place themselves in order, three abreast, and are led by a sergeant without beat of drum. Behind comes the Governor [William Bradford], in a long robe; beside him, on the right hand, comes the preacher [Elder Brewster], with his cloak on, and on the left hand the captain, with his side-arms and cloak on, and with a small cane in his hand; and so they march in good order, and each sets his arms down near him."

We get an insight into this Plymouth meeting-house also on a later and somewhat special occasion, when Plymouth enjoyed the residence of two ministers, and was receiving Governor Winthrop and Rev. John Wilson of Boston as its guests. Winthrop records in October, 1632:

"On the Lord's day there was a sacrament, which they did partake in; and, in the afternoon, Mr. Roger Williams [then living at Plymouth] (according to their custom) propounded a question, to which the pastor, Mr. [Ralph] Smith, spake briefly; then Mr. Williams prophesied [i.e., preached]; and after the governour of Plimouth spake to the question; after him the elder [Brewster]; then some two or three more of the congregation. Then the elder desired the governour of Massachusetts and Mr. Wilson to speak to it, which they did. When this was ended, the deacon, Mr. Fuller, put the congregation in mind of their duty of contribution; whereupon the governour and all the rest went down to the deacons' seat, and put into the box, and then returned."

On such an occasion the congregation in the rude cannon-topped meeting-house at Plymouth might well feel that in the liberty to practice the polity and worship in which they believed they had their reward for fidelity to their covenant promise "to walke in all his wayes . . . whatsoever it should cost them"; and what it had cost, the wind-swept graveyard and the rude street of hewn-plank houses bore mute witness.

CHAPTER IV.

THE PURITAN SETTLEMENT OF NEW ENGLAND.—PURITANISM CONGREGATIONALIZED.

IN the preceding chapter the struggles and sacrifices by which Congregationalists of the Separatist type brought their institutions from England through Holland to the American wilderness have been passed in rapid review. It has been seen that the Plymouth colony, after ten years of contest with perils within and without, was possessed of a population of about three hundred, and had arrived at a condition of stability which promised the continuance of its institutions in church and state, unless disturbed by influences from outside. But had Plymouth been left to its slow development such disturbance must almost certainly have come. Its supply of immigrants from the Leyden congregation was at best small, and by 1630 had practically reached its limit; it could hope for little direct increase from English Separatists, for they were few and poor; and though the sobriety and industry of the Pilgrim colony had enabled it to make head against the ill-managed attempts of Weston, Gorges, and Morton to found inimical settlements about Massachusetts Bay, it could be only a matter of time when the more fertile lands about the Charles and the superior fishing privileges of Cape Ann would people those regions with Englishmen more in number than those of Plymouth, who would inevitably force the Separatist colony into conformity with their wishes, should the principles of Plymouth be obnoxious to them. That the work of Plymouth was preserved, and that the larger English settlements, when they came to be erected on New England soil, were friendly rather than hostile, was due to the fact that, owing to causes the working of which was unforeseen when the Pilgrims crossed the ocean, the great Puritan party of England, within less than ten years after the landing at Plymouth, had begun the occupation of Massachusetts Bay in force, and, in spite of its opposition to Separatism in England, had come into essential ecclesiastical harmony with the Separatists of the New World.

Throughout the later years of Elizabeth and the reign of the first of the Stuarts the two types of Puritanism, noticed in the first chapter of this volume, continued without any very sharp discrimination, since the opposition of the government was continually driving Puritans of every shade to more and more radical positions. But between even the most advanced Puritan of the school of Cartwright and the Separatist there was one important point of disagreement. Alike in doctrine, both extreme Calvinists, agreeing also that the Bible is the ultimate rule of church polity as well as the final test of faith, both questioning the rightfulness of the ceremonies, liturgy, and government of the Establishment, they differed chiefly in their attitude toward that church itself. To the Separatist of the type of Browne, Barrowe, or Johnson, it was an antichristian imitation of the true church of God, from which duty should compel a Christian to withdraw himself as speedily as possible. Robinson and Brewster, indeed, as they advanced in years, came to think less harshly of the legal church, but even they regarded it as a body from membership in which a Christian man should hold himself aloof. But to the extremest Puritan the Church of England was still a true church, though in error. He agreed largely with the Separatist as to what the officers of the church ought to be; he felt that its membership ought to be purified, for Puritanism was above all a movement of ethical power anxious that men should live godly lives; but he clung to the idea of a national church, and hoped that its purification would be brought about by the assistance of the government. And if this was true of the extreme Puritan, it was even more true of the large wing of the party that continued in the attitude which had been that of all the Puritans before Cartwright, viewing the service as marred by Catholic ceremonies, the Prayer-Book as defaced by superstitious prescriptions, the membership of the church as in sore need of discipline and its ministry of education, objecting to the tyranny of the High Commission and its imposition of vestments and rites, and looking for the abolition of all these evils from the government, without going so far as to join with the extremer Puritans in condemning Episcopacy *per se*, or the Prayer-Book as a whole.

Nor did this hope of general reform by the civil authority, cherished by all types of Puritans, appear to be vain for many years after the Puritan movement had begun. True, the Puritans were frowned upon by Elizabeth and imprisoned by Whitgift and other bishops under her encouragement; but all through the reign of that great queen their numbers steadily increased. It did not require a long memory for the Puritan to recall that Henry VIII. had torn the church from Rome and given it an English Bible, while leaving its doctrines essentially Catholic; that the government which ruled in the name of Edward VI. had given the same church an English liturgy and Protestant articles; that Mary had led the way back to Rome; that Elizabeth had brought it once more to at least partial Protestantism; and that all these changes had been concurred in by Parliament and extended at once, in theory at least, to the remotest hamlet of the kingdom. Why should not a growing party feel confident that the time would come, if not under Elizabeth, yet speedily, when for a fifth time within a century the sovereign and Parliament would once more undertake the reformation of the often altered Church of England, and make it more fully what the Scriptures taught that a church should be? And this hope seemed the better grounded because Parliament, while not yet mainly Puritan, had been gaining rapidly in sympathy with Puritanism, and in a sense of its own right to take an increasing share in the government of the nation, during the closing years of Elizabeth's reign.

It was with this hope that about seven hundred and fifty Puritan ministers of the Church of England approved the Millenary Petition, with which James I. was met on his way up to London to take possession of the throne vacated by Elizabeth in 1603. This prayer did not ask for extensive changes, it represented the wishes of the moderate rather than the extreme Puritans; and the petitioners would have been satisfied could they have secured the abolition of the surplice, the sign of the cross, and similar ceremonials, together with non-residence and other grave ministerial faults, and the change of a few passages in the Prayer-Book. They had some reason to hope, in spite of the efforts which James had made in his Scotch kingdom to give real power to the bishops, to whom Scotch law had long allowed a nominal existence, that the well-known Calvinism and the Presbyterian training of the new English sovereign would incline him to grant what they asked. But in this they found themselves grievously disappointed. In the Hampton Court Conference of January, 1604, which resulted from this petition, and where these and some other changes desired by the Puritans were debated before and by the king, James fully committed himself to the Anglican side. His great desire was the assertion of his own authority, and he was shrewd enough to see that a system which made him the appointer of the bishops, and them the regulators of the church, gave him a power which had never been his in Scotland—a power which would be impaired just in proportion as concessions were made to the Puritans. "No Bishop, no King," was the "short Aphorisme" in which the royalist sympathizer Barlow says James expressed his position at the conference; and his hostility to all proposed changes in church government led him to declare that Scotch Presbyterianism "as wel agreeth with a Monarchy, as God and the Deuill. Then *Iack* & *Tom*, & *Will*, & *Dick*, shall meete, and at their pleasures censure me, and my Councell, and all our proceedinges." To the Puritans, who had treated him with the greatest respect throughout the conference, he announced: "I shall make thē conforme themselues, or I wil harrie them out of the land, or else doe worse." No wonder these declarations of their new sovereign were pleasing to the bishops; but were it not told by the sympathetic Dean of Chester, one could hardly believe that any member of that order could have exclaimed, as one did with delighted servility, that "hee was fully perswaded, his Maiestie spake by the *instinct of the spirite of God.*"

This triumph of the High Anglican party was followed by another. The Convocation which met under the presidency of Bancroft, then Bishop of London, in the summer following the Conference, passed a series of stringent canons enforcing uniformity, and declaring that to question the apostolical character of the Church of England in its existing form, to condemn its Prayer-Book, rites, and ceremonies as superstitions, or its officers—such as archbishops, bishops, deans, or archdeacons—as repugnant to the Word of God, or to affirm that any ministers or laymen may make rules for church government without the sanction of the king, is to become *ipso facto* excommunicate, and incapable of restoration to communion by any officer less in rank than the archbishop himself, and then only after repentance and a public revocation. Under the stress of these stringent regulations, which were soon promulgated with the royal approval, a number of ministers, estimated by some at three hundred, were driven from their livings.

Archbishop Whitgift died in February, 1604, and was succeeded in the see of Canterbury by Bancroft, who now brought the *jure divino* theory of episcopacy to the highest ecclesiastical post in the kingdom. His elevation strengthened, of course, all the forces opposed to Puritanism.

But while Puritanism thus suffered a loss of influence over the administration of the church, rather than a gain, through the accession of James it made a decided advance in another quarter—the English Parliament. Under the Tudors Parliament had reached its lowest ebb of power. The destruction of the old noble families during the War of the Roses had removed from Parliament that which had been its main strength in the Lancastrian days; it required several generations for the power of the landed gentry to develop sufficiently to raise the lower House to something of the importance which had once belonged to the upper. It was during the reigns of the five Tudor sovereigns that this transfer of the parliamentary center of gravity took place, and while it was in process parliamentary independence amounted to little. But before the close of Elizabeth's reign the strength of the Commons was considerable; and if it was not much exercised in opposition to the will of a popular sovereign such as the great queen was, the latent forces were there which would be sure to rise into strength when resisted by a king who was unpopular. And James, through his arbitrary assertions of his claims, alienated his first Parliament, that of 1604. He sought to interfere in the election of members, he pressed measures for a union with Scotland which the Commons regarded with suspicion, he quarreled with the Commons as to whether they were a "court of record" or no, and thus roused a high degree of irritation. This opening Parliament of his reign was not predominantly Puritan, but it was sufficiently under Puritan influence to believe that some of the reforms desired by the Puritans might wisely have been granted. And with the beginnings of parliamentary opposition to the king the religious and the political opponents of the arbitrariness of the crown naturally recognized that they were in a measure fighting the same battle; the Puritan way of thinking inclined, moreover, as truly toward the limitation of royal absolutism by precedent and by law as the High Anglican to assert the royal supremacy. As the reign of James went on the Commons came into more and more hearty sympathy with the religious ideas of the Puritans. James's own feeling had been right, that Puritanism, like Scotch Presbyterianism, "as wel agreeth with a Monarchy"—as he wished a monarchy to be—"as God and the Deuill."

The reign thus begun in hostility to the Puritans, and to the spirit of constitutional government which soon came into full alliance with Puritanism, went on with increasing bitterness, though not always with increasing severity, toward the Puritan party. Under Bancroft the repressive policy of Whitgift was continued and strengthened; but George Abbot, Bancroft's successor in the see of Canterbury from 1611 to 1633, was a pronounced Calvinist, in some degree sympathetic with the Puritans, and willing to overlook some departure from the prescribed vestments and ceremonies. During his early archbishopric, till the rise of Laud and his school, the Puritans felt more encouragement, though they at no time obtained the favor of the king. With Parliament James fell into more and more hopeless quarrel. The nation as a whole looked upon Spain as its natural enemy; its strong hatred of Catholicism feared any alliance with Spanish interests; but the king hoped to promote the peace of Europe and fill his depleted treasury by effecting a marriage between his son and a Spanish princess—a hope which the diplomacy of Spain used for years to tie the hands of the English Government when all England except a few extreme royalists and Catholics were longing to go to the aid of German Protestantism, struggling from 1618 onward in the death-grapple of the Thirty Years' War. Nor was James's home policy more representative of the best feeling of England than his foreign. Corruption was less concealed in his court than in that of his immediate predecessors; successive favorites, Carr and Villiers, with no other claim to elevation than the fancy of the king, dispensed the royal favors; unusual taxes were imposed by royal order; and monopolies for manufacture and trade were granted which were popularly supposed to be enormously profitable, and which angered the people against their possessors. Parliament disliked James's administration at home and abroad, in church and state alike, and the quarrel culminated in 1621 and 1622 in the royal prohibition that the Commons should discuss affairs of state—a prohibition which was met by the famous declaration that all concerns of church and state were proper subjects of parliamentary debate, and that in their consideration every member should have freedom of speech. James expressed his opinion of this assertion of right by tearing the page on which it was recorded from the journal of the Commons with his own hand, declaring, as he did so: "I will govern according to the common weal, but not according to the common will."

All these events, and especially the proposed Spanish marriage and the non-interference in behalf of the hard-pressed Protestants of Germany, strengthened Puritanism and gave it a hold on the national affection which it had never enjoyed under Elizabeth. As the average Englishman saw James agree, in 1623, that if his son should marry the Spanish princess the future queen should have public Catholic worship to which every man might have unmolested access, that Catholics everywhere in the kingdom should have freedom of worship in private houses, and that the children of the proposed marriage should be under their mother's charge till ten years of age and hence have their early training in the Roman faith, no wonder he felt that the party which maintained the most positive type of Protestantism at home and which would go, if it could, to the aid of oppressed Protestants abroad was the party for him, rather than that which exalted royal absolutism and preached the doctrine of unquestioning obedience to the behests of so unrepresentative a king. Nor was this feeling of the common Englishman lessened when, after his brief period of joy over the failure of the Spanish marriage negotiations, he saw the heir to the throne betrothed to the daughter of the king of France under an agreement pledging nearly as great concessions to English Catholics as had been offered to propitiate Spain.

Thus it came about that when James died, in 1625, he left the affairs of his kingdom in a situation which only the wisest and most conciliatory statesmanship could master, and he left them to an obstinate, self-willed young man—Charles I.—who, though outwardly more dignified than his father had been, had an evil trait not markedly present in the older Stuart king, a capacity to make promises which he never intended to fulfill; and who was, if anything, more persuaded than James of the divine authority of kings. Such a king could only make matters worse.

The accession of Charles was followed by his marriage to the French Catholic princess; the establishment of her Catholic chapel, which soon became a popular place of resort; and the loan of English ships to Richelieu to fight against French Protestants as part of the price—in justice to Charles be it said an unexpected part of the price—of the French marriage. His first Parliament he dissolved after it had sat for less than two months in the first year of his reign because the Commons refused to vote money which they believed would be squandered by the all-powerful favorite, George Villiers, who as Duke of Buckingham was Charles's most trusted adviser. His second Parliament he sent home in 1626 to save the favorite from impeachment. His third Parliament wrung from him the famous "Petition of Right" in June, 1628, but was dissolved in March of the following year because it attempted to enforce the Puritan hatred of Catholicism and Arminianism, and to prevent the levying of taxes unauthorized by the Commons. For the next eleven years Charles reigned without Parliaments—a time of oppression which, while it was marked by evidences of commercial prosperity and external good order, was one which made good men despair of the future of English liberty, and so fed the flames of dissatisfaction that when they burst forth once more they destroyed for a time the whole fabric of royal absolutism which had been so laboriously erected.

The hostility to Arminianism displayed by the Parliaments of the reign of Charles was a manifestation of Puritan opposition to the change in doctrinal position which had been going on among the High Anglicans since the beginning of the reign of James. Arbitrary as their domineering policy was, it would be an injustice to the bishops and clergy who supported Charles in the opening years of his rule to fail to recognize that they now represented not merely a tyrannous insistence on ceremonial and governmental uniformity in the church, they stood in a measure for doctrinal freedom. The older Anglicans, like Whitgift, had no serious doctrinal dispute with the Puritans—they were alike Calvinists. But there was an intensity in the Calvinism of the Puritans which made them endeavor to strengthen and enforce the Calvinism they found in the Thirty-nine Articles. To Puritan thinking, right views regarding the divine decrees were essential to all true Protestantism and all successful resistance to Rome. This feeling had led the Puritans at the Hampton Court Conference vainly to propose the introduction into the Articles of the English Church of the Lambeth Articles of 1595, which, though approved by Whitgift and others of the Anglican party at the time of their composition, are the most extreme statement of Calvinism ever put forth with any show of authority in England. But, contemporary with the reign of James, the Arminian controversy ran its violent course in Holland. That discussion awakened much interest in the English Church, which was represented by commissioners at the Synod of Dort in 1618–19; and though James approved the Calvinistic decisions of that body, the Arminian theories there condemned impressed a section of the High Anglican clergymen, and, through the influence of William Laud, it is said, even modified the theology of the old king himself.

Under Charles, Arminianism became increasingly characteristic of the High Church party; and Arminianism in England under the Stuarts, whatever it may have signified in Holland or in the Wesleyan revival, while implying an increase of intellectual freedom in doctrinal matters, was characterized also by a less strenuous Protestantism, by a willingness to coquet with some features of Catholicism, and a decreased sympathy with the Calvinistic churches of the Continent, with which the Church of England had thus far held itself in cordial fellowship. During the reign of James, also, the *jure divino* view of episcopacy, introduced by Bancroft and Bilson in the later years of Elizabeth, had become that of the Anglican party; and by the accession of Charles to the throne the devotion of that party to the royal absolutism had risen to an absurd height under the stimulus of constant royal favor and increasing opposition from the majority of the nation. The High Church party stood chiefly by the favor of the king, and it is not surprising that its members exalted the hand that upheld them.

Over against this Arminianism and absolutism of the High Anglican party, Puritanism in the church and in Parliament desired absolute uniformity of belief. Neither of the parties favored toleration, but the unity sought by the one was not that looked for by the other. To the Puritan the prime necessity was unity in acceptance and in strengthening of the historic Calvinism of the English Church; to the Anglican it was a submission to the regulations imposed by a divinely authorized king and a God-appointed order. To the Puritan the spiritual and doctrinal condition of England was the all-important matter; to the Anglican its external uniformity and submission to constituted authority. The Puritan would have men believe alike; the Anglican would have them worship alike.

This feeling that the Protestantism of England was threatened by doctrinal innovation as well as its liberty imperiled by the assertion of royal absolutism, induced Parliament, now decidedly Puritan, to proceed against some of the High Church party. In 1625 the Commons reproved Dr. Richard Montagu for denying that Calvinism was the doctrine of the Church of England and speaking favorably of Rome—a reproof which they soon carried to the extreme of imprisonment. The king's answer was the appointment of Montagu first to a chaplaincy and later (1628) to the bishopric of Chichester. Nor were the voices of the Anglican royalists less loudly raised in favor of the king's claims, or his recognition of their services less exasperating to the Puritans. In 1627, when Charles was endeavoring to raise taxes without the consent of Parliament, Dr. Robert Sybthorpe, vicar of Brackley, printed a sermon in which he declared that subjects were not authorized to resist even if the royal command was counter to the laws of God or nature, or impossible of fulfillment. These views were too exaggerated for the Puritanism of Archbishop Abbot to approve their publication; but the Bishop of London did so, and they were so acceptable to the king that Abbot was disgraced for his opposition, and practically set aside. About the same time Rev. Roger Manwaring declared in a sermon before the king that Parliament was a cipher, and that the king's command, without the consent of Parliament, bound the subject to pay any tax imposed, on pain of eternal damnation. The royal approval of Manwaring's theory was expressed by ecclesiastical advancement. In 1628 Charles and his bishops published a declaration, still prefixed to the Articles of the Church of England, affirming that in order that unprofitable discussion should cease these Articles were henceforth to be taken in their literal meaning, and no private interpretation should be put upon them. In one sense this declaration tended to theological liberty; but its real purport was to bar the Puritans from insisting on a Calvinistic interpretation of them as the only admissible one, and thus to aid in the spread of theological views which a majority of the nation deemed inimical to Protestantism.

The most conspicuous illustration of opposition to Puritanism and of what was best and worst in High Anglicanism was William Laud, who was Charles's most trusted clerical adviser from the beginning of his reign, and after the assassination of Buckingham in 1628 Charles's right hand in the ecclesiastical and largely in the civil administration of the kingdom. Laud was born in 1573, and had his education in St. John's College, Oxford, where he was distinguished for his anti-Puritan sentiments. Preferment came to him slowly at first, but by 1616, when he became Dean of Gloucester, he was one of the most marked and influential of the extreme Anglicans. In 1621 James made him bishop of St. David's; 1624 saw him a member of the High Commission; in 1626 he became Bishop of Bath and Wells; and now in 1628 he was raised by Charles to the see of London, the most important and most Puritanly inclined of the bishoprics of England, and only less in influence than the archiepiscopate of Canterbury, to which Charles advanced him in 1633.

Laud was unquestionably sincere, devout, mentally acute, of indefatigable energy, a lover of learning, and devoted to the interests of the church as he understood them; but he was also narrow-minded, cruel, and domineering. He never learned that conciliation and forbearance are sometimes desirable; he believed that the best method of securing uniformity was by crushing opposition by force. He regarded unity in form and worship as of the highest importance, and in his willingness to persecute those who differed from him he resembled the pre-Reformation prelates whose ideals of the church were so largely his own. A firm believer in the necessity of the episcopate and of apostolic succession, a representative of the anti-Calvinistic theology of the High Church party, and a devoted supporter of the royal absolutism, Laud was more than the chief exponent of the views of his party, he was a leader such as few men in the history of the English Church have been. To his mind there came the pleasing but unhistoric conception that subjection to the papacy and the Reformation were but incidents in the life of the Church of England; that that organization had presented substantially the same doctrine at all times in fundamentals, and that those fundamentals were better preserved in the Roman Church, in spite of its errors and its subjection to the papacy which he denounced, than in the non-prelatical churches of the Continent. A strong sacramentarian, though he did not materially differ with Calvin regarding the nature of Christ's presence in the Supper, he attached greater importance to the sacraments than the Calvinistic Reformers had done. Above all he was a ritualist, whose piety craved a showy service, whose mental habit attached great importance to bowings at the name of Jesus, who saw irreverence in placing the communion table in the body of the church as the Puritans did, and desired to rail it off at the end as the altar had been in Roman days; while his martinet-like spirit inclined him to force all that he deemed fitting in worship on clergy and people, to whom these changes seemed nothing but a return to Rome. Laud was the first of Anglo-Catholics; he was not a Roman Catholic. But it is no wonder that neither the Puritans nor the Roman Catholics of his age understood him, and that both parties sincerely believed that his object was to lead the Church of England back to Rome—a belief which led to the offer to him on two occasions of a cardinal's hat. If it is true that his views of worship and of the sacraments have largely become those of the English

Church, it is also true, as Gardiner has remarked, that this has been brought about "by a total abandonment of Laud's methods. What had been impossible to effect in a church to the worship of which every person in the land was obliged to conform became possible in a church which any one who pleased was at liberty to abandon."

But to Laud's thinking, the enforcement of conformity seemed not at all impossible, and he set himself to the work, now that he was master of the great diocese of London, with a vigor that made many a Puritan despair of the religious future of England. To the Puritan the spiritual elevation of the people seemed impossible without the aid of a learned, preaching ministry, inculcating Scriptural doctrines, reproving sins, and above all setting forth an active type of religious life, of which conversion by the power of the Spirit of God was the source, and a strenuous morality the fruit. In order to secure such a ministry the Puritans had established in many parishes what were known as "lectureships"—that is, pecuniary provision was made by which a preacher of Puritan inclinations, generally in priests' orders but not always so, could have maintenance and "lecture" on Sunday afternoons in parishes where the incumbent was absent, or incompetent, or obnoxious. This system had been partially tolerated by Abbot, though in 1622 James had issued orders through Abbot that no preacher less in rank than a dean should discuss predestination or grace before a general audience. As these subjects were uppermost in Puritan thought, the aim of the order was distinctly inimical to the lectureship system. To Laud the lectures were intolerable, and he set himself on entering on his diocese of London, and even more when Archbishop of Canterbury, to their suppression. By Laud's persuasion Charles issued directions that afternoon sermons should be reduced to mere catechising by question and answer, and that every lecture must be preceded by the service, read by the lecturer in surplice and hood. To the Puritan this hostility of Laud and the king seemed a deprivation of the means of salvation.

Perhaps even more impressive to the ordinary Puritan mind than these general orders was the savage relentlessness with which Laud pursued men whose only offense was that they spoke what half the nation was thinking, and what the Puritan believed to be the truth of God. A universally notorious illustration is that of Alexander Leighton, father of the celebrated Scotch archbishop. Leighton was an extreme Cartwrightian Puritan, who printed in the "month wherein Rochell was lost" (October, 1628) a fierce outburst against the bishops and the Catholic queen, entitled "Sions Plea against the Prelacie." The book was a burning attack upon the influences which had led to a great disaster to the Protestant cause and a great disgrace for English foreign policy. For its writing Leighton was sentenced by the Star-Chamber Court in June, 1630—while Laud with uncovered head gave thanks to God for the decree—to degradation from the ministry, to life imprisonment, to the hopelessly exorbitant fine of £10,000, to the pillory, to whipping, to the loss of his ears and the slitting of his nose, and finally to branding on his cheeks as a "sower of sedition."

Leighton's attack upon the authorities of the church had been bitter, and his punishment merciless. He certainly was an extremist. Possibly, therefore, Laud's more usual methods of harassing Puritanism and enforcing uniformity may be better understood from a much less flagrant case, where the minister was no fanatic, but was notably learned, spiritual-minded, able, and devoted—a man who might well be deemed an ornament to any communion. Thomas Hooker, later one of the founders of Connecticut, had filled for two years, when Laud became Bishop of London, a notably successful lectureship at Chelmsford. His opinions on the great problems which agitated the state in those stormy years had no doubt been positive, but his chief activity had been the preaching of the doctrines of grace in a deep, spiritual, searching, and intensely Calvinistic treatment of the relations of the soul to God. A man of profound piety, he had preëminently sought the conversion and upbuilding of his hearers. This preaching, though its themes contravened the orders issued by James in 1622, was received with great popular favor—as one of Laud's agents wrote in 1629: "Our people's pallats grow so out of tast, y[t] noe food contents them but of M[r] Hooker's dressing." But Laud had been less than a year Bishop of London before his hand was stretched out against Hooker, and the Chelmsford lecturer was under bonds for appearance when wanted. Renewed preaching brought him in a few months more again to Laud's attention. But now his beneficed neighbors among the clergy to the number of forty-nine, and, it is interesting to note, the rector of Chelmsford, in whose parish he had labored, petitioned for his retention as a man "for doctryne, orthodox, and life and conversation honest, and for his disposition peaceable, no wayes turbulent or factious." A few days later forty-one of the ministers of the county sent in a counter-petition asking that uniformity be enforced. Hooker had to abandon the lectureship, and now taught school for a few months, with John Eliot as his assistant; but even this change of occupation did not shelter him from Laud. In July, 1630, he was ordered to appear before the High Commission; but his friends at Chelmsford paid his forfeited bail, and he escaped with difficulty to Holland. Certainly when such men as Hooker were forced to abandon the pulpit—and his case was neither striking nor exceptional—it was paying pretty dear for ceremonial uniformity; and the prohibition of discussion of those doctrines which the Puritans deemed essential to all spiritual growth was a sorry way to advance theological freedom at a time when the chief need of the Establishment was an educated and worthy ministry, a better instructed membership, and a stricter moral life. No wonder Milton cried out in his noble lament for Lycidas, nine years after Laud became Bishop of London and eight years after Charles had put in force his determination to rule without Parliament:

> Last came, and last did go,
> The pilot of the Galilean lake;
> Two massy keys he bore of metals twain,
> (The golden opes, the iron shuts amain,)
> He shook his mitered locks, and stern bespake:
> "How well could I have spared for thee, young swain,
> Enow of such as for their bellies' sake
> Creep, and intrude, and climb into the fold?
> Of other care they little reckoning make,
> Than how to scramble at the shearers' feast,
> And shove away the worthy bidden guest:
>
> . . . . . .
>
> The hungry sheep look up, and are not fed,
> But, swollen with wind and the rank mist they draw,
> Rot inwardly and foul contagion spread:
> Besides what the grim wolf with privy paw
> Daily devours apace, and nothing said."

Under such circumstances of increasing discouragement a few of the more adventurous of the Puritans began to look across the Atlantic with the thought of founding on the shores of a new continent the institutions that were denied them in the old. This inclination was doubtless stimulated by the example of the Plymouth Pilgrims, whose experiences, told in Mourt's "Relation" and Winslow's "Good Newes from New England," were given to the English public in 1622 and 1624. But religious considerations did not exclusively control the first Puritan motions toward the settlement of Massachusetts. That impulse had its apparent beginnings in the south-of-England borough of Dorchester, where Rev. John White, a distinguished Puritan, was rector. From all this coast of England vessels resorted annually to American waters for fishing; and as larger crews could be employed in taking the catch than were required for the homeward voyage, the thought occurred to some of those interested in the trade that a permanent settlement could be formed in New England, where the superfluous fishermen could remain, and where supplies could be raised and stored. For this purpose a Fishing Company was organized at Dorchester through White's influence, and by this company a settlement was begun on Cape Ann late in 1623 or early in 1624. To this colony Roger Conant, a vigorous Puritan, came as its superintendent, in 1625, and with him Rev. John Lyford, who had been with him at Plymouth, and whose experiences in the Pilgrim colony have already been noted. But the Cape Ann enterprise was unsuccessful, and when most of its settlers went home to England in 1626, Conant, and a few like-minded men, removed to the more fertile spot which was afterward known by the name of Salem.

As the project had gone on White's thoughts had grown broader, and he now determined to organize, if possible, a Puritan colony, in the formation of which religion rather than trade should be a prime consideration. To this end he now labored to enlist Puritan sympathy and obtain a patent which would give a legal basis for his new enterprise. In both attempts he was successful. The Plymouth (England) Council, a body of which Sir Ferdinando Gorges was the leading spirit, and which by a charter of

November, 1620, claimed jurisdiction over New England, granted by a patent of March 19, 1628, such portion of its territories as lay between three miles north of the Merrimac and an equal distance south of the Charles rivers to a Puritan land company having John Endicott as one of its members. Under the auspices of this new association Endicott and an advance guard of settlers left England in the summer of 1628, landing at Salem, where Conant had been for about two years a resident, on the 6th of September.

The enterprise thus launched was pushed rapidly on. Through the instrumentality of White and others, Puritans from all over England were interested, and new members of increasing prominence were rapidly added to the company. Influential support was secured at court; whether Charles I. really seriously concerned himself with what must have seemed to him an insignificant colony in an out-of-the-way part of the world may be doubtful; possibly he felt that a Puritan exodus might free him of a few of his opponents; but through the influence of Lord Dorchester and the Earl of Warwick the king granted a direct charter to this enlarged company—a document which was sealed on March 4, 1629, and which authorized the "Governor and Company of the Mattachusetts Bay," thus created, to elect officers, admit new members, and make laws for the administration of its domain. Thus equipped with a charter granting extensive privileges, the company strongly attracted Puritan colonists, so that within a few months after its creation a large reinforcement was sent to Salem, arriving there in June, 1629. Even more important for the future of the enterprise was the agreement entered into by John Winthrop, Sir Richard Saltonstall, Thomas Dudley, Increase Nowell, Isaac Johnson, William Pynchon, and others at Cambridge, August 26, 1629, to go to New

England the next spring, provided the government and charter of the company should be transferred to Massachusetts. This gave the undertaking not only the support of men of character and position, it made the new colony practically a semi-independent, self-governing state, instead of an ordinary corporation for the development of a new country administered by a board in England, which was doubtless all that the king had in mind when the charter was granted, if that act caused him any serious thought at all. The decision to make the company wholly domiciled in New England led to the election of John Winthrop to the governorship, since Matthew Cradock, the first governor, was unable to emigrate; and in the spring and summer of 1630 the Puritan exodus ran full tide. Probably at least a thousand persons came from England to Massachusetts in that year alone—more than three times as many as the Plymouth colony numbered after ten years of struggle—and by 1640, when the advent of the Long Parliament and the evident speedy downfall of the tyranny of Charles and Laud checked Puritan emigration, it is estimated that the number who had crossed the ocean had risen to more than twenty thousand. The summer of 1630 saw the settlement of Dorchester by a company organized into church-estate through the influence of Rev. John White before leaving England; and the same weeks witnessed the beginnings of Winthrop and his immediate following at Charlestown and Boston; while at the same time settlements were made at Watertown and elsewhere about Massachusetts Bay.

These emigrant companies, like that at Plymouth, all experienced a period of disease and death which robbed them of many of their best members within a few weeks of their landing. But their contrast to the Plymouth Pilgrims in all that goes to make for worldly esteem and probable success was extreme. Their membership contained men of humble position, it is true, but their leaders were from good station in England, many of them of the country gentry, men of wealth, character, and education. Their ministers, as there will be ample occasion to see, were the peers in learning and ability of any in the Puritan wing of the Church of England; they were men reverenced and admired not only in the colonial hamlets to which they came, but by wide circles in the home land. Probably no colony in the history of European emigration was superior to that of Massachusetts in wealth, station, or capacity. The religious motive, ever predominant in the beginning of the enterprise, had enabled it to draw on the best elements of a great party in England, and to attract men whom no mean or ordinary aims would have drawn across the sea. Religion had equally animated the Plymouth enterprise; but Plymouth had no constituency in England from which to draw strength; its Separatist principles had been despised in the home land by Anglican and Puritan alike, and its true-hearted membership had come from the humble Leyden exiles, or the equally humble occasional emigrant sent directly from England by the merchant-partners or self-impelled to cast in his lot with the struggling community. It had a few men of ability, like Brewster and Bradford and Winslow, it had men of character in abundance; but it was wholly deficient in men of wealth or university education, while its pulpit, never conspicuously strong after Robinson had been left at Leyden, was filled by no higher officer than a ruling elder when the Puritan colonists began their work at Salem.

Nor were these Puritan emigrants men easily impressible by outside influences or tolerant of dissent. Puritanism crossed the ocean with no such general intention of seeking civil and religious liberty as has often been attributed to it. As compared with the Puritans, the Pilgrims of Plymouth indeed showed a considerable measure of toleration, perhaps because of Dutch example, more probably by reason of the kindly spirit infused into them by Robinson and maintained by Brewster, Bradford, and Winslow—a spirit the more readily cherished on account of the comparative feebleness of the colony. But neither Pilgrims nor Puritans had any thought of establishing liberty for men to do as they please; nor would any general toleration, such as we now justly value, have furnished motives definite enough to have led our ancestors to the New World. The Puritans who settled Massachusetts had little if any more disposition to tolerate dissent from what they believed to be the right path in church and state than had Archbishop Laud to allow departure from the ceremonial observances which he enjoined. They had no intention of separating from the Church of England as the Pilgrims had done. If Mather was correctly informed, one of the two ministers of the first Puritan church on Massachusetts soil, Francis Higginson, had exclaimed when the last headlands of their island home faded from the view of his fellow-voyagers:

"We will not say, as the separatists were wont to say at their leaving of England, 'Farewel, Babylon!' . . . but . . . 'farewel, the Church of God in England! . . . We do not go to New England as separatists from the Church of England; though we cannot but separate from the corruptions in it.'"

Certainly, in 1630, Winthrop, Dudley, Johnson, and other of the most prominent of the Massachusetts Company joined in the declaration, as they started on their voyage:

"Wee desire you would be pleased to take Notice of the Principals, and Body of our Company, as those who esteeme it our honour to call the *Church* of *England*, from whence wee rise, our deare Mother. . . . Wee leave it not therefore, as loathing that milk wherewith we were nourished there, but blessing God for the Parentage and Education, as Members of the same Body, shall always rejoice in her good."

And in 1631 the extremely Separatist Roger Williams refused to supply the pulpit of the Boston church because that body still considered itself unseparated from the Church of England.

All the more remarkable is it, then, in view of the worldly and educational superiority of the Puritans over the Pilgrims, and their anti-Separatist feelings, that the Puritan churches organized in New England adopted the principles of Separatist Plymouth in their formation and government. No step in the development of Congregationalism is more obscure or more important than this Congregationalizing of English Puritanism. To understand it we must go back to the winter of 1628–29, when Endicott and the vanguard of the Puritan emigration were laying the foundations at Salem. Illness had borne hard on the little company, and in their distress Endicott had obtained the ministrations of the only physician then on the coast, Dr. Samuel Fuller, deacon of the church at Plymouth. Before Fuller's coming, Endicott, like most Puritans, had regarded the Plymouth Separatists with suspicion; but in conversation with his guest prejudices melted away, and he was able to write to Bradford on May 11, 1629, as follows:

"I acknowledge my selfe much bound to you for your kind love and care in sending Mr Fuller among us, and rejoyce much y^{t} I am by him satisfied touching your judgments of ye outward forme of Gods worshipe. It is, as farr as I can yet gather, no other then is warrented by ye evidence of truth, and ye same which I have proffessed and maintained ever since ye Lord in mercie revealed him selfe unto me; being farr from ye commone reporte that hath been spread of you touching that perticuler."

That Endicott was readily impressed by the expositions of the Plymouth deacon was natural. Puritans and Separatists had never had doctrinal disagreement; both were pronounced Calvinists. Both alike believed that much of the worship required by the English Establishment was superstitious. Both held that in the Bible God has set forth all his will. Both welcomed preaching on the doctrinal issues of the day. Both had left their native land to escape High Commission Courts and requirements of uniformity, that they might practice "the positive part of church reformation." Neither could have felt any desire to see the continued rule of bishops; for, apart from the hostility of the Separatists and extremer Puritans toward the spiritual claims of an episcopal order as unwarranted by Scripture, no Puritan in Endicott's company could have remembered a time when the bishops, as a whole, had not been hostile to the Puritans. Nor was the Prayer-Book likely to have a place in the affections of a generation of men who had vainly striven to amend what they deemed its evils, and had seen its use required in its entirety as a badge of that spiritual system which the Puritan and the Separatist were alike trying to escape. The more advanced Puritans had held, from the time of Cartwright at least, that there should be no ministers at large, but that every minister ought to be bound to a particular congregation, which ought in some way to have a voice in his selection; and they had been of the opinion also that the local church should be so purified by discipline that practically only persons of Christian character should remain in it. In addition to these characteristics of the extremer type of Puritanism in general which would incline to a ready acceptance of Plymouth theories, there is reason to think that some of the Puritans associated with White in the initial stages of the Salem undertaking were moving in directions hitherto distinctive only of English Separatism. How far this was the case is a question the answer to which is of great obscurity. The use of a distinct covenant as the basis of the local church is one of the fundamental principles of Congregationalism which never found acceptance with English Puritanism as a whole, but was typical of the system of Browne, Barrowe, and Robinson. The ordination of its ministers by the local congregation, in addition to their election, was also a distinctly Separatist doctrine. But certain considerations seem to show that the former of these usages, if not also the latter, may have been favorably regarded in the circle from which Endicott came. Rev. Hugh Peter, for example, who was among the earliest members of the Massachusetts Company of 1628, and whom Endicott must have known personally, employed a covenant in the church at Rotterdam of which he became colleague pastor on his flight from England in 1629. Perhaps he may have argued in favor of the practice in Endicott's hearing before the Salem settlers left England; but more probably Peter's own adoption of the covenant was due to the influence of his associate in the Rotterdam charge, Dr. William Ames, whose Separatist leanings were decided. Of more importance as showing possible inclination toward covenant organization in the circles of southwestern England where White labored is the fact that the church which was organized through White's efforts at Plymouth, England, in March, 1630, and which afterward settled at Dorchester, Mass., seems to have had some more definite uniting pledge than was usual in Puritan parishes, though reasons will be given when the organization of that church is more minutely described for doubting whether that agreement implied an exclusively regenerate membership. And if the statement is true, as seems hardly credible, that at the officering of that church the ministers were not only chosen but ordained by the congregation, it is evident that the Puritans of southwestern England were far more radical than Puritanism as a whole.

But while it is thus clear that Endicott and the first emigrants to Salem were nearer to the Plymouth Pilgrims in belief than they at first realized, their conceptions of polity and government were still in the gristle, and we may safely conjecture that the discussions with Fuller embraced four or five features of church life, in regard to all of which general Puritan custom differed from that of Plymouth: the power of a local congregation to ordain its own chosen officers; the participation or non-participation of the church as a whole in matters of discipline; the use of a covenant; the conduct of public worship; and relationship or non-relationship to a national church whose nearest congregation was three thousand miles away. On all of these points except the last the practice of Plymouth won over or confirmed the inclinations of the Puritans at Salem; the last point was not yielded, and most of the Massachusetts Puritans continued to view themselves for a considerable time as members of the Church of England. But if the soil was thus prepared for the seed which Dr. Fuller sowed, his planting was of the first importance. Agreed as Endicott found that he was with the men of Plymouth, the discovery of that agreement was in no small measure due to the persuasive skill of the Plymouth physician.

The Plymouth advice resulted speedily in the formation at Salem of a Congregational church, the first Puritan church, and the second Congregational church in New England. The historians of the latter part of the seventeenth century, and even Rev. John Higginson, son of the first teacher of the Salem church and himself one of its most honored ministers, dated its formation from August 6, 1629; but a contemporary letter shows that by July 20th of that year a covenanted church on the Plymouth model existed at Salem, which on that day chose and ordained its pastor and teacher. It is quite possible that this church was organized, at least to the extent of the union of its first members by a covenant, in the late spring of 1629, before the coming of the large immigration in June. Be this as it may, the covenant by which this church was constituted was, like almost all early Congregational covenants, extremely simple. As far as its content is now known it was embraced in a single sentence:

"We Covenant with the Lord and one with an other; and doe bynd our selves in the presence of God, to walke together in all his waies, according as he is pleased to reveale himself unto us in his Blessed word of truth."

While Endicott had thus been battling with the New England winter and coming into friendly relations with the Separatists of Plymouth, the company in England whose agent he was had been rapidly growing, it had obtained its royal charter, and was prepared in the spring of 1629 to send over a numerous body of colonists. Prominent among the cares of the company during this busy winter had been its negotiations with clergymen of Puritan sentiment to take spiritual charge of its American enterprise and attempt the conversion also of the savage natives of New England. In this search aid was rendered by Rev. John White and by Rev. John Davenport, later to be the first pastor at New Haven, Conn. Three ministers were obtained, Francis Bright, Francis Higginson, and

Samuel Skelton, all of whom were ordained clergymen of the Church of England; and with them came a fourth minister who had obtained passage in the company's ships, Ralph Smith, whose strict Separatist views had not been understood at first by the company; but how little the enterprise savored of general toleration is manifest from the direction given to Endicott that unless Smith should be "conformable" to the government established at Salem he should not be permitted to remain. Acknowledged fellowship with Separatist Plymouth was still far from the desire of the managers of the enterprise in England, who, aside from their own objections on religious grounds, doubtless feared the hostility of the English Government should the Salem colony become known as "Brownist." By the end of June, 1629, these ministerial reinforcements had crossed the Atlantic.

On July 20th, about three weeks after their arrival, Endicott appointed—so Charles Gott wrote to Bradford, ten days subsequent to the event—"a solemne day of humilliation, for y choyce of a pastor & teacher." The morning of that day was spent in prayer and preaching as a preparation for the main event; and in the afternoon Higginson and Skelton were asked to express their view as to the proper call to the ministerial office. Both had had episcopal hands laid on them in ordination; but both now affirmed that a true call embraced two elements, one of which at least was not deemed an essential in their original episcopal vocation—an inward sense of fitness, and an election by the free suffrages of the male members of "a company of beleevers . . . joyned togither in covenante." Such a covenant church the Salem congregation evidently felt itself to be, for, the church approving these answers, "every fit member wrote, in a note, his name whom the Lord moved him to think was fit for a pastor, and so likewise, whom they would have for teacher; so the most voice was for Mr. Skelton to be Pastor, and Mr. Higginson to be Teacher."

This election was followed by an act of great importance —one which would scarcely have been performed save for the influence of Plymouth teaching. As Gott records of the pastor and teacher just elected: "They accepting ye choyce, Mr Higgison, with 3. or 4. of ye gravest members of ye church, laid their hands on Mr Skelton, using prayer therwith. This being done, ther was imposission of hands on Mr Higgison also."

By this laying on of hands Higginson and Skelton broke with the whole system of episcopal succession which Laud maintained, and illustrated the wholly congregational conception that it was within the province of every Christian congregation not only to choose but to ordain its own officers—a conception which had been held in its fullness only by Separatists and Anabaptists.

But another Congregational principle was to be illustrated in the formation of this first New England Puritan church besides that of the autonomy of the congregation. At least one ruling elder and one or more deacons were elected on this memorable 20th of July; but their ordination was delayed in order that there might be no repentance if the incoming ships should bring immigrants better qualified for these posts, and August 6th was fixed for the completion of the work. News of the events past and to occur was sent to Bradford at Plymouth by a private correspondent, though it is hardly probable that the statement of the Plymouth historian Morton is correct, that representatives from Plymouth were formally invited by the Salem church. However this may have been, Bradford and some others of the Plymouth church appear to have gone to Salem to welcome the new enterprise, and though the voyage proved longer than they hoped, they came into the Salem assembly in time to give the first illustration on American soil of that communion of churches which is so important a trait of American Congregationalism by holding out "the right hand of fellowship."

Yet though Endicott and Higginson and Skelton were profoundly influenced by Plymouth example, they wished to steer a narrow course of their own between such a conformity to the methods of worship of the English Establishment as the more moderate Puritans in England practiced, and full Separatism. Not all the inhabitants even of the little Salem community were of their way of thinking. Two of the most prominent of the newcomers of 1629, John and Samuel Browne, were dissatisfied with the form and worship of the new church. To their thinking it was Separatist, and its abandonment of the Prayer-Book was distasteful to them. They gathered a few like-minded spirits and held separate services at which the liturgy of the Establishment was used. The situation was now not unlike that from which Endicott and his friends had fled in England, only the strength of the parties was reversed. The moderate Puritans at Salem who deserted the congregation and held their Anglican service were now the nonconformists of the little commonwealth, and as such they were sent back to England by Endicott before the summer of their arrival was past. On the other hand, Endicott desired to have no real Separatists in the colony, much as he inclined to the other features of Plymouth worship and government; and it was not long before Rev. Ralph Smith, who was apparently a decided Separatist, found it well to leave for desolate Nantasket, whence he was brought to Plymouth by a kindly crew from that place, to meet a more friendly reception than at Salem, and to become for a time the minister of the Plymouth church. Of the causes of dissatisfaction which led Francis Bright, one of the three ministers sent out by the company, to return to England in 1630 little is certainly known; but the writers of New England history in the latter half of the seventeenth century believed that he, like the Brownes, was too much of a conformist wholly to relish the Salem innovations.

That so radical a departure was not expected or relished by the Puritan members of the company who remained in England there is abundant evidence. On news of what had been done by Endicott regarding the Brownes his superiors wrote to him: "Wee may haue leave to think that it is possible some vndigested councells haue too sodainely bin put in execučon, wch may haue ill construcčon wth the state heere, and make vs obnoxious to any adversary."

It is evident, too, that the English Puritans believed the Salem novelties to be due to Plymouth influence. A year after the formation of the Salem church, 1630, Winthrop, Dudley, Johnson, and Coddington were denied the Lord's Supper by Skelton, and baptism was denied to Coddington's child, since they were not members of any local church. On news of this refusal of the sacraments to those who certainly were members of the Church of England, supposing a national church to have any rightful existence, Rev. John Cotton, then of Boston, England, but later to become the teacher of the church of Boston, Mass., and a chief defender of the position he now attacked, wrote to Skelton in distress, declaring: "You went hence of another judgment, and I am afraid your change hath sprung from New Plymouth men."

The story of Salem beginnings has thus been told at some length because it is a turning-point in Congregational history. Had Endicott, Higginson, and Skelton moved in any other direction than that they took, Congregational development would have been vastly other than was actually the case. They might have maintained the moderately conformist position of the Brownes; but had they done so, the Plymouth influence would have been scarcely felt, and the Puritan and Pilgrim streams could hardly have flowed together. They might have become wholly Separatist; but that would have been to break with the company which had sent them out, and to have been discredited in large measure by the army of immigration that was to follow them. As it was, they disowned one feature of Plymouth polity—that of Separation—which was not very strenuously insisted on at Plymouth, and which had little practical importance across the Atlantic, save as a stimulant to English prejudice. But all other essentials of Plymouth practice they adopted, and made thereby characteristics of Puritan Congregationalism. The pathway thus marked out was one easy to follow by those who came after them. And the credit of this fusion is due primarily to two laymen, Dr. Samuel Fuller and Governor John Endicott.

The effect of the adoption of full Congregationalism by the Salem church in molding subsequent Puritan organizations is clearly apparent in the constitution of two of the three Massachusetts churches that were formed in 1630—those of Charlestown-Boston and of Watertown. The church immediately subsequent in origin to that of Salem had indeed a peculiar and an interesting beginning. Of all Puritan churches in New England, only one, represented now by the church at Windsor, Conn., and possibly by the First Church, Dorchester, Mass., traces its continuity back to English soil. Its origin was in a company gathered by that unwearied friend of Massachusetts colonization, Rev. John White, in 1629 and 1630, drawn largely from the southwestern counties of the island, which left England on March 20, 1630, and settled at Dorchester early in June. This body assembled in the New Hospital at Plymouth, England, just before sailing; and there, under the guidance of White, chose as its officers two clergymen of the Church of England, from Exeter and its neighborhood, John Maverick and John Warham. Here, as at Salem, the choice was solemnized by a fast and preceded by a sermon; but it may well be doubted whether the ministers were ordained by the church. Roger Clap, who was present as a young man, and whose vivid recollections written out many years later constitute our source of knowledge of the details of the scene, would hardly have omitted so essential a feature. White, who was no extreme nonconformist, and was afterward much more of a Presbyterian than a Congregationalist, as evidenced by his later attitude in the Westminster Assembly, could scarcely have countenanced it; and the thought of ordination in addition to election in this transaction at Plymouth would probably be at once rejected, were it not for the direct statement of the learned eighteenth century New England annalist, Rev. Thomas Prince, that ordination took place. Prince based his statement on a manuscript letter, but whose or when written does not appear; and the inherent improbabilities seem so great that one may well hesitate before accepting the allegation as proven. Whether this body possessed a covenant before leaving England is also not easy to decide, and competent New England historians have held the affirmative and the negative. Roger Clap, of whom mention has been made, though present as a member of the expedition at the election at Plymouth, was "admitted into the Church Fellowship at the first beginning in *Dorchester*, in the year 1630." This would seem as if some agreement had been entered into before sailing to which the young and humbly ranked Clap was not a partner. But whether this agreement implied a covenant entered into by regenerate persons only as the basis of the church, is made doubtful by Warham's opinion, expressed to Fuller just after the arrival of the Dorchester company on American soil, that the "church may consist of a mixed people, godly and openly ungodly"—a view which comports with the English Puritan theory better than with that of Plymouth. But whatever imperfections there may have been in the Congregationalism of this Dorchester body at its coming, it is easy to see that it was moving in a direction which would incline it to look favorably at what Endicott and his Salem associates had done, and feel kindly toward Plymouth, whose physician, the indefatigable Fuller, was ministering to the sick of the Dorchester company, and talking church polity to sick and well, within a month of their arrival.

Before the Dorchester fellowship had much more than begun the erection of their dwellings the main portion of the immigration of 1630 had come and entered on the hard life of colonial beginnings at a number of other places about Massachusetts Bay—the chief interest being of course at Charlestown, and speedily at Boston, where Governor Winthrop and his immediate following were located, and at Watertown, where Sir Richard Saltonstall was the most prominent settler. With Winthrop was Rev. John Wilson, a Puritan clergyman of the Church of England who had been conspicuous for his nonconformity during an interrupted ministry at Sudbury, in Suffolk; with Saltonstall was Rev. George Phillips, a clergyman of even stronger anti-Anglican tendencies, from Boxford, in Essex. As yet none of these infant communities were gathered into Congregational church estate; they had indeed been advised to consult with the people of Plymouth by a minister held in great esteem among them, John Cotton, of Boston, England, who was three years later to become the teacher of the church at Boston, Mass. But his counsel appears to have been of the most general character, and these immigrants came to Massachusetts Bay with their conceptions of church organization still in the formative stage. In this condition they fell under the molding influence of Fuller, and of his earlier convert Endicott, whom the Plymouth physician now describes as a second Barrowe in his zeal for the Congregational way.

The sickness incident to new settlements in those days of little sanitary knowledge afflicted Winthrop's company at Charlestown severely. In their distress Winthrop appealed to the Salem church for advice. At Salem there were present, on the reception of this request, three of the more prominent members of the Plymouth body, Fuller, Winslow, and Allerton, and, as was natural, they too were consulted as to the problem presented by the Massachusetts governor. By the joint counsel of the Salem church and of the representatives of that of Plymouth, Friday, July 30, 1630, was appointed as a fast in view of the sickness, and by the same advice covenanted churches were organized on that day at Charlestown and Watertown. At Charlestown such care was exercised in admission to this new fellowship that on the day of beginning only four, Governor Winthrop, Isaac Johnson, Thomas Dudley, and Rev. John Wilson, were united—a number which was rapidly augmented during the ensuing weeks. It is interesting to observe that at Charlestown, as was probably the case at Salem, the organization of the church by union in covenant considerably preceded its choice of officers. It was not till August 27th, after salaries, to be raised by taxation, had been voted to Wilson and Phillips by the assistants of the company on August 23d, that the

Charlestown-Boston church chose and installed John Wilson as teacher, Increase Nowell as ruling elder, and William Gager and William Aspinwall as deacons. It is curiously illustrative of the conservatism of this Puritan congregation that, as Winthrop tells us, they "used imposition of hands, but with this protestation by all, that it was only as a sign of election and confirmation, not of any intent that Mr. Wilson should renounce his ministry he received in England"—of course at the hands of a bishop. But the trend of the Charlestown-Boston church toward the full realization of the Plymouth ideals was decided. Though Roger Williams found it still "unseparated" in 1631, in November, 1632, when Wilson was transferred from its teachership to its pastorate, he was "ordained by imposition of hands" of the elder and deacons, and Winthrop records no reservation as to previous ministry; and when, on October 10, 1633, the distinguished John Cotton, already for twenty years vicar at Boston, England, was made its teacher, he was "chosen by all the congregation testifying their consent by erection of hands," and then ordained by the pastor and ruling elders, who, "speaking to him by his name, . . . did . . . design him to the said office, in the name of the Holy Ghost, and did give him the charge of the congregation, and did thereby (as by a sign from God) indue him with the gifts fit for his office; and lastly did bless him."

Absence of a chronicler like Winthrop makes it impossible to follow the course of events at Watertown as closely as at Charlestown-Boston, but there is reason to think that the tendency in polity Plymouth-ward there was even more rapid. The minister, George Phillips, told Fuller a month before the gathering of the church, that if his people "will have him stand minister, by that calling which he received from the prelates in England, he will leave them"; and the tradition reported by Hubbard and Mather concerning him was that he was more advanced toward the Separatist ideals in his Congregationalism than most of the early New England pastors.

Enough has been said to show that Plymouth example, as interpreted and somewhat modified by Salem, found ready approval with the three Puritan churches which originated in 1630. Thus influentially established by those who were to be leaders in all early Massachusetts history, the way was made easy for the adoption of full Congregationalism by the Puritan immigration that came after; and this tendency to conform to the type developed in 1629 and 1630 was doubtless stimulated by the prescription of the Massachusetts General Court in May, 1631, that the franchise should be limited to those in church-membership. This enactment, characteristic of Massachusetts and New Haven colonies, and not to be found in Plymouth or Connecticut, was doubtless intended to establish a semi-theocratic government, wherein the religious element should rule and from which all disaffected with the Puritan way, especially all Anglican sympathizers, should be excluded; but its effect could have been scarcely less in giving fixity to the pattern of church organization set at the beginning of the colony. It made Congregationalism essentially a state church, and insured that all later coming bodies of Christians, not violently out of sympathy with the views of the founders, would organize themselves after the pattern with which the founders had connected the franchise, and which was in so many respects attractive to the advanced Puritan. Like the whole trend of the English Reformation movement, of which it was a radical manifestation, this religious commonwealth was essentially controlled by laymen. No charge is more baseless than that which represents early New England as "priest-ridden."

The minister was reverenced and consulted as perhaps in no other British territory; but a jealous public sentiment excluded him from political office, and kept the ultimate control of the churches and of the state in the hands of the General Court. It was Endicott rather than Higginson that gave form to religious institutions at Salem, and crushed out incipient dissent by expelling the Brownes. It was the General Court, whatever urging may have come from the ministers, that banished Williams and Anne Hutchinson. It was the same legislative assembly that called, in 1646, the Cambridge Synod that gave definite written form to the polity of New England. And in Massachusetts after 1631 the Court was a body of lay church-members. The vote of that year was the completion of the Puritan reaction against the condition of affairs in England. There every man was accounted of the church by reason of his membership in the state; in Massachusetts a voice in the state was now conditioned on membership in the church for all who were admitted to the privilege after 1631, and this continued to be the rule till 1664; and really in spirit, though not in letter, till the revocation of the charter in 1684.

The rapid immigration of the fourth decade of the seventeenth century led to the speedy formation of new churches, often by companies already well acquainted with one another on English soil, and under the charge of ministers whose services had been prized by their New England hearers before leaving the mother-country. No church was organized in 1631; but in July, 1632, that at Roxbury came into being with Thomas Welde as pastor, and before the close of the year with "Apostle" John Eliot as teacher. The same year saw the beginnings of a church at Lynn, and the separate organization of the members of the Charlestown-Boston church, whose natural meeting-place was at Charlestown. In Plymouth colony also the first ecclesiastical swarming from the parent hive took place in 1632, and resulted in churches at Duxbury and Marshfield. The year 1633 saw the completion of a strong church at Newtown, now Cambridge, with Thomas Hooker as pastor, Samuel Stone as teacher, William Goodwin as ruling elder, and John Haynes, successively governor of Massachusetts and Connecticut, as its chief lay member—a church that in process of time became the First Church in Hartford. In 1634 churches were established at Ipswich in Massachusetts and at Scituate in Plymouth; while 1635 beheld the origin of churches at Newbury, Weymouth, and Hingham; 1636 added to the roll of Massachusetts churches that of Concord, and new churches at Cambridge and Dorchester to take the places of those which had gone from these places to Connecticut. Possibly the church at Wethersfield, Conn., was formed also in the year last named. Springfield in Massachusetts and Taunton in Plymouth followed in 1637; in 1638 Massachusetts received Salisbury and Dedham, Plymouth added Sandwich; and three churches were founded in what is now New Hampshire, at Hampton, Dover, and Exeter. In 1639 came the churches of Quincy and Rowley in Massachusetts, of Yarmouth and a new church at Scituate in Plymouth colony, and those of New Haven and Milford in New Haven colony. Thus, in a few months more than ten years from the formation of the Salem church, the churches of New England probably numbered thirty-three. Of these the churches of Newbury and Hingham had pastors inclined to Presbyterianism in internal administration, and rather critical of the polity of the majority; but the others were all of the full Congregational type.

Mention has been made in the preceding paragraph of

churches in Connecticut and New Haven colonies. The founding of these plantations was the most noteworthy territorial extension of Puritanism in New England, important as giving strategical control of southern New England to the settlers who had hitherto occupied only a narrow fringe on the eastern coast, but chiefly noteworthy in our story as allowing room for the development of independent types of civil government and church polity, closely resembling those of Massachusetts, but possessed of individual peculiarities, since Connecticut and New Haven were never mere echoes of the larger colony; and ultimately giving to American Congregationalism a broader variety in form and a more diversified doctrinal life than if its development had been confined to Massachusetts alone.

The settlement of Connecticut was chiefly the work of the inhabitants of Newtown (now Cambridge) and Dorchester, together with a few from Watertown and other Massachusetts towns. Its causes are somewhat complex; and it seems strange at first sight that men who had miles of unsubdued forest almost at their doors should so soon find the limits of the first settlements too narrow. But the founders of New England had all the land-hunger of pioneer communities of our more modern West; like all frontier societies, they were marked by restlessness and love of change. The valley of the Connecticut, with its long stretches of fertile, treeless meadows, was a garden spot compared with the hard soil about Massachusetts Bay. There was serious danger that it would be taken by the Dutch or the men of Plymouth, who both had posts on the river by 1633. This was incentive enough for emigration thither; but there is reason to believe that other motives, of a nature less easily expressed in public debate, may have urged the removal quite as strongly. The Newtown people were a wealthy and homogeneous company, led in spiritual matters by Hooker and Stone, and in civil concerns by John Haynes, men easily the peers of any in the colony. They may well have desired to go where these leaders could have a little freer scope than in the immediate neighborhood of Winthrop and Cotton—the more so that Hooker seems to have had a somewhat more democratic theory of government than prevailed in Massachusetts, and to have disapproved of the limitation of the franchise to church-members. The Dorchester company, too, though it did not enter into the emigration quite as fully as that of Newtown, will be remembered as somewhat peculiar in origin and distinct in composition. At all events, unrest soon manifested itself in these towns. By 1634 the people of Newtown were petitioning the General Court for leave to go to Connecticut, and the same year a few adventurers from Watertown were beginning the settlement of what is now Wethersfield. The emigration of the petitioners was delayed, but before the close of 1635 many inhabitants of Dorchester and Newtown had found their way to what became Windsor and Hartford. In the spring of 1636 this emigration reached its greatest height, when Hooker and Stone, with a large part of their congregation, made their way overland to Hartford; and probably during the same season the surviving minister of the Dorchester church, John Warham, took up his abode at Windsor, whither many of his flock preceded or accompanied him. Thus two of the most prominent Massachusetts churches were transferred to Connecticut, the continuity of their organization being uninterrupted by the change; while on the soil which they had abandoned, and where some of their former members still remained, new churches had to be gathered to take their place. Connecticut, though a small colony, had thus from the first a strong ministry and a completely ordered Congregational ecclesiastical system, while its early tendencies were a little less theocratic than those of Massachusetts.

New Haven, the youngest of the early Congregational colonies, had its origin in a Puritan company gathered chiefly from London by Rev. John Davenport, who had been curate of St. Lawrence Jewry, and afterward vicar of St. Stephen's in that city, till Laud's opposition caused him to fly to Holland in 1633. Davenport had been interested in the Massachusetts enterprise almost from the beginning, and by the close of 1636 his friends were making ready for the voyage. Chief among them was his parishioner, Theophilus Eaton, a London merchant, and the whole company was conspicuous for wealth and high character. In sympathy with this London movement two small emigrant parties were formed in other regions of England, in Hereford under the spiritual leadership of Rev. Peter Prudden, and in Kent, Surrey, and Sussex by men who chose as their minister Rev. Henry Whitfield, of Okely, in Surrey; and settlers from Yorkshire also added their strength to the enterprise. Davenport, Prudden, Eaton, and a large proportion of the future New Haven settlers sailed from England in the spring of 1637 and landed in Boston on June 26th, where they met a warm welcome from the Massachusetts authorities, who would gladly have received so valuable an accession of strength to their own colony. But the emigrants desired independence; Davenport was a man of positive opinions as to the ordering of church and state; and while the newcomers agreed substantially with the leaders of Massachusetts, they preferred to be their own masters. Accordingly, after some exploration and a winter spent in the vicinity of Boston, they removed to the site afterward known as New Haven, reaching their goal in April, 1638. From the first the colony had a stronger theocratic tendency than any of its predecessors, and one of the earliest acts after setting foot on New Haven soil was an agreement that church and state alike—laws, officers, and problems of government—should be ordered by the Word of God. But as yet no church was formed, though worship was regularly maintained. It was not till more than a year had elapsed after the beginnings at New Haven, and Prudden with his Hereford associates had determined to establish the neighboring plantation of Milford, that on June 4, 1639, the permanent civil and ecclesiastical government of New Haven was determined. After considerable debate, in which the point of contention was the restriction of the suffrage to church-members, the landed proprietors of the infant colony, led by Davenport and Eaton, voted that the "Scripturs doe holde forth a perfect rule for the directiō and gouernmt of all men in all duet[ies] wch they are to performe to God and men as well in the gou'mt of famylyes and comonwealths as in matters of the chur[ch]"; and renewed their pledge of the previous year that they would be governed by biblical rules in the organization of a church and in the "choyce of magistrates and officers, makeing and repealing of lawes, devideing allottmts of inheritance and all things of like nature."

They then voted to limit the franchise to church-members, thus bringing their practice into accord with that of Massachusetts, and departing from that of Plymouth and Connecticut; and, in order to establish the church, this assembly of "free planters," still guided by Davenport, proceeded to nominate twelve men, who should select seven from among themselves as the foundation members of the church to be. Thus by the voluntary action of the New Haven founders the franchise and tenure of office were restricted to a portion of the community.

After more than two months of deliberation the New

Haven church was formed by the seven pillar-members chosen by the committee of twelve, on August 21 or 22, 1639, Davenport and Eaton being included in its original fellowship; and on October 25th following these seven church-members organized the civil government of the little community, elected Eaton as magistrate or governor, and extended the franchise to those (only three in number) who had been admitted to the New Haven church up to that time, and also to those who were "members of other approved churches." Though they had no royal charter, this new government felt itself authorized five days later to execute an Indian for murder. The new church, like that at Boston and probably that at Salem, was at first a covenanted association without officers, but the tradition when Benjamin Trumbull wrote his "History of Connecticut," a century ago, was that not long after its organization the infant church chose Davenport its pastor, with the presence and assistance of Hooker and Stone of Hartford in his installation; though the circumstances of the officering of the Milford church make this Hartford assistance doubtful.

The transactions thus narrated concerned only the inhabitants of New Haven, for in Davenport's colony, unlike Massachusetts and Connecticut, the towns were at first wholly independent of each other; and no central authority had jurisdiction over them all till 1643. While the New Haven church was being organized Prudden and his Hereford company were still in New Haven, though as intended residents of Milford they were looked upon as independent. Evidently, however, they approved of the course of the New Haven settlers, for on August 22, 1639, the same day that the New Haven church was formed, or possibly the day after, seven prominent men chosen by their company organized the Milford church at New Haven.

Of these seven Prudden was one, and on April 18, 1640, he was ordained its pastor at Milford with imposition of hands by three of the six men who had originally entered into covenant with him. In this it may well be believed that Milford simply followed what New Haven had already done in the case of Davenport. By November, 1639, this company were in their Milford home, and on November 20th the planters there voted that the franchise should be confined to church-members. This prescription was speedily modified, and six non-member landholders were allowed the ballot. But when Milford was admitted into union with New Haven and other towns of the colony in October, 1643, these non-church-members were expressly denied a direct voice in matters of general colonial concern.

The company from Kent, Surrey, and Sussex, under the leadership of Rev. Henry Whitfield, of which mention has been made, arrived in New Haven by direct voyage from England during the summer in which the churches of New Haven and Milford were formed. On this voyage they had entered into a written covenant to be faithful one to another, but expressly reserving the formation of their church till they should be settled in their new home. Established at Guilford before the close of 1639, their affairs were temporarily ordered by committees until they could accomplish the "main end" of their coming—the establishment of "the ordinances of God in an explicite congregational church way." There is some reason to believe that the New Haven restrictions on the suffrage were not satisfactory to the people of Guilford, and therefore the formation of their church was delayed; but though they had been originally politically independent, the formation of the Colonial Union of Massachusetts, Plymouth, Connecticut, and New Haven in 1643 made it seem desirable for Guilford to unite in a common jurisdiction with

New Haven and Milford; and accordingly, in the spring or summer of 1643, probably June 19th, seven men entered into covenant as at New Haven, and the Guilford church was constituted. Two of the seven were ministers, Whitfield and John Higginson, who became pastor and teacher, though some doubt exists as to whether Whitfield, at least, was not esteemed so far a minister by virtue of his episcopal ordination that he was not specially ordained to this charge.

The formation of churches by a select few was no peculiarity of the New Haven colonies: that at Charlestown-Boston had been constituted by four men. But the number seven, based doubtless on Proverbs ix. 1, was certainly unusual elsewhere in New England. The church gathered at Dorchester in 1636, after the departure of Warham to Windsor, was constituted by the covenant vows of seven persons, but there is nothing to show that the number there was more than accidental.

As New Haven colony was the last of the Puritan colonies, so in some respects it marks the most radical departure of any from English ecclesiastical ideals. Its civil state was even more distinctly based on a compact than that of Plymouth. Its code of laws was avowedly the Bible. It almost seems as if the theory of churchly independency which these colonists represented was carried over to the state in the complete autonomy of each local community in which they began. The system they would maintain was truly a theocracy, for it was an attempt to be ruled in all things by the Word of God. Yet even in this extremest form New England Puritanism never absolutely merged church and state. The condition of a voice in the state was membership in the church, but when that voice was expressed it was not as the church, but as the civil "court" of legislation and adjudication. Church and state might and sometimes did trench on each other's borders; but in early New England theory, and largely in practice, they were distinct. The chief peculiarities of New Haven, including its restriction of the franchise, passed away on its union with Connecticut in 1664–65.

It has thus been seen that Puritan ecclesiastical institutions on New England soil shaped themselves essentially on one model—a model largely that of Plymouth. Minor unlikenesses existed between church and church; dissimilarities of considerable importance, like the extent of the franchise, distinguished one colony from another; but when all these have been taken into consideration, the conclusion remains that the churches of early New England were singularly alike. They everywhere presented the conception of a church as a body of persons of religious experience bound together by a covenant, choosing its own officers, administering its own affairs, and independent of other ecclesiastical control. They stood everywhere, also, for a free, unliturgical form of worship, an educated ministry, and a strenuous moral discipline. But if the model set at the beginning led to a high degree of local independence, other characteristics of early New England ecclesiastical life, some of which have already been touched upon, and others of which will be noted in the next chapter, prevented this centrifugal tendency from becoming mutual indifference. The connection of these churches with the state, the repressive measures adopted toward dissenters, with the consequent necessity of the formulation of their own standards, led also to the growth of a spirit of fellowship which ultimately developed that sense of responsibility of one church for another that distinguishes American Congregationalism from that of England, and has made our churches something more organically knit together than a convenient grouping of local congregations similar in polity.

CHAPTER V.

THE DEVELOPMENT OF FELLOWSHIP.

It has already been pointed out that the settlers of New England came with no intention of establishing general freedom of worship or extended religious toleration. Their belief in the Scripture was profound, their feeling that the Church of England as then administered did not represent the biblical model was intense, and their great desire was to set up the institutions which they believed the Scriptures required. Had they approved a general toleration, the majority of them would probably have never left their English homes. It was their confidence that the beliefs they maintained were, within narrow ranges of possible divergence of opinion, the only beliefs that were true, that nerved the emigrants for the sacrifices involved in leaving their native island and gave much of its strength to the New England character. And once in possession of a country where they could establish institutions of their own, they did not propose to imperil their work by allowing extensive dissent from their methods either in church or state. This attitude of mind, more conspicuously illustrated in the Puritan colonies than in Plymouth, and most of all evident in Massachusetts, led to acts of banishment and repression scarcely more defensible in some instances than those of Laud, which constitute an unattractive chapter in the story of men otherwise so conspicuous for statesmanship, Christian character, and lofty purposes. But it is a chapter that cannot be passed over if we are to understand the founders of New England; and it is of great importance for the history of Congregationalism, since the measures undertaken to repress dissent and to secure uniformity crystallized the at first somewhat solvent polity, gave to it standards of government and faith, and by compelling consultation and united action emphasized the principle of fellowship in Congregationalism. The methods by which dissent was suppressed often deserve censure; but this exclusive dominance of the Congregational system enabled it to mold popular thought in church and state, to become developed along the lines of its own genius, and by fashioning the ideas of successive generations to affect American civil and religious life as it might not otherwise have done.

During all of their seventeenth century history, save when England was under the Commonwealth, the New England colonies were in a most difficult position; and this was especially true of Massachusetts, which, as the largest and most representative, had to bear the brunt of criticism. On the one hand, their leaders were determined to maintain the religious system and the civil institutions of which they approved; on the other, none of the colonies save Massachusetts had a royal charter till Connecticut received one in 1662, and though the Massachusetts charter was liberal in its provisions for a trading and colonizing company, it required considerable stretching of its conferred powers to make it the basis of a semi-independent state. Hence the Massachusetts colony was always liable to be called to account by those unfavorable to its ecclesiastical system or its political methods; and the great anxiety of the Massachusetts authorities was to prevent any disturbances within the colony or appeals from its jurisdiction which should give occasion for questioning its action or its institutions; and hence, also, their acts of repression had almost always a twofold motive, the one aiming at the preservation of religious and political uniformity, the other having regard to the prevention of interference from England. This dual aspect of the repressive acts of colonial governments, and especially of Massachusetts, has often been forgotten by historians, and the actions of the civil authorities have either been denounced as pure religious bigotry, or excused as entirely due to political necessity. In point of fact, both elements entered into the motives of the leaders of early New England, and it is often impossible to say which predominated; and while we may wish that New England might have exhibited the toleration displayed by Holland under very different circumstances, it may well be questioned whether a general toleration would have produced that sturdy spirit of independence which ultimately secured political freedom from Great Britain, or whether internal commotions would not have given the ever ready English Government excuse for disastrous interference when as yet New England institutions were in the formative stage. It was because the leaders of New England believed that they had a cause worth defending that they were so tenacious in its support against opposition at home and abroad. Doubtless the same is true of Laud or Philip II.; but the situation of New England was essentially unlike that of England or Spain. A few feeble colonies maintaining their institutional integrity in the face of a powerful and menacing home government were not in the condition of countries whose independence and autonomy were practically unshakable. Probably the New England leaders would have had little sympathy with extensive divergence from their views under any circumstances; but the peculiar situation of New England was such as to provoke and intensify repressive measures, for it added fear as to the permanency of the state itself to feelings of religious concern. No estimate of the attitude of the fathers of Puritan Congregationalism toward those who differed with them is correct which ignores the influence of a situation of extreme public peril in intensifying the antipathy which they felt toward that which they deemed subversive of the principles they had made such sacrifices to put into practice.

The interference of the civil authorities of New England in matters of faith and practice began early. The case of the Brownes at Salem has already been noticed, and the uncompromising action of Endicott has been seen in sending them out of the colony when their separate worship, even though that of the English Establishment, threatened to divide the scanty inhabitants of the wilderness plantation. From the first, the Massachusetts authorities exercised the power of ridding their territories of persons obnoxious in civil or religious affairs by what was practically banishment, even though that word of somewhat technical legal import be strictly applicable only to a sentence of Parliament. Thus in September, 1630, the court directed the notorious Thomas Morton of Mount Wollaston to be sent to England, his goods seized to pay the cost of his passage, and his house burned. In March, 1631, six persons were ordered back to England as "vnmeete to inhabit here"; in May of that year two were sentenced to leave the colony before October 20th, their offense being "contempt of authoritie & confrontinge officers"; in June following Philip Ratliffe was "banished," in addition to the loss of his ears and a fine of £40, "for vttering mallitious & scandulous speeches against the gou'm^t & the church of Salem"; and during the next September Henry Lynn was "whipped and banished . . . for writeing into England falsely & mallitiously against the gou'm^t & execuc̄on of justice here."

These cases, most of which did not involve religious considerations in the remotest degree, show that banishment was no unusual remedy for the ills of the body politic, nor one that was first employed in the case of Roger Williams. This able, personally lovable, but exceedingly erratic man was probably a Londoner by origin, who graduated from Cambridge in January, 1627, and then held a chaplaincy to Sir William Masham, of Otes, county of Essex. Here he adopted Separatist views, and as a Separatist in feeling he came to New England in 1631. As such he refused to minister to the Boston church, or even to enter its membership, because he "durst not officiate to an unseparated people," and "because they would not make a public declaration of their repentance for having communion with the churches of England while they lived there." With this illiberal attitude, Williams, like Robert Browne, combined a view in another direction quite in advance of the current opinions of his age. With Browne he held that the civil ruler should not enforce the observance of "first table," i.e., the first four commandments, which the theory of that age held to cover the field of right belief and worship. The particular form of magisterial interference to which Williams objected was the punishment of "the breach of the Sabbath." Shortly after his refusal to serve the Boston church, Williams was called to the teachership made vacant at Salem by the death of Higginson—that church having advanced, it would appear, to a more distinctly Separatist position than the Boston congregation occupied. On news of this call the six members of the Court of Assistants, which met on April 12th, sent an informal letter to Endicott advising delay. Probably this letter interrupted the action of the Salem church, for from the autumn of 1631 to the summer of 1633 Williams assisted Rev. Ralph Smith in the care of the Plymouth church, and there began the study of the Indian tongues, which he was to put to so conspicuous use. From Plymouth, where he left the impression on Bradford of being "a man godly and zealous, having many precious parts, but very unsettled in judgmente," Williams returned to Salem, and after assisting Skelton, he succeeded within a few months of Skelton's decease to the pastorate of the Salem church.

The time was one of special peril and anxiety in the colony. Sir Ferdinando Gorges had obtained the ear of Laud in 1634, and had set the machinery in motion for the revocation of the Massachusetts charter, the suppression of the New England Puritans, the establishment in the Puritan colonies of the Church of England, and the appointment of Gorges himself as governor of the reconstructed territories. The danger for the next five years was very real. The colonial authorities temporized, they fortified Boston Harbor, they stirred up all the friends they could muster in England; but had Gorges had more money to fit out an expedition, or had not the resistance of the Scotch to Laud's attempt in 1637 to introduce episcopacy into their churches distracted the attention of the royal government, it would have gone hard with Congregationalism in America. Such a time of anxiety demanded unity at home, or at least the avoidance of all acts that might precipitate the forcible overthrow of their governments which the colonies feared.

But Williams was not a man to be moved by considerations of expediency. During his stay at Plymouth he had written an essay to prove that royal charters were worthless, since not the king but the Indian natives had a right to give title to the land; that King James was a liar and blasphemer in that he had called Europe "Christendom" and spoken of himself as "the first Christian prince that had discovered this land"; and that King Charles was aptly described in Revelation xvi. 13, 14, xvii. 12, 13, and xviii. 9; and that it was the duty of the colonists to repent of their sin in receiving such a patent. Aside from the inexpediency of insulting powers already sufficiently hostile, there seems to be reason to doubt whether Williams had ever read the charters of 1620 or 1629, for the passages of which he complains do not appear in them; and the company had been explicit in its directions that Indian claimants should be satisfied. Nor does it add to our estimate of the worth of Williams's criticisms to learn that he himself gave them so little weight as to own a house at Salem, which by his own principles must have been held ultimately on a dishonest title. On hearing of the existence of this dangerous document Governor Winthrop asked for it, and submitted it to his brother magistrates on December 27, 1633. Admonished by the magistrates, Williams now disclaimed any intention to make trouble, and offered to allow his book to be burned; and so the matter rested for a little.

Whether Williams instigated, as Endicott certainly effected, the mutilation of the English flag at Salem in November, 1634, by cutting out the cross "as a relique of Antichrist" is possibly uncertain, though exceedingly probable and characteristic in its perilous disregard of the critical situation of the colony. But by December, 1634, Williams was once more "teaching publickly against the king's patent, and our great sin in claiming right thereby to this country," and denouncing the churches of England as "antichristian." In the previous April King Charles had appointed a commission, having Laud as its head, with power to recall charters and inflict any form of punishment; and it seemed probable enough that Massachusetts would be speedily deprived of any legal title without the aid of denunciations by her own inhabitants.

Williams soon advanced to more annoying if less vital criticisms. In its peril the court ordered, in April, 1634, that all residents of the colony should take oath to obey its laws and reveal plots against its welfare. But to Williams's thinking an oath was an act of worship, and since it was a sin to "have communion with a wicked man in the worship of God," no magistrate had a right to call on any unregenerate person to make oath. Just about the time that Williams began to vent these opinions, the church at Salem, which had enjoyed his ministry for more than a year, ordained him to its pastorate. The views of the minister and the action of the church caused great alarm to the magistrates, and as a consequence, Williams was summoned before the court in July, 1635. Here he was charged with teaching that the civil ruler had no right to punish breaches of the "first table," that the oath could not be tendered to an unregenerate man, nor could a man pray without sin with his own wife or child if they were unregenerate. The court called on the ministers of the colony for advice, and "the said opinions were adjudged by all, magistrates and ministers, . . . to be . . . very dangerous"; and the action of the Salem church in "calling of him to office, at that time, was judged a great contempt of authority." The court gave the Salem church and its pastor till its next meeting to think matters over.

It was at the same court which thus severely criticised the Salem minister and church that a petition, presented by the representatives of Salem, and claiming title in the name of the town to certain lands, was laid on the table pending the settlement of these disputes. The action of the court in so doing was no more than might be expected of ordinary human nature probably; but it was a mixing of two distinct questions, which should have been kept separate. Possibly the court doubted a little the loyalty of the Salem people; but the tabling of the petition looks more like a disposition to punish the Salem church-members for their certainly exasperating course. But Williams met it with an act which showed that whatever might be his theory as to the wrongfulness of coercion by magistrates in matters of worship, Sabbath-keeping, and belief, he had no hesitation in applying churchly censure to compel votes in purely secular questions. With the approval of the Salem church, he now sent letters to the other churches whose members had voted in the court on the land question, calling on them to discipline these magistrates for the action taken on the petition. On receipt of these letters some of the churches, and notably those of Boston and Newtown under the lead of Cotton and Hooker, remonstrated with the Salem communion, and with such effect that the majority of that body began to be ashamed of their course and critical of the wisdom of their pastor. On perceiving that he had lost his hold on his own congregation, Williams now turned on it, and by a letter of August 16, 1635, announced to it that he had separated from all the other churches of Massachusetts, and would renounce communion with that of Salem unless it would follow him in cutting off fellowship with its sister congregations "as full of antichristian pollution." The majority of the Salem church had no sympathy with this demand; but Williams was fully determined, refusing even to hold family prayers or say grace at table in the presence of his wife so long as she continued to worship in the congregation of which he was still in name pastor.

On its assembly at Cambridge in September the court took cognizance of the censorious letters of the Salem church designed to bring church censure to bear upon the magistrates, by ordering home the Salem deputies, and directing that Salem should send its representatives to the court when the major part of its voters (of course church-members) had disclaimed the offensive epistles. They complied; but the court showed no haste in dealing with Williams himself. It was not till more than a month had elapsed after its first meeting that Williams was brought before it. Here, the advice of the ministers of the colony having been had, Williams was taken to task on October 8th for his letters defamatory of the Christian character of the Massachusetts churches, and for his other well-known opinions; and, on his defense of his views, was offered a month for further thought. This he refused, and Rev. Thomas Hooker was appointed to argue with him. As far as any evidence of the nature of the debate has come down to us, it was of an exceedingly dialectic and hair-splitting sort, turning on the right of a Christian to share in oaths, grace at table, and the like, with non-Christians. But, as was probably to be expected, Hooker "could not reduce him from any of his errors." The court therefore proceeded on October 9, 1635, to pass sentence upon him: "Whereas Mr Roger Williams . . . hath broached & dyvulged dyvers newe & dangerous opinions, against the aucthoritie of magistrates, as also writt l[ette]res of defamacõn, both of the magistrates & churches here, & that before any convicc̃on, and yet mainetaineth the same without retracc̃on, it is therefore ordered, that the said Mr Williams shall dep'te out of this jurisdicc̃on within sixe weekes nowe nexte ensueing."

Governor Haynes, the most prominent layman in Hooker's congregation, and later to be a leader in Connecticut, summed up the case and spoke the verdict. In his speech he charged Williams with four errors: his attack on the charters, his denunciation of oaths and acts of worship shared in by the unregenerate, his affirmation that it was a sin to hear ministers of the Church of England in the home country, and his denial of authority to magistrates in matters of belief. The fourth point in Haynes's summary, which we know only from Williams's own report, is of course the most famous; but neither Williams nor the court regarded it as the chief ground of his banishment.

By the strict letter of the sentence Williams would have been compelled to leave the Massachusetts colony for England, Plymouth, or the unsettled regions about Narragansett Bay whither Winthrop had advised him to go, by November 20th; but before that time he was ill, and the Massachusetts authorities consented to his stay at Salem till spring, on condition that he would not make proselytes. This was doubtless too hard a condition for a man of Williams's disposition—at all events, he gathered hearers in his house, did "preach to them, even of such points as he had been censured for," and had drawn "above twenty persons to his opinion." The chief burden of this preaching was still the old cry of the impurity of the Massachusetts churches in that they allowed their members who returned on visits to England to listen uncensured to the ministers of the Establishment. For this renewed act of opposition the court proposed to ship Williams to England, but he anticipated their designs by flight, and after a hard winter sojourn among the Indians, he began laying the foundations of Providence with the aid of sympathizers who accompanied and followed him. Here he came to doubt his English baptism—a matter not surprising in one so stoutly Separatist in his attitude toward the English Church—and, apparently under the influence of these doubts, he developed Baptist opinions not held while in Massachusetts. As a result, he was baptized by Ezekiel

Holliman in 1638, and to Holliman and ten others he in turn administered the rite. Yet Williams did not long remain in the fellowship of this first American Baptist Church. After three or four months of walking in the Baptist way he declared "that their baptism could not be right, because it was not administered by an apostle"; and from thenceforward to his death, in 1684, he remained a "seeker," ready to preach or pray with all, but holding that the church and its ordinances could be reëstablished only by a new apostolic manifestation.

Doubtless it would have been better, taking the wide future into view, if the Massachusetts government had allowed Roger Williams to turmoil the Salem community, to denounce the charters, to decry the oaths of fidelity, and to refuse to admit to his congregation those who did not repent of once having been of the communion of the Church of England. Doubtless Massachusetts lost something of variety, and it may be of breadth of thought, in depriving itself of the stimulus of so constant and so conscientious a critic as Williams. It is a loss to any community to lose any good man, and especially if he be a man of talent and in any way a man of progress, as Williams undoubtedly was in his doctrine of freedom of belief. But there are times in nascent communities, as well as in plant life, when rest seems the condition of taking root, and to the men of Massachusetts there was much in the hard-pressed situation of the colony to make the most kindly of them believe this to be such a time.

Williams's banishment was for reasons affecting the peace of the state and the churches rather than their doctrine; but it led to results of permanent influence on American Congregationalism. As has been seen, Williams in his attack upon the magistrates appealed in the name of the Salem church to its sister churches; and they in turn labored with the Salem body, and not in vain. The dispute brought out, as nothing before in the brief history of New England had done, the sense of fellowship and mutual responsibility between churches, which had been foreshadowed in Bradford's right hand of fellowship to the Salem church in 1629, but which is so characteristic a feature of American, as distinguished from English, Congregationalism. All these tendencies were strengthened by the action of the Massachusetts General Court in the spring of 1636—action which was but the logical outcome of its restriction of the franchise to church-members in 1631, but which was occasioned apparently by the divisions of Williams's Salem congregation and a dispute which had arisen at Lynn involving a possible schism in the church there on personal grounds. In March, 1636, the court voted that no body of men associated after the passage of this law should be approved as a church, "without they shall first acquainte the magistrates, & the elders of the great^{r} p'te of the churches in this jurisdiccōn, with their intencōns, and have their approbacōn herein."

This course of procedure had been voluntarily adopted by the company, which organized a church at Cambridge on the 1st of February previous to this vote, and there is reason to believe that it had been followed in other cases; but it was now made obligatory. The consent of the ministers and the magistrates (themselves church-members) was now essential to the gathering of a church. Though not in form a Congregational council, it made such a council practically a necessary step in church-formation, and thus immensely strengthened the sense of mutual responsibility between churches. The statute was no meaningless enactment. In April, 1636, less than a month after its passage, Rev. Richard Mather and his Dorchester associates sought the prescribed approval for their gathering in church estate. Their case was duly investigated, and though their "confession of faith" was approved, so strong were the doubts felt as to the Christian experience of most of the applicants that it was not till the following August that their desire was granted. Indeed, had the court's wishes been fulfilled, Congregationalism would have reached a greater degree of consolidation as a consequence of the Williams dispute than it actually attained. A year before the vote just quoted, in March, 1635, the court had requested "of the elders & brethren of eu'y church within this jurisdiccon that they will consult & advise of one vniforme order of dissipline in the churches, agreeable to the Scriptures, & then to consider howe farr the magistrates are bound to interpose for the preservacon of that vniformity & peace of the churches"; but nothing had come of it, nor was it to bear full fruitage till the Cambridge Synod of 1646–48.

This impulse toward Congregational consolidation, growing out of the Williams controversy and the consequent measures adopted in church and state, was greatly strengthened by a second and more purely theological dispute, which arose speedily after Williams's banishment—the so-called Antinomian episode. In this discussion the colonial authorities acted on a larger scale and with less political justification than in the affair of Williams, and the consequences were correspondingly greater. The source from which this new commotion had its origin was a warm-hearted, magnetic, and keen-tongued woman, Mrs. Anne Hutchinson, who, with her husband, William Hutchinson, had come to Boston in 1634, having been a warm admirer of Cotton in old England, and being attracted across the ocean by his example. A woman of much skill in nursing, and self-sacrificing in her devotion to those of her own sex who needed her services, she soon endeared herself to a large circle in the little colonial seaport. To these friends she talked on what was the great theme of interest—religion; and especially on the merits and demerits of the discourses of the colonial ministers. These meetings, at first confined to her own sex, grew rapidly in popularity, and as they increased in attendance enlarged in scope, until they became a religious power in the little community. The views which Mrs. Hutchinson unfolded to her admiring auditors were those now known as "perfectionism," or the "higher life." To her thinking, the Holy Spirit dwells in every believer in a personal union so as to become one being with him, and so as to preclude the need of any other evidence of sanctification than a consciousness of this divine conjunction to prove a man a Christian. In fact, to argue the existence of Christian character from betterment of morals, delight in God's worship, or anything short of a conscious feeling of union with God, was to rest in a "covenant of works"; while to one under the "covenant of grace" divine illumination, complete confidence, and undoubted salvation were assured.

The labors of Mrs. Hutchinson, at first approved by the authorities, and especially by Cotton, did not come to their full fruitage till 1636, when two other forces of turmoil had been added to the Boston community. In October, 1635, Henry Vane, later to be Sir Henry and one of the most conspicuous figures of the great drama of the English Commonwealth, landed at Boston. Young, handsome, and popular, above all the son of an influential royal counselor at a time when Massachusetts needed all possible aid at the Court of Whitehall, Vane was eagerly taken up by a colony which had temporarily tired of Winthrop and had tried Thomas Dudley and John Haynes in the gubernatorial chair. In May, 1636, Vane was elected governor. From his coming to Boston Vane was actively in sympathy with Mrs. Hutchinson, and through their influence the Boston church, to which they both belonged, came to be chiefly of the same way of thinking. Its pastor, Wilson, and Winthrop opposed the movement. Cotton, though he said little, was counted its friend. The second element of strength added to the Hutchinsonian side was due to the coming into the colony in May, 1636, of Mr. Hutchinson's brother-in-law, Rev. John Wheelwright, a graduate of Cambridge and a minister of the Church of England of pronounced Puritan beliefs.

By the time of Wheelwright's arrival the Boston church was in a divided state. Mrs. Hutchinson and her friends desired to have him as one of the ministers of that church. Wilson opposed, and was now openly attacked, as under the "covenant of works." The projected calling of Wheelwright failed through the hostility of Winthrop, in a debate which involved Vane, Cotton, and Wheelwright himself; but he was given a ministerial position at Mount Wollaston, then a Boston territorial appendage. Yet if the feeling of Boston was warmly Hutchinsonian, that of the churches and ministers of the other towns supported Winthrop and Wilson; and on October 25, 1636, a meeting of ministers at Boston tried in vain to heal the breach. By the out-of-Boston party Winthrop was looked upon as the champion of good order, while the majority of the Boston church held to Vane, who more and more represented the Hutchinsonian theories. By December, 1636, the ministers of the colony appeared before the magistrates, where Hugh Peter, the Salem pastor, openly rebuked Vane as responsible for much of the confusion; and they next debated with Mrs. Hutchinson herself, who maintained her favorite position that while Cotton and Wheelwright preached the "covenant of grace," the rest of the ministers were under the "covenant of works," not having received the "seal" —or, as some theological circles of the present day would say, a "second blessing." On the last day of 1636 the Boston church, led by Vane, endeavored to censure Wilson; but its rule requiring unanimity in important action prevented, though Cotton admonished his colleague before the congregation. And at a fast held on January 20, 1637, Wheelwright, preaching before the Boston church, added fuel to the flame by describing those under the "covenant of works" as "Antichrists." As Winthrop recorded, "it began to be as common here to distinguish between men, by being under a covenant of grace or a covenant of works, as in other countries between Protestants and Papists."

When the court met in the following March, Wheelwright was censured for this sermon by the majority, in spite of the protests of Vane and of a large portion of the Boston church. The dispute had now involved the whole colony, and on it the election of May, 1637, turned, with Winthrop and Vane as representatives of the rival interests. At this election Vane and his friends were dropped from office, but were promptly chosen as representatives of Boston as a reply of that defiantly Hutchinsonian town to the substitution of Winthrop for Vane in the governorship. The successful party made an ungenerous use of their victory by enacting a law forbidding the entertainment of strangers for more than three weeks without the consent of the magistrates—a law general in form, but really designed to prevent the settlement in the colony of friends and relatives of the Hutchinsonian faction whose immigration was expected.

The supporters of the "covenant of grace" were now politically beaten in the larger field of colonial interests; but in Boston they were dominant, and expressed their dislike of their opponent heartily. The Boston halberd-bearers, who had lent official state to the governor on public occasions, refused to honor Winthrop. The Boston levy for the Pequot campaign largely declined to serve in the little army of the colony, because the Boston pastor, Wilson, was chaplain, and he was under the "covenant of works." Certainly affairs seemed moving perilously near to civil conflict.

What might have happened had Vane remained in New England is impossible to say; but the Hutchinson party received a staggering blow when Vane, who had not recovered from his disappointment occasioned by the loss of the governorship, sailed for England, August 3, 1637. Two days after Hooker and Stone of Hartford and other prominent ministers and laymen came to Boston, called to the first general Congregational council, or, as they styled it, "synod." The suggestion of this assembly originated with some of the Massachusetts ministers, but the plan was submitted to the magistrates for their consent, and with magisterial approval "sundry Elders were sent for, from other jurisdictions, and messengers from all the Churches in the Country." Though its summons is unrecorded in the Colonial Records, so much was it deemed a creature of the General Court that the board of its attendants from Massachusetts and the traveling-expenses as well of those from Connecticut was paid from the colonial treasury. Soon after Hooker's arrival in Boston with the other Connecticut delegates, the date of the synod's opening was fixed by the ministers, in consultation with the magistrates, for August 30th, at Cambridge. Here, on the day appointed, in the rude meeting-house that possessed the distinction of having "a bell upon it," there gathered not only "all the teaching elders through the country, and some new come out of England, not yet called to any place here, as Mr. Davenport," later of New Haven, numbering perhaps twenty-five in all, but with them "others sent by the churches"; and with these members of the synod proper there sat the Massachusetts magistrates, as assistants in debate rather than as voters. It was no longer a mere assemblage of ministers such as had frequently gathered at the request of the magistrates. The body was distinctly representative of the churches, and, as such, contained the deputies of the ordinary membership which distinguished a Congregational council from a ministerial convention, and gave to Congregationalism, even in its most theocratic period, a democratic character compared with other polities. It marked the highest expression yet attained of that sense of community and responsibility, of fellowship in churchly concerns, which had been growing in New England since the days of Fuller's ministrations at Salem, and distinguishes American Congregationalism from English Independency.

But while this gathering was thus momentous for Congregational history, its proceedings exhibited no more toleration than those of the court. Under the joint moderatorship of Thomas Hooker of Hartford, Conn., and Peter Bulkeley of Concord, Mass., and with John Higginson as its scribe, whom the New England ministers had been educating out of love for his short-lived father, the synod held its sessions for twenty-four days. Some eighty-two errors, said to be entertained by the Hutchinsonian party or deducible from its beliefs, or at least held by some in New England, were enumerated and condemned by the overwhelming majority of the assembly, though the delegates of the Boston church protested, and some of them left the synod. As the session went on, Cotton more and more came over to the majority, so that Wheelwright was left alone. Mrs. Hutchinson's large "set assemblies" for women were "agreed to be disorderly"; and the public questioning of a minister by a "private member" at the close of his sermon was only to be "very wisely and sparingly done."

A result so generally harmonious was so satisfactory to Winthrop in particular that the governor proposed that synods should be annually held; but for this development Congregationalism was not ready, and the suggestion was disapproved. A second proposition of Winthrop, that the synod should decide upon the method of ministerial support, was laid aside by the ministers with a high-mindedness usually characteristic of the New England clergy, "lest it should be said that this assembly was gathered for their private advantage." On September 22d the synod adjourned.

Since the Hutchinsonian party remained openly defiant of the synod's conclusions, the court felt the more disposed to take sharp measures against it. At the November session Wheelwright and Mrs. Hutchinson were sentenced to banishment, the latter after claiming direct divine revelations; and, by an arbitrary stretch of authority, the remonstrance which the people of Boston had addressed to a previous legislature in March, 1637, praying that the court would not interfere with Wheelwright, was now interpreted as constructive sedition, and those of its signers who would not express their contrition were disarmed and some of them disfranchised. With the fifty-eight thus deprived of their arms in Boston, seventeen persons in five other towns, were joined by the court. The result was the complete break-down of opposition. Public feeling in Boston changed, or at least was silenced; Cotton was now wholly identified with the majority. In March, 1638, Mrs. Hutchinson, who had been permitted to remain through the winter in Massachusetts, was brought before the Boston church, of which she was a member, and where she had formerly enjoyed the sympathy of the majority; and, after a trial reflecting little credit on any concerned, she was excommunicated. Going to Rhode Island soon after her excommunication, she lived near the present Newport till 1642, when she removed to Manhattan Island, then under Dutch jurisdiction, and was there murdered by the Indians with most of her family in August of the next year. Her connection, Wheelwright, began the hard wilderness life anew in the winter of 1636–37 at Exeter, N. H.; but ultimately returned to Massachusetts, and died in 1679 as pastor of the church at Salisbury. Mrs. Hutchinson's sympathizer, William Coddington, became one of the founders of Rhode Island institutions.

The main actors in these proscriptions naturally desired to make the religious element in them seem as slight as possible, while they emphasized the civil breach of peace which these troubles threatened. No doubt they sincerely believed the danger of political division, especially in the threatening attitude of the English Government, a very real peril. No doubt, too, they sincerely feared an outburst of fanaticism such as men had associated for a century, for the most part wrongly enough, with "Anabaptism" or "Antinomianism." But the religious motive was the leading impulse on both sides, and if it led on the one to mystical and erroneous views, it led on the other to persecution as real as it was unjustifiable. It led also, as our story has pointed out, to a remarkable development of the principle of fellowship in Congregationalism, which involved the calling of the first general council.

Unfortunately, the spirit of persecution once aroused was not easily checked. The political necessities which largely justified the treatment of Williams by Massachusetts were much less of a factor in the Hutchinsonian dispute, though still present; in the proscription of Baptists and Quakers they were hardly of weight at all. Persons of Baptist principles were to be found among the Puritan settlers of New England from the beginning; but so long as they did not violently attack infant baptism or the churches practicing it they were let alone.

As early as December 14, 1642, three women of Lynn and Salem were before the quarter court for their Baptist views. A little later, February 28, 1643, William Witter, of Lynn, was brought to answer by the same tribunal, having "called our ordenonce of God a badge of the whore." Witter made apology; but in February, 1646, he was again before the court of Salem "for saying that they who stayed whiles a child is baptized doe worshipp the dyvell." This case, and one or two others, induced the General Court to take action in November, 1644, when a law was passed threatening all opponents of infant baptism with banishment. For his Baptist sentiments, Henry Dunster, the first president of Harvard College, was compelled to resign his post in 1654. But Plymouth colony was by no means as severe in this matter as Massachusetts; and the patience and persistence of the Baptists at last broke down the opposition of the Massachusetts authorities themselves. In 1665 a Baptist church was organized in Boston, which soon worshiped on Noddle's Island. The court intervened, and in 1668 sentenced three of these dissenters to banishment; but protests from prominent men of the colony and from leading English Congregational ministers prevented the full execution of this decree; and by 1674 this Baptist church was transferred to Boston. By the close of the century Cotton Mather could write of the Baptists: "We are willing to acknowledge for our *brethren* as many of them as are willing to be so acknowledged."

This spirit of persecution manifested itself in far more violent forms against the Quakers than against the Baptists, in proportion as their own conduct was more exasperating. The Baptist at least claimed to stand with the Puritan on the Word of God. The Quaker asserted a divine illumination which made his actions and his testimony directly inspired of God; and however necessary such a protest as his may have been against the literalism of the Puritan's interpretation of the Bible, there can be no doubt that the early New England Quaker by conduct and speech convinced the Puritan that he was an enemy against decency and order rather than a messenger of the Lord. Probably the extremer forms of Quaker demonstration were aggravated by the repressive measures from which the Quakers suffered; but much that they did would, if done in our own day, have brought them before the police-court and into examination as to mental sanity. First arriving in the colony in July, 1656, they were imprisoned and sent away; and in October of that year a law was passed by the General Court, now presided over by Endicott and Bellingham, two of the sternest of Massachusetts Puritans, as governor and deputy-governor, ordering that all Quakers should be whipped, imprisoned, and transported out of the country. Similar laws were enacted in Plymouth, Connecticut, and New Haven colonies. Yet Quakers continued to come, claiming "a message from the Lord"; and in 1658 the penalty for return after banishment was, by recommendation of the commissioners of the four colonies, increased in Massachusetts to death. The three other colonies failed to follow the advice of their commissioners, and the Massachusetts lower House passed the statute by a majority of only one. But the Quakers were persistent. Under what they believed to be divine impulse, they continued to return to Massachusetts in order to denounce its institutions and revile its ministers and magistrates. In accordance with this law, two men were executed at Boston in 1659, one woman in 1660, and a man in 1661. But opposition to these severities was strong in the colony, and in May, 1661, the law was greatly alleviated. In 1677 the last instance of punishment of Quakers by whipping occurred; and though Massachusetts still looked upon them with disfavor, they, like the Baptists and all other Protestants, received freedom from molestation by the new charter granted to the colony in 1691.

The shortcomings of a neighboring people are slight excuse indeed for national failings; but it is not without interest to observe that the repressive measures of the New England Puritans were nothing peculiar to them. Indeed, if the severity rather than the spirit of the statute be made the test, American Puritanism appears lenient in comparison with the mother-country, or with the other great English colonial experiment of the period, the Church-of-England colony of Virginia. Under what has recently been described as the "wholesome discipline" of Sir Thomas Dale, high marshal of that colony from 1611 to 1616, a code of laws of military strictness was established. By these statutes continued absence from daily services was punishable with six months in the galleys, and similar neglect of Sunday worship with death. This harsh rule was probably never fully enforced, and it was modified when the colonial assembly of Virginia began its existence in 1619; but the worship of the Church of England still remained the exclusive legal form, and attendance on its services "both forenoon and afternoon" was enjoined on "all persons whatsoever," under a fine established by statute in 1623, as a hogshead of tobacco for a single willful absence, and of £50 for a month's neglect. Yet, in spite of this enforced uniformity, an appeal came from some of the people of Virginia to Boston in 1642 asking for Congregational missionaries. New England heard the request, and in response Rev. Messrs. William Tompson of Braintree, John Knowles of Watertown, and Thomas James of New Haven went thither with the commendation of their ministerial associates. Yet, though they had some slight success, their mission was a failure, owing to the opposition of the government, which drove out the ministers, and, though the dissenters numbered a hundred and eighteen, "made an order that all such as would not conform to the discipline of the Church of England should depart the country by a certain day." So effective were the drastic measures of the Virginia assembly that Governor Spotswood was able to write in 1710, two generations after this expulsion: "It is a peculiar blessing to this Country to have but few of any kind of Dissenters." Certainly the New England Puritan was not more bigoted than the Virginia Episcopalian.

But it should not be forgotten, in any estimate of Puritan New England, that it had in itself a principle that ultimately worked the cure of its limitation of religious freedom. It believed profoundly in the authoritative character of the Word of God; but in the interpretation of that Word, as John Fiske has pointed out, it employed no aid save reason, enlightened by whatever of learning men could attain. In this regard it was beyond all other Christian countries of the age rationalist. It appealed to no standards of interpretation fixed in bygone centuries, or by authoritative councils. It claimed no insight into the

Scriptures for its ministers beyond what any layman might and ought to reach by a similar degree of education and study. It laid down no dictum as to the meaning of the Bible which it did not believe to be grounded on the same bases of rational argument that it applied to the concerns of law or business. Its ministers were no priestly order demanding reverence as the exclusive expounders of divine oracles, or claiming any inherent right to direct the affairs of state. Their influence, great as it was, had no other basis than that of special knowledge obtained through ordinary processes of learning addressed to themes which the community deemed of first importance. It was largely because Mrs. Hutchinson and the Quakers claimed other sources of authority, substituting for study of the Bible and logical deductions from its teachings what they affirmed to be divine revelations, that they seemed so obnoxious to the New England Puritans. Such a system of scholarly investigation implies, however dimly the implication may be apprehended, the possibility of revision, which no dogmatic or confessional system allows without revolution. And though the Congregationalists of the seventeenth century adopted elaborate statements of faith as expressions of the beliefs of the body of New England churches, by allowing each church freedom of creed-formation and autonomy in government within the general limits of fellowship they unintentionally made the way easy for local modification and adaptation to advancing discussion.

Nor did the ministry of early New England manifest any jealousy of laymen either in theologic discussion or in church administration. There were no fountains of divine knowledge not open to the ordinary church-member. By the votes of laymen the minister received the "call" which gave him all the ministerial title he possessed; and though when in office a minister had a more authoritative position than he enjoys in modern democratic Congregationalism, the doctrine, discipline, and increase of any particular church rested ultimately on the decision of its non-clerical membership. In all synods and councils the lay element was present, and usually during the seventeenth century in larger numbers than the ministers. It was this working together of the religious community as a whole which renders the repressive acts of which account has been given the work of no one class, and which made it certain that as soon as public sentiment in general was ready for toleration repression would cease.

One other feature of the Congregational life of the seventeenth century shows that in spite of whatever narrowness it may have exhibited it was in a healthful state, and had in it seeds of future freedom. New England Congregationalism believed that education was one of the chief safeguards of the Christian life. Such a conception was the natural outcome of the importance it attached to the Bible, and especially of the method by which the truths contained therein were thought to be discoverable. The Puritan had no sympathy with the doctrine that ignorance is the mother of faith; to his thinking, education is the road to knowledge in divine things. The New Englanders of the seventeenth century, judged by modern standards, were not a reading people; but compared with the common people of the land from which they had come forth, they were educated; and their ministry was from the first a conspicuously learned body of men. Moved by the desire to train up successors worthy of the graduates of Cambridge and Oxford who occupied New England pulpits, the Massachusetts General Court, on October 28, 1636, voted £400 for a "colledge." The same court that exiled Mrs. Hutchinson in November, 1637, ordered that it should be at Newtown, soon after named Cambridge, doubtless in honor of the English *alma mater* of nearly fifty of the inhabitants of the colonies; and to this college the name of Harvard was given in March, 1639, in honor of its principal benefactor. The first commencement at this seat of learning was held in 1642, and from that time till the founding of Yale College, in 1701, it was almost the sole source from which the New England ministry was replenished.

Lower education also soon attracted the attention of the colonial governments. Boston had a school by 1635; in Hartford one was in existence by 1637, and by 1643 the town voted to pay the tuition of any whose parents were "not able to pay for their teaching"; New Haven established a school in 1642. The example thus set was enforced by the colonial legislatures. In November, 1647, Massachusetts thus ordered: "y^{t} ev^{r}y towneship in this iurisdiction, aft^{r} ye Lord hath increased y^{m} to ye number of 50 houshold^{rs}, shall then forthwth appoint one wthin their town to teach all such children as shall resort to him to write & reade; . . . & . . . y^{t} where any towne shall increase to ye numb^{r} of 100 families or househould^{rs}, they shall set up a gram̄er schoole, ye m^{r} thereof being able to instruct youth so farr as they may be fited for ye university."

This Massachusetts statute was copied verbally in the code of laws enacted by the Connecticut Court in May, 1650. And the reason given in both cases is that men might have a better understanding of the Word of God: "it being," as the court expressed it, "one cheife proiect of y^{t} ould deluder, Satan, to keepe men from the knowledge of ye Scriptures."

Certainly a community in which the autonomy of the local church was preserved; in which separate colonial jurisdictions grew out of and perpetuated somewhat divergent theories as to the extent of the theocratic principle in the administration of the state; in which laymen were concerned in the definition of doctrine and the management of ecclesiastical affairs to a degree nowhere else exemplified; and in which the interpretation of the fundamental religious rule, the Scriptures, was based solely on studious investigation and argument—was a community having in its constitution principles which must lead to religious freedom, in which repression could be only a passing phase of development, and which was certain to produce strong, intelligent, intellectually acute, Christian men and women.

As a matter of fact, in spite of the repression of the extremer forms of dissent from what was practically an established church, discussion of polity—and, to a considerable extent, of doctrine—was a necessary characteristic of early New England life, and from these debates continued progress in the development of the principle of fellowship resulted. The form which these discussions took was largely determined by the changing state of public affairs in England—a change which led, in 1640, to the summons of the Long Parliament, and in 1642 to war between Parliament and the king and the dominance in parliamentary counsels of Presbyterian Puritanism. To some extent, also, debates as to the extent of church-membership and consequent right to baptism, which were to turmoil the New England churches in the sixth and seventh decades of the seventeenth century, made their beginnings felt soon after the Hutchinsonian dispute.

Naturally the rapid development of Congregationalism in New England excited the curiosity, and to some extent the concern, of the Puritan party in the mother-country. Through the influence of Cartwright and other of its early leaders the nonconformity of that party inclined toward Presbyterianism. To many of its leaders the Congregationalism of Massachusetts and Connecticut seemed a falling away under Plymouth example into dangerous Separatism. Accordingly, as early as 1636 or 1637 the English Puritans sent across the ocean two sets of queries as to the constitution of a church; membership; forms of worship; the use of a liturgy; ministerial election, ordination, and standing; councils; and, in fact, the whole range of ecclesiastical life. The shorter of these inquiries, entitled "A Letter of Many Ministers in Old England, requesting The judgement of their Reverend Brethren in New England concerning Nine Positions," was replied to by Rev. John Davenport, of New Haven, under the caption of "An Answer of the Elders of the Severall Chvrches in New-England unto Nine Positions," and both the query and the reply were printed at London in 1643, after they had circulated several years in manuscript. The longer series of questions, thirty-two in number, were replied to in 1639 by Rev. Richard Mather, of Dorchester, but his tractate, like that of Davenport, did not appear in print till 1643, and bears the title of "Church-Government and Church-Covenant Discvssed, In an Answer of the Elders of the severall Churches in New-England To two and thirty Questions." These elaborate expositions of the various aspects of New England Congregationalism evoked plentiful reply, and were soon followed by others. Thus, not long after Mather's tract was composed, Rev. John Cotton, of Boston, wrote a manuscript defense of New England methods, which reached England in an imperfect or undigested copy, and after circulating in manuscript for several years was printed in 1645 as the "Way of the Churches of Christ in New-England." Even more important as one of the formative expositions of American Congregationalism was Cotton's "Keyes of the Kingdom of Heaven," published at London in 1644. These works led to many opposing treatises, especially after the call of the Westminster Assembly and the adoption of the Covenant by Parliament in 1643 made Presbyterianism dominant in England. Perhaps the most weighty of these replies, in the estimate of the founders of New England, was the "Due right of Presbyteries," published by Professor Samuel Rutherford, of the University of St. Andrew's, in 1644. To this work Mather rejoined in 1647 by his "Reply to Mr. Rutherfurd," and Cotton in 1648 by his "Way of the Congregational Churches Cleared"; but the most important answer was that of Rev. Thomas Hooker, of Hartford, in his "Survey of the Summe of Church-Discipline," the original manuscript of which was sent from New Haven by the celebrated "phantom ship" in January, 1646. Its destruction in the mysterious loss of the vessel to which it was intrusted led to its ultimate publication, in 1648, from an exceedingly imperfect manuscript, after the death of the writer; yet fragmentary as it is, Hooker's "Survey" ranks with Cotton's "Keyes" as one of the chief settings forth of early New England Congregationalism.

This formulation of the Congregational system in elaborate treatises, only the more important of which have been named, was chiefly the result of inquiry and criticism from beyond the sea; but even more positive consequences in the way of definition flowed from home debates. Not all of the founders thought alike upon polity. At Newbury, Mass., the pastor and teacher, Thomas Parker and James Noyes, were so far inclined toward Presbyterianism that they did away with the participation of the ordinary membership in church acts save in ministerial election. At Hingham, Rev. Peter Hobart was of the same opinion. But to the majority of the ministry of New England this denial to the brethren of a share in admissions, dismissions, and discipline seemed a serious error; and therefore a convention of the ministers of the Congregational colonies was held at Cambridge in September, 1643, with Cotton and Hooker for its moderators. It was not a synod, like the council of 1637, though that name has sometimes loosely been given to it, for it had in it no delegates from the lay membership of the churches. By this assembly the Newbury ministers were labored with, though not convinced; and it shows the advance toward consolidation that the few years of establishment on American soil had effected, that the suggestion vainly proposed by Winthrop in the Synod of 1637 was approved with added emphasis by the convention, which agreed, "that Consociation of churches, in way of more general meetings, yearly; and more privately, monthly, or quarterly; as Consultative Synods; are very comfortable, and necessary for the peace and good of the churches." It is hardly needful to point out that the word "consociation" was not used by the first two generations on New England soil in the technical sense later attached to it in Connecticut; what the convention had in view more nearly resembles the modern Congregational "conference."

It was natural that the unhealed difference between the ministers at Newbury and Hingham, the manifestation of Baptist sentiments here and there among the membership of the churches, and above all the growing prominence of the questions as to the extent of church-membership and the right to baptism out of which the Half-Way Covenant discussion was to grow, should incline men who had just expressed their approval of frequent meetings of the churches to desire a new general council to determine the questions at issue, and to give to the churches the "one vniforme order of dissipline," the propriety of which had been urged by the Massachusetts General Court as early as March, 1635. But other causes impelled toward the formulation of Congregational order. Parliament was at war with the king, and in that struggle had the hearty sympathy of the New England colonies. But Parliament and its Scotch supporters were violently Presbyterian. The Westminster Assembly had been engaged since July, 1643, in preparing a Presbyterian Confession and ecclesiastical constitution for England. Moreover, Parliament, in November, 1643, had established a board entitled "The Commissioners for Plantations," with power "to provide for, order, and dispose all things" for the colonies, and in fact exercise all the authority formerly possessed over them by the king. It seemed no idle fear that when the Westminster Assembly had done its work Parliament would force the acceptance of its results on New England, as it seemed likely to do on other parts of the realm. This fear was strengthened by a formidable movement in 1645 and 1646, led by William Vassall, of Plymouth colony, and Dr. Robert Child and a number of associates in the Massachusetts jurisdiction. These men, dissatisfied with the limitation of the suffrage to church-members in Massachusetts, and with the strenuous barriers which Congregationalism everywhere placed between the sacraments and all who could not unite in church covenant on the basis of personal religious experience, petitioned the courts of Massachusetts and Plymouth for the privileges which they would have had in church and state in England, and threatened that if their desires were not granted they would appeal to Parliament for redress. Certainly they had much reason to feel that their complaint was just; yet had the courts granted their requests, the fabric of New England institutions would have been profoundly altered. And had they not been frustrated in their attempt to secure parliamentary interference by the great political reversal which in 1647 made Cromwell and the army, rather than Parliament, masters of England, New England institutions would probably have been forcibly changed by a parliamentary power no less arbitrary than that of King Charles himself.

It was under these circumstances of internal discussion and dreaded interference from without that some of the Massachusetts ministers obtained from the General Court of that colony, in spite of considerable hesitation on the part of the representatives of the towns in the lower House, the summons of a synod by a call dated May 15, 1646. By this legislative invitation the churches of Massachusetts, Plymouth, Connecticut, and New Haven were asked to send their ministers and delegates to meet at Cambridge on the 1st of September following, "there to discusse, dispute, & cleare up, by the word of God, such questions of church governm^t & discipline . . . as they shall thinke needfull & meete."

The particular questions which seemed to the court to be the most pressing were "those about baptisme, & ye p'sons to be received thereto"; but the invitation doubtless was intended to allow freedom to formulate the whole round of ecclesiastical practice.

Yet, in spite of the call of the court, four Massachusetts churches were unrepresented when the 1st of September came. Hingham was doubtless disinclined, owing to a recent quarrel with the colonial authorities; at Concord the minister was unable to go, and no brother of the church was deemed gifted enough to be its delegate; but at Boston and Salem considerable portions of the congregation had doubts as to the wisdom of synods by legislative authority. These scruples were overcome after much argument; but this discussion consumed a number of days, and the attendance from other colonies than Massachusetts was small, and therefore, having appointed

Rev. Messrs. John Cotton of Boston, Richard Mather of Dorchester, and Ralph Partridge of Duxbury each to draught a "model of church government," the Synod adjourned to June 8, 1647. At that time it reassembled, but an epidemic caused its speedy adjournment for the second time.

Soon after its second recess the court laid a new task upon the Synod. The Westminster Assembly was well known to have prepared a Confession of Faith, which, though presented to Parliament in December, 1646, was not approved by that body till after much revision, in June, 1648. Till adopted by the Scotch General Assembly on August 27, 1647, it had been held secret; and its exact nature was in all probability unknown in New England when the General Court of Massachusetts met in October of that year. It doubtless seemed to many in New England that it would be well for the Synod to be ready with a confession of its own should that of Westminster prove unsatisfactory, and therefore the court requested seven of the Massachusetts ministers each to prepare "a breife forme of this nature, & p'sent ye same to ye next session of ye synode."

Meanwhile affairs in England were rapidly assuming an aspect satisfactory to the New England Congregationalists. Child and his friends had gone thither to prosecute their complaints, and the Massachusetts authorities had sent Gov. Edward Winslow of Plymouth thither, in December, 1646, as its agent to prevent the English governmental interference which Child proposed to invoke. In this mission Winslow was entirely successful, not so much on account of his own labors, though he was skillful and energetic in high degree, as by reason of the downfall of the Presbyterian ascendency owing to the rise of the army to political supremacy in 1647 and 1648. When the

Synod met, therefore, for its final session on August 15, 1648, the political horizon seemed brighter than at any time in its history. Two draughts certainly of the three models of church government requested by the Synod were presented; and that of Rev. Richard Mather was preferred to that of Rev. Ralph Partridge, though much abridged and somewhat modified by the assembly. In particular, the extension of baptism to the children of those who, though themselves baptized offspring of parents in church-covenant, were not persons of Christian experience —the system later known as the Half-Way Covenant— though given a place by Mather and Partridge in their draughts, and though prominently in the thought of the court as a question to be determined by the Synod, was left undecided, after considerable debate, owing to the strenuous opposition of a few to the innovation. The defeat of Child and his friends made it seem a less pressing question than at the call of the Synod. Thus revised, Mather's draught became the celebrated "Cambridge Platform." At the same time the Synod fulfilled the further request of the court, that a confession of faith should be adopted, by approving "for the substance therof" the doctrinal parts of the Westminster Confession, which had now reached New England. With these acts the most important of early Congregational councils came to an end.

The "Platform," provided with a preface by Rev. John Cotton elucidating certain features of Congregational polity and defending the orthodoxy of the New England churches, was printed at Cambridge in 1649, and presented to the Massachusetts court at its October session in that year. By that legislative body it was commended to the churches for their consideration and report—a request which was repeated as an order in June, 1650, when the churches were also desired to express their opinion on the Westminster Confession. The churches seem generally to have approved, though a considerable number of criticisms regarding the "Platform" were offered, which were answered by the ministers, at the request of the court, through the pen of Rev. Richard Mather. And at last, in October, 1651, the court expressed its guarded approval of the result, voting that its members "account themselues called of God (especially at this time, when the truth of Christ is so much opposed in the world) to giue theire testimony to the s'd Booke of Discipline, that for the substance thereof it is that we haue practised & doe beleeue." Yet from this very cautious commendation fourteen of the town representatives in the lower House dissented, including the entire delegations from Boston and Salem, showing thus that the distrust which had there led to a tardy recognition of the Synod had not died out. But no serious opposition to the "Platform" developed among the churches, and the "Platform" continued the recognized standard of Congregationalism in Massachusetts throughout the colonial period, and in Connecticut till the Saybrook Synod in 1708.

The Westminster Confession of Faith, approved at Cambridge as an adequate expression of Congregational belief, was superseded in Massachusetts in 1680, and in Connecticut in 1708, by a slight modification of its Savoy revision of 1658. But early Congregationalism in America stood uncriticisingly on the doctrinal basis of the great Puritan party in the home land, and there is no evidence that the adoption of the Westminster Confession aroused anything like the interest excited by the "Platform." One point, indeed, that of "vocation," raised a little debate in the Synod; but neither that body nor the churches seem to have felt in any critical spirit toward the Confession, which Parliament had just made the doctrinal standard of England.

The "Cambridge Platform" is an ecclesiastical constitution in seventeen chapters, built upon the proposition that "the partes of Church-Government are all of them exactly described in the word of God." It attempts to ascertain the Scripture pattern of the church; the character and conditions of its membership; its powers; its officers, their appointment and duties; its discipline; its expression of fellowship with other churches; the right of councils to advise in its affairs; and the authority of the magistrate in ecclesiastical concerns. The "Platform" represents Congregationalism as the New England fathers pictured it after half a generation of experience in its practical administration. To the thinking of the Synod, Congregationalism was vastly less democratic than modern Congregational practice conceives the system to be. It was viewed as of exclusive divine authority, and as subject to the interference of the civil ruler should its churches swerve in doctrine or administration from the God-given standard. But though the "Platform" in these and other particulars reflects the temporary rather than the permanent characteristics of the system, it pictures with great clearness the abiding principles of Congregationalism. The covenant as the basis of the local church, the autonomy of each congregation, coupled with its dependence on other churches for fellowship and counsel, the representative character of the ministry, above all the absence of all final authority in doctrine or polity save the Word of God, are the essential features of the "Platform" which have given it permanent worth and have partially justified the veneration with which this monument of early New England Congregationalism has been regarded.

The preparation of the "Cambridge Platform" and the

adoption of the Westminster Confession as general expressions of Congregational faith and practice by a body representative of the New England churches as a whole marks the completion of that movement toward confederation which characterized early American Congregationalism from the arrival of the Puritans, which was greatly strengthened by the establishment of Congregationalism as a state church, and had its strongest impulse from the efforts of the civil and ecclesiastical forces of the new settlements to guard their institutions and their faith from what they deemed dangerous encroachments. Congregationalism was thus placed almost from the first in New England in a totally different position from what it has ever occupied in England—in the home land it has always been a somewhat radical element protesting against an established system; in New England it necessarily became conservative, since it was the legally recognized polity, and such a position is one requiring definition and leading to united action. No general council of all Congregational churches in America met again till the Albany Convention of 1852; but the impulse toward fellowship which marked these early years developed principles recognized from the first in the system, but which had not come into practice to any considerable extent in England or Holland, and so developed them that they gave a fraternal character to the relationship of churches one to another and a corporate consciousness to the Congregational body which survived the strongly decentralizing tendencies of the eighteenth century, and is increasingly valued in our own day.

CHAPTER VI.

CONGREGATIONALISM FROM 1650 TO 1725.

It was one of the pleasant incidents of the second session of the Cambridge Synod in June, 1647, that, as Winthrop tell us, "Mr. Eliot preached to the Indians in their own language before all the assembly.". The missionary enterprise thus publicly exhibited had not long before been inaugurated. To bring the savage inhabitants of America to Christianity had, indeed, been one of the objects which attracted the Leyden Pilgrims across the ocean; and the Massachusetts Company had declared, in 1629, that "the propagating of the gosple is the thing [wee] doe professe aboue all to bee o^{r} ayme";—a propagation which included the evangelization of the Indians, as well as the establishment of English religious institutions in New England. But though various efforts were made in the early days of the colonies to carry this purpose into execution, no systematic plan was at first pursued, and scanty results were accomplished. The barriers of language and especially of thought and manner of life made easy communication between the two races difficult. It is to be remembered to the credit of Roger Williams that while at Plymouth, probably as early as 1632, he began the study of the Indian tongues and cultivated that familiarity with Indian life which made his words influential with the savage warriors.

But the most important movement for Indian conversion was initiated by the Massachusetts court,—the body which was responsible for so much that was good and evil alike in early New England religious life, and which served in so many ways as a General Assembly regulative of the churches. In November, 1644, the court expressed its desire that the Indians should receive religious instruction, and soon invited the ministers to express their opinions as to the most fitting methods. And two years later, November 4, 1646, the same legislative body ordered the ministers to choose two of their number at the annual election every year to engage in missionary work with the aid of such volunteers as might join them. Probably the latter action of the court was hastened by the knowledge of missionary labors which had been begun a week before its enactment. Rev. John Eliot, the teacher of the Roxbury church, had been for some time studying the Indian dialect, with the aid of a young native who had learned English as a servant; and on October 28, 1646, Eliot and three friends went to an Indian village near Watertown, and there the Indian apostle preached his first sermon. The movement excited the general interest of the churches, and such assistance as could be given was cheerfully rendered. These direct efforts for the conversion of the savages were accompanied by attempts to give them the rudiments of education and to bring them to English modes of life, in which Eliot had the support of the court and the colonial treasury.

Contemporary with these missionary exertions of Eliot, or possibly a little earlier in their beginning, were the independent labors of the Mayhews on the island of Martha's Vineyard, where the father and son established themselves as proprietors by purchase, the former in 1644 and the latter even earlier. Tidings of these events, published by friends of New England, aroused great interest in the mother-country, and led, in July, 1649, to the formation of a corporation by act of Parliament under the title of

"The President and Society for the Propagation of the Gospell in New England," designed to raise money by a "general collection" in England for the furtherance of the work. The dispensing agents of this society in New England were the commissioners of the four united colonies of Massachusetts, Plymouth, Connecticut, and New Haven. Nor were the sums given in charity in England under the Commonwealth inconsiderable: amounting by 1656 to a total of £1700, and reaching by 1661 to more than £600 a year. To these gifts the inhabitants of New England added what they could, giving, a contemporary observer declared, "far more, in proportion, than their countrymen in England." Under the instructions of Eliot, the Mayhews, and others, the work soon showed results. In 1650 Eliot organized his converts into a community at Natick, where they might not only worship, but learn trades and husbandry and be drilled in the exercise of civil government. By 1655 a similar Indian town was begun at Punkapog, later known as Stoughton, and others were soon formed near Grafton and Concord. In Martha's Vineyard the labors of the Mayhews were as successful; and attempts of a less fruitful nature were made to reach the Indians at Sandwich in Plymouth, near Norwich in Connecticut, and at Branford in New Haven Colony. The most notable literary fruit of this enterprise was the publication at the cost of the English Society in 1661 at Cambridge, Mass., of Eliot's translation of the New Testament into the language of the Massachusetts Indians,—a work which was followed two years later by the issue of the whole Bible from the same press. This monumental undertaking was followed by a number of translations, embracing treatises by Cotton, Increase Mather, Shepard, Baxter, as well as the "Cambridge Platform" and the Confession of 1680, the publication of which extended over a period of nearly sixty years. By 1674 the "Praying Indians" numbered not far from four thousand, gathered in part into at least seven churches, and enjoying the religious instruction of teachers of their own race, as well as the general oversight of white missionaries, in many settlements in Massachusetts, Plymouth, and the islands. Of these churches, four, and of the Indians, some eighteen hundred, were on the islands of the Martha's Vineyard group.

But an unexpected tempest largely wrecked the Indian missions thus auspiciously begun. Contrary to the representations sometimes made, the Puritan settlers of New England treated the Indians well. Except for the short, sharp conflict with the Pequots in 1637, the two races were at peace. The white inhabitants of the colonies carefully secured their lands by purchase, and defended Indian rights by law. The New England Puritan of the first two generations seems to have been as honorable in his dealings with the red men as the Pennsylvania Quaker. But the situation was one, thanks to Indian politics, where permanent peace between the two races was impossible. Thrust in between Massachusetts and Plymouth on the east and the settlements of Connecticut on the west were a number of tribes, of which the most powerful were the rivals, the Mohegans and the Narragansetts. To keep on good terms with both was difficult, and the situation was doubtless made all the harder by a complete misunderstanding on the part of these more powerful tribes of the motives of Eliot and the other missionaries. The "Praying Indians" were mostly from feeble tribes, like the Massachusetts and the Pokanokets. As Mr. John Fiske has pointed out, to the stronger Indian clans, who could have comprehended little of missionary intentions, it probably seemed that Eliot, by his villages and churches, was strengthening the white man's tribe by the familiar Indian method of adoption, causing it thus to be an increasing menace to Indian independence. The unexpected attack upon the settlements, known as Philip's War, from the English nickname of the chief of the Wampanoags, who organized the tribal confederacy designed to effect the destruction of the settlements, began on June 20, 1675, and the terrible struggle lasted till the death of Philip, August 12, 1676. In this contest the Indian power in New England was forever broken, the Narragansetts, the Nipmucks, and the Wampanoags were largely blotted out; but the cost to the colonies was frightful. More than half of the eighty or ninety towns in Massachusetts and Plymouth were partially destroyed, ten or twelve were utterly consumed. Nearly six hundred men, besides scores of women and children, lost their lives,—many of them by the torments in which Indian cruelty has always delighted. And what made the settlers doubly incensed was that not a few of the implicitly trusted "Praying Indians" went back to their savage kinsmen, and were the equals in cruelty of any who attacked scattered farm-houses or frontier villages.

Fortunately most of the Indian converts were faithful, and they had devoted friends in Eliot and Captain Daniel Gookin, who from 1656 to his death, in 1687, was by appointment of the General Court "ruler," or superintendent, of the Massachusetts converts. But the war wasted the missions. When it was over the work was taken up once more; and while a large proportion of the Indians who had professed Christianity were gathered once more in their old settlements, those who had been partially civilized and were in process of training were mostly lost forever. It was a crippled work; but it shows the true missionary spirit of the New England churches that, in spite of the bitter feeling of hostility which the war excited, the publication of books in the Indian tongue and the gathering of Indian churches was carried forward with persistent energy. Eliot continued his work almost till his death, in 1690. The real failure of these missionary enterprises to make permanent Indian churches was due to the disappearance of the Indian tribes in the eighteenth century, chiefly through the dying out of the red race, in part also through the intermarriage of its remnants with negroes, causing the Indians to be absorbed in the colored population of New England.

After the "Great Awakening" had aroused renewed religious activity in New England during the fourth and fifth decades of the eighteenth century, new attempts at Indian Christianization were begun, notably that among the Housatonic Indians of western Massachusetts, devised by Rev. Samuel Hopkins of West Springfield (uncle of the more famous Samuel) in 1734, and carried out by Rev. John Sergeant at Stockbridge, till his death, in 1749, who was in turn succeeded from 1751 to 1758 by the greatest of New England theologians, Jonathan Edwards. Equally important was a school for Indian instruction in the household of Rev. Eleazar Wheelock of Lebanon, Conn., which received as its first pupil the Mohegan Samson Occom in 1743,—a school which developed in 1769–70 into Dartmouth College. This picturesque Indian preacher, who was welcomed by the pulpits of Great Britain as well as of New England, is still remembered by his hymn, beginning:

> "Awaked by Sinai's awful sound;"

and he was, on the whole, the most conspicuous fruit of these Indian missions; for, though a native of Martha's Vineyard, Caleb Cheeshahteaumuck, climbed the long road from barbarism to the Bachelor's degree at Harvard in 1665, this sole Indian graduate of New England's oldest college died at the age of twenty. The well-nigh complete extinction of the New England aborigines by the close of the eighteenth century ended the possibility of further missionary labors within the ancient borders; though some effort has been put forth by the Congregational churches down to the present time to reach the fast-receding tribes to the westward.

While the beginnings of these missionary activities were occupying the attention of Eliot and his associates and exciting a degree of interest in the churches immediately after the Cambridge Synod, the Congregational body was profoundly stirred by the first general discussion in which it engaged on American soil,—that known as the Half-Way Covenant controversy. This dispute, often though most erroneously ascribed to political motives, really sprang out of the dual theory as to entrance into church-membership entertained by the settlers of New England. Unlike any other division of Protestantism at that day except the Anabaptists, Congregationalists maintained that only adult persons of Christian experience,—in the phrase of that day, "visible saints,"—should be admitted to the covenant union which constituted the local church; but they also held that, as in the Jewish church of old, children shared in their parents' covenanting and were therefore truly members of the church to which their parents belonged. This infant-membership was not the result of baptism; rather it was the covenant relation already acquired by birth in a Christian household that gave right to this sacrament. But the fathers of New England at their coming held that it extended only to the immediate offspring of professed Christians, and hence restricted baptism to children one of whose parents, at least, was a declared believer, in fellowship with some church. This restriction was comparatively easy at first, in spite of the twofold mode of entrance into church-membership,—by profession and by birth,—because the leaders in the emigration were men of tried religious experience, generally able to give a reason for their faith. The line of distinction was sharp between the consciously regenerate and that considerable class even among the first settlers who made no claim to a regenerative change. But with the growth of the children of these first-comers the question was made much more difficult. These members of the second generation naturally showed some decline from the ardent type of piety which marked many of the founders. They were prevailingly of moral life, anxious for the religious training of their children, and desirous of throwing about them the safeguards of church-watch and discipline; but in many instances they could point to no conscious work of divine grace in their own personal experience.

What to do with these persons was not easy to decide. To admit them to the Lord's Supper would be to break down the whole theory of regenerate church-membership; and though Robert Child and his associates in Massachusetts, and a few years later William Pitkin and his friends in Connecticut, desired that all who would have been accounted members of the Church of England at home should be admitted to the full privileges of the New England churches, if of respectable character, this extension of access to the communion was not put in practice by any of the churches during the first half-century of their existence, save at Presbyterianly inclined Newbury.

On the other hand, to deny some church standing to these non-regenerate children of the church came to seem not only difficult but dangerous to the thinking of many of the leaders of New England. If these persons were by birth members of the church to which their parents had belonged, when did their membership cease? Could they be cast out of covenant save by excommunication, and could any be excommunicated save for actual transgressions of moral law or heretical opinions, with which these persons were not chargeable? And if their membership was denied, what hold had the church upon its children for that discipline which Puritanism in general believed so essential for the spiritual upbuilding of the community?

To avoid this dilemma the New England churches, after a long period of agitation, adopted a rather illogical compromise. The non-regenerate offspring of the church were held to be sufficiently in church-covenant to transmit the same degree of church-membership, and its accompanying right to baptism, in turn to their children, on condition of acquaintance with the main truths of the gospel and a sincere promise to walk in fellowship with and under the discipline of the church of which they were members,—a promise called "owning the covenant," into which they had been born. But while the abiding membership of this earnest but non-regenerate class was thus clearly recognized, its representatives were debarred from a place at the Lord's table or a vote in church government or in the choice of church officers. They were not members in "full communion." A double classification of members was thus introduced, and those whose non-regenerate character limited their church privileges to a single sacrament and the disciplinary oversight of the church were said to be members in what its opponents of the eighteenth century nicknamed the "Half-Way Covenant."

The establishment of this serious modification of the system of original New England was the result of a prolonged discussion, in which the leaders were the ministry of the churches rather than the class for whose benefit the modification was made. It was not political impulse that led to the change. Save in the applications of Child in Massachusetts and Pitkin in Connecticut for the full introduction of English theories of church-membership,—requests for something very unlike the Half-Way Covenant,—the political note is nowhere heard in the whole debate. No political advantages came to the Half-Way member in Connecticut or Plymouth; in Massachusetts the approval of the system by the Synod of 1662 was followed in two years by the modification of the restriction of the franchise to church-members, and the most strenuous debates over its adoption by individual churches occurred after the change of the basis of the electorate in 1664. No mention of political considerations occurs, as far as the writer is aware, in any of the voluminous discussion which the Half-Way Covenant Synod and Convention produced. Nor was a share in the government of the churches an impelling cause. The Convention of 1657 and the Synod of 1662, as well as the votes of local churches, forbade the Half-Way member any part in ecclesiastical administration; and how consonant this prohibition was with the general feeling of the time is shown by a declaration of the Massachusetts court. as late as October, 1668, that while "euery church hath free liberty of calling, election, & ordination of all her officers, . . . this Court doth order & declare, & be it hereby ordered & enacted, that by the church is to be meant such as are in full comunion only."

The real impelling motive in the adoption of the system was the desire of the ministers and many of the churches to maintain a hold over those whose parents had been actively Christian, but who themselves seemed slipping away from the churches. It was as a religious question that the Half-Way Covenant discussion had its only importance.

The question first presented itself, it would appear, in

1634, when a grandfather of the Dorchester church asked baptism for his grandchild,—the immediate parents of the child not being persons of professed Christian experience. The request was referred to the Boston church for advice; and that body counseled compliance, on the ground that though the immediate parents were not regenerate, they were not so far "pagans and infidels" as to debar their offspring from baptism on the strength of the grandfather's membership. This position was not generally approved a few years after, even by those who apparently countenanced it in 1634, for Cotton, Hooker, and Richard Mather all expressed the opinion in their early works on Congregational polity that only the immediate offspring of believing parents were to be admitted to the rite. But the problem grew increasingly pressing, and opinion shifted. Though Hooker and Davenport never departed from the early strictness, by 1645 Mather argued in favor of the baptism of the children of those whose church-membership rested on birth rather than experience, and similar expressions within the next six years from men as influential, and as scattered, as Rev. Messrs. Thomas Shepard, of Cambridge, John Norton, of Ipswich, Samuel Stone, of Hartford, John Warham, of Windsor, Henry Smith, of Wethersfield, Ralph Partridge, of Duxbury, and Peter Prudden, of Milford, show that the system commended itself to leading men in all four colonies. No wonder that the Massachusetts court in its call of the Cambridge Synod in 1646 specified "baptisme, & ye p'sons to be received thereto" as a prime topic for discussion by that assembly.

Probably the Half-Way Covenant would have been adopted by the Cambridge Synod had it not been for strenuous opposition on the part of a few members, apparently led by Rev. Charles Chauncy, then of Scituate, but to become, in 1654, the second president of Harvard College. Both Richard Mather and Ralph Partridge gave the system a place in the tentative platforms which they prepared at the direction of the Synod, but that body passed the point by in rather ambiguous terms.

All the more by reason of the non-action of the Cambridge Synod the topic became one of increasing debate. But the practice was first adopted by the church at Ipswich, Mass., of which Rev. Thomas Cobbett was minister, in 1656. In May of the same year the General Court of Connecticut was moved to attempt the settlement of the problem by a ministerial convention, and appealed to the Massachusetts court to assign a time and place of meeting and to notify the other colonies, accompanying its request with a series of questions for debate in the proposed assembly. The Massachusetts authorities did as asked, appointing thirteen prominent divines of their jurisdiction to meet at Boston on June 4, 1657, with those ministers whom the other colonies might send. The notification of this action and the request for coöperation sent by Massachusetts to the other colonial courts was variously received. Connecticut, of course, approved and appointed four ministerial representatives; Plymouth took no action; while New Haven, influenced by Davenport, not only refused to have a part in the convention, but sent an earnest letter of protest against change and insistence that the old ways be kept.

Though representative of the ministers of Massachusetts and Connecticut only, the Convention met for a fortnight in June, 1657, and formulated a series of answers to the questions which the Connecticut legislature had asked. These conclusions of sixteen or seventeen ministers heartily supported the Half-Way view; and declared that the non-regenerate member by birth was entitled to transmit the same status to his children, and obtain baptism for them, provided he accepted the obligations of his membership, as far as he was able without the full transforming grace of God, by solemnly acknowledging his intellectual belief in the principles of the gospel and his willingness to submit to the discipline of the church to which he belonged and to promote its welfare. On the other hand, it was affirmed that nothing but a full Christian profession would fit the member by birth, or any other person, for the Lord's table or a vote in ecclesiastical affairs.

The Ministerial Convention of 1657 had no effect in allaying debate; the question continued as divisive as before. The Massachusetts court therefore determined to try the healing virtue of a true synod, or council, in which all the churches of the commonwealth should be represented by their ministers and delegates. On December 31, 1661, the legislature issued an order to the churches of the colony to convene at Boston, March 11, 1662, and decide the question, "Who are the subjects of baptisme?" and, at the request of the same civil authority, the ministers of Boston and vicinity propounded a second query for the council's consideration, as to "Whither, according to the Word of God, there ought to be a conscociation of churches, & what should be ye manner of it." It is well to remember that what these divines meant by "a conscociation" was not the peculiar institution later known by that name in Connecticut. The word has as yet no strictly technical usage; what was to be discussed was the nature and conditions of fellowship between churches.

On the day appointed the Synod gathered, with an attendance of more than seventy, including the most prominent survivors of the first generation of Massachusetts ministers, like Richard Mather, John Wilson, and Charles Chauncy, and the rising lights of the second generation, such as Jonathan Mitchell and Increase Mather. From the first, the question at issue was hotly disputed. About an eighth of the membership, having a weight disproportionate to their numbers by reason of the able leadership of President Chauncy of Harvard and including Increase Mather, strenuously opposed any departure from the stricter practice, and circulated writings by Rev. John Davenport, of New Haven, denunciatory of the Half-Way Covenant. The vast majority, however, led by Jonathan Mitchell, Richard Mather, and John Norton, favored the larger practice and determined the result of the Synod,—a result which was reached at its third session, in September, 1662. The conclusions arrived at were essentially those of the Ministerial Convention of 1657. The right to bring his children to baptism was extended to the non-regenerate member who owned the covenant; but, as before, access to the Supper and a vote in church affairs were denied to all whose Christian experience would not warrant membership in full communion.

The baptismal question was the only problem of moment before the Synod of 1662, and the body therefore very hastily and practically unanimously approved a few brief principles governing church-fellowship, not materially divergent from the prescriptions of the "Cambridge Platform." This second question for the Synod's consideration had been a ministerial after-thought and one which evidently aroused little interest.

The Synod of 1662 was representative of Massachusetts only; but the publication of its results increased, rather than diminished, the heat of the controversy in all the colonies. No New England discussion of the seventeenth century aroused such interest as this, and the rivals on the floor of the Synod continued their strife in a war of pamphlets after its close. The chief effect of this discussion was that Increase Mather was convinced of the justice of the Half-Way Covenant position, and became a defender of the Synod's conclusions which he had at first opposed.

In Connecticut the division of feeling was intensified by the forcible union of the colony of New Haven with Connecticut by the charter granted the latter by the recently restored Charles II. in 1662,—a union completed in 1665. Under the influence of Davenport the predominant sentiment of New Haven favored the older strictness; the sentiment of Connecticut proper was more divided, but inclined to the larger usage. At Hartford, a quarrel begun in 1666, in which the colleague ministers, Whiting and Haynes, took opposing sides, led in 1670 to the establishment of a second church. The Stratford and Windsor churches were similarly rent; while Rev. Abraham Pierson, of Branford, led a considerable colony of settlers from the old New Haven jurisdiction to Newark, N. J., where they might be free from Half-Way Covenant innovations, and could continue the restriction of the franchise to church-members which had once characterized New Haven, but which the union with Connecticut abolished. After vain attempts to call a Connecticut Ministerial Assembly in 1666 and 1667, the Connecticut court voted toleration for both parties in the dispute in 1669. But the course of events inclined the ecclesiastical founder of New Haven, Rev. John Davenport, to look with misgiving on the scene of his labors for nearly thirty years, and when a call came to him from the First Church in Boston, a majority of the membership of which shared Davenport's opposition to the Half-Way Covenant, he accepted the invitation, although nearly seventy years of age. The result was unhappy for him and for the church,—since that portion of its membership which favored the larger view and had opposed his coming withdrew and formed the Third or "Old South" Church of Boston.

But though vigorously opposed by many churches and some ministers, and never universally adopted, the Half-Way Covenant won its way into use in the vast majority of New England churches, and so continued till the beginning of the nineteenth century. And as it became more familiar in the usage of our churches, especially under the influence of the low type of piety prevailing in the eighteenth century, it became a far less strenuous and worthy spiritual instrumentality than it had been planned to be by the leaders in the Assemblies of 1657 and 1662. In its original intention it had been confined exclusively to those in the covenant of the churches by birth into the household of a church-member; and the owning of the covenant by these unregenerate persons had been looked upon as a solemn association with the people of God, by which a man pledged himself to do all in his power to seek a Christian hope and lead a religious life. But by the early part of the eighteenth century it became the frequent custom to admit all applicants of unblamable character to Half-Way Covenant membership and their children to baptism. In times of religious interest the Covenant came to be administered to large bodies of young people. Instead of being, as it was intended, a means of retaining those under the watch and discipline of the churches who were members by birth and yet seemed slipping away, it became a method of entrance into the church for those also who could advance no birth-right claim. This was a detrimental modification of the original theory, and one that undoubtedly did much to lower the spiritual tone of the churches. It vastly augmented that which was the main evil of the Half-Way Covenant system always,—the toleration of a partial

Christian profession, allowing men who might have been led to a full Christian experience to rest content with an imperfect and merely intellectual religious life.

A modification of the Half-Way system, the beginnings of which became apparent within less than a score of years after the Synod of 1662, deserves notice. The original advocates of the larger practice barred the non-regenerate member from any share in the eucharist or in church administration. But to some this seemed an undue restriction, and as early as 1677 advocates of the full extension of churchly privileges to the non-regenerate but earnest-minded members of the churches were to be found among the New England ministers. This view was, however, most elaborately set forth by Rev. Solomon Stoddard, who served the church at Northampton, Mass., from 1669 to 1729, and who was in his day the most influential minister in the Connecticut valley. Advocated by Stoddard at the "Reforming Synod" of 1679, this theory, often called "Stoddardeanism," was argued by him in print in his "Instituted Churches" of 1700; and though attacked by Increase Mather, was further defended by Stoddard in a sermon published in 1708, and especially in his "Appeal to the Learned" of 1709. Though not adopted by Stoddard's own church till after 1706, this theory, largely through his influence, became widespread in western Massachusetts and Connecticut during the eighteenth century, and did not lack defenders in other parts of New England, though it always remained the view of a fraction only of the churches.

The Stoddardean theory held that the Lord's Supper was designed for "all adult Members of the Church who are not scandalous." It was to be "applyed to visible Saints, though Unconverted, therefore it is for their Saving good, and consequently for their Conversion." In

Stoddard's judgment "visible saints" were "such as make a serious profession of the true Religion, together with those that do descend from them, till rejected of God." This was essentially an importation into New England of the inclusive membership theories of England or Scotland which the New England fathers had abandoned, though it differed from those conceptions of church-relationship in that it laid stress on covenant-membership as the basis of access to the Lord's table. It did not, as has often erroneously been represented, encourage every respectable person in the community to come to the communion. On the contrary, it was for the "visible saint," for the church-member by birth, even though "in a Natural Condition," as well as for the member by profession of Christian experience, that the sacrament was declared to be instituted.

Stoddard was a man of unusual piety and ability. Living in an age of low spiritual life, his ministry was marked by a succession of revivals. It is perhaps useless to attempt to pry into the processes by which he reached his peculiar sacramental views. His "Instituted Churches" shows a large sympathy with a theory of the church more akin to the Presbyterianism of his day than to early New England Congregationalism. But there is a tradition, dating back certainly to Rev. Joseph Lathrop, pastor at West Springfield, Mass., from 1756 to 1820, which affirms that Stoddard began his Northampton ministry in an unregenerate state, and became converted at the Lord's table. Yet, to the present writer, it seems quite as probable that family experiences may have emphasized any tendency toward insistence on participation in the Supper as a duty incumbent on all church-members which was inherent in Stoddard's general cast of thought. His wife was a daughter of Rev. John Warham, of Windsor, Conn.; and one of the few facts known regarding Stoddard's father-in-law is that, though a deeply religious man, he spent much of his later life under such a burdening sense of unworthiness to partake of the consecrated elements that, while he administered the communion to his flock, he often refused to share in the Supper himself, and this state of melancholy self-distrust continued till his death, in 1670. Brought thus into his own family as a practical question, it is not surprising that Stoddard came to the conclusion that it was the duty of all church-members to come to the Lord's table, without a continual torturing self-examination as to whether they were really regenerate or not.

Yet though Stoddardeanism became considerably widespread, and by the time that Cotton Mather wrote his "Ratio Disciplinæ" was practiced peacefully side by side with the Half-Way Covenant or the older New England strictness, it was a complete denial of the original Congregational conception of the church. The revival of the ideal of an exclusively regenerate membership, and the attack upon all departures from it, begun by Jonathan Edwards, in 1749, and continued by his disciples and spiritual successors, Joseph Bellamy, Chandler Robbins, Cyprian Strong, Stephen West, Nathaniel Emmons, and other representatives of the so-called "New Divinity," led to a general abandonment both of the Half-Way Covenant and of Stoddardeanism by the beginning of the nineteenth century, though in a few instances the Half-Way practice survived till 1820, and in one church,—that at Charlestown, Mass.,—till 1828.

This brief sketch of the later story of the chief discussion which disturbed the first century of New England Congregationalism has carried us beyond the seventh and eighth decades of the seventeenth century, to which we must now return. By the time of the meeting of the Synod of 1662 the founders of New England were passing rapidly off the stage. Many had indeed gone before: Hooker had died in 1647; Cotton, in 1652; Winthrop, in 1649; and Bradford, in 1657. Yet in spite of the prominence of men of the second generation, like Jonathan Mitchell and Increase Mather, in the Half-Way Covenant discussion, the chief weight in the decision seems still to have been that of the surviving leaders of the settlement. But ten years after the Synod we are clearly in the time of the second generation; and, notwithstanding the survival of a few patriarchs of the older time like the Apostle Eliot, the most powerful influence in the New England of the children of the founders was Increase Mather.

The ablest of his distinguished family, Increase Mather has been most variously judged. He was essentially a conservative, he was far from universally popular in his own lifetime; but there was no man in the New England of his day who compared with him in ability, leadership, or influence, or who labored more sincerely for what he deemed the interests of the kingdom of God. Born in 1639 in the Dorchester home of his father, Richard, he graduated from Harvard College in 1656, and soon sailed for England, where he found acceptance as a preacher in the closing days of the Commonwealth, but whence he returned speedily after the Restoration, possessed of a wide and useful acquaintance with English men and affairs. On his arrival in his native New England he began to preach to the Second Church of Boston, though he did not accept the office of teacher till 1664, and in the service of this church he remained till his death, in 1723. The post was probably the most conspicuous in influence of any in the colony, especially after the crippling and division of the Boston First Church consequent upon the Half-Way Covenant discussion and the settlement of John Davenport. For the last forty years of this distinguished pastorate he had as his colleague, and in the fullest sense as his associate, his gifted though less able son, Cotton Mather, who survived him till 1728. During the last three decades of the seventeenth century Increase Mather was in the forefront of every ecclesiastical action in Massachusetts, and his prominence in educational and political affairs was hardly less conspicuous. From 1685 to 1701 he was president of Harvard College. In the stress of colonial affairs after the downfall of the first charter, it was Increase Mather who was sent to England in 1688 to plead the Massachusetts cause against Andros with James II.; and it was Mather who secured for Massachusetts more than any other American could have obtained in the new provincial charter of 1691. So preëminently did Mather stand forth as the first citizen of his colony that the English Government, in granting the charter, made him the nominator of those who should first bear office under it. Yet even the cares of this arduous political mission could not draw him away from that interest in ecclesiastical affairs which was always his chief concern. His stay in England was marked by the formation, chiefly through his agency, of the union of Presbyterian and Congregational ministers in and about London, in 1691,—a union which, indeed, fell apart soon after Mather's return to America, but which was, while it lasted, the only extensive association of the two English bodies which the seventeenth century beheld, and which had as its basis the "Heads of Agreement," of which there will be occasion to speak in treating of the "Saybrook Platform." But with all his preëminence, it was Increase Mather's misfortune to be to some extent passed by in the drift of events, so that his old age was a period of disappointment; yet he was never without influence, and was as long as he lived the foremost of the New England ministry, alike in the merit of the services which he had rendered to his country and its churches and the reverence which his abilities compelled.

This leadership of Increase Mather in the second generation was exhibited in the summons of the next Synod which followed that of 1662,—the "Reforming Synod" of 1679–80,—an assembly which has the distinction of being the last Congregational Synod of Massachusetts. The gathering of this council was not occasioned by any general discussion such as centered public interest in the Half-Way Covenant. On the contrary, it met to deplore the spiritual deadness of the times, and to devise a remedy for their evils. Its immediate occasion was what the leaders of New England believed to be a series of divine judgments consequent upon religious decay. As has already been pointed out, the second generation manifested little of the religious zeal which had animated the fathers of New England. The fire of the first enthusiasm had spent much of its force,—it is the universal experience of mankind that ideals which profoundly stir one age lose something of their power in the next epoch,—and while New England was still an intensely religious land when judged by the standard of contemporary England, the type of piety was less warmly experiential, the additions to the churches were fewer, and serious cases of discipline seem to have been more common than in the days when the enterprise had more of novelty. New England was becoming more provincial. Its founders had been leaders in a great cause which had been that also of thousands in the home-land who never crossed the seas. Till the Restoration they still continued actors, in a measure, on the national stage. But with the return of the Stuarts New England ceased to have weight in the mother-country. The party whose principles it represented was defeated and proscribed; other interests than those for which the Puritan cared largely engrossed English thought. New England was no longer a formative factor in English religious life; while the second generation, brought up in the hard battle with the half-tamed wilderness, lacked that generous training gained from the institutions of an old and stable civilization and developed by participation in struggles of national importance, which the fathers so richly enjoyed. Doubtless it was well for the future of America that sympathy in thought between Old England and the New was thus interrupted, and that political bickerings added to the separation between the two lands, for it made the development of New England a hardy and independent growth; but its immediate effect was to stunt the life which drew its sustenance from the scanty colonial soil. All through the later colonial period fancy looked back with almost pathetic lamentation to the early days as a golden age of piety and an era of men of strength; and though there was much of exaggeration in this view, there was a measure of truth also, for the later New England was poorer in enthusiasm, poorer in men of conspicuous leadership, less endowed with a sense of a mission to fulfill than the New England of the founders.

In the eighth decade of the seventeenth century material losses enhanced this feeling of spiritual decline. Disastrous conflagrations in Boston in 1676 and 1679, visitations of the smallpox, and above all the destructive struggle of 1675–76 known as Philip's War, brought distress to all parts of Massachusetts; while the threatening movements which resulted in the overthrow of the charter had already begun to make themselves felt.

To Increase Mather it seemed desirable that a Synod should assemble to consider the situation; and therefore, at his motion, a petition, bearing his name and that of eighteen others of the Massachusetts ministry, was presented to the General Court at its session beginning May 28, 1679, praying that such a council should be called. The court heard the request, and ordered that the Synod should meet on September 10th, at Boston, "for the reuisall of the platforme of discipljne agreed vpon by the churches, 1647, and what else may appeare necessary for the preventing schishmes, hæresies, prophaness, & the establishment of the churches in one faith & order of the gospell,"—a problem embodied more succinctly in the two questions handed in by the petitioners and approved by the court, "What are the euills that haue provoked the Lord to bring his judgments on New England?" and "What is to be donn that so those evills may be reformed?"

Pursuant to this call, the representatives of the churches gathered at Boston at the time appointed, and after a session of ten days adopted a document draughted by Increase Mather setting forth the Synod's sense of the decay of godliness in the land; of the increase of pride; neglect of worship; sabbath-breaking; lack of family government; censurings, intemperance, falsehood, and love of the world: and recommending, as means for combating these evils, insistence on strictness in admission to communion; the strengthening of family and church discipline; the appointment of a pastor, teacher, and ruling elder in each church, as at the beginning of the New England churches, instead of having only a single minister, as had already become the rule; the payment of adequate ministerial salaries; the careful execution of law, especially of the statutes regulating the sale of spirits; a renewal of church covenants; and care for schools, especially for Harvard College, then the sole source of ministerial supply. At the same time, and as a measure for religious betterment, the Synod "unanimously approved" the "Cambridge Platform," "for the substance of it."

This enumeration of evils and suggestion of remedies undoubtedly did good in that it stirred up the churches to renewed self-examination, and led, for a time at least, to greater painstaking in the instruction of the young, as well as to special meetings designed to awaken their attention to religious things. But the most permanently memorable, if least discussed, action of this Synod was the result of the appointment of a committee on the last day of its first session to "draw up a Confession of faith" and report it to a second session on May 12, 1680. Though the Cambridge Synod had approved the doctrinal parts of the Westminster Confession in 1648 as "very holy, orthodox, & judicious," and had therefore "freely & fully" consented to it "for the substance therof," that Confession had been revised by English Congregationalists at a Synod held at the Savoy Palace in London in 1658; and in addition to the changes introduced by Parliament when the Confession had been declared the religious standard of England, the English Congregationalists had rewritten a number of articles, leaving their doctrinal significance essentially unaltered, but amending the phraseology here and there, and changing every passage incompatible with Congregational theories of church government. To the minds of the leaders of Massachusetts it doubtless seemed well that a similar readaptation of the Westminster Confession should bear testimony to the common faith of New England.

The committee on the creed was made up of Urian Oakes, acting-president of Harvard, and Rev. Messrs. Increase Mather, Solomon Stoddard, Samuel Torrey, of Weymouth, James Allen, of the Boston First Church, Samuel Willard, of the Boston "Old South," John Higginson, of Salem, and Josiah Flynt, of Dorchester. It was a body as able as any that could have been gathered in Massachusetts, and undoubtedly might have formulated an original Confession of learning and force had it so chosen; but three of its most prominent members had been in England at the time of the preparation of the Savoy Confession about twenty-two years before, and the desire of all was strong that the essential unity of belief between the Congregational churches of Old England and the New should be expressed, if possible, by a common Confession. Nor had there been as yet any serious doctrinal discussions in New England. The churches still stood, as at their origin, on the basis of the general Puritan theology of England as it had been in the time of their beginnings. Increase Mather could say with truth, as he said in the preface commending the results of this session of the Synod in 1680: "It is well known, that as to matters of Doctrine we agree with other Reformed Churches: Nor was it that, but what concerns Worship and Discipline, that caused our Fathers to come into this wilderness." The setting forth of a new Confession aroused no general interest, for no one could doubt what its essential content would be,—it was simply one of various devices for the betterment of the churches in this time of loss and, as it was believed, of judgment.

It was natural, therefore, that when the Synod met for its second session, under the moderatorship of Increase Mather, the committee recommended and the Assembly adopted the Savoy Confession, changing a word here and there, asserting more distinctly the church-membership of children of Christian parents which the Half-Way Covenant discussion had brought into prominence in New England; but making no serious alteration except to substitute for the guarded expressions of the Savoy symbol concerning the interference of magistrates in religious matters an article chiefly in words borrowed from the Westminster Confession, which more positively set forth the authority of the state in doctrinal questions,—a change which cannot be deemed an improvement. The lengthy Confession was twice read to the Synod; but it awakened no debate of consequence, and a session of two days sufficed, under Mather's energetic leadership, for the establishment of what has since been known by the title of the "Confession of 1680" as the public testimony of the Massachusetts churches to their faith.

So came into existence a creed which the Congregational churches of America have always held in veneration, and which the National Council in 1865 affirmed in its "Burial Hill Declaration" substantially embodies their faith. It was not imposed on individual churches, nor was it intended as a substitute for local creeds. Two churches did indeed employ it as their own creedal expression,—the First Church, Cambridge, and the "Old South," Boston, though in the latter case, at least, it is doubtful whether it was ever adopted by formal vote of the church. No Congregational church has been bound by it in the sense in which every Presbyterian church is bound by the Westminster Confession. But it remains the fullest and the most respected testimony to the faith of those churches as that faith appeared to the men of the last quarter of the seventeenth century.

The adoption of this Confession was an event of less immediate concern to the people of Massachusetts than the great political overturn of five years later, which threatened for a time to make profound alterations in the state, and which led to a considerable modification of the ecclesiastical policy of the colony. The charter of 1629, as interpreted by the founders of Massachusetts, rendered that commonwealth practically self-governing, and had therefore long been looked upon with disfavor by the Stuart sovereigns. It had been earnestly defended by the early settlers against the encroachments of Charles I. and of Parliament; but Charles II. was now attacking it, and the situation on both sides of the Atlantic favored such an onslaught. In the mother-country the opponents of the religious system of New England were in authority; in the colony the old sturdy Puritan type of the Winthrops and Dudleys had, to some extent, given place to a society swayed by prospects of political advantage, especially in the chief towns,—a society whose aspirations and affiliations favored rather than discountenanced closer connection with the royal authorities. In 1683 that enemy of Massachusetts, Edward Randolph, succeeded in serving upon the colonial government a writ summoning it to show cause before the English courts why the charter should not be vacated. Though the Upper House of the legislature favored submission to such a revision of the charter as the king might choose, the Lower House, representing as it did the still strongly Puritan sentiment of the common people and the country towns, refused. But the blow fell. In June and October, 1684, the English Court of Chancery declared the charter vacated. All that the founders of Massachusetts had held dear in civil liberty, ecclesiastical polity, or even personal property, was without legal safeguard. A revision of the powers of the Massachusetts government by the English authorities was doubtless sure to come at some time. The charter of Charles I. was an anomaly as soon as the colony grew powerful enough to be in any sense a rival to the mother-country. The privileges which it granted were too nearly those of independence to have continued in a large colony in the seventeenth century without civil war; though the smallness of Connecticut eventually preserved to her rights similar to those which Massachusetts now lost. It was well, too, that a broader policy of religious toleration and a wider extension of the franchise than Massachusetts had heretofore allowed should be established. The colonial government had been neither tolerant nor conciliatory toward those who had differed from its way in church or state. But such a desirable revision was very different from the revolution which the annulling of the charter accomplished. By that act every corporation created, every town government established, every sale of land effected by virtue of powers conferred by the charter of 1629, was made void. The whole legal establishment of the churches, the entire body of colonial law, was swept away.

These radical changes in the organic law of Massachusetts were effected under Charles II., but that monarch died on February 6, 1685, without having arranged for the new governments which were to take the place of the old in New England, though it had been the king's intention to make Colonel Piercy Kirke governor, a man soon to become notorious for his cruelties in the suppression of Monmouth's rebellion. So turmoiled were the early days of James II. that it was not till 1686 that the new government was set up. After the brief presidency of Joseph Dudley, beginning in May of that year, the governorship of all New England was taken by Sir Edmund Andros, who arrived at Boston on the 20th of the following December. Under the new form of government, which asserted itself in a few months over all the Puritan colonies, directly representative institutions no longer existed. At the head of the colonies was a governor of royal appointment, instead of chief magistrates chosen by the freemen. For his assistance there was a council, designated by the king. To this non-elective body, which took the place of the popular legislatures, the law-making power was committed, and by governor and council taxes could be laid. And to the New England Congregationalist of the old school not the least of the offensive features of the political situation was the open countenance given by Randolph to the efforts which had been begun in 1679 to introduce Episcopacy into the colonies and which resulted in the formation of an Episcopal congregation in Boston,—that of the famous King's Chapel,—on June 15, 1686. This feeling of dread was strengthened when Andros and Randolph demanded the use of the "Old South" meeting-house for worship in conformity with the usage of the Church of England during such time as it was not occupied by its regular Sunday congregation. A modern Congregationalist, conscious that the laws under which he lives will permit no other religious body to fetter him in the free exercise of his worship, and accustomed to see members of Christian communions of various names labor side by side with mutual respect and sometimes with fraternal coöperation, may find it hard to sympathize with the feeling displayed by his ancestors against the introduction of a form of worship which was that of the mother-country. But his sense of surprise disappears when he recalls the fact that Episcopacy was still the sole legal form of worship in England, that Congregationalism was still proscribed in the home-land, that the political institutions of New England were prostrate, and the feeble colonies were wholly at the mercy of a government avowedly disposed to support Episcopal interests. It seemed no very improbable supposition that a power which had not hesitated to vacate the title of every Massachusetts farmer's homestead and do away with all popular representation in the government might enforce on reluctant New England something of that Episcopal uniformity which was legally maintained in the home-land. The New Englander's fears may have been exaggerated. His worst forebodings were not realized. Andros showed himself, on the whole, a well-intentioned man, who fulfilled the duties of his office with honesty and with as much fairness as could be expected of a courtier out of sympathy with the political and religious ideas of the land over which he was called to administer. But had he been a far better governor than he really was, his rule would have been none the less a tyranny, for he represented the Stuart attempt to take away the liberties which the colonies had enjoyed and modify essentially the institutions which they had created.

Fortunately for New England, the revolt of Old England from James II. made the dominance of the Stuart system in New England brief; and happily, also, Massachusetts was represented at this juncture by Increase Mather at the royal court. The foremost exponent of the old Puritan spirit which still dominated all the community except a portion of the trading and political class chiefly to be found in Boston, Mather slipped out of Massachusetts early in April, 1688, as the informal representative of the people of his native colony. Arrived in London, he presented his case before James II. and was received with personal favor, though the requests which he made were not granted. But meanwhile he diligently cultivated the friendship of the leading non-conformists, and obtained, to some extent, the favor of the Whig leaders, so that when the revolution of the autumn of 1688 drove James from his throne and substituted the joint sovereignty of William and Mary, Increase Mather was able to approach the new government with some prospect of a favorable hearing. Such an advocate was needed, for on the tardy arrival of news of the landing of William in England, the people of Boston arose on April 18, 1689, and made Andros and his official following prisoners. In Massachusetts and Connecticut the old governments were restored by popular insistence. But only the timely efforts of Mather prevented the issue of an order from William directing that Andros continue in authority. Yet, though proceedings for the voiding of the Connecticut charter had not advanced so far as to make it impossible for the ancient government of that colony to resume its sway now that what men deemed the usurpation of Andros was over, the charter of Massachusetts was gone forever. For a moment, in January, 1690, it seemed likely that Mather would secure its restoration by act of Parliament. But William proved at first almost as intractable as his Stuart predecessor, and it was soon evident that a full restoration of the ancient privileges of Massachusetts was out of the question. The old thought of a theocratic state, in which one form of worship should be allowed, where the rulers should be Christian men, and in which a self-governing class of the population should administer all affairs in a spirit of semi-independence, was impossible of revival, partly because New England had in a measure grown away from it, but chiefly because William, like James, wished to hold the prosperous colony closely under his administration.

But though the Massachusetts of the fathers which Mather loved was not to be reproduced, Mather rescued much that was dear to the New England Puritan. He prevented the annexation of Plymouth Colony to New York, and secured its incorporation with Massachusetts, thus honorably and naturally terminating the separate existence of the Pilgrim commonwealth, the independence of which could not longer be maintained. He obtained a new charter for Massachusetts in 1691, in spite of the opposition of the agents whom the colony had associated with him and who impracticably held for the old charter or nothing. This charter was, indeed, distasteful to Mather in its limitations; it reserved to the king the appointment of the highest offices of government, and a right to reject obnoxious laws. It swept away all ecclesiastical tests for the franchise, even such indirect and partial tests as had continued since 1664; it granted freedom of worship to Protestants of all shades. But it left to Massachusetts a legislature the Lower House of which was directly chosen by the people, and in which the Upper House was still measurably under the control of the popular representatives,—a legislature, too, which held the purse, and hence had a potent means of control over all branches of the government. The old local governments of the towns were left undisturbed; and this, with the power of taxation which was in the hands of the legislature, insured the ascendency of the form of ecclesiastical polity which had heretofore been dominant in New England. An express provision, confirming all grants made by the General Court in time past, secured to individuals and to churches the possession of their lands, and the maintenance as far as possible of the old order of affairs. Certainly Congregationalism owed much to the influences that preserved its essential features unfettered by the English Government at the conclusion of this momentous political change.

Such a profound disturbance of public thought as occurred all over New England during the Andros episode gave occasion, as such events customarily do, to movements of more or less intensity in other directions than merely political. It would be unwarranted to say that the grim tragedy of Salem witchcraft was caused by this state of the public mind. New England, like Old England and Scotland, firmly believed in the possibility of witchcraft; and the laws under which executions took place in the mother-country as late as 1712, and which were not repealed till 1736, had their counterparts in these colonies, where an occasional victim had been put to death by legal process in Massachusetts and Connecticut. But no New England community had thus far been crazed with excitement, as Salem now was; and the excessive violence of this mental epidemic may in this case be justly attributed to the fevered state of the public mind. Fortunately the outbreak was local and its duration brief. Beginning with the strange actions of children in the household of Rev. Samuel Parris, of Salem village, now Danvers, Mass., in February, 1692, it chiefly involved Salem and Andover, and before the executions ceased, in September, 1692, nineteen men and women had been hanged, and one pressed to death in accordance with the barbarous English penalty for refusal to plead. All this was done under a special judicial commission appointed by the new royal governor, Sir William Phips, himself, like the members of the commission, of New England birth; and the habit of mind by which it had been made possible had been fostered by the teachings of the two Mathers, especially of Cotton Mather. But it is illustrative of the good sense fundamental to the New England character that the excitement passed by almost as quickly as it arose; and though belief in witchcraft did not immediately die out, men speedily felt that there had been no proper sifting of evidence, and it is to their credit that some of the chief actors in these scenes, such as the high-minded Samuel Sewall of the judicial commission, and some of the jurymen themselves, publicly acknowledged that they had been in error and entreated forgiveness. Indeed, the government of the province, in appointing a fast-day in January, 1696, though maintaining the satanic origin of the tragedy, prayed the divine forgiveness for "whatever mistakes . . . had been fallen into"; and at a later time, 1711, gave pecuniary compensation to the heirs of the victims. When Cotton Mather believed that he had discovered a case of demoniac possession in Boston a year after the Salem executions, his views were combated by Robert Calef, a merchant of that place; and this discussion led to an elaborate criticism of the transactions of 1692 and of those prominent in them, issued by Calef in 1700. Though popular trust in the reality of satanic compacts continued in New England, as in other countries, into the eighteenth century, the Salem executions ended the infliction of death for this widespread delusion, and it is not without significance, as illustrative of the comparative mildness of New England punishment, that the Salem witches were hanged, while in Scotland these miserable creatures were burned as late as 1722.

To turn from a grim outburst of popular delusion to the peaceful establishment of a new agency for the expression of Congregational fellowship is an abrupt transition, but the disturbed years of waiting between the downfall of the government of Andros and the grant of the new Massachusetts charter saw the beginnings of permanent Ministerial Associations. There had been meetings of the ministry of the scattered settlements as early as 1633, and these voluntary gatherings had continued for some years; but fears lest they should result in a Presbytery, it would appear, led to their abandonment not far from the middle of the seventeenth century. But the year 1686 saw the addition to the ranks of the New England ministry of Rev. Charles Morton, a prominent Dissenter, who had made his English home a theological seminary even under the restored monarchy of Charles II., and who was settled, speedily after his arrival, over the church at Charlestown,

Mass. Morton had been a member of a Ministerial Association at Bodmin, Cornwall, in the days of the Commonwealth, and now, on October 13, 1690, an association, having the same rules as the Bodmin body, was formed, doubtless through his efforts, embracing the ministers of Boston and its neighbor towns, and meeting regularly in the college building at Cambridge. It was a purely voluntary, club-like organization, having for its aim "to debate any matter referring to ourselves," and "to hear and consider any cases that shall be proposed unto us, from churches or private persons." Such an institution met a real want; and by 1692 two other associations, one having its headquarters at Salem, were in existence. By 1705 they numbered five. From 1690 onward they became a permanent feature of New England Congregationalism, though their full development did not come till the consociational movements of 1705 and 1708 in Massachusetts and Connecticut, to which reference will speedily be made.

Another token of the upheaval of public thought is to be seen in certain innovations on established ecclesiastical usage which made themselves felt in the last decade of the seventeenth century, particularly at Boston,—innovations in themselves of no great importance, but which gave rise to more or less successful attempts to establish a stricter and more Presbyterian type of Congregational government. A group of youngerly men, connected with Harvard College, were inclined toward change, and, as it seemed to them, a liberalization of the usages of earlier New England. The most conspicuous members of this party were John Leverett and William Brattle, who had become tutors at Harvard in 1685, and had controlled the college during Increase Mather's absence in England,—a position which Brattle exchanged in 1696 for the more influential post of pastor of the Cambridge church. Associated with Brattle, and of even greater prominence than he, was his older brother Thomas, the college treasurer; and Ebenezer Pemberton, a tutor and later colleague pastor of the "Old South" Church of Boston. These men desired the abandonment of public relations of religious experience in admission to church-membership; and they wished that all baptized adults who shared in a minister's support, whether in full communion or not, should have a voice in his election. These were the two main features of their innovations, but they desired also the baptism of all children presented by any Christian sponsor; the reading of the Scriptures without comment, instead of with explanation verse by verse, as was the Puritan custom; and the liturgical use of the Lord's Prayer.

The first two of these changes were opposed by Increase Mather with great vigor, and in a way to provoke his liberalizing associates in the Harvard faculty and in Boston. The result was the building by Thomas Brattle and his associates of a new meeting-house at Boston in 1698; and an invitation by its builders and others to Rev. Benjamin Colman, a Harvard graduate of 1692, then in England, to become their pastor. The well-known conservative sympathies of the three Congregational churches existing in Boston induced Brattle and his friends to recommend that Colman should procure ordination at the more friendly hands of the London Presbytery, and when Colman came to Boston in November, 1699, it was as a minister enjoying Presbyterian ordination, but of course no minister in the eyes of strenuous Congregationalists, who insisted, as the fathers had done, that a pastor was to be ordained only by the congregation which he served, and was a minister only in connection with a particular church. Having secured their pastor, the associates organized Brattle

Church on December 12, 1699. All this was done without the countenance of the other churches of the colony; it was clearly un-Congregational when judged by the standards of American usage. It would be thought grossly irregular at the present time. And the movement was strenuously opposed by the Mathers, especially by Increase, who attacked it in his vigorous tractate of 1700, "The Order of the Gospel." But, in spite of the Mathers and other conservatives, Brattle Church won recognition; and Increase Mather himself saw the control of Harvard slip from his own hands to those of sympathizers with the innovators in 1701, partly as a result of this quarrel, and partly by reason of political grudges and of his own unwillingness to live in Cambridge.

In itself this Brattle Church episode amounted to little. Brattle Church soon took a place practically indistinguishable from that occupied by the other churches of Boston; and its minister, Rev. Benjamin Colman, became in the course of a few years more prominent for conservatism than for any other characteristic. But its formation was the apparent cause of an attempt to secure a stricter ecclesiastical government in Massachusetts, which is of great importance,—an attempt in which not only the Mathers, but, curiously enough, Benjamin Colman and Ebenezer Pemberton, of the sympathizers with the Brattle Church movement, had a part.

The first public manifestation of the movement was in the Ministerial Convention of Massachusetts,—an annual gathering of all the ministers of the province at the time of the May General Court, which had begun in the informal coming together of the ministers in the earliest days of the colony, and had crystallized sufficiently by about 1680 to have a moderator, a dinner, and a sermon. The body still has a feeble existence as a joint meeting of

Trinitarian and Unitarian ministers and the custodian of a fund for the relief of the widows and daughters of Massachusetts ministers. Though in no sense a judicial assembly, or one directly representative of the churches, the Convention was accustomed to discuss the state of religion in the commonwealth, and had made suggestions to the legislature and the churches. This Convention now, on June 1, 1704, approved a circular letter to the churches, signed by Samuel Willard, of the "Old South" Church of Boston, Ebenezer Pemberton, Benjamin Colman, Cotton Mather, and twenty-two other of the Massachusetts ministers who were distinctly and widely representative. It urged more diligent pastoral labors in behalf of the young, a general enforcement of discipline, and "that the Associations of the Ministers in the several Parts of the Country may be strengthened." In the following November this vote was transmitted to the various ministers of the province through the agency of the Association meeting at Cambridge, of the formation of which, in 1690, an account has already been given.

As a result of these appeals, and perhaps of further action of the Ministers' Convention in 1705, nine ministers, including Willard, Pemberton, and Cotton Mather, came together at Boston on September 11, 1705, as representatives of five Massachusetts Ministerial Associations—apparently all that then existed in the province—and in a two-days session drew up an elaborate series of Proposals essaying seriously to modify the type of church government thus far characteristic of New England.

The plan involved two main features. The first of its recommendations was that Ministerial Associations should be formed where not already existing, and that pastors take their advice in all difficult cases. A suggestion of great importance, borrowed from the English "Heads of

Agreement" of 1691, which was the basis of the union of London Presbyterians and Congregationalists effected largely by Increase Mather, was that ministerial candidates be examined and licensed by these associations. Heretofore each church had given whatever warrant any man had to preach to it simply by asking, formally or informally, to hear him. But with this recommendation of 1705 the present New England method of ministerial licensure was introduced. "Bereaved churches," as those without ministers were called, were advised to apply to the associations for candidates. The associations were furthermore to inquire into the state of religion, examine charges brought against the character, belief, or conduct of any minister of their membership, and elect delegates to an annual General Association of the entire province.

The second division of this scheme recommended that the pastors connected with these associations and delegates from the lay membership of their churches should constitute "standing councils," to "consult, advise, and determine all affairs that shall be proper matter for the consideration of an ecclesiastical council within their respective limits." The results of these councils of "consociated churches" "are to be looked upon as final and decisive"; and in case of refusal to accept the decision, after the case has been heard by a second and neighboring standing council, the churches represented in the council "are to approve, confirm, and ratifie the sentence, and with-draw from the communion of the church that would not be healed."

The Proposals here briefly outlined were transmitted to the various associations by the Cambridge-Boston Association in November, 1705, and were approved by the Ministerial Convention at Boston on May 30, 1706. But though thus approved by men representative of all parties in existent Massachusetts Congregationalism as its discussions had heretofore developed, these Proposals were only partially carried into effect. Associations were stimulated, a system of ministerial licensure was established; but the most essential feature of the plan, the system of standing councils, was never put in operation in Massachusetts. The truth is that the Proposals encountered at once a considerable degree of opposition, both from ministers and from their congregations, as inimical to Congregational liberty. The system which it commended, though approved by a majority of the pastors, encountered too much hostility to be put in full practice without legislative support; and under the new charter, with a governor, Joseph Dudley, who coquetted with Episcopacy, and a legislature whose acts were subject to royal revisal, such support was unattainable.

These Massachusetts Proposals of 1705, which thus failed in large part in the commonwealth of their origin, were substantially adopted in Connecticut three years later. As compared with Massachusetts, the life of Connecticut in the latter half of the seventeenth century had been peaceful. Though Connecticut troops had borne their share in Philip's War, her towns had been spared the devastation that fell on Massachusetts and Plymouth; the government of Andros had extended to the colony, but the superior foresight of her General Court had assured to her citizens their lands, while those of Massachusetts were in doubt; no popular delusion, like the witchcraft craze, had frenzied any of her towns; her people were a homogeneous, fairly well-to-do agricultural population, ruled by a semi-independent government, under a charter even more liberal than that which Massachusetts had enjoyed before 1684.

But if the special trials of Massachusetts' political and

ecclesiastical life had no full counterparts in the Connecticut of 1700, the general causes modifying Congregational usage were at work there as in the larger colony. As has been already pointed out, the Congregationalism of the founders was of the type of Barrowe rather than of Browne. It recognized clearly the right of the ordinary membership to elect their ministers and to admit members, it held that no act of discipline was valid unless with the consent of the church; but it placed the initiative in the hands of the officers, and practically limited the share of the brethren in ordinary church acts to assent to or dissent from propositions presented by them. As the "Cambridge Platform" expressed it: "Church government, or Rule, is placed by Christ in the officers of the Church; . . . yet in case of mal-administration, they are subject to the power of the church; . . . the work & duty of the people is expressed in the phrase of obeying their Elders." And one of the duties laid on ministers by the same constitution is that of calling "the church together upon any weighty occasion, when the members so called, without just cause, may not refuse to come: nor when they are come, depart before they are dismissed: nor speak in the church, before they have leave from the elders: nor continue so doing, when they require silence, nor may they oppose nor contradict the judgment or sentence of the Elders, without sufficient & weighty cause."

The authoritative position here given to the ministry was difficult to maintain in a country like New England; but it became much more arduous when, instead of a pastor, teacher, and one or more ruling elders, to constitute a governing body, as in the larger churches at the first, the eldership was reduced to a single minister. This change from the original custom was induced rather by motives of economy than by any alteration of theoretic polity, and was deplored as already general by the "Reforming Synod" of 1679; but it is easy to see that a single pastor who attempted to exercise the extensive prerogatives wielded originally by an eldership of three or four officers, was not unlikely to fall into quarrel with his flock. Such disputes did occasionally occur, and they explain why it was that many in Connecticut, even in the absence of special problems such as disturbed the vicinity of Boston, were ready to look with favor on a revisal of the standards of church government.

The first decade of the eighteenth century was a time of much activity in Connecticut. In 1701 the long-cherished desire for "a nearer and less expensive seat of learning" than Harvard was carried into effect by the organization of Yale College, with ten of the ministers of the colony as its trustees. The meetings of these trustees at once became the most important ministerial gatherings in Connecticut; and as early as March 17, 1703, those present at one of these sessions sent forth a circular letter to ascertain whether the approval of the Massachusetts Confession of 1680 by the legislature of the colony would not be agreeable to the ministry as a whole. The efforts of the framers of the Massachusetts Proposals of 1705 also were well known to the leaders of Connecticut, many of whom sympathized with the Mathers and other prominent Massachusetts conservatives. But the Connecticut movement for stricter government was greatly aided by the election of Rev. Gurdon Saltonstall, of New London, to the governorship in December, 1707. In May following, and largely through Saltonstall's influence, the court issued the call for the Saybrook Synod,—the last Synod called by governmental authority in New England, except the "General Consociation" approved by the Connecticut legislature in the excitement of the "Great Awakening."

By this vote the legislature ordered the representatives of the churches to come together in the various county towns on June 28, 1708, there to draw up tentative schemes of church government and to choose delegates to a general assembly which should meet at Saybrook, at the Commencement of the infant college; when the delegates to this general council should, in turn, prepare a form of government, on the basis of the several county plans, for submission to the legislature. This rather elaborate direction was obeyed; and on September 9, 1708, the Synod met at Saybrook with an attendance of twelve ministers and four laymen.

The work of the Synod was threefold. It approved the Confession of 1680,—itself a slight modification of the Savoy revision of the Westminster symbol,—as the doctrinal standard; and the somewhat divergent views of its members regarding the proper strenuousness of church government were met by the adoption of the rather liberal and loose-knitted "Heads of Agreement" of 1691, and fifteen close-compacted Articles, the "Saybrook Platform" proper. These famous Articles, the most important and only original part of the Synod's symbols, were based essentially on the Massachusetts Proposals of 1705, though worked out in more elaborate detail. They provided that the churches should be grouped in "consociations" or standing councils, one or more such bodies in each county. To these "consociations" all cases of discipline difficult of settlement within the local church where they originate should be brought, and the decision then rendered shall be considered final save in cases of great difficulty and moment, when the next neighboring "consociation" should meet jointly with that having original cognizance of the case. The help of the "consociation" should be sought by each church belonging to it "upon all occasions ecclesiasticall," which included, of course, ministerial ordinations, installations, and dismissions. In a similar way, all the ministers of the colony were to be distributed into "associations," for consultation, ministerial licensure, and recommendation; and by their delegates an annual "General Association" of the whole colony should be constituted.

These recommendations were at once approved by the legislature, and were carried into effect in February, March, and April, 1709, when consociations and associations were formed in the several counties. In May the first General Association met, thus inaugurating what is now by far the oldest of the State organizations representative of Congregationalism, except the feeble and never very well compacted Massachusetts Convention. But though adopted in all parts of Connecticut, the Saybrook system encountered considerable opposition. While Hartford and New London counties accepted the new rules as they came from the Synod, Fairfield County made them more strenuous by a Presbyterianizing interpretation put on record when its consociation was formed, and New Haven County abated their strictness by the same method. It is clear that, unless backed by the legislature, they would have failed of adoption in Connecticut as the similar Proposals of 1705 did in Massachusetts. But in Connecticut they remained the legally recognized standard till 1784, and the rule of the vast majority of the churches, though with ever-decreasing strictness, till after the middle of the present century.

The adoption of this stricter Congregational system in Connecticut and its failure in Massachusetts put the two chief Puritan colonies on somewhat divergent paths, and led to certain minor differences in their types of Congregationalism which continue, though in much-abated distinctness, to the present day. Under the influence of consociationism, especially as the eighteenth century drew toward a close, Connecticut's sympathies went out increasingly toward fellowship with the Presbyterian Church of the Middle States. Massachusetts, on the other hand, came to represent an increasingly independent type of Congregationalism. In our own century the two types have once more approximated, though each has contributed elements to present denominational life.

This divergence of the characteristics of Massachusetts and Connecticut Congregationalism was stimulated by a keen satire upon the Proposals of 1705, published in 1710, by Rev. John Wise, pastor of a parish then in Ipswich, but now known as Essex, Mass., under the title of "The Churches Quarrel Espoused,"—a work which Wise followed in 1717 with his "Vindication of the Government of New England Churches." These brilliant little books doubtless came too late to have much effect in bringing about the rejection of the Proposals; but they stirred and stimulated Congregational thought, and ultimately did much to change the Barrowism of early New England into a more democratic type of Congregationalism. Wise was a graduate of Harvard of the class of 1673, who had suffered fine, suspension from the ministry, and imprisonment under the government of Andros for leading his town in a refusal to collect taxes not imposed by a representative assembly, thus being the first conspicuous American opponent of taxation without representation. His abilities as a leader of men in other experiences than those of a parish were attested also on a laborious campaign against Canada, in which he served as chaplain; and his enlightenment by his opposition to the witchcraft delusion of 1692. Altogether, Wise combined an intense love for the New England of the fathers with a clear-sighted perception of the democratic tendencies of American life that made him unconsciously prophetic of the future, while defending from innovation, as he believed, the best features of the past; and he clothed his work in a literary form more attractive than that of any other colonial writer of his age. In his little books of 1710 and 1717 Wise seems to have thought that he was simply defending the "Cambridge Platform" against the consociational movements of Massachusetts and Connecticut. But he really entered, especially in the second of these volumes, on a broad discussion of the fundamental principles of government in church and state alike, and his view was far more democratic than that of the "Platform." Wise based his defense of a democratic Congregationalism not only on the Bible and on the prescriptions of the New England fathers as he understood them, but very strikingly and prophetically also on natural law, declaring that "it seems most agreeable with the light of nature, that if there be any of the regular government settled in the church of God it must needs be a Democracy." "Power," he asserted, "is originally in the people." And Wise conceived it to be one of the chief merits of Congregationalism that it best illustrates the principles of the most valuable forms of civil government. In his views of civil society Wise showed his agreement with the most advanced of the European publicists of his day, holding the "compact" theory, so popular later in his century; asserting that men are "all naturally free and equal," that "civil government" is "the effect of human free-compacts and not of divine institution"; and that "the formal reason of government is the will of a community, yielded up and surrendered to some other subject, either one particular person or more," in order that men "may be secured against the injuries they are liable to from their own kind." This government may take the form of a democracy, an aristocracy, or a monarchy. Of these democracy is the oldest in the civil world, it "is a form of government which the light of nature does highly value, and often directs to as most agreeable to the just and natural prerogatives of human beings." So, too: "If Christ has settled any form of power in his church he has done it for his churches safety, and for the benefit of every member: Then he must needs be presumed to have made choice of that government as should least expose his people to hazard, either from fraud, or arbitrary measures of particular men. And it is as plain as daylight, there is no species of government like a democracy to attain this end."

These quotations from Wise's "Government of New England Churches" of 1717 show that he presented a new and forceful treatment of Congregationalism, making its claims no longer dependent on its superior conformity to the scattered hints of Scripture alone, but basing its merits also on the broad principles of democracy which were to be the mainspring of so much of American thought and action. In so doing he emphasized the democratic element in Congregationalism as no previous writer had done. His books were forces in Congregational thought from their publication. Yet his presentation was so novel and so in advance of his time that the influence of these tracts was not at first wide. Their greatest power as directive of public thought was more than half a century after they were first put in print. In 1772, when their author had been forty-seven years silent in death, their real hour came. Then, in the excitement anticipatory to the great struggle for political independence, Massachusetts welcomed two editions of Wise's works in a single year; and the democratic principles which he declared the essentials of Congregationalism, and which a slowly increasing number had recognized since his day, were the theories which men welcomed in church and state alike.

But while Wise must be reckoned thus as one of the men to whom modern Congregationalism is most highly indebted, the Massachusetts churches of his lifetime were more under the dominance of the views of the Mathers than his own. On May 27, 1725, just seven weeks after Wise died, the Ministers' Convention, by the pen of Cotton Mather, petitioned the legislature of the province to call a Synod in the old-time fashion, to consider "What are the miscarriages whereof we have reason to think the judgments of heaven, upon us, call us to be more generally sensible, and what may be the most evangelical and effectual expedients to put a stop unto those or the like miscarriages." The Upper House favored the request, the Lower House disapproved at first, but afterward joined in referring the question to the next session of the court, and this disposition met the approval of William Dummer, who, as lieutenant-governor, was the highest royal representative at the time in Massachusetts. But the Episcopalians of the province were determined that the Synod should not take place, and appealed to the Bishop of London, by whom the English authorities were induced to administer a sharp rebuke to Dummer and to forbid the meeting, giving as their reason: "It is thought here that the clergy should not meet in so public and authoritative a manner without the king's consent as head of the church, and that it would be a bad precedent for dissenters here to ask the same privilege, which, if granted, would be a sort of vying with the established church. It has also been insinuated that this Synod would have come to some resolutions to the prejudice of the Church of England."

Thus by Episcopal interference the churches of Massachusetts were made to feel that their privileges under the charter of 1691 were not what they had been in the days of the founders, or what Connecticut still enjoyed. But probably it was well that it was so. Congregational consolidation, the development of fellowship, had been the main characteristic of the seventeenth century. That development had gone to semi-Presbyterian lengths in Connecticut; it had nearly reached the same goal in Massachusetts. It was time to assert the other element of the polity, that of local autonomy; and the difficulty of calling Synods by government authority, the democratic principles of Wise, and the political situation, all tended tc make that assertion, rather than the further development of fellowship, the characteristic of the next century and a quarter.

CHAPTER VII.

EARLY THEORIES AND USAGES.

THE failure of the attempt to secure the summons of a Synod by the Massachusetts legislature in 1725 was the concluding incident of the last chapter. Though not in itself a matter of great importance, it may well serve as a convenient terminal mark for the story of early Congregationalism. It emphasized the decline of that intimacy of relationship of the civil and ecclesiastical leaders which had been more and more evident since the downfall of the first Massachusetts charter. The Synod itself was proposed to devise a remedy for a state of affairs largely illustrative of the passing away of the ideals of earlier New England. Already another theory of the claims of Congregational polity than that maintained by the founders had been propounded by Wise; and if one advances beyond this date there speedily appear new religious movements, new discussions, and different problems from those which had engrossed Congregational thought heretofore. It is proper, therefore, to pause in the narrative at this point and to glance at the characteristic features of the institution with which we have had to do—the Congregational Church—as those features appeared in this important division of Congregational history which has been under review.

As has already been pointed out, the first century and a half of Congregationalism was not a period of theologic contention. Not that doctrinal themes were not presented in sermons and in lectures with the utmost fullness. In no country were the intellectual principles of the Christian faith more laboriously and persistently set forth than in New England. But till well into the eighteenth century, save in one or two isolated instances, no disposition was manifested to depart from the strenuous type of Calvinism which the early English Congregationalists had defended and which had been characteristic of the Puritans of the reigns of Elizabeth and James I. In reading the sermons of Hooker or Cotton or Shepard, marked by a clear assertion of election, of the absolute powerlessness of man by nature in conversion, of the necessity of entire submission to the divine will, and of the infinite blessedness and comfort which flow to all who receive the justifying and preserving grace of God,—even more characterized by a strenuous and reiterated insistence on the necessity of personal godliness of life and a lofty conception of the requirements and the privileges of the Christian calling,—one is reading discourses of the same type as those of Whitaker or Perkins or Preston, the Puritan lights of the University of Cambridge; and these characteristics continued the uniform and practically unquestioned marks of New England preaching for over a century after the settlements were begun.

A few ripples did, indeed, disturb this doctrinal calm. The Hutchinsonian dispute, in the early days of Massachusetts, has already been described; the Baptist and Quaker beginnings have been glanced at; but none of these episodes affected any considerable portion of New England or modified the type of preaching there exhibited. Still less influential was the publication of a theory of the atonement at variance with the Anselmic view then prevalent in all Puritan thinking, by William Pynchon, the founder of Springfield, Mass., and one of the few laymen to contribute to theologic literature during the colonial period of New England. His book of 1650, the "Meritorious Price of our Redemption," denied that Christ suffered the torments of hell, or was under the wrath of God, or paid the exact penalty of our sins divinely imputed to him; and affirmed that the price of our salvation was his mediatorial obedience—the voluntary offering of himself—which disposed the Father to forgive sin. Thoughts similar to some of these were to appear in a modified form in that conception of Christ's work which the younger Jonathan Edwards was so successfully to advocate in the closing years of the eighteenth century, that it has become known as the "New England theory"; but New England was not ripe for such speculations in 1650.

The Massachusetts legislature ordered Pynchon's book to be burned, and appointed Rev. John Norton, of Ipswich, to make reply. Pynchon was not convinced, but he founded no new school of thinking, and his pamphlet led to no permanent results. Indeed, so uniform was the pattern of New England belief that Cotton Mather was able to say in his "Ratio Disciplinæ," published in 1726: "There is no need of Reporting what is the Faith professed by the Churches in New England; For every one knows, That they perfectly adhere to the Confession of Faith, published by the Assembly of Divines at Westminster, and afterwards renewed by the Synod at the Savoy: And received by the Renowned Kirk of Scotland. The Doctrinal Articles of the Church of England, also, are more universally held and preached in the Churches of New England, than in any Nation; and far more than in our own [England]. I cannot learn, That among all the Pastors of Two Hundred Churches, there is one Arminian: much less an Arian, or a Gentilist. . . . It is well known, that the Points peculiar to the Churches of New England, are those of their Church Discipline."

It is when we turn to the polity of Congregationalism that we see that which was most peculiar to our churches in their first century and a half. As defined by the "Cambridge Platform," and as held from the beginnings of Congregationalism, "a Congregational Church, is by the institution of Christ a part of the Militant-visible-church, consisting of a company of Saints by calling, united into one body, by a holy covenant, for the publick worship of God, & the mutuall edification one of another, in the Fellowship of the Lord Iesus." The "saints by calling," who are the members of a church, are: "Such, as haue not only attained the knowledge of the principles of Religion, & are free from gros & open scandals, but also do together with the profession of their faith & Repentance, walk in blameles obedience to the word," with their children; in number not greater than "may ordinarily meet together conveniently in one place: nor ordinarily fewer, then may conveniently carry on Church-work." The covenant which joins a company of otherwise disconnected Christians into a church, and which is a fundamental characteristic of the Congregational system, is a "voluntary agreement" "wherby they give up themselves unto the Lord, to the observing of the ordinances of Christ together in the same society." This covenant is best when it is "express & plain"; but the Puritan Congregationalists of New England, though they firmly denied the proper existence of any organized churches except Congregational bodies, were far from believing with the English Separatists that the English parish churches were antichristian. On the contrary, the "Cambridge Platform" asserted that a verbal covenant was not the only form of the basal agreement, for "a company of faithful persons" express such a union "by their constant practise in comming together for the publick worship of God, & by their religious subjection unto the ordinances of God"; and hence they held that though there was no true Church of England, there were many true churches in the bounds of the Establishment.

A church was organized in early New England by the entrance into formal covenant one with another of those inhabitants of a definite territory, a township or a division of a township, who were "satisfied of one another's faith & repentance." From 1636 onward in Massachusetts and from 1658 in Connecticut the consent of the civil government and the approval of other churches was a prerequisite to this act,—a consent which was based not only on the type of religious character exhibited, but on the ability of the petitioners to support the necessary expenses of divine worship. In general these fundamental covenants were remarkably free from doctrinal expression, being usually a simple promise to walk in fidelity to the divine commandments and in Christian faithfulness one to another. Nor was anything of peculiar sanctity supposed to lie in the form of words adopted at a church's beginning. Such covenants were renewed, made more explicit against definite forms of prevalent sin, or otherwise amended, with much freedom, to meet the exigencies of ecclesiastical life. In fact, it was widely the custom for each new minister to draught the particular agreement to which he took the assent of candidates for church-membership, without necessarily submitting his form of words to the approval of the church. The essential matter was the agreement, not its verbal expression. Local confessions of faith were to be found in a few instances in early, though apparently not in the earliest, New England, as at Wenham, Mass., by 1644, or Windsor, Conn., in 1647. A large portion of the elaborate local creeds of the Congregational churches of the present day had their beginnings in the discussions of the opening years of the present century.

Yet it would be a serious error to conclude that the churches of New England had no doctrinal tests for membership. The absence of written local creeds was chiefly due to the prevalent doctrinal uniformity of the first century of New England life. But the ordinary requirements for admission to membership show that the tests applied were severe. The candidates for fellowship made their desire known to the officers of the church. They were then obliged to submit to an examination by the teaching and ruling elders, usually in private, though frequently in the presence of the more prominent members of the flock, as Cotton declares, both as to "their knowledge in the principles of religion, & of their experience in the wayes of grace, and of their godly conversation amongst men." The "Cambridge Platform" indeed directs that "the weakest measure of faith is to be accepted," and that "severity of examination is to be avoyded"; but the evidence seems clear that this threefold test implied not only a searching inquiry into the candidates' experience and reputation, but into their acquaintance with the principles of Christian doctrine. Once approved by the officers, the candidates were propounded to the church that objection to their admission might, if necessary, be made. No difficulties having been raised, the candidates would appear before the church as a whole, unless excessively timid, and make a "relation" of their beliefs and religious experiences. With men this usually took the form of oral statements of some length, or question and answer; in the case of women written confessions were usually read by a church officer. But, however presented, the most essential portion of the transaction was the act of the church itself, which, after hearing these statements, voted on the candidates' admission. If accepted, they assented to the covenant and were accounted of the church.

This early strenuousness, which kept probably a majority of the inhabitants of the colonies out of the churches even in the first days of the settlements, was relaxed as the seventeenth century wore on. When the Half-Way Covenant had become the rule, those baptized under it, as already of the church, were admitted to "full communion" in some places, on the strength of a private examination by the officers, without the elaborate propounding and relations still required of those who had had no parental connection with the churches. But these public relations were felt by many to be a formidable matter,—their abandonment was one of the innovations insisted upon by Brattle Church in 1699,—and though they still continued in extensive use at the close of the first quarter of the eighteenth century, and were favored by conservatives like the Mathers, private examination by the ministers more and more took the place of the public ordeal, especially in the larger towns.

The organization of a church was followed by its choice of officers. As with the English Separatists, these officers were theoretically held to be pastor, teacher, elders, deacons, and widows. But actual New England practice underwent a very rapid change in the direction of simplicity during the seventeenth century, so that by 1700 few New England churches had any other officers than pastor and deacons. These officers were at first chosen by the votes of all the adult male members of the church which they were to serve, and members in which they were required to be,—the deacons continued to be so selected always. But certain changes, due primarily to the share of all the inhabitants of a township or precinct in a minister's support, of which more will be said later in this chapter, led to the recognition, toward the close of the seventeenth century, of the right of the legal voters of a town or parish, irrespective of their church-membership, to a coöperant part in a minister's selection, thus establishing the dual organization of New England Congregationalism, the church and the "society," or parish, as joint factors in the choice and settlement of a minister. As long as all legal voters in Massachusetts, or the overwhelming portion of the enfranchised in Connecticut, were church-members, the provision of a minister's support or the erection of a meeting-house by town authorities was the act of substantially the same persons who as church-members had the selection of the minister. But the growth into political prominence of those who were not of the churches altered the situation. In spite of the declaration of the Massachusetts court in 1668 that none but members in "full communion" should join in a minister's election, exceptions occurred at Salem as early as 1672 and at Dedham in 1685. In 1666 the Connecticut court asked the ministers to give advice "whether it doth not belong to ye body of a Towne collectively, taken joyntly, to call him to be their minister whom the Church shal choose to be their officer?" but nothing came of the inquiry at the time. Massachusetts statutes of 1692–93 directed that the church should select the minister, and that the choice should then be submitted to the inhabitants, both church-members and non-members, for approval; if approved by a majority, the tax-payers of the town or parish should be bound to provide his support. In cases of disagreement a Massachusetts law of 1695 declared that a council of neighboring churches should decide; but the law practically necessitated a concurrence of communicants and tax-payers in ministerial settlement. A law of 1708 in Connecticut gave legal sanction to a similar system; and in both colonies these statutes were but expressions of the sentiment that there should be no taxation without representation. Indeed, in this matter Connecticut practice in the latter part of the period under review allowed the parish in many instances larger influence than it obtained in Massachusetts. New settlements in Connecticut, and parish districts of older settlements in which churches were not yet formed, usually selected a minister and contracted for his salary before, in some instances a number of years before, a church was organized. Having thus taken the initiative at the beginning, the society sometimes kept it after the organization of a church, and called the minister, leaving to the church a confirmatory or rejecting power. In eastern Connecticut, especially New London County, this uncongregational outgrowth of early colonial conditions continued in force throughout the colonial period. This joint action of church and society in ministerial selection led to the theory, adjudged to be the law of Massachusetts in the Dedham case of 1820, that a church has no legal existence save in "connection with some regularly constituted society,"—a legal interpretation which has been much disputed, and which has been practically voided within the last few years by laws in Massachusetts, Connecticut, and other New England States allowing the incorporation of a church without the appendage of a society. But this union of church and society, the one having to do with the spiritual and the other with the secular concerns of ecclesiastical life, still continues the almost universal rule among the churches of New England even in these days of voluntaryism, while outside of New England it has never very extensively obtained.

Election to office was followed by ordination in the case of all officers in early Congregationalism; though at the close of the first century on American soil, the primitive custom had become so modified that ordination of deacons was falling into disuse, and reimposition of hands upon ministers who had held previous pastoral charge was already abandoned for the ceremony of installation. In the undeveloped and somewhat tentative state of Congregational fellowship during the few years which immediately succeeded the arrival of the Puritans, as in the Congregational churches of England and of the Dutch exile, ordination was accomplished by the church which the minister was to serve; and the establishment of the pastoral relation was effected without the advice of other churches. But from the time that Governor Bradford went to Salem in 1629 to extend the right hand of fellowship to the newly ordained Skelton and Higginson it became increasingly the custom for sister churches to recognize the new relation, and soon to advise in it, so that when the church at Watertown ordained Rev. John Knowles in 1640 without "giving notice thereof to the neighboring churches, nor to the magistrates," Winthrop declares that they differed "from the practice of the other churches." During the early part of the first century of our churches on American soil opinion as to the proper persons by whom ministerial ordination was to be performed underwent a rapid change. At the beginning, where a church had no officers, as at Salem in 1629, ordination was at the hands of "3. or 4. of ye gravest members of ye church," or where a church had officers, as at Boston, in 1633, when Cotton was added to the ministerial equipment, by the existing pastor, teacher, or ruling elders. But as the fellowship of sister churches was increasingly expressed by the presence and advice of their representatives in ministerial ordination, it became increasingly the custom to call upon ministers of other churches to lay consecrating hands upon the three classes of church officers included under the title of "elders," the pastor, teacher, and ruling elder. As far as the writer is aware, the ordination of deacons, when practiced, always remained the work of the church which chose them to office. This transitional stage in the ordination of "elders" is illustrated in the "Cambridge Platform" of 1648, which inclines toward the older method of consecration, but admits that "in such Churches where there are no Elders, & the Church so desire, wee see not why Imposition of hands may not be performed by the Elders of other Churches." But the newer method made rapid progress. In spite of such conservative examples as that of the Salem church, which ordained John Higginson in 1660 by the hands of two deacons and a brother in the presence of a council of neighboring churches, or of the Milford church in ordaining Roger Newton by its ruling elder, deacon, and a brother, in the same year, the system of consecration at the hands of ministers of the vicinage, gathered in council at the request of the church which had called the candidate, became speedily universal.

Though Congregationalism has always attached much importance to ordination, it has never attributed to this rite the supreme value ascribed to it by some Protestant bodies. As defined in the "Cambridge Platform," it was "nothing else, but the solemn putting of a man into his place & office in the Church wher-unto he had right before by election, being like the installing of a magistrat in the common wealth." Choice by a church was the real title to ministerial office, for "ordination doth not constitute an officer, nor give him the essentials of his office." It followed that since "church-officers are officers to one church," and not to the churches as a whole, that "hee that is clearly loosed from his office-relation unto that church wherof he was a minister, canot be looked at as an officer, nor perform any act of Office in any other church, vnless he be again orderly called unto Office." The logically consistent position, thus stated in the "Cambridge Platform," which denied the ministerial character of all persons not in office, was accepted after a little hesitation even by those of the Puritan immigrants, like the founders of Boston, whose affection for the English Establishment was warm; but the feeling that one who had once been set apart to the pastoral office was in some way authorized to administer the sacraments, and was possessed of an undefined ministerial character, even though he had not been for years the officer of any local church, caused this stricter theory to be generally laid aside in practice by the close of the seventeenth century.

Ordination, or installation, was always accomplished with ceremony, the church making the occasion one of fasting, and the neighboring pastors extending fellowship. As the mutual responsibility of churches was speedily developed, the occasion became one for the assembling of an advisory council, of more or less examination of the candidate, and the conduct by the minister-elect of a public service, including prayer and a sermon, before the council and the congregation gathered for the occasion. This public exhibition of the candidate's powers, designed originally to "give some Discovery, that he understands the Work, to which he is now to be Separated," yielded place gradually in the early part of the eighteenth century to the prayer and preaching of "elder divines" as "more decent"; though occasional instances long continued. After the sermon, the moderator of the council asked the church to ratify its election and the candidate to renew his acceptance. Then followed the prayer of ordination, with imposition of hands; next a charge intended to impress upon the newly ordained minister the duties of his office; and finally an extension of the right hand of fellowship by one of the assembled pastors in the name of the churches. The "charge to the people," now usual on such occasions, was not one of the customs of early New England. In installation the services were the same, save that a prayer commending the new relation to the blessing of God took the place of the prayer of ordination and its accompanying laying on of hands.

Church officers were divided into two main groups in the classification of early Congregationalism, "elders" and "deacons." To the "elders," constituting the "presbytery" of the local church, the power has been committed by Christ "to feed & rule the Church of God." Elders in turn were divisible into two subclasses, embracing the "teaching," i.e., pastor and teacher, and the "ruling" eldership; and in theory the diaconate was separable into two groups, the "deacons" proper, and the "widows" or deaconesses. The diaconate "being limited unto the care of the temporall good things of the church, it extends not unto the attendance upon, & administration of the spirituall things thereof, as the word, and Sacraments, or the like."

As defined in the "Cambridge Platform," "the office of Pastor & Teacher, appears to be distinct. The Pastors special work is, to attend to exhortation: & therein to Administer a word of Wisdom: the Teacher is to attend to Doctrine, & therein to Administer a word of Knowledg: & either of them to administer the Seales of that Covenant [i.e., sacraments], unto the dispensation wherof they are alike called: as also to execute the Censures." It is easy to see, however, that this distinction, though held to be of theoretic importance, was hard to maintain in practice. The more prominent of the early churches, except that at Watertown, which had colleague pastors, provided themselves with the two classes of "teaching elders" at the beginning; but the shade of difference was too indistinct to be readily discriminated, and the expense of supporting two such officers in a small community where one could really do the work was a serious burden, so that with the death of the first generation of ministers the distinction speedily ceased to be observed, and the New England churches came prevailingly to have a single minister. Even where, as at Boston, the wealth and populousness of the place made two ministers the rule throughout the period with which we have to do, associate pastorships took the place of the ancient pastorate and teachership in most instances before the year 1700, though that eminent conservative, Increase Mather, remained "teacher" of the Boston Second Church till his death, in 1723.

No office established by Congregationalists in their attempt to revive the New Testament model was more strenuously insisted upon by the early New England expounders of polity than the ruling eldership, and scarcely any was more speedily abandoned in practice. The ruling elder of Presbyterianism is a layman; but early Congregationalism was a little uncertain whether he was a minister or a layman, though inclined to class him in the ministry. Thus Congregationalism reckoned him to the "presbytery" of the local church, ordained him not infrequently at the hands of ministers gathered in council from other churches, and paid him a salary as it did the teaching elders; but did not allow him to administer the sacraments, and permitted him to preach, as Brewster did at Plymouth, only when a "teaching elder" was wanting. In its exposition of Congregationalism the "Cambridge Platform" thus sets forth his duties: "The Ruling Elders work is to joyn with the Pastor & Teacher in those acts of spiritual Rule which are distinct from the ministry of the word & Sacraments committed to them. of which sort, these be, as followeth. I to open & shutt the dores of Gods house, by the Admission of members approved by the church: by Ordination of officers chosen by the church: & by excommunication of notorious & obstinate offenders renounced by the church: & by restoring of pœnitents, forgive by the church. II To call the church together when there is occasion, & seasonably to dismiss them agayn. III To prepare matters in private, that in publick they may be carried to an end with less trouble, & more speedy dispatch. IV To moderate the carriage of all matters in the church assembled. as, to propound matters to the church, to Order the season of speech & silence; & to pronounce sentence according to the minde of Christ, with the consent of the church. V To be Guides & Leaders to the church, in all matters what-soever, pertaining to church administrations & actions. VI To see that none in the church live inordinately out of rank & place; without a calling, or Idlely in their calling. VII To prevent & heal such offences in life, or in doctrin; as might corrupt the church. IIX To feed the flock of God with a word of admonition. IX And as they shall be sent for, to visit, & to pray over their sick brethren. X & at other times as opportunity shall serve therunto."

Here was a series of obligations requiring peculiar wisdom and tact, some of them very irksome in their nature, sure to bring criticism upon the efficient ruling elder, while his position had not the popular strength which comes to the pastor from the administration of the sacraments and the regular preaching of the Word. In some of his prerogatives the ruling elder trenched on the powers of the pastor and teacher, in others he limited the rights of the brethren. He was a superfluous officer, and Congregationalism speedily found him so, partly by reason of a growing doubt whether more than one kind of "elders" was spoken of in the New Testament, and even more because the office was hard to fill and difficult to administer. In a large proportion of the churches of New England the ruling eldership did not survive the first generation of the settlers. Some instances of continuance to a much later period may, indeed, be found. Thus the post was occupied at Plymouth till the death of Thomas Faunce, in

1746; the New North Church, Boston, had a ruling elder till 1775; while the North Church, Salem, chose one as late as 1826; yet, in spite of these rare examples of survival, the statement of Cotton Mather, published in 1726, is true, that the office had been "almost extinguished . . . within the half of One Century."

Turning now to the distinctly lay offices, we find the only one represented in New England practice was that of the deacon. The duties of members of this rank were clearly set forth in the "Cambridge Platform," as follows: "The office and work of the Deacons is to receive the offrings of the church, gifts given to the church, & to keep the treasury of the church: & therewith to serve the Tables which the church is to provide for: as the Lords Table, the table of the ministers, & of such as are in necessitie, to whom they are to distribute in simplicity." They were to furnish the sacramental elements, to raise the salaries of the elders, and to have the oversight of the church poor. As such they had charge of the contributions of the churches. Like the pastorate, the diaconate has survived to the present day as a characteristic of American Congregationalism. But its duties early became somewhat more restricted in practice than the "Cambridge Platform" implies. The salaries of the ministers came speedily to be generally raised by taxation; church poor were few, especially in hard-working rural New England; and when Cotton Mather published his "Ratio Disciplinæ," he could say that the reason why the early custom of ordination had been extensively abandoned was "because in many of our Churches, the Deacons do little other Work, than provide the Elements for the Eucharist; and a solemn Ordination to nothing but this, appears hardly a Congruity." The statement is still largely true, though the more democratic nature of modern Congregationalism, the development of social meetings for prayer and conference, and the disappearance of all other ministerial officers save the pastor, have given the deacons a place since Cotton Mather's time as the minister's most efficient aids in the conduct of the more informal services and his advisers in church administration,—a place not theirs in early New England.

The other lay office recognized by early American Congregationalism was that of the deaconess or "widow," to give "attendance to the sick, & to give succour unto them, & others in the like necessities." But as far as New England was concerned this office was purely theoretical. No instances of deaconesses appear here in the period with which we have to do; perhaps for the reason given by Cotton in his "Way of the Churches," that "wee finde it somewhat rare to finde a woman of so great an age (as the Apostle describeth, to wit, of threescore years) and withall, to be so hearty, and healthy, and strong, as to be fit to undertake such a service." The London-Amsterdam church, which enjoyed the ministry of Johnson and Ainsworth, had a deaconess of whom Governor Bradford has left a picturesque account. "She honored her place," he records, "and was an ornament to the congregation. She usually sat in a convenient place in the congregation, with a little birchen rod in her hand, and kept little children in great awe from disturbing the congregation. She did frequently visit the sick and weak, especially women, and, as there was need, called out maids and young women to watch and do them other helps as their necessity did require; and if they were poor, she would gather relief for them of those that were able, or acquaint the deacons; and she was obeyed as a mother in Israel and an officer of Christ." Certainly many women in the churches of all epochs have shown similar aptitude in smoothing the rough places of life for their fellow-members, but it was only at Amsterdam that early Congregationalism put its theory in this matter into practice by the appointment of a "widow." The ancient office, thus exemplified in a single instance, is being revived with profit by a few churches of the Congregational order at the present day, but the movement is of recent origin.

The support of the ministry was a matter of much importance in early American Congregational life. Though salaries were small when judged by the standards of the present day, when estimated by the style of living in the new-formed communities, and by the remuneration of civil officers, they were fairly liberal. Congregational human nature was no more exempt from niggardliness, at times, than human nature generally; but the feeling was prevalent that a minister should be supported in a manner worthy of the best type of colonial life. It was the theory of Separatist Congregationalism, as expressed, for instance, in the "Points of Difference" in which the Amsterdam exiles summarized their criticisms of the Church of England in 1603, that the "due maintenance" of ministers "should be of the free and voluntarie contribution of the Church." This system the Pilgrims brought with them to America. The Massachusetts Company entered into definite agreements with the first ministers that it sent over, Bright, Skelton, and Higginson; and the colonial court voted on August 23, 1630, to pay the salaries of Wilson, of Boston, and Phillips, of Watertown, "att the comon charge." But after 1630 the Puritans of Massachusetts, probably moved by Plymouth example, tried the voluntary plan till 1638. At Boston the raising of ministerial salaries by general taxation never regained a footing, and free contribution continued the rule throughout much of the colonial period, though modified there after a time by the system of pew assessments.

There is every reason to believe that the early New England Congregationalists of the Pilgrim and the Puritan types alike attempted the voluntary system as a matter of Christian duty. But it was not long before it was found that the heavy expenses for church building and for ministerial support were met with difficulty in many towns. Church attendance was obligatory in Massachusetts by a law of March, 1635, and the feeling of the time was that "not only members of Churches, but all that are taught in the Word, are to contribute unto him that teacheth." So unequal were the gifts of different towns that Governor Winthrop raised the question of ministerial maintenance at the Synod of 1637; but the ministers there assembled laid it aside lest their motives should be thought mercenary. Yet the question was a pressing one, and in September, 1638, the Massachusetts General Court met it by a law rehearsing the frequent failure of those who were not church-members to bear a share in church expenses, and ordering that every "inhabitant who shall not volentarily contribute, p'portionably to his ability, wth other freemen of the same towne, to all comon charges, as well for vpholding the ordinances of the churches as otherwise, shalbee compelled thereto by assessment & distres to bee levied by the cunstable, or other officer of the towne, as in other cases." This drastic measure was intended to apply only to those who failed to do their duty voluntarily; but it changed the basis of ministerial support to taxation wherever it was not made a dead letter by public sentiment, as in Boston permanently, and for a time at least in other towns. Similar action was speedily taken in other colonies. One of the first acts of the commissioners, after the four congregational commonwealths entered into the union of 1643, was to recommend (September, 1644) to the courts of Plymouth, Massachusetts, Connecticut, and

New Haven the enactment of laws directing "that euery man voluntaryly set downe what he is willing to allow to that end & vse [ministerial support], and if any man refuse to pay a meet p'porcon, that then hee be rated by authoryty in some just & equall way, and if after this any man wthold or delay due payment the ciuill power to be exercised as in other just debts." This suggestion, which kept the appearance of voluntariness while rendering ministerial maintenance really a public tax, was made the statute of Connecticut on October 25, 1644. Plymouth colony, where the old Separatist idea of free contribution was deep-rooted, held out yet longer; but on June 5, 1655, it passed a mild enactment authorizing magistrates, in the case of obstinate neglecters, "to use such other meanes as may put them upon their duty." Two years later this law was somewhat strengthened. The statutes of New Haven colony, printed in 1656, but most of them enacted considerably earlier, provided that where negligence appeared the deputies and constable of each town should summon all inhabitants and have them pledge what they would individually give toward the minister's support. In case of refusal or delay, or of a niggardly subscription, the authorities should assess and collect a proper sum, if necessary, by legal execution. This was essentially the recommendation of the commissioners of 1644. Thus, within a comparatively few years of the settlement, though the principle of free contribution was still recognized as the ideal, the law collected the expenses of the churches as truly as it did the maintenance of the state, and the colonial records give ample evidence that threats of legal process against delinquents were often carried into action.

The pathway of legal prescription once entered upon was easily followed yet further. Thus, in November, 1647, the Massachusetts General Court authorized towns to levy taxes to supply their ministers with houses. In August, 1654, the same body directed that the county courts, upon complaint, should fix ministers' salaries and collect them by distraint. In Connecticut even the appearance of voluntaryism preserved in the statute of 1644 was in time abandoned. An official report to the English authorities in 1680 declared that ministers' maintenance was "raysed upon the people by way of a rate," i.e., a tax; and a law of May, 1697, provided that salaries due from any town or society "shall be levied and assessed on the several inhabitants in each town or plantation according to their respective estates as from time to time they shall be in the gen^ll list," and collected "by such person or persons as the respective townes shall from year to year choose and appoint for that end." Collections were to be made by the same process of constraint as in case of other taxes, and, lest a people should grow negligent, they were to be made even in case the pulpit was vacant, being then placed in the hands of the court of the county to be retained for the benefit of the ministry when once more established in the town. This law was made more explicit in October, 1699; and its provisions were the subject of occasional strengthening or modification during the eighteenth century.

Naturally when dissenters from the established religious system of New England arose they regarded as a serious grievance the necessity laid on all inhabitants of the colonies, save those of a few towns like Boston, to contribute to the support of the Congregational ministry under penalty of seizure of goods. Agitation for exemption commenced as soon as dissenters began to multiply in the eighteenth century. As a result, in 1727, Episcopalians in Massachusetts were allowed to pay their assessment to a clergyman of their faith, instead of to the Congregational pastor, in towns where there was an Episcopal minister. In Connecticut, where a law of 1708 had allowed the same toleration secured in Massachusetts by the new charter of 1691, an exemption law was passed for the benefit of Episcopalians in 1727, ordering that all inhabitants should be taxed at the same rate for the support of the ministry, but that wherever a resident clergyman of the Church of England was to be found, the taxes of those regularly attendant on his ministrations should be paid to him; and providing also that Episcopalians should not be chargeable with the erection of Congregational meeting-houses. Similar relief was extended by Connecticut in 1729 to Quakers and Baptists; and Massachusetts granted exemption to these two classes of Christians in 1728–29. In both colonies release from payment to the legally recognized churches was obtained only by a formal signification of connection with another denomination. The laws were interpreted with strictness; in the excitement of the "Great Awakening" in Connecticut some of the privileges were temporarily withdrawn. But on the whole the system of taxation and exemptions worked to the upbuilding of other denominations at the expense of Congregationalism. If a quarrel occurred in a Congregational parish during the colonial period, a second Congregational church could not be formed without legislative permission, since all Congregational inhabitants of the parish were legally bound to support the duly settled minister. But the disgruntled faction, by becoming Baptists, Episcopalians, Presbyterians, or Quakers in name, could be relieved from all payment to the Congregational minister. Not a few churches, especially of the Baptist faith, had their origin in this state of the law, which made it easier for the minority in church quarrels to become connected with another denomination than to found another church of their own order.

As the eighteenth century wore on religious freedom increased, especially after the discussions of the revolutionary period. The Massachusetts Bill of Rights of 1780 declared it the duty of the legislature to require the support of Protestant worship, and continued to it authority to compel attendance thereon where conscientious scruples did not prevent the individual citizen. But it left each town or parish free to choose such a minister as the inhabitants pleased, without stipulating that he should be of the Congregational order, and only requiring that all taxes paid for the support of worship by any resident not of the same belief as the majority of the parish should go to a "public teacher" of the denomination to which he belonged, provided there was such a minister whose services he attended. Some difficulty was made for dissenters under these provisions by the hesitation of judges to look upon the clergy of voluntary religious bodies as "public teachers." Four years after the ratification of this Bill of Rights, Connecticut granted even greater freedom to its dissenters by a change in the statutes (1784). Both commonwealths still maintained the principle that all persons should be taxed for the support of religious institutions, and that there was one standard polity and faith in each town or parish from which all others were dissenters; and both still required that this dissent should be expressed by the deposit with the town-clerk of a formal certificate in order to secure exemption. But this system came to an end in Connecticut by the adoption of the present constitution in 1818, by which all religious bodies were made equal before the law and all connection between church and state was severed; and a similar disestablishment took place in Massachusetts in 1834. Thus, after about two hundred years of ministerial maintenance by state aid, New England Congregationalism reverted to its original system of voluntaryism. Outside of New England the Congregational churches have never enjoyed the support of civil government.

The "meeting-house" was the religious and social center of colonial New England. It was alike the place of worship and of political discussion. No impropriety was seen in using the meeting-house for legislative and town assemblies, for no special sacredness was held to attach to the structure itself,—the "church" in strict Congregational thought has always been the association of Christian believers, though loose usage has often affixed the title to the place of their worship. It has often, though erroneously, been intimated that New England meeting-houses were studiously mean. On the contrary, they were, from the first, the most elaborate structures that the comparatively unskilled carpenters and masons of colonial days could erect. Ecclesiastical symbolism was scrupulously eschewed; but the steady improvement in the material elements of early New England life finds its reflection in the constantly advancing elaborateness of the meeting-houses.

The "meeting-house" of colonial days was prevailingly a square, or slightly oblong, structure, entered by a door on the side and at each end, and having within a pulpit well raised up on the side wall opposite the main door, from which, nearly to the pulpit, a broad aisle ran. In earliest New England two pews at different heights faced the congregation from the front of the pulpit, the more dignified for the elders, the lower for the deacons. The congregation sat on benches; the men on one side of the house, and the women with the smaller children on the other, while the boys and young men, under the watchful eyes of a tithing-man, occupied the gallery, if the edifice was elaborate enough to boast such a structure. As in England, seats were assigned in the meeting-house in accordance with the supposed social dignity of the occupants—a custom productive of much discussion and heart-burning; but this separation of families and "dignifying" of seats continued in some parts of New England to a very late period. Husbands and wives sat apart at Glastonbury, Conn., till 1757; while seats were assigned by social rank at East Hartford till 1824, and at Norfolk, Conn., in form at least, till 1875. The original system of benches or "slips" was early modified in part by the erection of "pews," at first nearly square inclosures, often constructed at the expense of the occupant, and placed in any convenient position which the vote of the society would assign for his use, usually around the sides of the house. In these "pews" whole families sat together, and gradually they grew to be held as property, or subject to a fixed rent. No method of heating New England churches was employed during the colonial period.

The first of the two Sabbath services began at nine in the morning, the congregations being summoned by a bell in a few of the more wealthy communities, but more generally, at least during the seventeenth century, by a drum, a conch-shell, a horn, a flag, or some such inexpensive device. Once gathered in the building, the services were begun, where a church had a full complement of the officers prescribed by early Congregationalism, by a prayer of "about a quarter of an houre" by the pastor,—of course wholly unliturgical, for the founders of New England delighted in their liberty of making their wants known unto God in words suited to their immediate necessities. Members of the congregation in illness or trial were accustomed to request the supplications of the church by "bills" read by the pastor before this prayer.

Following the petition, the teacher read a passage of the Bible, expounding it section by section. This form of

Scripture-reading was deemed the only fitting method by the New England fathers, "dumb-reading," or reading without comment, being supposed to savor of the liturgical usages from which they had fled. But by the close of the seventeenth century New England practice was undergoing a twofold change. In some churches in the larger towns, like that of Brattle Street in Boston, the custom of Scripture-reading without comment had begun; but in many places Scripture exposition had fallen into disuse with the abandonment of the office of teacher, and the Bible was not read in the services of the Lord's day. At Newburyport, Mass., the regular use of the Scriptures was approved by the church in 1750; at West Newbury, in 1769; while the General Association of Connecticut as late as 1765 recommended "the Public reading of the Sacred Scriptures" to the churches of the colony, and in 1810 the Litchfield South Consociation repeated the exhortation to the churches under its care.

Next in order in the morning worship came a psalm, lined off by the ruling elder, or where such an officer was lacking, by a brother "whom the Pastor desires to do that Service," that the congregation might sing. New England singing was indeed a dolorous performance. Instrumental music was disapproved till far into the eighteenth century, as forbidden by Amos v. 23; and this feeling is well illustrated by the refusal of so innovating a body as Brattle Church in 1713 to accept an organ bequeathed to it by William Brattle, its most prominent founder and leading worshiper. Thus, deprived of instrumental music, and using books, when books were used at all, which, like the Bay Psalm-Book, were without notes, the tunes retained by tradition were few, and became almost hopelessly corrupted. Even Cotton Mather, in his "Ratio Disciplinæ" of 1726, writing when the dawn of improvement was perceptible, could find no higher praise than that New England worship of song "has been commended by Strangers as generally *not worse* than what is in many other parts of the World," "and more than a *Score* of Tunes" are to be heard. When Mather thus described the state of music about Boston, a vigorous reform was in progress. In 1714 Rev. John Tufts, of West Newbury, Mass., had published a little tract in favor of singing by note, and containing twenty-eight tunes. Eleven editions were called for in the next few years. The musical impulse thus given to the churches rapidly spread. Within the next twenty years the agitation had involved nearly all New England, and the newer method of notes and printed tunes, instead of lining off and memoriter singing, though violently opposed as a dishonor to the fathers and a dangerous step Rome-ward, won its way into favor by reason of its obvious superiority. The choir did not gain much footing till about the time of the Revolution.

The psalm was followed by the sermon, always esteemed the central element in the Congregational service. New England discourses were habitually based on a text, and in the seventeenth century were expected to be about an hour in ordinary delivery, an hour-glass often being placed on the pulpit; though special occasions were thought to warrant more protracted efforts. The preaching of the first two generations of the settlers was almost exclusively memoriter or from brief notes, though with very painstaking preparation since, as Cotton Mather remarks, "well studied Sermons are those which among Judicious Christians in these Churches find the best Acceptance." By the first quarter of the eighteenth century, however, fully written discourses had "become extremely Fashionable," somewhat to the detriment of freedom in delivery, for "no doubt some Sermons are the better Composed for it, tho' it will require good Management if they be not the less Affecting." A glance at a few of the hundreds of manuscript sermons that have come down to the present day shows good reason for the caution quoted from the "Ratio Disciplinæ," since, owing to the expensiveness of paper, they were customarily written on pages as small as a modern postal-card, and in writing almost microscopic in its minuteness. Such manuscripts must have been held close to the eyes to be read at all, and the difficulty of their decipherment must have prevented all freedom in delivery. In the early days of the colonies, as among the English Puritans, it was a frequent usage for some of the auditors to take notes of the sermon during its progress, but this rather laborious custom hardly survived the decline of the first religious enthusiasm of New England.

After the sermon the teacher, when there was such an officer, or if there was not, then the pastor, made "a shorter Prayer," asking the divine blessing on the sermon; and the congregation was dismissed with the benediction. When Cotton Mather wrote, at the close of the period under review, a second psalm was often sung between the prayer and the words of blessing in dismission.

Between the services of morning and afternoon there was an intermission of several hours in the larger towns, and of less duration in the country, where the distance of the meeting-house from the homes of many of the congregation and the badness of the roads made an early termination of the worship imperative. The interval of waiting was spent in social intercourse, and as the only occasion on which the scattered inhabitants of a rural community had an opportunity of exchanging news and gossip, this friendly hour doubtless did as much as any statutory enactment to secure the general attendance of all inhabitants at the meeting-house from Sunday to Sunday. But occasionally a church felt that a more spiritually profitable method of employing the time of waiting might be devised, and instances are recorded, especially in seasons of religious interest, where men were appointed "to tarry at the meeting-house by turns, and read some suitable discourse between the public services, for the benefit and edification of such as tarry at noon." It need hardly be said that such an infringement on the one general, if rather sober, rural visiting-hour of the week was never very widely adopted.

At two o'clock, or earlier in the afternoon, the second service began,—a service which was substantially a repetition of that of the morning, save that where a church had both a pastor and a teacher, the minister who had not preached in the morning usually delivered the sermon. At the afternoon service also, a collection was taken in such churches as supported public worship by voluntary gifts, and in others, as occasions for benevolence presented themselves,—a duty to which the congregation was summoned in the early days of the churches by one of the deacons, who exhorted "as God has prospered you, so freely offer." At Boston and Plymouth, and probably elsewhere, no plates were passed; but the congregation rose and filed by the deacons' seat, putting their money or written pledges into a box, and occasionally offering ornaments or articles of merchandise, like the "faire gilt cup" which Lechford saw given at Boston, and then returning to their places.

Once a month, at the conclusion of the morning service, as Lechford noted, "is a Sacrament of the Lords Supper, whereof notice is given usually a fortnight before, and then all others departing save the Church, which is a great deal lesse in number then those that goe away, they receive the Sacrament, the Ministers and ruling Elders sitting at the Table, the rest in their seats. . . . The one of the teaching Elders prayes before, and blesseth, and consecrates the Bread and Wine, according to the words of Institution; the other prays after the receiving of all the members . . . the Ministers deliver the Bread in a Charger to some of the chiefe . . . and they deliver the Charger from one to another, till all have eaten; in like manner the cup, till all have dranke, goes from one to another. Then a Psalme is sung, and with a short blessing the congregation is dismissed." Though participation was confined to church-members, all persons who wished were permitted to be spectators at the Supper.

Baptism was held by Congregationalism to be the seal or witness to the membership of a believing adult, or of a child or ward of a Christian household, in the divinely appointed fellowship of some covenanted church, and should not therefore be administered privately, but before the congregation. At Boston, in Lechford's day, the rite was granted at the close of the afternoon service whenever desired, at the hands of "either Pastor or Teacher, in the Deacons seate. . . . The Pastor most commonly makes a speech or exhortation to the Church, and parents concerning Baptisme, and then prayeth before and after. It is done by washing or sprinkling."

While the Sabbath was thus filled with services in which the element of preaching was made central, the New England church of the seventeenth and eighteenth centuries had none of that wealth and variety of societies and meetings for different types of Christian work which engage the efforts of so large a portion of the membership at the present day. In the larger towns from the first a weekly "lecture" was maintained,—in Boston and Hartford on Thursdays, though elsewhere often on other days of the week. On these occasions a sermon was preached, though custom favored a somewhat freer and more secular range of topics for discussion than on the Sabbath. It was the especial occasion for the treatment of questions of politics and morals, though always with primary reference to the Scriptures. In the first years of enthusiasm these meetings were so popular that the legislature of Massachusetts in 1639 sought to limit their "length and frequency," lest running about from one town to another to be present at "two or three in the week" should seriously interfere with business; but a century later (1740) Rev. Benjamin Colman had to say of the Boston "lecture," that it had "been shamefully neglected by the Town."

The "preparatory lecture," anticipatory of the Supper and now characteristic of Congregationalism, was begun March 4, 1720, just at the close of the period under review, by the joint action of the Brattle Street and First churches of Boston, where the lecture was held for many years, monthly, on Friday afternoons.

Evening meetings of a public character were regarded with suspicion in early New England as possible occasions of disorder in the larger towns, while scattered rural communities even now find them difficult of maintenance. After our period, especially in the revival season known as the "Great Awakening," a few evening services were instituted in populous places, as, for example, at Boston, on October 21, 1740; but they were not an approved measure, and did not become so till the revivals which marked the dawn of the nineteenth century.

Besides these set occasions, many days of fast and of thanksgiving were appointed by public authority or observed by individual churches, on which the services were similar to those of the Sabbath, though the sermon bore distinctly on the themes of the special assembly. It need hardly be said that saints' and holy days were scrupulously disregarded.

These public services of the churches did not indeed embrace all the agencies for religious nurture by which early New England Christian life was characterized. Not only was there careful catechising in families and schools; ministers from time to time took heed to their flocks "by goeing from hous to hous" in order to ascertain how they were "p'fitting by ye word"; and young people were gathered together in any season of religious interest for special pastoral instruction. Private meetings of the brethren with or without the minister were not infrequent, and from 1705 onward many towns had voluntary societies of church-members, to "consider what may be for the good of the Town in general, especially the churches in it, and more particularly our Church."

In two features of social life, now deemed by Congregationalists, as by other Christians, occasions peculiarly appropriate for religious service,—weddings and funerals, —the customs of early New England were unlike those of the present day. Like the English Separatists, the founders of New England held that ministers were not to be "burthened with the execution of Civill affaires, as the celebration of marriage, burying the dead, &c. which things belong aswell to those without as within the Church." The feeling which prompted this prohibition was due in part to reaction from the Roman conception of marriage as a sacrament and from the Catholic practice of prayers for the dead, in part also to the thought that a minister had pastoral duties only to the particular body of covenanted believers whom he served. Therefore early New England marriages were celebrated by the magistrates, but not without the asking of the divine blessing on the unions, for these civil officers, themselves almost invariably professing Christians, "not only gave the Marriage Covenant unto the Parties, but also made the Prayers proper for the Occasion," as Cotton Mather tells us. But the usage of the church universal was stronger than the Separatist theory in this matter, and in 1686 the first instance of marriage by a clergyman occurred in Massachusetts, while in Connecticut ministers were permitted to join in marriage by a law of 1694.

Though no word of prayer cheered an early New England funeral, there was no want of respect to the dead. Lechford records in his book of 1642, that "at Burials, nothing is read, nor any Funeral Sermon made, but all the neighbourhood, or a good company of them, come together by tolling of the bell, and carry the dead solemnly to his grave, and there stand by him while he is buried. The Ministers are most commonly present." But as in marriage, so here, the peculiar usage at length disappeared. In 1685, at Roxbury, there occurred the first instance in the Congregational colonies of prayer at a funeral,—the occasion being the burial of a minister, Rev. William Adams. Yet these religious observances won their way slowly. When Cotton Mather published his "Ratio Disciplinæ" forty-one years later, he found that "in many Towns of New-England the Ministers make agreeable Prayers with the People come together at the House, to attend the Funeral of the Dead. And in some, the Ministers make a short Speech at the Grave. But in other Places both of these Things are wholly omitted."

The relation of one church to another was that of sisterly equality, since of each church Christ is the immediate head; and to New England thinking, especially as developed through the experiences narrated in preceding chapters of this book, this relation was anything but one of indifference. The "Cambridge Platform" enumerated six ways in which "the communion of Churches" was to be "exercised." The first was that "of mutuall care in taking thought for one anothers wellfare." A second way was that "of Consultation one with another," in all questions of difficulty; and, as we have seen, in all ministerial settlements and dismissions the advice of a council of the representatives of neighboring churches and ministers was sought. But sometimes a church would fall into what seemed to its neighbors dangerous error or reprehensible quarrel, and yet asked no advice. Congregationalism would remedy such a situation, if possible, by methods similar to those laid down by the Saviour for dealing with an erring brother within a local church; and this gave rise to the "third way" of communion,—that of "admonition." In the exercise of this duty, any church which perceived that a sister church was in error should first admonish its wandering associate, as one Christian might a sinful brother. Should this exhortation produce no amendment, the admonishing church was to acquaint several other churches with the offense and ask them to join in reproof. Should they too be unheeded, they were to call a council of neighboring churches to advise in the case, and should this advice be unfavorable to the accused church, such churches as approved the result were to declare a cessation of communion with the offending church. This system was strengthened in the "Saybrook Platform" by making the membership of the council definite, and its methods more exactly prescribed, but the underlying theory was the same. A fourth, and more agreeable, mode of communion the "Platform" styled that of "participation"; which permitted members of one church providentially with another to join with the church of their sojourn in the sacraments. Closely connected with this method was the fifth way,—that of "recommendation," by which members going from one church to another for a more permanent stay transferred their relationship by letters of recommendation or dismission. And finally, the sixth manifestation of fellowship was in the way of "reliefe & succour," when a more gifted church supplied a needy sister either with "able members to furnish them with officers," or "outward support" of a pecuniary character, —a twofold thought, which contains the germ of the whole modern home missionary activity of Congregationalism.

But no account of the ecclesiastical system of colonial New England would be complete without mention of the general supervision in ecclesiastical affairs exercised by the colonial legislatures. These general courts in Massachusetts and New Haven were composed for a generation exclusively of church-members, and throughout the period with which we have to do were predominantly made up of Christian men in all the colonies. They were therefore really representative of the churches, though indirectly and through laymen only. As the "Cambridge Platform" expressed it: "It is the duty of the Magistrate, to take care of matters of religion, & to improve his civil authority for the observing of the duties commanded in the first, as well as for observing of the duties commanded in the second table;" i.e., his authority extended both to matters of belief and practice. And the colonial courts acted fully on this theory. They called Synods; they authorized the organization of churches; they determined church quarrels; they reprimanded communities which were laggard in procuring a minister; they sometimes recommended ministerial candidates; they regulated the collection of the ministers' support, and heard the prayers of those pastors who were inadequately recompensed; they commended statements of faith and polity to the churches; they counseled weekly "lectures" and careful catechising. Sometimes, as when the Boston Second Church proposed to choose an uneducated pastor in 1653–54, they interfered with their advice; on one occasion at least, in 1652, the Massachusetts court enumerated the books of the Scriptures by name, and threatened banishment or possible death on all who should deny any of them "to be the written & infallible word of God"; at another time, in 1646, the Massachusetts legislature became a missionary society for sending the gospel to the Indians. The watchfulness of the general courts over the churches was incessant, minute, and not infrequently annoying.

Yet this governmental supervision had its distinct limits. The "Cambridge Platform" declared: "As it is unlawfull for church-officers to meddle with the sword of the Magistrate, so it is unlawfull for the Magistrate to meddle with the work proper to church-officers;" and this restriction represented fairly well the actual practice. Large as was the exercise of influence and authority by the legislatures over the churches, governmental authority did not appoint ministers, nor did it compel individuals to become church-members, or to offer their children for baptism. In general, the churches, even in the most theocratic portion of New England history, enjoyed local autonomy and a degree of individual freedom which has never characterized the churches of any other land where ecclesiastical affairs have been the subject of governmental cognizance.

It is difficult to fix an exact terminus to the period of governmental supervision in New England. Its more extensive manifestations were, of course, in the seventeenth century. The Massachusetts charter of 1691 greatly limited its possibilities in that province, so that throughout the eighteenth century the legislature interfered in ecclesiastical matters more in Connecticut than in the larger Puritan commonwealth. But this supervision tended to assume less and less pronounced forms. It slowly died out. Long before the Revolution it had come to amount to little more than the maintenance of a certain method of settling and recompensing a minister and defraying other ecclesiastical expenses; but a measure of connection between church and state, and consequently of potential state supervision, continued till the full disestablishment of these churches in our own century.

CHAPTER VIII.

THE GREAT AWAKENING AND THE RISE OF THEOLOGICAL PARTIES.

THE fourth decade of the eighteenth century witnessed the beginnings of a remarkable revival period which profoundly stirred the churches of New England and of the Middle Colonies, which gave rise to divisions and doctrinal discussions to a degree unknown in New England heretofore, and which led ultimately to the rise of a distinctly American school of theology. Interest in the discussion of polity had now become well-nigh exhausted, since few New Englanders were familiar with any type of church government other than the Congregational. From this revival movement onward till the middle of the nineteenth century New England religious thought concerned itself with doctrine; and polity did not rise again into importance till contact on a large scale with other forms of church life, after the narrow territorial bounds of New England had long been burst by her westward-streaming sons and daughters, once more turned the attention of Congregationalists to what they deem the peculiar excellencies of the system they profess.

The type of piety for half a century after the "Reforming Synod" was low and unemotional. There were indeed occasional manifestations of religious interest here and there in the churches, as, for example, in Northampton under the ministry of Solomon Stoddard apparently in 1679, 1683, 1696, 1712, and 1718; at Hartford in 1696;

at Taunton in 1705; at Windham in 1721; and a considerable and general, though brief, religious quickening followed the deep impressions produced by the great earthquake of October 29, 1727. But none of these movements were of any striking magnitude. The general type of preaching and of religious life which had come to characterize the third and fourth New England generations was not conducive to revivals. The intense preaching of the founders, directed to a class of men profoundly stirred by religious ideals, had been marked by "conversion," or a conscious change in a man's relation to God, often accompanied by deep conviction of sin and an intense spiritual struggle. The founders, in their strong Calvinism, had indeed represented man as wholly passive in this experience,—"conversion" was solely a work of God;—but they had made its attainment the one object of Christian hope, before which all minor acquirements and privileges, like birth in the covenant, sank into insignificance. They had insisted upon a strenuous morality; yet they had taught that morality was the fruit rather than the means of the Christian life. But the decline of the first intensity of religious enthusiasm inevitably produced a marked change in the emphasis of preaching, if not in its doctrinal content. "Conversion" was still held to be the work of God alone, it was still declared to be the all-important Christian experience; but there were "means" by which a man could put his soul in a position likely to receive the regenerating touch of God's Spirit. Such means were prayer, the study of the Scriptures, a moral life, regular attendance on divine worship, "owning the covenant" when one was of the church by birth, and, in churches into which Stoddardean views had entered, participation in the Supper.

It was but a following out of the characteristics of

human nature that when regeneration was looked upon as a change beyond human power, and at the same time many religious acts within a man's attainment were declared to be adapted to put the soul in a position of hopeful expectation, emphasis should be placed in men's thinking on the "means" which man could employ, even while it was still affirmed that the divinely wrought change was the all-essential matter. Nor is it surprising that, as the eighteenth century advanced, some ministers and some congregations began to question the extent of human inability and query whether God had not so conditioned regeneration on the employment of "means" that a "sincere" though necessarily imperfect obedience would bring saving grace to him who rendered it. This position, which was soon known as "Arminianism," was not very distinctly recognized at the beginning of the revivals, and was never accepted by the larger portion of the churches; but the discussions of the revival period brought it into fuller and more definite development, so that in the New England wherein Cotton Mather's "Ratio Disciplinæ" of 1726 had declared that no Arminian pastor could be found there were many ministers by 1740 who were accused of "Arminianism." The chief evil both of the old New England Calvinism and of the newer Arminianism was that responsibility for a full and personal obedience to God was practically denied. In the one case the nature of an unconverted man was represented as devoid of all present power to serve God; in the other a well-intentioned and serious attempt at obedience seemed to lay off upon God all further responsibility for a man's salvation.

It was into an atmosphere so filled with an unemotional reliance on the use of "means" that a new force came in the person and preaching of Jonathan Edwards, the greatest theologian that American Congregationalism has produced; and it came where a reaction was perhaps most needed, at Northampton, Mass., the source from which "Stoddardeanism" had flowed out. Jonathan Edwards was born at East Windsor, Conn., where his father, Timothy Edwards, was pastor, on October 5, 1703; and after a youth-time of brilliant promise graduated at Yale College in 1720. A period of study and of preaching ended in his settlement on February 15, 1727, as colleague with his maternal grandfather, the aged Solomon Stoddard, whose death two years later left him the sole pastor of the Northampton church. In Edwards there was a rare combination of fervor of feeling, of almost oriental fertility of imagination, and intellectual acumen, which clothed all that he said with glowing force, while beneath his words flowed the stream of a most carefully elaborated theologic system; and all these more exalted and impulsive moods were emphasized by the influence of his wife, Sarah, a daughter of Rev. James Pierpont of New Haven, a woman of remarkable intellectual force, but even more conspicuous for intense spirituality of nature.

Of Edwards's contributions to New England theology there will be occasion later briefly to speak, but perhaps the most far-reaching in its influence was his assertion of responsibility. An intense Calvinist, he felt the difficulty of the old Calvinism as keenly as the shortcomings of the new Arminianism; and, while he asserted the absolute sovereignty of God, and the entire right of the Creator to dispose of his creatures as seemed wise, he affirmed a distinction between moral and natural ability which had been advanced in less perfect form by the French theologian of the Saumur school, Moses Amyraut, in the first half of the seventeenth century, and had been hinted by the philosopher Locke, but which had been ignored by most Anglo-Saxon Calvinists. Man has not lost the power to turn to

God, and hence he owes to his Maker a full and perfect obedience and an unfeigned love. He should therefore be urged to begin an active Christian life by faith and repentance, without an undue reliance on "means." But while man has this power, he has not the willingness to turn to God, he is morally unable, and will so continue unable, though responsible, till God in sovereign mercy works in him a change of desires, by revealing himself to him as his highest good.

As far as any human origin can be assigned, the great revival began at Northampton in December, 1734, in connection with a series of sermons by Edwards which set forth the doctrine of justification by faith alone, exhorted to the duty of immediate repentance, and denied that any action, however good in itself, done by an "unconverted" man laid any claim either upon divine justice or the promises of grace. Soon the whole town seemed in deep spiritual concern. Little else was talked of besides the interests of religion; and these impressions were deepened by the vividness with which Edwards depicted the wrath of God, from which he exhorted men to flee. The movement was almost as marked among the aged as among the young, and by May, 1735, when it began to abate, more than three hundred persons were thought to have experienced a regenerative change. Soon the same impulse was felt in other towns of the Connecticut valley. From Northfield on the north to Windsor on the south it affected every settlement on the river, and in Connecticut it extended considerably widely, reaching points as far asunder as Lebanon, New Haven, Stratford, and Groton. News of these unusual events was sent to England by Rev. Dr. Benjamin Colman of Boston, and at the request of Colman's English correspondents, Rev. Drs. Isaac Watts and John Guyse, Edwards wrote his "Narrative of the Surprizing

Work of God," which was printed and circulated on both sides of the Atlantic in 1737–38, and turned public attention in all Anglo-Saxon non-prelatical circles to the American revival movement. Public interest in the subject was further heightened by considerable, though less extensive, manifestations in 1739–40 among the Presbyterians of New Jersey.

It was in a time, therefore, when popular thought had been widely aroused regarding revivals that Colman, in 1740, invited Rev. George Whitefield to visit New England. This eloquent English preacher was in the height of his youthful fame. Though but twenty-five years of age, his matchless oratory, his novel methods, and his fiery zeal had made his name familiar, and this popular curiosity was intensified by his anomalous position as a clergyman of the Church of England in sympathy with the doctrines and usages of the Presbyterians and Congregationalists. He had gone to Georgia in 1738 at the request of his friends, the Wesleys; and after his speedy return to England, he had crossed the Atlantic once more, reaching Philadelphia in November, 1739, and journeying through the colonies southward as far as Savannah. On this journey he made the acquaintance of William Tennent and his sons, especially the famous Gilbert, ministers of the Presbyterian Church in Pennsylvania and New Jersey, and second only to Edwards in their later influence in the revival movement. From Charleston, S. C., Whitefield sailed for New England, and on September 14, 1740, he was in Newport, R. I. All New England had been filled with religious excitement by the events of the last six years, and his reception was enthusiastic in the extreme. After three days of preaching to crowded assemblies at Newport, he went on to Boston, being received with the utmost cordiality by all classes of society. For the next ten days he discoursed to immense congregations, taxing the capacity of the largest meeting-houses, and assembling occasionally on the Common in the open air. He addressed the students at Harvard College; and from Boston he journeyed down the coast as far as York, Me., returning to the Massachusetts capital to repeat for a week his previous successes. Everywhere his audiences were profoundly moved. Under his oratory they were "melted"; men wept, and women fainted, numbers professed conversion. But with much that was excellent, Whitefield began to exhibit at Boston that censorious spirit toward ministers who differed with him which marred all his preaching. From Boston he wrote to John Wesley, of whose "perfectionism" he had heard, "Remember you are but a babe in Christ, if so much; be humble, talk little, think and pray much;" and this spirit of criticism led him to declare in the "Old South" meeting-house, in the presence of many ministers, that "the generality of preachers talk of an unknown and unfelt Christ; and the reason why congregations have been so dead is, because they have had dead men preaching to them." The charge was undeserved, for whatever their shortcomings, the hard-working, faithful pastors of New England were not an "unconverted ministry."

On October 13, 1740, Whitefield left Boston, kissed and wept over by Governor Belcher, who had been among the foremost to do him honor; and his hearers were as wax in his hands, as he journeyed by way of Concord, Worcester, Brookfield, and other towns, to Northampton, drawn thither by the fame of the revivals under Edwards. Here Edwards and his congregation were much moved, though the Northampton minister felt it necessary to remonstrate with his guest for giving too great heed to "impulses" as evidences of regeneration in his hearers, and for "judging other persons to be unconverted." But on this latter point Whitefield was irrepressible. At Suffield, Conn., as he records in his journal, "many ministers were present. I did not spare them." And so he went on his way, preaching at Westfield, Springfield, East Windsor, Hartford, Wethersfield, and Middletown; staying only a few hours at each place, but remaining nearly three days at New Haven, where he addressed the students on "the dreadful ill consequences of an unconverted ministry." Thence he went rapidly onward to New York, and spent the remainder of the year in a tour through the other American colonies. Never in the entire history of New England was a preacher possessed of such popular influence or received with such unbounded adoration by the community at large.

Whitefield's brief journey was followed by an outburst of evangelistic activity in New England. From December, 1740, to March, 1741, Gilbert Tennent continued in most effective labor at Boston, and soon followed up Whitefield's work in Connecticut. By the spring and summer of 1741 the movement was in full tide. Not only were revival manifestations widely extended, but many ministers were engaged in itinerant evangelism, of whom the most conspicuous were Rev. Messrs. Jonathan Parsons of Lyme, Benjamin Pomeroy of Hebron, Eleazer Wheelock of Lebanon, Joseph Bellamy of Bethlem, and John Graham of Southbury in Connecticut, and Jonathan Edwards of Northampton in Massachusetts. The preaching of all of these worthy ministers was accompanied by physical demonstrations which manifested the high pitch of spiritual excitement prevailing among their auditors. When Parsons discoursed at Lyme on May 14, 1741, he tells us that "great numbers cried out aloud in the anguish of their souls. Several stout men fell as though a cannon had been discharged and a ball had made its way through their hearts. Some young women were thrown into hysteric fits." When Edwards preached at Enfield, Conn., on July 8, 1741, taking as his theme, "Sinners in the hands of an angry God," "there was such a breathing of distress, and weeping, that the preacher was obliged to speak to the people and desire silence, that he might be heard." Men claimed to have visions of heaven and hell in which Christ showed them their names written in the Book of Life. And some of these extreme bodily manifestations were defended as representative of a true Christian experience even by Edwards, whose intense and spiritual-minded wife was wrought upon by the contemplation of divine things to a degree almost as great as the just awakened hearers at Enfield or Lyme.

It is no wonder, when such men looked with favor on a markedly emotional type of preaching and experience, that there were those who advanced to extremely radical methods. Such a man was Rev. James Davenport of Southold, Long Island, in regard to whom Whitefield, who was not conspicuous as a judge of character, had declared "that of all men living he knew of none who kept a closer Walk with God." Excited by the revivals, he journeyed through Connecticut and Massachusetts, haranguing large audiences in words of impassioned exhortation or denunciation, charging ministers who opposed him with being "unconverted" and "leading their people blindfold to hell." Wherever he went the scene of his preaching was almost a riot. At New London, on March 6, 1743, he built a fire of the books of Flavel, Beveridge, Increase Mather, and others, and declared to his followers that as the smoke arose from this pyre "so the smoke of the torment of such of their authors as died in the same belief was now ascending in hell." So extravagant was

Davenport that the Connecticut legislature and a Boston jury, both of which took legal cognizance of his actions, pronounced him mentally unbalanced; and it is charitable to suppose that their view was correct.

But with all these vagaries of method, the revival was an awakening such as has never been equaled in intensity in America. Coming after a period of profound religious inertia and followed by a half-century of similar spiritual coldness, the ten years from 1734 to 1744, and especially the years 1740–42, were a season of wonderful ingathering into the kingdom of God. Estimates are of course almost entirely conjectural. Careful historians writing a generation or more after the event have concluded that from 25,000 to 50,000 out of the population of New England, then perhaps 300,000, were converted or added to the churches. From such investigation as the writer has been able to make he believes that the smallest of these guesses is greatly in excess of the truth; but though these estimates may be disallowed, the fact remains that never has there been so extensive a manifestation of religious feeling in New England in any period of similar duration. It amply deserves the title of the "Great Awakening."

Enough has been seen, however, to cause no surprise that the movement awakened very divergent emotions among its contemporaries. While men like Edwards or Colman looked upon it as a blessing, others no less honest regarded it with distrust and hostility. Chief of these opponents was Rev. Dr. Charles Chauncy, the able, ascetic, unemotional, and doctrinally exceedingly "liberal" pastor of the Boston First Church, whose "Seasonable Thoughts on the State of Religion in New England," published in 1743, was the most notable opposing treatise that the "Great Awakening" produced. Two parties speedily divided New England. The one heartily supported the new methods of Christian work, approved the dramatic exhortations of itinerant evangelists, and insisted on a conscious experience of a change in a man's relations to God as the only proof that a man was truly a Christian. The other felt that the impulse that controlled the meetings was an evanescent enthusiasm, rather than an abiding force, and doubted whether the results of the labors of the itinerants were as permanent as those of the regular ministry; while they held also, that the surest way to become a Christian was to employ the ordinary means of grace with diligence. The party favoring the revivals was nicknamed the "New Lights," their opponents the "Old Lights"; and a similar division among the Presbyterians of the Middle Colonies led to the "Old Sides" and "New Sides." On the whole, a majority of the ministers of New England inclined to "Old Light" views; though generally laboring, as at Hartford, with the utmost diligence to reap the fruits of the evident work of God.

Between these two parties New England was speedily filled with controversy. The excesses of the revival were nowhere so conspicuous as in eastern Connecticut; and at its session in October, 1741, the Connecticut legislature approved a proposition of the ministers "to have a General Consociation of the churches in this Colony, consisting of three ministers and three messengers from each particular consociation," "hoping that such a general convention may issue in the accommodation of divisions, settling peace, love, and charity, and promoting the true interest of vital religion." This body, of which the colony bore the expenses, met at Guilford, November 24, 1741; and enjoys the distinction of being the last Congregational synod representative of the churches of a commonwealth called under the auspices of the State. It declared strongly against itinerant preachers as the chief source of existing disorders; and affirmed that no minister ought to preach or administer the sacraments in a parish not his own, "without the consent of . . . the settled minister of the parish." This expression of the representatives of the churches failing to improve the situation, the court, at its May session in 1742, passed a drastic and arbitrary enactment, forbidding itinerant evangelizing without the consent of the minister of the parish, under penalty of loss of right to collect his legal salary and subjection to bonds for good behavior in case the offender was a clerical resident of Connecticut, or expulsion from the colony if a stranger.

This action only added fuel to the flames. At Canterbury, Mansfield, Plainfield, Norwich, and many other places in eastern Connecticut, "Separatist," or, as they called themselves, "Strict Congregational," churches were formed during the next few years, chiefly by persons in humble circumstances. These bodies rejected the "Saybrook Platform," opposed the Half-Way Covenant, held that an educated ministry or premeditated sermons were unnecessary, attached great value to visions and to religious excitement in public meetings, and believed that the church was so possessed of the "key of knowledge" that it could discern by spiritual intuition who were the real Christians who alone should constitute its membership. In general they were made up of warm-hearted, spiritually-minded, though ignorant persons, who had been profoundly touched by the revival. In general, too, the principles which they held regarding the constitution and government of the churches were more nearly those of modern Congregationalism than the views of the established churches which they opposed. But ignorance, ridiculous fanaticism, and inordinate exercise of discipline soon distracted their congregations; they had upon them the heavy hand of the State, which deprived them of office, compelled them by distraint and imprisonment, even where in the majority, to pay taxes for the regular ministry, and till 1755 refused all petitions for their relief. When the two brothers Cleaveland of Canterbury attended a Separatist meeting during vacation with their parents in 1744 they were expelled from Yale College, as the saintly David Brainerd had been for reflecting on the religious character of tutor Chauncey Whittelsey and attending a Separatist meeting in 1741. Frowned upon by the authorities of the day, and torn by internal dissensions, the "Separatist" churches in many cases died out, while in some instances they became Baptist through the bodily transference of the organization to that communion or the adoption of Baptist sentiments by their leading members.

Naturally the excesses incident to the revival aroused much opposition from many of the ministry in Massachusetts, though owing to its restricted charter the colonial government, had it so desired, was unable to interfere as in Connecticut. An evidence of this opposition was the "testimony" of the Annual Ministerial Convention at Boston on May 25, 1743, "against several errors in doctrine, and disorders in practice, which have of late obtained in various parts of the Land." This body lamented itineracy; the preaching of "private Persons of no Education"; ordinations "at large"; the establishment of separate congregations; condemnation of non-sympathetic ministers "as Pharisees, Arminians, blind, and unconverted"; and "the disorderly Tumults and indecent Behaviours" which had defaced many of the revival meetings. This "testimony" encountered much opposition in the Convention from a large minority, and the thirty-eight votes by which it was declared adopted represented only a small portion of the ministers of Massachusetts. The supporters of revival measures, therefore, led by Joshua Gee of the Boston Second Church, Benjamin Colman and William Cooper of Brattle Street Church, and Thomas Prince and Joseph Sewall of the Old South Church in the same town, gathered a new and special "Assembly of Pastors" at Boston on July 7, 1743, with an attendance of ninety ministers drawn thither from Massachusetts and New Hampshire. This revivalistic convention affirmed it to be an "indispensable Duty" to bear witness "that there has been a happy and remarkable Revival of Religion in many Parts of this Land, through an uncommon divine Influence,"—remarkable "on Account of the Numbers wrought upon, . . . the Suddenness and quick Progress of it, . . . also in Respect of the Degree of Operation, both in a Way of Terror and in a Way of Consolation; attended in many with unusual bodily Effects." At the same time they acknowledged that "in some Places many Irregularities and Extravagancies have been permitted. . . . But who can wonder, if at such a Time as this Satan should intermingle himself, to hinder and blemish a Work so directly contrary to the Interests of his own Kingdom?" To this document the names of sixty-eight ministers were appended, and attestations were collected from forty-five more pastors scattered throughout New England,—the whole forming a list conspicuous for ability, position, and piety.

But it is not surprising that, in spite of the efforts of many anxious to advance the revival movement, the general religious interest passed away almost as suddenly as it had begun. Controversy turned men's thoughts away from personal spiritual concerns, the type of revival preaching was too emotional and too denunciatory not to produce decided reaction, and beginning with the attack on Louisburg in 1745 there followed a succession of wars and political discussions of the most engrossing character that lasted till the adoption of the federal constitution in 1788. So speedily did the great revival interest cease that the earnest Thomas Prince of the Boston Old South Church declared in November, 1744, that for a year previous there had been scarcely any conversions in the town of his ministry; and even Jonathan Edwards waited from 1744 to 1748 for any candidate to come forward for admission to the Northampton church.

When, therefore, Whitefield arrived in New England on October 19, 1744, for a second preaching tour it was hardly possible to expect a repetition of his previous successes; but he was now met with the warnings of the "Old Light" party; and this feeling of opposition was increased by the unguarded remarks concerning New England colleges and churches which had found a place in his published journals. On December 28, 1744, the faculty of Harvard issued a "Testimony against the Rev. Mr. George Whitefield and his conduct," and the authorities of Yale made a similar "Declaration" of opposition to his methods on February 25, 1745. As Whitefield journeyed through New England during the winter and spring of 1744–45, protests against his admission to the pulpits multiplied. Such dissuasives emanated from the Ministerial Associations of Essex County, at Cambridge, at Weymouth, at Marlborough, and from pastors in Bristol County in Massachusetts. In Connecticut the Hartford North Association took similar action on February 5, 1745; and on June 18th the General Association of the colony voted regarding Whitefield that "it would by no means be advisable for any of our ministers to admit him into their Pulpits or for any of our People to attend upon his Preaching and Administrations." The signers of these documents were not always anti-revivalists. Whitefield himself made partial explanation regarding some of the rash censurings for which he was criticised. But while many thus opposed him, he had vigorous friends. Prince, Gee, Foxcroft, and others of the Boston ministers upheld him; his non-clerical admirers there proposed to build the largest meeting-house in America for his use; but his influence was slight compared with that exerted on his first visit. Three times more he visited New England,—in 1754, 1764, and 1770,—and was always gladly heard by thousands. On his last visit he died at Newburyport, Mass., September 30, 1770; and his memory is that of one who with many faults of temper and of method yet with many virtues of heart and deep consecration of spirit was a prime human factor in the greatest religious overturning that New England has ever experienced.

The most permanent fruit of the Great Awakening was the doctrinal discussion of which it was the occasion,—a discussion which ultimately produced the only original contribution of importance given by America to the development of Christian theology, in the system worked out by Edwards and his followers and often nicknamed the "New Divinity" or "New England theology." Out of the general mass of New England Old Calvinism of the type of the Westminster Confession the Great Awakening developed two marked schools of thought, each carrying out tendencies already observable at the beginning of the revival movement, but both intensified and stimulated by that spiritual upheaval. These schools, both of which were small at first in comparison with the prevailing Old Calvinism, ultimately led to the division of the Congregational body into two unequal wings, the "Orthodox" and the "Unitarian," though the severance did not become formal till two generations had passed. Each illustrated one of two diametrically opposite tendencies exhibited by later Puritanism as represented in England and America.

It would be wrong to call them "Old Lights" and "New Lights," and divide them merely by their attitude toward the revivals, for the mass both of the supporters and the opponents of the measures of Whitefield and the itinerants were Old Calvinists; but the one party embraced almost to a man the most strenuous of the antagonists of the Great Awakening, while the other included its most zealous advocates. They were the two extremes between which the Old Calvinists constituted the center.

The first of these incipient schools, at both of which we have already glanced, was that of what was known at the time of the Great Awakening as "Arminianism"; though as it differed radically in spirit from the contemporary evangelistic Arminianism of the Wesleys, and as Arminian tenets were only a part of its characteristics, its most marked doctrinal distinction being a negative attitude toward the main features of historic Calvinism rather than a constructive genius, we will designate it by the name which its spiritual offspring of modern times prefer,—the rather indefinite title of "Liberal Theology." This tendency, which had aroused the concern of Edwards at the beginning of the revivals, was largely due, as has already been pointed out, to a reaction from the intense preaching of the founders of New England and especially to the importance attached by the ministry of the second and third generations to use of "means." It was a school which was stimulated, however, by the course of Puritan development in England, and especially by the writings of the prominent Dissenters of the eighteenth century, for all through the colonial period the degree of intercourse between the Nonconformists of the mother-country and the Congregationalists on this side of the Atlantic was very considerable.

The critical tendency of the eighteenth century, which

doubted so much that the seventeenth century had held to be established, which gave rise to Deism and Free-thinking, affected the English Dissenters profoundly, especially during that period of low spiritual life which preceded the Wesleyan revival. Arminianism, by the year 1700, had widely invaded English Nonconformist ranks. Arianism, foreshadowed by Milton and Locke, was presented in 1702 by Thomas Emlyn, once a Presbyterian minister at Dublin, in his "Humble Inquiry into the Scripture Account of Jesus Christ." It was popularized by William Whiston in a treatise entitled "Primitive Christianity Revived" of 1711; and was set forth in a lofty and seductive form by the distinguished Anglican divine, Samuel Clarke, in his "Scripture Doctrine of the Trinity" in 1712. Thus advocated by distinguished scholars within and without the Establishment, it found its chief acceptance among the English Presbyterians, by some of whose pastors it was adopted by 1717; and Arianism soon spread to such an extent throughout that denomination, which had been the largest body of Nonconformists at the passage of the Toleration Act, that by 1750 English Presbyterianism was prevailingly Arian, and half a century later became as generally Unitarian.

English Congregationalism resisted the Arian inroad, but its leaders, like Watts and Doddridge, though men of warm Christian feeling, defended the older Puritan Calvinism rather feebly in the face of the rising tide of Arminian and Arian speculations. In their reaction from the doctrinal strenuousness of the seventeenth century the religious classes of England, and especially the Dissenters, generally inclined to look upon creeds as man-made statements of dubious value, and claimed a large degree of tolerance for all shades of religious opinion. The favorite expression of the time was that questions of belief should be discussed with "candor,"—a phrase which signified practically that no sharp points of doctrinal definition should be obtruded. The works of the leading Churchmen and Nonconformists were read by the ministry of New England. English Arianism was indeed too wide a departure from New England doctrinal positions to evoke much sympathy, though it was not without fruit; but the less radical treatises of the Nonconformists made much impression on the American mind, especially in eastern Massachusetts, a region which by reason of its trade and its comparative wealth was brought into closer touch with the mother-country than the rest of New England.

The writings of two English divines were especially influential in molding the "Liberal Theology" of New England at the period of the Great Awakening. One of these was an Anglican clergyman, Daniel Whitby (1638–1726), who during the last half-century of his life was a rector at Salisbury. Whitby began his ministry as a Calvinist, but passed to Arminianism, and finally, under the influence of Clarke, to Arianism. During his Arminian period, in 1710, he published a "Discourse" on the five Calvinistic points which was four times republished and was esteemed an almost unanswerable argument in favor of the Arminian view. The second writer was even more influential. John Taylor (1694–1761) was a Presbyterian Arian divine of Norwich, who printed a treatise on "The Scripture Doctrine of Original Sin" in 1738, which soon ran through five editions; a "Key to the Apostolic Writings" in 1745; and a discussion on the "Scripture Doctrine of the Atonement" in 1750. These tracts were written in a remarkably simple and comprehensible style and appealed distinctly to the general reader. In the first, Taylor maintained that sorrow, labor, and physical death were the consequences to us of Adam's transgression; but we are in no sense guilty of Adam's sin; no curse was pronounced upon our rational powers; each of us is fully able to serve God, and, with the assistance of the divine Spirit, to obtain "Regeneration, or our gaining the Habits of Virtue and Holiness"; and the aid of the Spirit, though a most valuable help, is not given "as supposing any natural Corruption or innate Pravity of our Minds." In the last, Taylor rejected the idea that Christ suffered to satisfy divine justice or endured a vicarious punishment, and presented a conception of the atonement like the governmental theory of Grotius, though with insistence also on the moral influence upon the sinner of Christ's death.

The first New England work of importance which marked the greater definition of parties consequent upon the Great Awakening was Experience Mayhew's "Grace Defended," of 1744. Experience Mayhew was a worthy member of that missionary family which labored for five generations for the spiritual uplifting of the Indians. A grandson of the younger Thomas Mayhew, of whom mention has already been made, he spent his life among the natives of the Martha's Vineyard group; and though thus isolated and without a college training, he maintained a lively interest in New England religious progress and won recognition for his very exceptional talents. In his treatise of 1744 Mayhew affirmed himself to be essentially a Calvinist, declaring his full persuasion "of the Truth of the Doctrine of God's Decrees of Election and Reprobation, as the same is revealed in the Scripture, and for the Substance, as it is explained in our Confessions of Faith." But his contention was that "the Offer of Salvation made to Sinners in the Gospel comprises in it the Offer of the Graces given in Regeneration," and that "the best Actions of the Unregenerate are not properly called Sins, nor uncapable of being Conditions of the Covenant of Grace." The unregenerate cannot exercise saving grace, but they can, by diligent cultivation of the "means of grace," fulfill the conditions on which the free pardoning grace of God which will effect their regeneration is bestowed.

Perhaps the next treatise of moment as indicating the direction in which some men in eastern Massachusetts were moving was a sermon by Rev. Lemuel Briant, entitled "The Absurdity and Blasphemy of depretiating Moral Virtue," preached, among other places, at the West Church, Boston, and printed in 1749. Briant was a man of twenty-seven, of brilliant parts, and pastor since 1745 of the church of that portion of Braintree which is now Quincy, Mass. Taking as his text the much-abused declaration of Isaiah, "All our righteousnesses are as filthy rags," he affirmed that this prophetic utterance was never intended to be a description "of the personal Righteousness of truly good and holy Men." On the contrary, "the great Rule the Scriptures lay down for Men to go by in passing Judgment on their spiritual State, is the sincere, upright, steady, and universal Practice of Vertue." Some might object, Briant declared, that this was not preaching Christ; but, he answered, "to preach up chiefly what Christ himself laid the chiefest Stress upon (and whether this was not moral Vertue, let every One judge from his Discourses) must certainly, in the Opinion of all sober Men, be called truly and properly, and in the best Sense, preaching of Christ."

This discourse produced immediate reply. Soon after its publication, Rev. John Porter of what is now North Bridgewater, Mass., uttered a counterblast, from the same text, in the pulpit of another Braintree church, which was printed in 1750 as "The Absurdity and Blasphemy of substituting the personal Righteousness of Men in the Room of the Surety-Righteousness of Christ, in the important Article of Justification before God." To this sermon were appended the attestations of five of Porter's ministerial neighbors, who "rejoyce that this our dear Brother is enabled to stand up in Defence of the Gospel; and . . . lament the dreadful Increase of Arminiasm and other Errors in the Land, among Ministers and People." Rev. Thomas Foxcroft, the revivalistic colleague of Dr. Chauncy in the pastorate of the Boston First Church, also replied to Briant, though not by name, "at the Tuesday-Evening Lecture in Brattle-Street, Boston, January 30, 1749–50"; and from the text already twice preached on in the discussion. In Foxcroft's judgment the debate was between positions essentially Protestant and "Popish." Briant answered Porter at once, and in a tone of irony, though he says seriously enough, "I challenge you . . . to point out a single Passage in my Sermon where the Doctrine of Justification by the merit of Man's personal Righteousness is asserted. . . . All I contend for . . . is only to show that the Prophet did not design to brand the Vertues of real good Men with this odious Character of filthy rags. . . . I say expressly . . . Forgiveness of Sin and final Acceptance with the Father is thro' the Merits of the Son. . . . But I always tho't that so far as any Man is pure (let it be in a greater or lesser Degree) he is not filthy."

But Briant aroused other opponents. His aged neighbor in the Braintree ministry, Rev. Samuel Niles, after waiting in vain for a "laudable Retraction," and finding instead that Briant resorted to "Banter," put forth, in 1752, a lengthy "Vindication of Divers important Gospel-Doctrines," in which he accused his young neighbor of omitting the custom of catechising children practiced by former Braintree pastors, declared that the much-disputed sermon "disavow'd the orthodox commonly received Notions," asserted that Briant was "an Arminian or worse," and affirmed that the "main Design" of the present Vindication was "to put a Stop to the prevailing Contagion of Arminian Errors and other loose Opinions among us, which threaten to banish vital Piety out of the Land." By the time that Niles wrote, Briant's church was in turmoil, and in the closing weeks of 1752 a council tried to heal the situation, though without much success. A more certain termination speedily came to the strife as far as the chief actor was concerned. In October, 1753, ill-health compelled Briant's resignation, and a year later he was no longer of the living.

This story has been told at some length because it shows the type of discussion which prevailed in New England in the decade which followed the Great Awakening, and because it reveals also the incoming of a presentation of Christian doctrine akin to the contemporary views of many English Nonconformists, but a decided departure from the historic position of New England. Of course matters did not stop here. Eastern Massachusetts was in a general doctrinal ferment. In 1757 Rev. Samuel Webster, a Harvard graduate of 1737, and from 1741 to 1796 pastor at Salisbury, Mass., published an anonymous tract entitled "A Winter Evening's Conversation upon the Doctrine of Original Sin . . . wherein the Notion of our having sinned in Adam, and being on that Account only liable to eternal Damnation, is proved to be unscriptural." This leaflet, which bears evidence that Webster was a student of Whitby's and Taylor's writings, was reprinted the same year at New Haven, Conn., and, if one can judge by the commotion which it created, must be called "timely." In it Webster held "that even supposing that, which cannot be proved, that Adam was our federal head, or representative, . . . we only suffer the ill consequences of his folly; but are not . . . chargeable with his sin;" and that infants are "as blameless as helpless." To Webster Rev. Peter Clark, a Harvard graduate of 1712, and a much-respected minister at Danvers, Mass., till his death in 1768, responded in 1758 in "A Summer Morning's Conversation," fortified with a preface signed by five ministers of revivalistic sympathies, including Joseph Sewall, Thomas Prince, and Thomas Foxcroft, of Boston. In this reply Clark argued at much length in support of the doctrine of the inherent depravity of human nature as a consequence of Adam's transgression; and, as the attestors expressed it, criticised Webster for "making tragical Exclamations against the Doctrine of Original Sin . . . as if it imply'd, that Children dying in Infancy suffer the eternal Torments of Hell for the first Sin of Adam;—when it is well known, the Patrons of that Doctrine are wont to leave the future State of such among the secret Things which belong to God alone." Clark was confident that infants were not liable to punishment.

These two tracts aroused other contestants. Rev. Joseph Bellamy, the distinguished Edwardean of whom there will be occasion to speak later, replied anonymously to Webster in 1758, in a dialogue of considerable briliancy, advocating the theory of the imputation of Adam's sin to the race, and called attention to Edwards's "Original Sin Defended," then about to be issued from the press. Quite a different contribution to the debate was a tract, also anonymous, by the anti-revivalist Charles Chauncy of Boston, in criticism of Clark's answer to Webster. With a good deal of dialectic ingenuity Chauncy turned Clark's guns by asserting that "this Gentleman [Clark], no more than his Antagonist [Webster], is a friend to the Calvinistical doctrine, as it maintains the liableness of all Adam's posterity, without exception, on account of his first sin, to the eternal damnation of hell," thus accusing Clark of treachery to Calvinism in admitting the general salvation of infants. Other pamphlets by the principals in the debate and by two more anonymous writers followed; but the most important publication on this theme at the time was the work of Edwards which Bellamy had announced.

Edwards's elaborate treatise on Original Sin was begun and perhaps finished before Webster put forth his tract. It is an answer to the writings of John Taylor, the English Presbyterian Arian whose works have already been spoken of, and who furnished most of Webster's ammunition, rather than to the American deniers of original sin. But the occasion of its publication at this time rather than several other important works which Edwards held in manuscript was doubtless this discussion. It was passing through the press when Edwards died, in the spring of 1758. In this lengthy essay Edwards asserts that the universal prevalence of original sin is taught by experience and by the Scriptures. All mankind are by nature corrupt at whatever stage of their existence from infancy to old age. But the most peculiar portion of Edwards's argument is that in which he explains the nature of the Adamic relation. That primal sin is ours; but not by reason of any Augustinian existence of the sum of human nature in Adam. That which preserves personal identity, which makes the man of to-day the same being that sinned or was virtuous yesterday, is simply the constant creative activity of God. God, by a "constitution" or arrangement of things that is "arbitrary" in the sense that it depends on his will alone, sees fit to appoint that the acts and thoughts of the present moment shall be consciously continuous with those of the past; and it is this ever-renewed creation that gives all personal identity to the individual. In a similar way God has constituted the whole race one with Adam, so that his sin is really theirs and they are viewed as "sinners, truly guilty and children of wrath on that account." This may indeed come perilously near the verge of ascribing to God the authorship of sin; but it reveals a thinker of vastly greater powers than Taylor or Webster or Clark.

These discussions reveal a good deal of breaking down of the old Calvinism, especially in eastern Massachusetts, but other divines of that region went considerably further in their criticism. It will be remembered that Lemuel Briant's sermon of 1749 was preached to the West Church at Boston. The pastor of that church from 1747 to his death at the age of forty-five in 1766 was Jonathan Mayhew, son of Experience Mayhew, whose "Grace Defended" has already been spoken of. Mayhew was a man of most brilliant qualities, though too arrogant in discussion; a correspondent with prominent English Dissenters; and one of the earliest of the American patriots who foresaw and prepared the public mind for the revolutionary struggle—a friend of Otis and the Adamses. He was a marked man in every respect. Already at his settlement rumors accusing him of doctrinal unsoundness were rife, and several of the churches invited preferred not to be represented in the council by which the pastoral relation was established; but he gained public respect as a preacher of power, and grew to be a force in the town of his residence. Among his voluminous publications were a series of "Sermons" issued at Boston in 1755 and reprinted at London a year later. In these discourses Mayhew inveighed against "Creeds of human composition"; but his chief endeavor was to explain the method of salvation. The discussion led him to elaborate and carry much further the principles laid down by his father. "Those who imagine," he declared, "that, because we are saved by grace, obedience to the gospel is not necessary, as the condition on our part, in order to salvation, draw a conclusion which is very unnatural." To the objection that to assert this condition was to exalt human merit, Mayhew replied: "Good men may so far trust to their own righteousness, as to believe it will be available with a gracious God, thro' the Mediator; so as to procure eternal life for them."

But the chief innovation advanced by Mayhew in these sermons was his view of the Trinity. On that doctrine he was a high Arian of the school of the English divine, Samuel Clarke. "Tho' our obedience as Christians," he told his hearers, "is due more immediately to our Lord Jesus Christ, . . . yet it is ultimately referred to His Father and our Father, to His God and our God; who 'is greater than ALL'; and who has conferred this dignity and authority on the Son." "The Dominion and Sovereignty of the universe is necessarily one, and in ONE; the only living and true GOD, who delegates such measures of power and authority to other Beings, as seemeth good in his sight; but 'will not give his peculiar glory to another.' Our blessed Saviour does indeed assert the rights and prerogatives of his own crown; but never usurped those of his Father."

A more pronouncedly Arian footnote with which the passage in which these statements occur was accompanied aroused the anxiety of Jonathan Edwards, who was further moved by the anonymous publication of a reprint of Emlyn's Arian treatise of 1702, the "Humble Inquiry," at Boston in 1756. Edwards therefore wrote to Prof. Edward Wigglesworth, Hollis Professor of Divinity at Harvard, in February, 1757, asking him to take up the cudgels against Mayhew. But though Wigglesworth sympathized in the main with Edwards he did not feel a necessity of engaging in the struggle to which he was thus exhorted.

Though Mayhew was the most pronounced, he was not the only sympathizer with Arian views among the ministry of eastern Massachusetts. When the Unitarian struggle was at its height in 1815, President John Adams stated that "sixty-five years ago" (i.e., about 1750) Lemuel Briant of Braintree, Ebenezer Gay and Daniel Shute of Hingham, and John Brown of Cohasset, besides Mayhew, "were Unitarians." Probably this description is a little overdrawn, for even Mayhew does not appear to be more than a high Arian in his writings; but that the full divinity of Christ was being questioned considerably widely there is ample evidence. In 1768 Rev. Samuel Hopkins, the distinguished disciple of Edwards, preached a sermon at Boston on the Character of Christ, which is largely an answer to Arian positions, and which he said he wrote "under a conviction that the doctrine of the Divinity of Christ was much neglected, if not disbelieved, by a number of ministers in Boston." In a note to this discourse Hopkins remarked: "I desire it may be considered, whether the ordaining councils who neglect to examine candidates for the ministry, with respect to their religious sentiments, and they who zealously oppose such examinations, do not by this conduct openly declare that it is with them no matter of importance what men believe;" thus implying that much laxity in this particular already prevailed. Nor were Arian views confined to the immediate vicinity of Boston. In 1757 a council called to investigate charges of unsoundness preferred against Rev. John Rogers of Leominster, Mass., found that he did not "hold or believe the essential Divinity of Christ"; and in 1758 he was dismissed. In 1760, in a pamphlet wherein Bellamy attacked the theory that creeds as a test of orthodoxy should be abandoned, which Rev. James Dana had brought with him from his home under the shadow of

Harvard College to Wallingford, Conn., and which found other defenders, the Edwardean champion charged that the liberal party in New Hampshire "actually, three years ago, . . . ventured to new model our shorter catechism, to alter, or entirely leave out the doctrines of the Trinity, of the decrees . . . of original sin, . . . and to adjust the whole to Dr. Taylor's scheme." A catechism, apparently the one thus described, was issued at Portsmouth in April, 1757.

It is evident that twenty years after the Great Awakening Arminian and even Arian opinions were somewhat extensively disseminated in eastern Massachusetts, and were supported by men of ability and character. It is clear, too, that a large part of the stimulus toward such ideas came from the writings of thinkers across the Atlantic who had trod the same path from Calvinism to Liberal Theology somewhat earlier. But it is no less manifest that the development of some of the Puritan churches in America, especially some of those that most opposed the revival movement, had been leading them independently to results similar to those reached by the Presbyterian Puritans in England. That the development of Liberal Theology, in its outward manifestations, was not more rapid after 1765, and that Unitarianism did not become a recognized power till the beginning of the nineteenth century, was due in a measure to the early deaths of Mayhew and of Briant, but even more to the great political struggle which absorbed the thought of New England for more than twenty years. Men gave little heed to theology. But the type of belief that Mayhew and his sympathizers represented quietly spread, till forty years after his death it was that of a large proportion of the churches of eastern Massachusetts.

In polar opposition to these Liberal Theologians stood

the school of Edwards,—that of the so-called "New Divinity." The leaders in this movement were a remarkably able and strongly individual group of eight men, seven of them of Connecticut blood, and all except one trained at Yale College. All were warm sympathizers with the "New Light" party, though the five younger members were not actively contemporary with the Great Awakening. They were Jonathan Edwards and his two immediate friends, Joseph Bellamy and Samuel Hopkins; and the later representatives of the same impulse, Stephen West, John Smalley, Jonathan Edwards the younger, Nathanael Emmons, and Timothy Dwight.

Of the early life of Jonathan Edwards mention has already been made, and his share in the revival movement has already been pointed out. A man of more metaphysical genius than any other American, Edwards was a force such as few men have been in molding the thoughts of his friends and of three generations of the religious body to which he belonged. He was a man of warm friendships; but, in spite of his remarkable ability as a preacher, he was always something of the student rather than the man of affairs in dealing with his associates, and an autocratic strain inherited from his father gave him less of the sympathy of his ministerial neighbors than might otherwise have been his. A serious case of church discipline, and even more the hostile stand which the growing clearness of his own conception of the conditions of entrance into the kingdom of God induced him to take more than twenty years after his settlement against the "Stoddardean" system introduced by his grandfather and practiced in his own early ministry, led to his dismission from Northampton under very trying circumstances in 1750. This event was followed, in 1751, by his settlement in the then frontier town of Stockbridge as pastor of the church and missionary to the Housatonic Indians; and here he spent nearly seven years of great intellectual productiveness. Early in 1758 he accepted a call to the presidency of Princeton College, an institution in hearty sympathy with the "New Light" party; but he died, March 22, 1758, just as he was entering on his new duties.

Edwards was a mystic and a seer as well as a dialectic theologian; and partly by reason of this manifoldness of his nature, partly because death interrupted him in his labors, his system was not fully worked out on all points nor made in all respects logically consistent. But no small share of his power over those who have come in contact with him and with his writings is the feeling that he awakens that one is dealing not merely with an intellect of marvelous acuteness, but with a soul stirred by profound religious emotions, and a spirit that in a peculiar degree seemed to walk with God. It is a perception of this spiritual many-sidedness that has led others than those of the theological lineage that bears his name to lay claim to him as the master-key that unlocks the meaning of the most various tendencies in the later history of New England thought. But whatever germs of diverse fruitage may have been wrapped up in the profundities of his speculations, Edwards stands historically as the founder of a school of definite tendencies and easily recognized influence on New England theology and life. He aimed to raise up Calvinism, then sore pressed by the Arminian school of Whitby and Taylor; and he sought this restoration not because of any devotion to Calvinism as a system long maintained in the churches, but because the center of his own religious experience, like that of Calvin, was the recognition of the sovereignty of God. Yet he was equally convinced that Calvinism needed to be modified so that the responsibility of man should be more clearly taught. And a second aim was no less evidently his. Edwards sought to foster a warm, emotional type of Christian character, touched and vivified by a sense of immediate communion between God and the human soul.

Edwards's publications numbered twenty-seven in his lifetime, and nine volumes from his pen have been printed since his death, while it is said that even more material than has ever been published still remains in the voluminous manuscript fragments on which he recorded his thoughts. Five works, however, may be readily selected as the most characteristic.

The first of these publications of prime importance was Edwards's "Treatise Concerning Religious Affections," of 1746. It is a garnering up of the best results of the revival upon the author's thought regarding the problem which that movement had made prominent,—what are the characteristics of true personal religion. Edwards includes the will as well as the emotions in his conception of the affections. His work is a profound, somewhat mystical plea for the primacy of the emotions, and chief of all love, in religion; a warning against mistaken tests and signs of Christian character; and a definition of the nature of those affections which constitute the essence of personal godliness. The Holy Spirit does indeed operate on and overrule the actions of all men, but he enters into indwelling union only with the saints; by his power men are led to a new attitude of heart toward God, impossible for them to conceive in their natural state, but implying no new faculties of the soul not possessed before. This new attitude induces men to love God, not for any self-interest, but out of delight in his holiness; and from this primal love to God all other Christian virtues flow.

Holding such lofty views as to the essence of the Christian life, and so convinced of the spiritual worthlessness of all that fell short of it, it is no wonder that Edwards was led to renounce "Stoddardeanism" and the Half-Way Covenant with their admission of non-regenerate men to the sacraments, as he did in his second work of moment, the "Humble Inquiry . . . Concerning the Qualifications Requisite to . . . full Communion," issued in 1749.

But the most famous of Edwards's treatises was one written in his Stockbridge sojourn and published in 1754, —his "Careful and Strict Enquiry into the modern prevailing Notions of Freedom of Will." In this work Edwards sought to defend the Calvinistic doctrine of the complete sovereignty of God in conversion against Arminianism of the school of Whitby, by maintaining that human freedom implies simply the natural power to act in accordance with the choice of the mind. With the origin of the inclination man has nothing to do. Man is free to do as he chooses, as free now as ever he was, but not free to bend his inclinations hither and thither. The action of the will always follows the strongest choice, and follows it freely; but that inclination is determined by what seems the highest good. While man has full natural power to serve God, —that is, could follow freely a choice to serve God if he had such an inclination,—he will not serve God till God reveals himself to him as his highest good and thus renders the choice of obedience to God man's strongest determination. Moral responsibility lies in the choice, not in the cause of the choice; and hence a man of evil inclination is to be condemned, since choice is his own act, even though the direction in which the choices are exercised is not under his determination. Man cannot choose between various possible choices; nor can his choice originate without some impelling cause; but his will acts in the direction in which it desires to move and is not forced to act counter to its inclination. This philosophic conception, by which Edwards believed that he had demonstrated the absolute control of God while leaving freedom and responsibility to man, had its immediate philosophical antecedents in the speculations of Locke, Hobbes, and Collins, though Edwards appears to have known only the writings of the first-named thinker; but Edwards's own use of these ideas was profoundly original, and the work was long regarded by most Calvinists in America and Scotland as an unanswerable critique of the Arminian position.

The fourth work of special moment which Edwards issued was that "Christian Doctrine of Original Sin defended" which appeared in 1758. The peculiar argument by which he attempts to show the unity of the race with Adam by a divine constitution or appointment has already been noticed.

A final volume deserves particular attention,—that containing Edwards's essay on "The Nature of true Virtue" which was published in 1765, though written about ten years earlier. To his thinking, virtue is essentially benevolence, or love to intelligent being in general. God as the absolutely infinite and perfect being is the object of the highest love; men are objects of a real though far lesser love. The characteristic of this benevolence is that it seeks "the highest good of Being in general. And it will seek the good of every individual Being unless it be conceived as not consistent with the highest good of Being in general." Should any individual being be hostile to this general good, true virtue must of necessity oppose him and take satisfaction in his punishment. A second and inferior characteristic of virtue is the attraction which one possessed of general benevolence feels toward any other being who is animated by a like spirit. The actual exercise of benevolence brings a perception of spiritual beauty and joy which no other experience can equal. Self-love is the opposite of love for being in general and hence is hostile to true virtue. Of course virtue in God is the same in essence as in his creatures,—it is benevolence which leads him to seek what his wisdom declares is the highest good of being in general, or of the universe as a whole. But, as Edwards shows in his treatise "Concerning the End for which God created the World," which was printed with his essay on virtue, the manifestation of this benevolence is somewhat different in God from what it is in men. God, as the being before whose infinity the sum total of other being is infinitesimal, in manifesting benevolence to being in general, naturally and unselfishly loves himself and seeks primarily his own glory.

It is evident, from what has been said, that while Edwards exalted the divine sovereignty in creation, providence, and redemption to a higher degree than the Calvinism of the day had been accustomed to do, he also emphasized four positions which were essentially a departure from that historic Calvinism. The first was his insistence on the possession by the sinner of a natural ability to do the will of God, thus placing the sinner's inability to obey God not in lack of power, but in lack of inclination. This doctrine emphasized a change of the sinner's disposition or "heart," as not only the primary, but the only important thing in beginning a Christian life. It laid stress on "conversion"; it depreciated the value of "means," since by undue reliance on "means" a sinner might be kept back from that full surrender to God which was his first duty. It also, though unintentionally, tended to lessen the importance attached to the covenant relation of birth in a Christian family and of baptism, through the stress which it put on "conversion" rather than on Christian nurture. A second characteristic feature of Edwards's system was his theory of virtue, making it consist in disinterested benevolence,—in a love to being in general which is primarily that self-forgetful love to God which Edwards regarded as the essence of the religious life. In the third place, Edwards maintained that the divine action in salvation and punishment alike flowed from a single principle, that of a wise benevolence to the universe as a whole, which is at the same time a manifestation of his own glory. And finally Edwards represented the preservation of identity in the individual and of unity in the race as the effect of a divine constitution which was a constantly renewed manifestation of creative activity. But, besides these evident features of his system, Edwards dropped many hints and half-elaborated suggestions regarding other doctrines, like that of the atonement, which made his work the beginning of a development carried much further by his followers, rather than the framing of a system to be accepted as a completed whole.

The elder of the two immediate disciples of Edwards and contemporaries of his later years was Joseph Bellamy, a native in 1719 of what is now Cheshire, Conn., a graduate of Yale in the class of 1735, and from 1738 to his death, in 1790, the minister of the little town of Bethlem, Conn.,—a rural parish which he might have exchanged, had he been willing to do so, for a New York City pulpit. Bellamy was from the beginning of his ministry a warm personal friend of Edwards. He was the most gifted preacher of any of the Edwardeans,—a man of unusual pulpit abilities; and he threw himself heartily in the revivalistic current of the Great Awakening, becoming, for two years, an indefatigable itinerant evangelist. But his chief fame was as a writer and especially as a controversialist. He argued in his sermons of 1758 on "The Wisdom of God, in the Permission of Sin," that though sin was in itself a terrible evil, it was allowed by God as a necessary means of the best good of the universe as a whole. In a discourse of the same year on "The Divinity of Jesus Christ" he defended the doctrine of the Trinity which Mayhew had attacked. In a series of dialogues and tracts in 1769 and 1770 he attacked the Half-Way Covenant, which Edwards had opposed, and did more than any other man to bring about its abandonment. He was an ungenerous but most effective champion of the "New Divinity"; and it was largely by his blows and criticisms that opposition to it in Connecticut was broken down. Bellamy's most lengthy and most popular work,—next to Edwards's "Affections" the most generally influential book put forth by the Edwardean school,—was his "True Religion Delineated," of 1750, which Edwards read in manuscript and warmly commended in print. It is a vivacious, readable, yet severely logical presentation of the plan of salvation and of the Christian life substantially as Edwards conceived them. Bellamy's most marked doctrinal advance over his teacher is his clear assertion of a general atonement. Edwards had inclined to the limited atonement theory; but the view of Bellamy became that of the "New Divinity," and a further point of rupture with the older Calvinism.

All this influence was multiplied in the case of Bellamy by the reproduction of his theories in the teaching of numerous pupils. Bellamy's home practically became a theological seminary, in which more ministerial candidates were trained than in the house of any other New England minister except that of Emmons,—probably not less than sixty,—and almost every one of them bore the distinct stamp of his system.

Edwards's younger disciple and most intimate personal friend was Samuel Hopkins,—not an interesting preacher like Bellamy, nor so vivacious a writer, but a controversialist of even greater power, and a theological thinker who developed certain features of Edwards's teachings so fully that his own name was often given to the ultra-Edwardean school of which he was the founder. A man of great natural modesty, of self-denying Christian life, and one of the earliest of the New England opponents of human slavery, his personal character always commanded respect; but his theological opinions were assailed and defended with the utmost bitterness.

Hopkins was born, in 1721, at Waterbury, Conn., and, after graduating at Yale with the class of 1741, studied divinity in the household of Edwards at Northampton during the later months of the Great Awakening. He then became the pastor at what is now Great Barrington, Mass., from 1743 to 1769, being for seven years a near ministerial neighbor of Edwards while the latter was at Stockbridge. In 1770 Hopkins undertook the charge of the First Congregational Church at Newport, R. I., and in that office he remained till his death, in 1803.

The theologic positions most characteristically associated with Hopkins's teachings were all of them extensions of the theories of Edwards,—especially of Edwards's conception of "benevolence" as the essence of true virtue. Hopkins held that though man has entire natural freedom, and ought therefore to be exhorted instantly to repent, the elective and directing power of God overrules all his choices, whether good or evil; and since God acts on the principle of benevolence, or the largest good of being in general, God has not permitted any greater amount of sin than he sees is for the interest of the universe,—though this divinely wise permission of sin renders it no less evil in the sinner.

In the individual this benevolence, as with Edwards,

takes the form of a preference for the glory of God. Sin is selfishness. And hence the test of a true Christian is a willing and disinterested submission to the divine disposal. A soul is really submissive when it is content that God shall do with it what he deems for the best interest of the universe as a whole, even if that disposal be its damnation. This doctrine of unconditional resignation, so foreign to the feelings of most Christians, was not original with Hopkins; to say nothing of theologians in other branches of the church, it had been held by Hooker and Shepard in the early days of New England. It was a natural development from the principles of the Edwardean school; but as one reads the account which Mrs. Edwards gave of the profound religious experience which she underwent in the early weeks of 1742,—an experience turning on this resolution of absolute submission,—one wonders whether the impressionable young theological student, then an inmate of the Northampton home, may not have received something of his inclination toward this test of Christian character from the mystical, exalted, and winsome wife of his instructor.

In Hopkins's system this doctrine of benevolence led to a third conclusion, approached but not fully reached by Edwards. God has made no promises to the efforts of the unregenerate. The first duty is submission to the divine will; till that is rendered all acts are essentially selfish and sinful, and tend to harden the sinner in opposition to God. Hence, as Hopkins expressed it, "the unregenerate, under the greatest convictions, and in all their external reformations and doings, are more criminal and guilty than they were in a state of security." "The impenitent sinner, who continues obstinately to reject and oppose the salvation offered in the gospel, does . . . become, not less, but more vicious and guilty in God's sight, the more instruction and knowledge he gets in attendance on the means of grace." Yet "means" are desirable and even essential to a proper understanding of a man's sinful condition and the way of salvation; but they have no power in themselves to make a man better.

Closely connected with this doctrine is another feature of Hopkins's system which was carried much further by his pupil, Emmons, a feature having its roots ultimately in the speculations of Edwards on the will and virtue. All moral qualities, according to Hopkins, inhere in the choices or "exercises" of the will. Back of those exercises is a state or bias of the "heart" which in itself has no moral quality. In an unconverted man this bias makes it certain that his acts will be evil, yet these choices are his own. In regeneration this bias is changed by God to a bias or taste for good, and man is passive in this change. But now his choices are Godward, and to them are all the promises of the gospel. This doctrine that sin and virtue consist in exercises or definite acts led Hopkins to deny the responsibility for Adam's sin which Edwards had maintained. Men "are not guilty of his sin, are not punished, and do not suffer for that, any further than they implicitly or expressly approve of his transgression by sinning as he did." Yet God has so constituted man that present sin is an effect of Adam's sin; man sins as soon as childhood begins to act. The divine efficiency is the ultimate cause of all acts, good and bad; but since sin is in the act or exercise and not in its cause, sin belongs to man and not to God.

These views, advanced in an uncompromisingly controversial manner, naturally excited much opposition from the Liberal Theologians and the Old Calvinists alike, and were combated quite as much by the latter as by the former. Hopkins's first tract of importance was issued in

1759, the year after Bellamy's "Wisdom of God in the Permission of Sin," and bears its argument in its title: "Sin, through Divine Interposition, an Advantage to the Universe, and yet this no Excuse for Sin or Encouragement to it." But this created little discussion compared with his next essay. In 1761 Jonathan Mayhew put forth two sermons on "Striving to Enter in at the Strait Gate," in which he advocated his familiar position that regeneration was conditioned on the earnest efforts of good men to obtain it. After four years of waiting Hopkins replied in "An Enquiry concerning the Promises of the Gospel, Whether any of them are made to the Exercises and Doings of Persons in an Unregenerate State."

Mayhew did not live long enough to make reply; but the shot aimed at the Liberal drew abundant fire from the Old Calvinists. Jedidiah Mills, a venerable minister of "New Light" sympathies settled at what is now Huntington, Conn., answered Hopkins in 1767 in "An Inquiry concerning the State of the Unregenerate under the Gospel." The same year the distinguished Old Calvinist, Moses Hemmenway, who filled a pastorate at Wells, Me., from 1759 to 1811, put forth a volume of "Seven Sermons on the Obligation and Encouragement of the Unregenerate to labour for the Meat which endureth to everlasting Life." To the tract of Mills Hopkins replied in 1769 in his "True State and Character of the Unregenerate, stripped of all Misrepresentation and Disguise." But now the able and excellent William Hart, an Old Calvinist of "Old Light" sympathies who filled a distinguished pastorate at Saybrook, Conn., from 1736 to 1784, appeared in the arena in 1769 with a dialogue and a satirical sketch in which he opposed Hopkins's positions, and first used the epithet "Hopkintonian" to describe his system. To these arguments of Hart Hopkins replied the next year with a good deal of asperity. In 1771 Hart issued a vigorous criticism of Edwards's theory of virtue, and the year following Hemmenway put forth an elaborate reply to Hopkins's rejoinder to Mills. These two works, and one by the Old Calvinist, Moses Mather, of Darien, Conn., drew forth from Hopkins in 1773 his greatest and last important controversial treatise, "An Inquiry into the Nature of True Holiness."

In all this heated warfare of pamphlets, the question between the Old Calvinists and the champion of the "New Divinity" was as to the status of that class of men of upright, moral lives, but of no Christian experience, with which every religious community is familiar. Hopkins argued that they ought to use the means of grace; but that so long as they remained unconverted under those means they were growing worse rather than better. His Old Calvinist opponents replied that though a man who simply prayed and read his Bible and attended divine worship was not fulfilling his whole duty and was not yet regenerate, yet God commanded prayer and worship as well as repentance, and the man who used these and other means diligently was growing better rather than worse, and instead of moving away from God was coming into a position where God was likely to bless him with a full conversion.

Bellamy and Hopkins were companions of Edwards's later life; but the others of the Edwardean school to whom reference is now to be made may more properly be called successors, since they had little or no personal acquaintance with the Northampton divine. The earliest of these successors were two young men of Connecticut birth, Stephen West and John Smalley, who graduated from Yale in 1755 and 1756. Both exercised a wide influence through their training of theological students in their own households, as well as through their writings. West was the successor of Edwards in the Stockbridge pastorate from 1758 to 1818, and was brought from his original Arminianism to a high type of Edwardeanism by the influence of his neighbor at Great Barrington during the early part of his ministry,—Samuel Hopkins. As a controversialist West is best remembered for his "Essay on Moral Agency" of 1772,—a hyper-Edwardean defense of Edwards's "Freedom of Will" against the criticisms of Rev. Dr. James Dana, of New Haven; and his "Scripture Doctrine of the Atonement" of 1785, of which there will be occasion to speak in connection with the younger Edwards's more famous sermons on the same theme. Smalley's pastorate was at what is now New Britain, Conn., from 1757 to 1820. A pupil of Bellamy, he was in turn the teacher of Emmons. His doctrinal contribution to the "New Divinity" was a development along lines marked out by Edwards, of the theory of the natural ability of the sinner to serve God, as distinguished from moral inability.

A peculiar interest attaches to a third of these successors, in that he not only bore the name of Edwards, but in many incidents of his career strikingly resembled the founder of the Edwardean school. Jonathan Edwards the younger was in his thirteenth year at the death of his father, by whom he had been designed for a missionary to the Indians. His education was at Princeton College, where he graduated in 1765, and the reception of his degree was followed by a period of theologic training under Bellamy. A tutorship at Princeton was succeeded, in 1769, by his settlement over the North Church in New Haven—a conspicuous post, from which he was dismissed in 1795, really, though not ostensibly, by reason of doctrinal opposition. From New Haven he transferred his ministerial labors to the little town of Colebrook, Conn., and from there he was called to the presidency of Union College, in 1799. He died in his new office on August 1, 1801. Professor Park has thus summarized the curious likeness of this life to that of the elder Edwards: "The son, like the father, was a tutor in the college where he had been a student; was first ordained over a prominent church in the town where his maternal grandfather had been the pastor; was dismissed on account of his doctrinal opinions; was afterward the minister of a retired parish; was then president of a college; and died at the age of about fifty-five years, soon after his inauguration." In intellectual acumen the younger Edwards much resembled the elder; but he lacked the poetic nature and the warm mystical feeling which made the temperament of the father so rare a combination of the qualities of the intellect and of the heart.

Jonathan Edwards the younger was, like most of the Edwardean leaders, a successful trainer of ministerial candidates, numbering among his pupils men like Presidents Dwight of Yale and Griffin of Williams, or Rev. Drs. Samuel Nott and Jedidiah Morse. He edited his father's works; he expounded his father's system with originality and force; like Hopkins, he attacked negro slavery; he was a power in the churches always. But he gained his chief repute as a developer of the Edwardean system through a discussion in regard to the atonement which had its rise in consequence of the teachings of the introducers of Universalism into New England.

Universalism was first propagated on this side of the Atlantic by Rev. John Murray, once a disciple of Whitefield. Murray came to America from his English home in 1770, and founded a congregation at Gloucester, Mass., about 1779. From 1793 to his death, in 1815, he was pastor of a flock at Boston. His indefatigable itinerant labors, and those of his American associate, Elhanan Winchester, met with considerable response, especially among the Baptists; and his speculations won disciples, and led to the acknowledgment of somewhat similar opinions by several Congregational ministers. Of those who thus advocated the doctrine of ultimate universal salvation, though far from agreeing fully with Murray, the most noted was Rev. Dr. Charles Chauncy of Boston, the opponent of the Whitefieldian revival methods of forty years before. In an anonymous tract of 1782, entitled "Salvation for All Men Illustrated and Vindicated as a Scripture Doctrine," Chauncy published a number of excerpts from the writings of foreign Universalists, and taught the ultimate rescue of mankind, through Christ; though he held that many might undergo a protracted period of suffering hereafter. The next year Chauncy supported these beliefs in a second anonymous tract. These treatises were replied to by a number of ministers, both Edwardeans and Old Calvinists, and notably by Samuel Mather and Joseph Eckley of Boston, Peter Thacher of Malden, Timothy Allen of Granville, Mass., George Beckwith of Lyme, Conn., and the "New Divinity" leaders Hopkins and Emmons, during 1782 and 1783. But Chauncy persevered; and in 1784 set forth an anonymous, but hardly unacknowledged, book, —"The Mystery hid from Ages . . . or, the Salvation of all Men,"—defending his previous positions with great elaboration. To this work the younger Edwards gave an exceedingly able answer in 1790.

These outcroppings of Universalist sentiments were a sign of the general ferment of the times succeeding the Revolutionary War, and though not very extensive in the numbers affected, they were widely scattered, and created much alarm by appearing in the most unexpected places.

Such an instance was that of Rev. Joseph Huntington, of Coventry, Conn., who died, in 1794, supposedly in sympathy with his ministerial brethren, but whose posthumous "Calvinism Improved" of 1796 showed him a Universalist,—the "improvement" being the extension of the divine elective decree to include all mankind.

The title of Huntington's work shows the general doctrinal attitude of the early Universalists. While some believers in ultimate restoration, like Chauncy, were not Calvinists, many of this way of thinking were staunchly Calvinistic, and drew from the "satisfaction" theory of the atonement the strongest argument either for the immediate blessedness of all men at death or their final redemption. The younger Edwards thus stated their position in his "Brief Observations on the Doctrine of Universal Salvation" of 1784: "The doctrine is, that all mankind, without exception but none of the devils, will be saved; that this universal salvation will take place immediately after the general judgment, so that after that time there will be no punishment of any individual of the human race; that this deliverance from future punishment is obtained in the way of the most strict justice; that Christ having paid the whole debt, for all mankind, it is not consistent with justice that any man should be punished for sin in his own person." This position was naturally more difficult for the Edwardeans than for the Old Calvinists to answer, so long as the "satisfaction" theory of the atonement, historically characteristic of Calvinism, was maintained. The Old Calvinist could reply that all for whom Christ died would be saved; but that his atonement was limited, being only for the elect. But while the Edwardean maintained the doctrines of election and future punishment as vigorously as the Old Calvinist, he had also asserted, since Bellamy published his "True

Religion" in 1750, that the atonement was general, Christ having died for all men. It was to meet the difficulties of this situation that the younger Edwards introduced a theory of the atonement novel to New England.

This new Edwardean theory did not indeed spring from the exigencies which brought it out. Its principles lie back in the teachings of the elder Edwards and his contemporaries, though the full meaning of those principles was not perceived by them. In their exaltation of the sovereignty of God they had taught that not only the provision of redemption in general, but the rescue of each soul in particular, was a work of divine sovereignty. This position was a departure from the spirit of the Old Calvinism, which represented God as sovereign in election and in providing atonement, but held that after Christ had rendered satisfaction for each of the elect the salvation of the individual whose debt was thus paid was an act of justice, not of sovereignty. And taking this departure the Edwardeans must inevitably have reached eventually the position that the sinner's debt was not literally discharged by the sufferings of Christ, and hence that the atonement was not a "satisfaction." How certainly the minds of the theologians of the "New Divinity" school were moving in the direction reached by the younger Edwards is shown by the treatise entitled "The Scripture Doctrine of the Atonement," which West finished in the spring of 1785 and to which allusion has already been made. In this volume West maintained that the atonement was designed to manifest the divine attributes, to show the disposition of God's mind toward men for the breach of his law, and that it involved "no obligation on the justice of God, to pardon and save the sinner."

The full statement of the later Edwardean position was given in three sermons preached by the younger Edwards at New Haven in October, 1785, and printed the same year, under the title of "The Necessity of Atonement." In these discourses he maintained that "Christ has not, in the literal and proper sense, paid the debt for us." God forgives the sinner his sin freely. The atonement did not satisfy "distributive justice," i.e., the reward or punishment of the individual according to his "personal moral character or conduct." "This atonement constitutes no part of the personal character of the sinner: but his personal character is essentially the same, as it would have been, if Christ had made no atonement. And as the sinner, in pardon, is treated, not only more favourably, but infinitely more favourably, than is correspondent to his personal character, his pardon is wholly an act of infinite grace."

But "justice" may be used in another sense than "distributive." In "general" or "public" justice "any thing is just, which is right and best to be done"; and in this sense "the pardon of the sinner is entirely an act of justice. It is undoubtedly most conducive to the divine glory, and the general good of the created system." Though pardon is thus wholly an act of grace, an atonement was necessary in order that pardon could be bestowed. It is essential for the wise government of God and the best good of the universe that "the authority of the divine law" should be maintained. This can only be accomplished by the punishment of all offenders; or by an atonement "which, to the purposes of supporting the authority of the divine law, and the dignity and consistency of the divine government, is equivalent to the punishment of the sinner, according to the literal threatening of the law." Such an atonement Christ has made. By it "general justice to the Deity and to the universe is satisfied. That is done by the death of Christ which supports the authority of the law, and renders it consistent with the glory of God and the good of the whole system, to pardon the sinner." By it also "an exhibition" is "made in the death and sufferings of Christ, of the punishment to which the sinner is justly liable." The atonement flows from the divine benevolence; it enables God to pardon whomsoever he will, on whatever conditions he sees are wise to impose; it shows that the withholding of pardon is no act of injustice. The atonement is general. Christ's death makes it possible for God to pardon all men, it does not make it necessary for him to pardon all.

This theory, often called the "governmental" or "New England" view, resembles in many respects that advanced more than a century and a half before by the great Dutch Arminian Hugo Grotius. It differs from his theory chiefly in the clearer emphasis which it lays on the atonement as revealing the heinousness of sin, and in its presentation of benevolence as the central thought in the atonement itself. Developed by Smalley, Maxcy, Emmons, Griffin, Burge, Weeks, and Professor Park, it became speedily the dominant view in American Congregationalism; and though other conceptions of the work of Christ have gained a considerable currency within the last forty years, it is still the most widely accepted theory in the Congregational churches.

All of the Edwardean leaders were independent thinkers, and no one fully reproduced another. But with the two Edwardean divines who are now to be spoken of,—Emmons and Dwight,—the New Divinity may be said to have divided into two subschools, the one extreme and moving in the direction which Hopkins had pointed out, having Emmons as its representative; the other, of which Dwight was the leader, moderate and conciliatory.

Nathanael Emmons was a native of East Haddam, Conn.,

born in 1745, and a graduate of Yale in the class of 1767. His ministerial studies were in part under Smalley, but he became a warm friend of Hopkins; and from Hopkins, more than from Smalley, the pattern of his theology was derived. His only pastorate, from 1773 to 1827, was at Franklin, Mass., where he died at great age in 1840. A man of enormous industry, of much wit, and of exceeding keenness of mind, Emmons's best work was as a trainer of candidates for the ministry, of whom it is thought not less than a hundred passed under his molding touch. Of his influence on the development of Congregational polity there will be occasion later to speak. No man of his age was more widely a force in the religious life of New England.

In his theology Emmons developed yet further the positions taken by Hopkins, and which were known by the Hopkinsians as "Consistent Calvinism." Holiness and sin are "exercises" of the will; and though Emmons appears to have believed that some permanent substratum lies under these exercises, he so emphasized the idea that the mind exists solely in activity as to convey the impression that man's spiritual nature is simply a chain of acts or "exercises," each perfectly good or wholly bad. In these acts the will is free in the sense that it acts voluntarily, though the ultimate cause of all "exercises" is the divine efficiency. "If men always act under a divine operation, then they always act of necessity, though not of compulsion." "Though God does work in men to repent, to believe, and to obey, yet God does not repent, nor believe, nor obey, but the persons themselves on whom he operates." Though the efficiency of God is the cause of all action, yet "no created object . . . bears the least resemblance of the Deity simply because he made it. . . . It is, therefore, as consistent with the moral rectitude of the

Deity to produce sinful, as holy, exercises in the minds of men. His operations and their voluntary exercises are totally distinct."

Emmons, unlike Hopkins, represents man as active in regeneration. He is likewise active in sin, and derives no guilt from Adam, "for moral depravity consists in the free, voluntary exercises of a moral agent; and of consequence cannot be transmitted by one person to another." But "in consequence of Adam's first transgression, God now brings his posterity into the world in a state of moral depravity." Even in infants God "produces those moral exercises . . . in which moral depravity properly and essentially consists." Emmons asserted election and reprobation in the strongest terms. His Calvinism was of the Supralapsarian type. Yet he affirmed none the less distinctly that sin is the voluntary active transgression of known law, even in the case of young children, and that sinners should be exhorted to immediate repentance and holy love. Emmons wholly agreed with Hopkins that the essence of sin is selfishness, and that of holiness, disinterested love or benevolence.

In Emmons the Edwardean school reached its extremest development in the direction in which Hopkins had led the way; in Dwight it appeared in a much more moderate and conciliatory type of theology. Timothy Dwight was born at Northampton in 1752, and was through his mother a grandson of the elder Edwards. Like almost all of the Edwardean leaders, he graduated at Yale, his class being that of 1769. After service as tutor in the college, and as chaplain in the Revolutionary War, succeeded by a residence of several years in his native town, Dwight became pastor in Greenfield parish in the town of Fairfield, Conn., where he remained till his call to the presidency of Yale College in 1795. His election brought about the ascendency of Edwardeanism in that institution. Here he fulfilled a distinguished administration till his death, in 1817; but, what is of more moment for our narrative, here he also occupied the professorship of divinity, which required him to assume the pastorate of the college church and to give regular instruction to the students in theology, preaching a series of doctrinal sermons on Sunday mornings, designed to cover the outline of his system of divinity in four years. His own powerful personality, warm piety, and great ability gave these discourses wide popularity and much influence, not only over the students of the college, but with the Christian public. As "Theology Explained and Defended," they were published in 1818, and again in 1823.

Dwight earnestly opposed Hopkins's and Emmons's theory of the divine efficiency as the cause of sinful choices, and affirmed that their speculations led toward a Pantheism much like that of Spinoza. Unlike the more strenuous teachers of the Edwardean school also, he urged "that Ministers ought to advise, and exhort, sinners to use the Means of Grace." He held distinctly that as long as a man remains unregenerate all his acts are sinful; but on the question, "Whether the man, who performs the act merely, is any better for performing it, than if he had neglected or refused to perform it," Dwight took Old Calvinist, rather than Hopkinsian, ground, answering "that, supposing the man's disposition substantially the same in both cases, he is less sinful when he performs the act, than when he neglects or refuses to perform it." "In his preaching and advice, a minister is not to confine himself to the mere enjoining of Faith and Repentance; but is to extend them to any other conduct in itself proper to be pursued; while he universally teaches these great Christian duties, as the immediate end of all his preaching." Nor is it counseling sinners to sin to exhort them to pray and read the Bible, since Christ and the prophets directed those who were obviously unregenerate to call upon God.

A further divergence appeared between Dwight and Emmons. The latter taught that holiness or sin consists in acts of choice or "exercises," and was understood to hold that the soul was simply a chain of "exercises"; hence his system was often called the "exercise scheme." To Dwight's thinking something possessing moral qualities underlies choice; "there is a cause of moral action in Intelligent beings, frequently indicated by the words Principle, Affections, Habits, Nature, Tendency, Propensity, and several others." Elsewhere he speaks of this cause as a "disposition," and remarks: "Of the metaphysical nature of this cause I am ignorant. But its existence is, in my own view, certainly proved by its effects." This "disposition" is the cause of righteous or sinful choices; and regeneration consists in "a Relish for Spiritual objects, communicated to it by the power of the Holy Ghost." Yet, "after Regeneration the native character of man still remains; his relish for sinful pursuits and enjoyments still continues; and his relish for spiritual pursuits and enjoyments is never perfected on this side of the grave."

This conception that regeneration consists in the impartation to the disposition of a new relish or "taste," thus advanced by Dwight against Emmons's thought of regeneration as the production of "holy exercises" or "only love, which is activity itself," was elaborated, largely independently, by a contemporary of Dwight, Rev. Asa Burton, pastor at Thetford, Vt., from 1779 to 1836, and the instructor of nearly sixty ministerial candidates. In Burton's teaching it became known as the "taste scheme."

These divergent tendencies manifested in the Edwardean school by the close of the eighteenth century were continued and intensified in the early part of the nineteenth; and resulted, after further development by Nathaniel W. Taylor and others, in the creation in Connecticut of two theological seminaries, representative, in their early life at least, of the somewhat opposing theories of later Edwardeanism. Of these movements there will be occasion later to speak.

The Edwardean movement was a theological development of great force and originality; but its impulse was not primarily speculative. The New England mind has always been essentially practical. It cannot have escaped the reader's observation that the Liberal and the Edwardean movements alike had to do with what may not improperly be called the more practical doctrines of theology. Questions of the proper use of "means," of the nature of conversion, of the extent of human freedom and responsibility, of the essence of that holiness which is characteristic of the Christian life, of the relation of the atonement to the forgiveness of the individual transgressor's sins, constituted the chief themes of these debates. But practical as were these topics of speculation, it may be questioned whether the influence of the Edwardean party over the churches was not greater by reason of its warm, evangelic life, than by reason of its doctrinal discussions. The Edwardean leaders were not retired students, they were all of them pastors intimately associated with the life of the churches. They preached human responsibility and immediate repentance as New England had never heard these doctrines preached, even if they coupled this preaching with a high assertion of election and necessity. They advocated revival methods; they represented that which was best in the Whitefieldian movement. They urged a strenuous, self-forgetful type of Christian life. Edwardeanism was not merely, one is almost ready to say not chiefly, a doctrinal system; it was a moral and spiritual force.

The leaders of the Edwardean party were of Connecticut origin, and theirs gradually became the dominant influence in Connecticut and western Massachusetts. Unlike eastern Massachusetts, Liberal Theology of the Arminian type had not found much lodgment in the churches of western New England before the Edwardean movement became powerful. English writers were less read, the Episcopal Church had some existence in Connecticut and afforded a refuge for those of Arminian belief and strong dislike of emotional preaching. The separation between the Old Calvinists and the Edwardeans in western New England was long exceedingly bitter; but by 1758 the "New Light" sympathizers of both classes had gained control of the ecclesiastical machinery of Connecticut, and the most energetic and influential of the "New Lights" were the Edwardeans. Then, too, Edwardeanism, though largely a Connecticut product, had its leading expounders of the extremer type, like Hopkins and Emmons, outside of Connecticut borders. In Connecticut the younger Edwards and Dwight presented its principles in a form more conciliatory to the Old Calvinists; and though Old Calvinism continued, by the beginning of the present century Connecticut and western Massachusetts were thoroughly leavened with Edwardean views and methods. Edwardean opinions also spread widely among the Presbyterians of the northern Middle States, though opposed wherever Scotch or Protestant Irish influence was strong by an older form of Calvinism.

On the other hand, Liberal Theology of the type of Mayhew and Chauncy grew in influence in eastern Massachusetts till the end of the eighteenth century, and led to a large ignoring of the characteristic doctrines of Calvinism by many preachers who did not go to any such lengths as the two Boston ministers whose names have been cited. But though powerfully influential, Liberal Theology never gained so full control over eastern Massachusetts as Edwardeanism obtained in western New England.

The half-century following the Great Awakening was a period of spiritual deadness, and owing to this low religious life the growing divergence between the influences which were molding eastern and western New England was not as obvious as would otherwise have been the case; but the cleft between Liberalism and Edwardeanism ran deep, and the student who looks back upon this epoch can see that it was certain that if a new and general interest in religion should arise or the supporters of either type of theology should carry an aggressive campaign into territories where the other was strong, an open separation could be the only result. These conditions appeared in the last decade of the eighteenth and the opening years of the nineteenth centuries, and the consequence was the Unitarian division, of which some account will be given later in our story.

But while eastern and western New England were thus drifting really if not recognizedly apart, as the eighteenth century drew toward its end, the feeling of fellowship between the Edwardeans and those of the Presbyterians who sympathized with their views was constantly increasing. The old interest in polity which had marked the seventeenth century had largely been driven out by the new zeal for doctrinal debate. Doctrinal agreement made the people of western New England, and especially the Edwardeans, regard the differences in polity between Presbyterianism and Connecticut Consociationism as immaterial. Several of the Edwardean leaders, like the younger Edwards and Dwight, labored to secure the more intimate union of the two denominations; and in general the Edwardeans contributed little to the development of Congregational polity.

There was, however, one conspicuous exception. To Nathanael Emmons Congregational polity is more indebted than to any other leader of the eighteenth century, not excepting John Wise, and his thought ran in the same direction which Wise had already indicated. Emmons wholly abandoned the aristocratic conception of Congregationalism typical of the seventeenth century, which Wise had opposed. In his incisive style he declared that a Congregational church is "a pure democracy, which places every member of the church upon a level, and gives him perfect liberty with order." In a Congregational Church, in all matters of business, the pastor "is but a mere moderator; and, in respect to voting, stands upon the same ground as a private brother." Every church is wholly self-governing: "One church has as much power as another;" and "there is no appeal from the authority of a particular church to any higher ecclesiastical tribunal."

Emmons carried his doctrines of ecclesiastical independence to an extreme, as when he opposed the establishment of a State association in Massachusetts with the assertion: "Associationism leads to Consociationism; Consociationism leads to Presbyterianism; Presbyterianism leads to Episcopacy; Episcopacy leads to Roman Catholicism; and Roman Catholicism is an ultimate fact." Modern Congregationalism does not believe that voluntary organizations of a non-judicial character meeting at stated intervals lead to such a chain of results any more than it believes that the soul is a chain of "exercises"; but Emmons's teaching as to the absolute democracy of a Congregational church is the view of modern Congregationalism.

The development of the Congregational churches

throughout the eighteenth century was such as to make natural the teachings of Emmons regarding polity. The first two generations on American soil saw the growth of the principle of fellowship. That principle then became so imbedded in American Congregationalism that it has continued, and found constant manifestation down to the present day. But from the time of the Great Awakening, if not earlier, this centralizing tendency was supplanted by an emphasis on local independence. Many causes contributed to this result; the growth of democracy in political thought culminating in national independence, the doctrinal divisions, the differences of opinion as to method arising out of the revivals, the rapidly lessening interference of the civil governments in ecclesiastical affairs, all tended to make the local church free and democratic; while the new impulses toward voluntary union springing out of missionary efforts at home and abroad, which have tended to centralize modern Congregationalism in united endeavor, did not begin to appear till the very close of the eighteenth century.

CHAPTER IX.

THE EVANGELICAL REVIVAL.

WHILE the later theological movements described in the last chapter were in progress the great period of emigration had begun which was to carry thousands of the sons and daughters of New England beyond the borders of the original colonies, and ultimately to plant Congregational churches across the continent to the Pacific. But at first the "new West" was close at hand.

Vermont was the earliest of these territories to be opened up for settlement. Situated on the route between the older colonies and Canada, it was not a favorable region for husbandry till the conquest of the French possessions along the St. Lawrence in 1759–60 had removed the constant danger of attack from the northward. On the conclusion of the old French war, the few military settlements already existing in the territory were speedily supplanted by numerous peaceful colonies; and so preponderatingly was this immigration of Connecticut origin that a Vermont convention in 1777 contemplated the bestowal of the name "New Connecticut" on the region. Naturally, Congregationalism came with the more religious of the immigrants, and in 1762 the first church of Vermont was formed at Bennington. Other churches were organized in rapid succession,—Newbury in 1764, Westminster in 1767, Guilford and Windsor in 1768, Brattleboro in 1770, Chester and Thetford in 1773, Newfane in 1774, and Putney and Marlboro in 1776. The Revolution checked the growth of

Vermont for a time, but at its close, and especially after the admission of Vermont as the fourteenth State of the Union in 1791, the increase of population was very rapid and the multiplication of churches correspondingly great. By 1800 seventy-four Congregational churches had come into being in Vermont, and they had been united since 1796 in a "General Convention." The Congregational desire for education was exhibited in the granting of a charter to the University of Vermont in 1791 and to Middlebury College in 1800,—institutions largely Congregational in officers and membership, though undenominational in their constitutions.

A few Congregational churches were founded in eastern New York, besides several on Long Island, long before the Revolution. Thus churches of more or less permanence came into being at East Chester in 1665, at Bedford in 1680, at Gloversville in 1752, and elsewhere. But the settlement of central and western New York did not begin in force till after peace had been made with Great Britain. From that time onward emigration from Massachusetts and Connecticut across the Hudson was rapid. In 1791 Congregational churches were formed at Clinton, Paris, and Westmoreland, one at Franklin followed in 1792, others at Walton, Hamden, and Whitestown in 1793. Others yet more westward speedily followed, as at Madison and East Bloomfield in 1796, Lisle in 1797, Camden in 1798, and Canandaigua in 1799.

Yet the most westward of these new towns in which ecclesiastical beginnings were thus made was much eastward of the remoter settlements of the same period beyond the borders of New York. In April, 1788, a party of New Englanders began the first plantation in Ohio, at Marietta. Here worship was maintained from the beginning, and here on December 6, 1796, the first Congregational church of Ohio, and the first in the "Old Northwest," was gathered. The portion of Ohio most distinctively of New England settlement was, however, the southern shore of Lake Erie,—Connecticut's "Western Reserve." The year which saw the laying of ecclesiastical foundations at Marietta witnessed the beginnings of Cleveland; but the first church in the "Reserve" was that formed among the immigrants from Pennsylvania at Youngstown in 1799. The earliest Congregational church, and the second of any denomination in the "Reserve," was that of Austinburg, which dates from 1801. Under the impulse of immigration from New England and the Middle States Ohio rapidly grew, and by its admission into the Union in 1803 numbered about 40,000 inhabitants,—a population which had risen in 1810 to 230,000; and soon after 1830 reached a million.

The multiplication of churches which kept pace with this rapid spread of new settlements could not have been effected had it not been for the stirrings of missionary zeal in the Congregational churches of New England and the Presbyterian bodies of the Middle States. Connecticut, which contributed so largely to this outpouring, early felt this impulse. The General Association of that colony, at its meeting in Mansfield in June, 1774, voted in favor of raising funds and sending missionaries to "ye Settlements now forming in the Wilderness to the Westward & Northwestward," i.e., in New York and Vermont. The response of the churches was favorable, and in September of the same year the Association decided that two pastors should go forth on a tour of "5 or 6 months" "if the Committee are able to provide for their support so long,"—the journey to begin in the spring of 1775. But by the time the missionaries should have set forth the skirmish at Lexington had turned popular thought in other channels, and the

Association in June, 1775, had to record "that the perplexed & melancholly State of public Affairs has been a Discouragement to this Design, & a Reason why the Collections have not been brought in, as was expected." But some contributions were received, even in the dark days of the Revolutionary struggle; and in 1780 the General Association asked two pastors to go as missionaries to Vermont. Futher discussion followed in 1788 and in 1791; and in 1792 a missionary was approved. At the same time legislative countenance was sought for soliciting contributions. So successful were these appeals that in 1793 eight settled pastors were named as missionaries to go forth on tours of four months each, to receive four and a half dollars as their weekly compensation, together with an allowance of four dollars a week to supply the pulpits which their absence left vacant. The undertaking, launched with so much difficulty, was now pushed with vigor.

As the missionary labors of the Connecticut General Association grew more extensive, its own conception of the work magnified, and in 1797 it consulted the local Associations of the State regarding the formation of a Missionary Society. Encouraged by the response, the General Association on June 19, 1798, organized itself as a Missionary Society,—the first voluntary Congregational missionary society on this side of the Atlantic,—"to Christianize the Heathen in North America, and to support and promote Christian Knowledge in the new settlements within the United States." This organization was followed by the establishment of the "Connecticut Evangelical Magazine" in 1800, a periodical designed to promote acquaintance with missions, as well as for theologic discussion; and its profits were assigned to the Missionary Society. In 1802 the society was chartered by the Connecticut legislature.

These missionary movements in Connecticut led to similar results in Massachusetts. In 1798 the "Congregational Missionary Society in the Counties of Berkshire and Columbia" was formed, embracing representatives of the churches of western Massachusetts and of the New York county immediately adjacent. And on May 28, 1799, the "Massachusetts Missionary Society" came into being, under the presidency of that Edwardean champion, Nathanael Emmons, an organization identical in aim with the "Missionary Society of Connecticut." Like its Connecticut prototype, it soon began the publication of a periodical, the "Massachusetts Missionary Magazine," in 1803. This Massachusetts society was wholly the work of the Edwardeans and chiefly of their Hopkinsian wing. Two years later, September, 1801, the "New Hampshire Missionary Society" came into being, and in 1807 the General Convention of Vermont began acting as a missionary society.

In addition to these State organizations several smaller bodies of a missionary character were formed in this period. In October, 1800, the "Boston Female Society for Missionary Purposes," the first missionary organization of women, was constituted. Four years later the "Female Cent Institution" was founded in New Hampshire,—an association of pious women, pledged to contribute each a cent a week to the promotion of missions, which was extensively copied in other New England States. In 1802 Hampshire County in Massachusetts saw the beginnings of a local home missionary society; a similar local body was formed in eastern New Hampshire as the "Piscataqua Missionary Society" in 1804; and in 1807 representatives of the churches of the Massachusetts counties of Worcester and Middlesex joined in an "Evangelical Missionary Society." A similar impulse led to the formation of the "Vermont Religious Tract Society" in 1808, the "Connecticut Bible Society" in 1809, and the "Massachusetts Bible Society" during the same year. The development of these numerous organizations, many of which were not indeed peculiar to Congregationalism, revealed clearly the ready adaptability of the polity to meet new spiritual conditions by voluntary organization and effort.

Under the charge of these new agencies of evangelization, the Congregational churches began that extensive sending forth of laborers into the newer portions of the country which has continued to the present day, and which has done so much to impart a Christian character to the civilization of the great West. But these efforts soon gave rise to an important question of interdenominational comity, the solution of which profoundly affected the history of Congregationalism during the first half of the nineteenth century. The immigration into Vermont was almost exclusively of New England origin, and hence Congregational institutions were established in that State without question; but in New York, and even more in Ohio, the emigrant from New England encountered settlers from the old Middle Colonies whose training was in Presbyterianism and for whose spiritual instruction the Presbyterian Church was making efforts at the same time that the Congregational churches were sending forth missionaries. Presbyterian and Congregational missionaries met on the same ground, and labored for the same communities. It seemed desirable that some system of coöperation should be established.

This desire was the more natural since the Edwardean party, and to some extent the Old Calvinists, of Connecticut and western Massachusetts had for fifty years been coming into closer affiliation with the Presbyterians of the Middle States who largely sympathized with their doctrinal views. The elder Edwards was president of Princeton College, the younger Edwards was its graduate, nearly half the trustees of that institution at the time of Edwards's incumbency had had their education at Yale. The peculiar consociational system of Connecticut inclined many in that State to look upon the Connecticut churches as more allied in government with the Presbyterian bodies than with the churches of Massachusetts which held to the "Cambridge Platform." This feeling found frequent public expression. The churches of Connecticut were often designated by their own pastors and members as "Presbyterian." The Hartford North Association, in 1799, formally declared that the constitution of the Connecticut churches "contains the essentials of the church of Scotland, or Presbyterian Church in America." Even the General Association spoke of a plan offered in 1788 by which Presbyterians and Congregationalists should come into more intimate fellowship as "a Scheme for an Union of the Presbyterians in America," and described the "Saybrook Platform" in 1805 as the "constitution of the Presbyterian Church in Connecticut." More formal interrelation was naturally established. As a barrier against the introduction of an American episcopate,—an exercise of English governmental authority much feared by the colonies just prior to the Revolution,—an annual joint convention of representatives of the Synod of New York and Philadelphia and the Associations of Connecticut met from 1766 to 1775. After the war, a more intimate union was promoted, especially by the Edwardean leader Timothy Dwight, which, after discussion and correspondence in 1788, 1790, and 1791, resulted in an agreement between the Presbyterian General Assembly and the Connecticut General Association that delegates from each organization should regularly be sent to the session of the other body; and, at the request of the Presbyterians in 1794, these representatives were given full power of voting in the meetings to which they were accredited. Within the next few years a similar exchange of delegates was effected between the Presbyterian General Assembly and the State organizations of Massachusetts, Vermont, and New Hampshire. This arrangement continued in full force till the rupture in the Presbyterian body in 1837.

Relations between the two denominations being so friendly, and polity having been so little regarded during the doctrinal discussions which had prevailed since the Great Awakening, it was natural that union in missionary enterprises should be looked upon with favor. The motion to that effect originated, apparently, with the younger Jonathan Edwards, in the Connecticut General Association of 1800, where Edwards, then president of Union College, sat as a representative of the Presbyterian General Assembly. Thus moved, the Association empowered its delegates to the General Assembly to enter into negotiations "to promote harmony and to establish, as far as possible, an uniform system of Church government, between those habitants of the new Settlements, who are attached to the Presbyterian form of church Government, and those who are attached to the congregational form." The result was the adoption by the General Assembly in May, 1801, and by the Connecticut General Association in June of the same year, of the famous "Plan of Union." This agreement provided that missionaries should be directed to "promote mutual forbearance" between the adherents of the respective polities where they should labor; that churches of Congregational or Presbyterian preferences should continue to conduct their discipline in accordance with their chosen polity, even where their pastors were of the opposite type; that all cases of dispute between a pastor and a church of opposite inclinations should be determined, if both parties agreed to such a course, by the Presbytery or Association of which the minister was a member, but if agreement was impossible then by a mutual council of equal numbers of Congregationalists and of Presbyterians; that in mixed churches a "standing committee" of communicants should be chosen by the church to administer discipline, one member of which, chosen by the committee itself, should "have the same right to sit and act in the Presbytery as a ruling elder of the Presbyterian church"; and that appeals from the decision of such a "standing committee" should be allowed, in case of Presbyterian members of a mixed church, to the Presbytery, or in case of Congregational members, "to the body of the male communicants of the church." Appeals beyond the Presbytery were forbidden to members of a mixed church without the consent of the church itself; but an appeal might be taken by a Congregational member to the judgment of a "mutual council." The "Plan" clearly contemplated the formation of Associations as well as Presbyteries on the soil where it was to be put in operation.

This "Plan," which was afterward approved by other General Associations in New England besides that of Connecticut, continued in full force until repudiated by the "Old School" wing of the Presbyterian body in the General Assembly of 1837; and was then maintained in conjunction with the "New School" body until abandoned by the Congregationalists at the Albany Convention in 1852. It was a wholly honorable arrangement, and was designed to be entirely fair to both parties. Both Congregationalists and Presbyterians sacrificed important features of their polities in it. Its framers seem to have had little thought that the scanty settlements to which it was to be applied would grow to be among the strongest of American communities, and that what was well enough as a compromise arrangement by which feeble bands of Christians could be associated on the frontier would have a different look when the churches formed under it grew vigorous.

In its actual workings, the "Plan" operated in favor of the Presbyterians. They were nearer the scene of missionary labor; their denominational spirit was more assertive than that of the Congregationalism of the day; their Presbyteries were rapidly spread over the missionary districts, and the natural desire for fellowship where the points of separation seemed so few led Congregational ministers to accept the welcome offered therein. Moreover, the doctrinal discussions of New England and the development of Connecticut consociationism had created a widespread feeling in the older Congregational churches that Congregationalism could not thrive in unformed communities. It required the successful demonstration of experience wholly to remove this misconception from the New England mind; and even when western Congregationalism had shown its right to be, the rise of the Arminianly inclined theology of Oberlin, and other evidences of an independent spirit, led to unjust suspicions of infection with doctrinal unsoundnesses and somewhat retarded the growth of full cordiality of feeling between the churches of the East and those in the West who were struggling to maintain a pure type of Congregationalism. No wonder, then, that during the first half of the nineteenth century the Presbyterian body on the whole gained by the "Plan of Union"; and that its ultimate result was, if one may accept the figures given by the late Rev. Dr. A. H. Ross,—and no one has devoted more thorough study to the subject,—the transformation of "over two thousand churches, which were in origin and usages Congregational, into Presbyterian churches." It was under this "Plan" that the religious foundations of western New York, of Ohio, of Illinois, and of Michigan were largely laid.

This outflow of missionary activity was in part illustrative of that new manifestation of interest in the advancement of the Redeemer's kingdom characteristic of all Anglo-Saxon Christendom at the close of the eighteenth century; but its immediate apparent cause, aside from the burden of opportunity laid on our churches by the emigrations, was the new era of revivals which began soon after the long period of political distraction had been brought to an end by the adoption of the federal constitution. The excesses and excitement of the Great Awakening had been followed, as early as 1744, by a period of spiritual lethargy which made the era of the Revolutionary struggle the epoch of lowest spiritual vitality that our churches have ever experienced. Doctrinal discussion, as has been seen, was extensive. On the whole the ministry was brought into sympathy with a conception of the beginnings of the Christian life which made revivals desired, and which laid primary emphasis on "conversion" rather than on Christian nurture, though the opposite tendency was also developed in a considerable party in eastern Massachusetts; but the spiritual life of the churches was little affected. Slight popular interest was felt in religious questions, and ministers of the most opposing views associated in the same ecclesiastical fellowships and freely exchanged pulpits with one another.

This spiritual lethargy was ended by the new religious awakenings. No such general excitement marked the new revival era as had characterized the Great Awakening. No preacher of wide-extended fame, like Whitefield, aroused universal feelings of approval or of hostility for his methods. Bodily manifestations of nervous excitement and imagined visions were almost wholly absent; but the movement was continuous, far-reaching, and vastly more valuable in its permanent results than the Great Awakening. In 1791 a revival movement occurred in North Yarmouth, Me.; in 1792, Lee, Mass., East Haddam and Lyme, Conn., were similarly visited. The spiritual quickening thus quietly begun extended in increasing force all over New England, the Middle States, and the new West. Rev. Dr. Edward D. Griffin, then pastor at New Hartford, Conn., recorded of this period: "I saw a continued succession of heavenly sprinklings . . . in Connecticut, until, in 1799, I could stand at my door in New Hartford, . . . and number fifty or sixty contiguous congregations laid down in one field of divine wonders, and as many more in different parts of New England." These spiritual awakenings, though local, were often of great strength, and they appeared here and there in New England and beyond her borders year after year. The powerful revivals of 1799 were prolonged at least till 1805, and then, though lessened, did not wholly cease. In 1802 Yale College was greatly stirred. The years 1807–08 were seasons of quickening in Rhode Island and western Massachusetts. From 1815 to 1818 a sixth of all the towns in Connecticut were visited, Massachusetts and New Hampshire were much moved, while in Rutland County, Vt., there was almost a spiritual revolution. Again in 1820–23 extensive revival movements appeared in New England and the West, and once more in 1826–27; but these were surpassed in turn by the religious interest of 1830–31. Yet later, in 1841–42, and in 1857–58, very extensive awakenings took place. Thus, for two generations, the revival became the characteristic feature of Congregational religious life. These manifestations of religious interest had a distinct character. They were prevailingly accompanied by a profound conviction of sin, a sense of peace through submission to God, and a conscious change of purpose. The way was prepared for them in New England and the form of experience which they exhibited was determined in large measure by the doctrine and preaching of the Edwardeans; and the revivals in turn made the Edwardean theology and its methods almost the exclusive type among evangelical Congregationalists during the later two thirds of the period of their continuance. But the revivals were far more than the result of any special pattern of doctrine or method of Christian work; they were a general and profound influence, quickening and uplifting the religious life of the nation as a whole, and their effect on Congregationalism was almost that of a new birth.

The revivals stimulated all forms of religious activity. They led to the introduction into New England of the Sunday-school, which Robert Raikes had originated at Gloucester, England, in 1780; they brought about, speedily after their beginning, the extensive adoption of the evening prayer-meeting in the larger towns, which had heretofore been looked upon with distrust. But three of the consequences of this revival epoch, all manifested early in its history, are worthy of more minute attention,—the extension of missionary enterprises, the Unitarian separation, and the new systems of theologic instruction.

Of the beginnings of home missionary activity enough has already been said in speaking of the westward extension of Congregationalism at the close of the Revolution and of its coöperation with Presbyterianism. It has been seen that though the Connecticut General Association showed a missionary spirit as early as 1774, its work did not begin on an extensive scale till 1793, after the revivals had commenced, and the rapid organization of missionary societies in the New England States was from 1798 to

1807, when the first great wave of revival impulse was at its height. It was natural that when the thoughts of so many were turned toward the evangelization of the newer parts of their own country, the vision of missionary labor on a yet larger scale should rise before a few.

Doubtless the example and appeals of the English foreign missionary associations, especially of the "London Missionary Society," which came into being in 1795, prepared American religious sentiment to favor foreign missionary activity; but, as far as any single human origin may be assigned, its inception in the Congregational churches was due to Samuel John Mills,—"the father of foreign mission work in Christian America." Mills was born in 1783 at Torringford, Conn., where his father, of the same name, was pastor. The father was a man well fitted to give a missionary impulse to his son. An Edwardean preacher of power, he was one of the missionary pastors sent out by the Connecticut General Association in 1793, and an editor of the "Connecticut Evangelical Magazine"; while his own church experienced remarkable revivals in 1793 and 1799. Brought up thus in a missionary atmosphere, the younger Mills entered Williams College in 1806, and here in 1808 he organized "The Brethren," a little association "to effect, in the persons of its members, a mission or missions to the heathen." In the spring of 1810, following his graduation in 1809, Mills and his society were transferred to the newly instituted Theological Seminary at Andover; and there his missionary zeal enkindled or confirmed the consecration of at least six of his student associates. These were Adoniram Judson, a graduate of Brown; Samuel Newell of Harvard, Samuel Nott of Union; besides Luther Rice, Gordon Hall, and James Richards, with whom Mills had been associated at Williams College. These friends, after consultation with the Andover professors and with Rev. Messrs. Samuel Spring and Samuel Worcester, determined to apply to the General Association of Massachusetts,—a ministerial body similar to the ancient General Association of Connecticut, which had been formed in 1803 and which represented the Old Calvinists and Edwardeans of Massachusetts rather than the Liberals,—for support and direction in their chosen work. A memorial drawn up by Judson and signed only by Nott, Mills, Newell, and himself, lest a greater number of candidates should imperil the enterprise by affrighting the churches, was presented to the Association at Bradford, Mass., on June 27, and on June 29, 1810, that body instituted the "American Board of Commissioners for Foreign Missions," to put the request of their petitioners into execution. From the first it was intended that the Board should be more than a Massachusetts enterprise, though it was not at first planned to go beyond the borders of Congregationalism for its membership; and therefore of the nine original commissioners chosen by the Massachusetts Association, four were from Connecticut, including Governor Treadwell and President Timothy Dwight, the other five being Massachusetts men and numbering among them Rev. Messrs. Samuel Spring and Samuel Worcester, and William Bartlett, the benefactor of Andover Seminary. The first meeting of this Board was held and its organization effected at the house of Rev. Noah Porter, father of the president of Yale, at Farmington, Conn., on September 5, 1810.

The undertaking thus inaugurated met with the immediate approval of the Congregational churches; the foreign missionary cause took a strong hold on their affections, and led in a comparatively short time to large consecration of men and money to the work. But it was not easy to send the first missionaries to the heathen. It was uncertain at the beginning how far the churches would support the work. The great European wars, and the struggle between England and the United States which began in 1812, but of which the premonitory signs had been visible for some time before hostilities commenced, made the problem of transportation to India, whither the first missionaries desired to go, one of difficulty and their reception uncertain. Even the Massachusetts legislature, from which a charter was obtained in 1812, was persuaded with some difficulty to create a corporation to send money out of the country. It was not till February, 1812, after an encouraging bequest of $30,000 had been received from Mrs. Mary Norris of Salem, Mass., that the pioneer missionaries, Judson, Newell, Nott, Hall, and Rice, were sent forth to India. Mills, who had been so instrumental in awakening a missionary spirit, was unable to go with his friends, though he did a noble work as a home missionary and an organizer of Bible societies, and died at sea, in 1818, off the coast of Africa, whither he had gone on a voyage designed to ascertain the prospect of advancing the cause of Christ on that continent through the just formed "Colonization Society." But even with the arrival of the five American missionaries at Calcutta, the difficulties of the undertaking seemed almost insurmountable. The East India Company, then the ruler of such portions of India as were under British control, forbade them to preach lest commercial interests should be endangered by religious prejudice. The result was that Judson went to Burmah, while, after months of negotiation, Hall and Nott obtained a footing at Bombay, where at length Newell joined them. But the perplexities of the missionaries and the Board were not yet over. On the long voyage India-ward, Judson had adopted Baptist principles, and Rice soon followed him. Thus two of the most valued of these missionaries who had been sent out with so much labor withdrew at once from the service of the Congregational churches; but the event was not without its compensations, for it led, in 1814, to the founding of the "American Baptist Missionary Union," and the enlistment of that great body of churches in the cause of foreign missions.

The American Board was purely Congregational in its origin; its original commissioners were chosen by the Massachusetts General Association, with the understanding that as soon as the Connecticut General Association should ratify the plan it should elect a proportion of the number. This was actually carried out in 1811. But the act of incorporation, procured from the Massachusetts legislature in 1812, made the Board, as it still is, a self-perpetuating body or close corporation. The same feeling of fellowship with other Calvinistic religious bodies that had been exhibited in the "Plan of Union" of 1801 now prompted the Board, at its meeting in September, 1812, to choose eight Presbyterians to its membership; and, in 1816, to include also a representative from the Reformed (Dutch) Church. Even before the establishment of this connection, the Board had been recognized (June, 1812) by the Presbyterian General Assembly as a proper channel for the gifts of Presbyterian churches, and this approval was repeated in more positive terms in May, 1826. The connection with the Reformed Church was not quite so cordial, but for a quarter of a century after 1832 it secured decided intimacy of association. The American Board thus continued to be interdenominational in its basis for many years, and the process of its return to its original estate was a gradual one. In 1837 the "Old School" wing of the Presbyterians withdrew and constituted a Board of its own. Twenty years later the Reformed Church severed its connection; and finally, on the reunion of the "Old School" and

"New School" divisions of Presbyterianism in 1870, the latter withdrew in favor of its own denominational agency, leaving the American Board exclusively Congregational, though individual Presbyterians still continue in some instances their places in its membership.

The Board thus constituted has had a history of honor. Its original mission station in India was supplemented in 1816 by a mission in Ceylon; in 1817 and 1818 missionaries began work among the Cherokees and Choctaws, then in Georgia and Mississippi; 1819 saw the sailing of laborers for the Hawaiian Islands and for Palestine. Syria became the seat of a mission in 1823, China in 1829, Constantinople in 1831, Persia in 1833, the Madura district of India in 1834, Zululand in 1835, the Micronesian Islands in 1852, Japan in 1869, Spain, Mexico, and Austria in 1872, and Central Africa in 1880. These, with their various subdivisions and branches, constitute a field of labor of infinite variety, as well as great extent. By 1840 the Board could report that it had sent out 694 missionaries in the thirty years which then embraced its history, and that it had gathered 17,234 members into the churches which it had established. The number of its missionaries during its first half-century was 1258; while in 1894 it could declare that it had sent 2066 persons to the mission fields and had received 125,584 members into its churches. It has Christianized the Hawaiian and some of the Micronesian Islands, it has profoundly altered the life of Bulgaria and Asia Minor for the better, it has made creditable progress in India, China, and Japan. Such a missionary record may well be a cause of just satisfaction.

A further illustration of the new spirit of voluntary united action in effort essentially of a missionary character is to be seen in the organization at Boston on August 29 and December 7, 1815, of the "American Society for Educating Pious Youth for the Gospel Ministry," which was at first broadly interdenominational and speedily became the "American Education Society." Assistance to enable needy young men to secure a ministerial training had already been afforded by various synods among the American Presbyterians to candidates of their own order; and a local society for this purpose had been formed on March 6, 1804, by the Congregational association meeting at Pawlet, Vt. The work was now taken up on a large scale; and, in the spirit already exhibited in the "Plan of Union" and the American Board, the "Education Society" opened its membership and extended its aid to others than to Congregationalists, especially to Presbyterians. But as the Presbyterian General Assembly organized its own "Board of Education" in 1819, this connection was never very extensive, and the "Education Society" has long been, as it now is, distinctively Congregational. In 1874 the "American Education Society" joined with the "Society for the Promotion of Collegiate and Theological Education at the West," an organization formed at New York June 29, 1843, to aid in establishing Christian institutions for higher education. The combined body took the name of the "American College and Education Society," which it bore till 1893, when, becoming united with the "New West Education Commission" formed in 1879 to promote "Christian civilization in Utah and adjacent States and Territories," it reverted to its earlier name,—the "American Education Society." During its useful history this society has aided more than eight thousand candidates for the ministry, and its efforts in behalf of about thirty colleges have been largely instrumental in building up the cause of higher education, in which Congregationalism has always felt a deep interest, throughout the newer regions of the land.

It has already been seen that the home missionary activity of Congregationalism led to the formation of many comparatively local missionary societies. The examples of organizations on a national scale, like the American Board and the "Education Society," led to the creation at New York on May 10, 1826, of the "American Home Missionary Society,"—a body formed on the basis of a joint association of Presbyterians and a few members of the Reformed (Dutch) Church which had been organized under the title of the "United Domestic Missionary Society" in 1822. The new "Home Missionary Society" was of course voluntary and interdenominational, and it carried on its work in the spirit of the "Plan of Union."

At its beginning the new society was largely Presbyterian in its membership; but the local home missionary bodies of New England rapidly became auxiliary to it, without generally surrendering their own organization. It was at first heartily approved by the Presbyterian General Assembly; but on the division of the Presbyterian body into "Old School" and "New School" in 1837, the "Old School" party withdrew its countenance, declaring the work of the society "exceedingly injurious to the peace and purity of the Presbyterian Church." The "New School" wing continued its support, however, and, as a committee of that party affirmed in 1860, were "accustomed to regard it as, in a sense, peculiarly their own." But with the growth of denominational consciousness relations between the elements in the society became more strained, and by 1860 the body had become predominantly Congregational, drawing five sevenths of its receipts from Congregational sources and reckoning seven tenths of its mission fields to the same denomination. As a result, the "New School" Presbyterians withdrew in favor of more distinctly denominational agencies of their own on May 27, 1861, and the society became wholly Congregational,—a change which was tardily recognized in 1893 by the alteration of its name to the "Congregational Home Missionary Society." It has done an immense work in spreading Christian institutions throughout the West and in supporting feeble churches in all parts of the land. By 1893 it could report that it had organized 6121 churches, of which 2978 had become self-supporting. In that year it had 2002 missionaries on its rolls, and was conducting regular religious worship at 3841 stations.

It is evident that the New England of the new revival epoch that began about 1791 was a much more spiritually awakened and active land than the New England of most of the eighteenth century; and it was fortunate for the Congregational churches that this outburst of missionary zeal and this new sense of Christian privilege and obligation took place just before the separation between church and state was effected which altered the whole system of financial support on which the New England churches had depended. The changes of 1818 in Connecticut and of 1834 in Massachusetts found the churches filled with a new vitality, and ready to profit rather than to receive harm by being made wholly dependent on their own voluntary efforts.

The second result of the new period of revivals was the Unitarian separation,—an outgoing due to causes long operative, but which did not become completely accomplished till the nineteenth century had begun. In the preceding chapter some account has been given of the rise of the Liberals of eastern Massachusetts,—of their beginnings in the old Arminianism that was at first largely a disbelief in the sharper points of Calvinism; of their strengthening during the reaction from the excesses of the Great Awakening; of the influence of English Arminian and Arian writers; and of the teachings of men of talent and in many ways of worth, like Lemuel Briant, Jonathan Mayhew, and Charles Chauncy. It has been seen that by the end of the Revolution there were, or had recently been, pastors in eastern Massachusetts who openly denied the total depravity of man, who publicly controverted the doctrine of eternal punishment, and who advocated high Arian views of the Godhead. These men naturally dwelt in their preaching on the moral duties and on the cultivation of the virtues, rather than on their doubts and disbeliefs. Preachers who are unopposed usually prefer to be positive rather than negative; and till the Unitarian position was fully brought out by the criticisms of its opponents, the sermons, and doubtless the thinking, of the Liberals were more marked by omissions than by actual denials. Then, too, the prominence given by the Revolution and the subsequent era of political creation to the rights and duties of man made it natural for ministers of no great keenness of doctrinal interest to make ethical questions their main burden of discourse; and no ministers were more patriotic in the Revolutionary struggle or more hearty in entering into discussion of the problems which it involved than the Massachusetts Liberals.

The first organized avowal of anti-Trinitarian beliefs was made by the congregation worshiping in King's Chapel, —the oldest Episcopal body in Boston. The rector of that society, Rev. Henry Caner, had fled to Halifax with his loyalist friends when Boston was evacuated by the British in 1776, and it remained without a minister till 1782, when the congregation called Rev. James Freeman, a young man of twenty-three. Both minister and people found that their views were so strongly anti-Trinitarian that the expressions of the Prayer-Book were distasteful, and they proceeded in 1785 to revise the formulæ of prayer,—a course of action which Freeman warmly defended from the pulpit. But such radical anti-Trinitarian changes naturally led Bishops Seabury of Connecticut and Provoost of New York to refuse ordination, and therefore on November 18, 1787, the representatives of King's Chapel congregation themselves set Freeman apart to his office, much as an early Congregational church might have ordained its minister.

This action of the ancient Episcopal congregation of Boston was regarded as extreme, and it produced no immediate effect on the Congregational churches of the town; but the general prevalence of anti-Trinitarian sentiments among them is evidenced by the publication in 1795 by Rev. Dr. Jeremy Belknap, pastor of the Congregational Church in Federal Street, of a "Collection of Psalms and Hymns." This aid to worship, which soon came into extensive use in Boston and vicinity, while expressing the utmost affection for the Saviour and giving him a high Arian exaltation, omitted or altered all references to him as God or all intimations of a Trinity in the divine existence. A new collection of "Extracts" from Emlyn's "Humble Inquiry" was once more put forth, in 1790; and in 1795 Rev. John Clarke, Chauncy's cultivated and scholarly associate and successor in the pastorate of the First Boston Church, published "An Answer to the Question, Why are you a Christian?" which, though it ascribes a lofty function to Christ and holds full faith in his miracles, dwells primarily on the ethical aspects of the gospel, and is exceedingly "liberal" in tone. Yet Boston was not ready for a bald Socinianism, like that of Priestley, and a proposition to invite the English Unitarian leader to come thither in 1794 found no considerable encouragement. But by May, 1796, Freeman could write to an English friend: "The Unitarian doctrine appears to be still upon the increase. I am acquainted with a number of ministers, particularly in the southern part of this State, who avow and publicly preach this sentiment."

While these theories had been spreading in eastern Massachusetts, the Edwardean teachings of western Massachusetts and of Connecticut had also been gaining a foothold in the region. At Plymouth Chandler Robbins, a pupil and friend of Bellamy, held the pastorate of the old Mayflower Church from 1760 to 1799; at Newburyport the able Hopkinsian Samuel Spring was pastor from 1777 to 1819; Charlestown had for its minister, from 1789 to 1820, the gifted and polemic Jedidiah Morse, a pupil of the younger Edwards; while Nathanael Emmons, the most powerful leader of the ultra-Edwardean school, made his home a theological seminary and his pulpit a theologic fortress at Franklin from 1773 to 1827. With the beginning of the revivals and the new sense of religious privilege and obligation which began to manifest itself in a missionary spirit during the last decade of the eighteenth century, the influence of these men was greatly increased. They and their party had been the advocates of a more spiritual and evangelical type of religion in the depressed period before the revivals began, and the new revival spirit at once made Edwardean men and measures popular wherever the Liberal theology had not won complete control. As the eighteenth century drew toward a close the more conservative churches began to awake. In Essex County, for instance, during the decade of 1791 to 1801, "the churches are aroused to scrutinize more carefully the doctrinal views of their pastors; and when a pulpit is vacated by the removal of an Arminian, or a semi-Arminian, it is somehow pretty sure to be filled with a man of a more Orthodox stamp"; and the same thing was true, only in less degree, of other districts of eastern Massachusetts. The

Edwardeans and Old Calvinists, without wholly ignoring their differences, felt that they had a common cause to defend,—the cause of what they loved to designate as that of "evangelical truth." As the new evangelical movement became more pronounced and aggressive, ministers and churches who sympathized with it began to recognize how far some of their associates had drifted almost unperceived into Liberalism, and to wonder how such changes could have taken place around them without concealment. But such a charge, though a few passages to support it may be quoted from the writings of Freeman and others, is an essential injustice to the Liberals; it was rather that the more conservative element had been asleep.

Evidence of the evangelical awakening began to be patent by the close of the eighteenth century, and with the rising tide of Edwardean and revivalistic feeling the conservative elements became decidedly aggressive and determined to purge the anti-Trinitarians from the Congregational body. In 1798 a council refused to install Rev. Clark Brown at Brimfield, Mass., among other reasons, on account of denials of the divinity of Christ similar to the Arian speculations which he put forth to the world the next year in his tract, "The Character of our Lord and Saviour Jesus Christ." This refusal aroused much opposition. An anonymous pamphlet was at once published at Springfield, Mass., under the title of "Popish Hierarchy suppressed by Buonaparte in Italy: and his Holiness exerting his Influence, in a late Ecclesiastical Council at Brimfield," in which the action of the council was denounced as ecclesiastical tyranny. A more compliant council settled Mr. Brown a few months later. In 1799 the "Massachusetts Missionary Society" was formed, as has been already narrated; and in 1803 the foundations of a new state ministerial gathering were laid,—the Massachusetts General Association,—an assembly additional to, and more efficient than, the ancient Ministerial Convention. The new organization came into favor with some difficulty. It was recognized and opposed as the work of the evangelical party; but the extreme Independency of Nathanael Emmons led him and his Hopkinsian friends to show the same hostility to the enterprise that the Liberals manifested for other reasons. Its formation, however, was a distinct proof of the increasing strenuousness of the opponents of advancing Liberalism, and of the growing tightening of theological lines.

The first church to be divided by the rising contest,—unless the rather obscure schism at Taunton in 1792 be an exception,—was, curiously enough, the old Pilgrim Church at Plymouth. After the death of Rev. Chandler Robbins, in 1799, the Plymouth Church called Rev. James Kendall, —a man of "liberal" sentiments,—as their pastor, by a small majority of the communicants but with the well-nigh unanimous approval of the parish. His ordination was followed after some months by the withdrawal, on October 1, 1801, of almost exactly one half of the members of the ancient church, and their constitution into a church of the ancient faith, while the Mayflower Church, as an organization, passed fully to the party soon to be known as Unitarian. A year later, September 8, 1802, Rev. Samuel Worcester was dismissed from his charge at Fitchburg, Mass., because of a Calvinism displeasing to the parish, though not distasteful to the church.

But the first real test of strength between the two parties that was tried on any considerable scale took place over the choice of a successor to the decidedly Old Calvinist, Rev. Dr. David Tappan, whose death, in August, 1803, left vacant the Hollis Professorship of Divinity in Harvard College,—a choice which determined what influences were to be dominant in that seat of learning. The importance of the decision was keenly felt, and both sides put forth their efforts. At the time of Tappan's death the corporation was equally divided and no choice was made. The candidate of the Liberal side was Rev. Henry Ware, of Hingham, Mass., his opponents favored Rev. Jesse Appleton, of Hampton, N. H., soon to become president of Bowdoin College. In them the two types of theology were brought into opposing contrast. Death having changed the complexion of the corporation, the struggle issued on February 5, 1805, in the election of Ware, and in the manifest passage of New England's oldest college to the control of the anti-Trinitarians.

The decision as to the future attitude of Harvard College aroused public attention as nothing yet had done; it was the immediate occasion of the foundation of Andover Seminary, as there will be cause to note a little later in this chapter; and it was speedily followed by a bitter literary warfare. In 1805 Rev. Dr. Jedidiah Morse, of Charlestown, attacked the whole transaction in his "True Reasons on which the Election of the Hollis Professor of Divinity in Harvard College was opposed." But more permanent weapons than ephemeral pamphlets were also resorted to. In November, 1803, several prominent Boston Liberals had established the "Monthly Anthology," a magazine decidedly sympathetic with their cast of doctrine, but showing also that tendency toward literature which was so marked and so fruitful a characteristic of the early New England Unitarians. And now, in June, 1805, and largely through the influence of Morse, the "Panoplist" was founded, as an active defender of ancient faith, "by an Association of Friends to Evangelical Truth," who were broadly Calvinistic rather than Hopkinsian. From the first it was an aggressive, vigorous magazine; and there can be no doubt that it did much to compel the Liberals to define their position. United with the decidedly Hopkinsian "Massachusetts Missionary Magazine" in 1808, it ultimately became in a certain sense the ancestor of that non-polemic medium of Congregational missionary intelligence, the "Missionary Herald," which is published by the American Board to the present day.

One more publication of the year 1805 attracted wide attention,—the work of Rev. John Sherman, of Mansfield, Conn., entitled "One God in one Person only, and Jesus Christ a Being distinct from God, dependent upon Him for his Existence and his various Powers." This was the most positive anti-Trinitarian treatise that had yet originated in New England. Sherman was in a region where Liberalism found little ministerial sympathy, and he was promptly dismissed by a mutual council, though approved by a large portion of his congregation. The transaction caused much discussion, and coming so speedily after the Harvard College controversy, added fuel to the flames of public excitement.

Meanwhile the Liberal pulpit of Boston had received two notable accessions in the persons of Rev. William Ellery Channing,—on the whole the most distinguished of American Unitarians,—who became pastor of the Federal Street Church in 1803 at the age of twenty-three; and of Joseph Stevens Buckminster, who entered the service of Brattle Church in January, 1805, when not quite twenty-one, and died seven years later, but who lives in tradition even yet as one of the most gifted of American preachers. Both these ministers greatly advanced the popularity of Liberalism in the town of their labors; and the situation became one increasingly demanding positive action if the evangelical party was not to be driven from the local field. It was with this feeling, doubtless, that Rev. Dr. Morse, the evangelical champion of Charlestown, procured the settlement of Rev. Joshua Huntington, a Yale graduate, who had studied theology under President Timothy Dwight and under Morse himself, as colleague pastor of the Old South Church,—the most conservative of all the Boston churches,—in May, 1808. A few months later,—December, 1808,—the Second Church in Dorchester settled an actively evangelical minister in the person of Rev. John Codman, destined to fill a prominent place in the theological conflicts of the next few years. But it illustrates the still outwardly undivided state of Congregationalism that at the first of these installations Morse and Channing took part together in the services, and at the second Channing preached the sermon.

A much more positive and aggressive evangelical advance was the organization, on February 27, 1809, partly as a result of the recent preaching of Rev. Dr. Henry Kollock, of Savannah, Ga., of a new church in Boston which was soon known as that of Park Street. With the countenance of Morse and Codman this body was made illustrative of a strict type of Calvinism in its doctrinal basis, and on the settlement of Rev. Dr. Edward D. Griffin,—a pupil of the younger Edwards,—as its pastor in 1811, its eloquent and able pulpit presented a positive Hopkinsian type of theology such as Boston had not heard before, and presented it with great power. Such preaching was sorely needed, for, in his sermon at the Ministerial Convention of 1810, Rev. Dr. Eliphalet Porter, of Roxbury, had declared of the doctrines of "Original Sin, a Trinity in Unity, the Mere Humanity, Super-Angelic Nature, or Absolute Deity of Christ, and the Absolute Eternity of Punishment, . . . I cannot place my finger on any one article in the list of doctrines just mentioned, the belief or rejection of which I consider essential to the Christian faith or character."

The ancient New England custom approved far more frequent pulpit exchanges than are customary at present,—in many towns as often as once in three or four weeks,—and about the time of Griffin's settlement the evangelical party began to draw what eventually proved the line of separation between them and the Liberals by refusing to exchange with those whose soundness they suspected. Rev. John Codman, whose settlement at Dorchester has just been noted, was a leader in this movement, and the defense of his right thus to refuse ministerial fellowship caused him a bitter contest with a part of his parishioners, resulting in the calling of two councils, in 1811 and 1812, and his maintenance of his pastoral position only by the casting vote of the moderator of the latter of these bodies.

The position of exclusion from fellowship thus taken by Codman and others toward the Liberals was a sign of the growing strength and self-respect of the evangelical party; and the breach now opening was rapidly widened by an event of the year 1815. In 1812 Rev. Thomas Belsham, of London, who since the death of Priestley had been the leader of the English Unitarians, had published a "Life of the Rev. Theophilus Lindsey," in which he had printed letters from Freeman and other prominent citizens of Boston giving accounts of the progress of Liberalism in that community. For some reason the work attracted little notice at first; but in 1815 the portions relating to America were republished in a pamphlet at Boston, probably at the instance of Morse, under the title of "American Unitarianism; or, A Brief History of the Progress and Present State of the Unitarian Churches in America." This publication aroused great commotion; and its real significance was evident in its title. The word "Unitarian" at that day popularly signified an asserter of the mere humanity of Christ, and a semi-materialist in religion, such as Priestley had been. Such a "Unitarian" Belsham was to a large extent. But the Boston Liberals, with possibly one exception, were still Arians and supernaturalists, they were not "Unitarians" in the then odious sense of that word. Yet Freeman and William Wells, Belsham's correspondents, had spoken of the movement as "Unitarian," and Belsham, who was a "Unitarian" in the Priestleian sense, had naturally made the most of the epithet, though Wells at least took prompt occasion to declare that he had used the term to indicate "a Christian, not a believer in the doctrine of the Trinity," rather than in the narrow significance that Belsham attached to it. But the Liberals had all along asserted that their departures from the ancient faith were moderate and non-destructive, and in this pamphlet they seemed identified wholly with the extreme English party which was generally looked upon as little better than infidel. In a very able review of the pamphlet in June, 1815, probably from the pen of Jeremiah Evarts, the "Panoplist" pushed this identification, asserting: "We shall feel ourselves warranted hereafter, to speak of the fact as certain, that Unitarianism is the predominant religion among the ministers and churches of Boston," and declaring that "Unitarianism and Infidelity are nearly related indeed. Mr. Wells, who is a hopeful pupil of the Priestleian school, says that they are identical. 'Unitarianism,' says he, 'consists rather in *not* believing.'"

This extreme characterization of the Liberal party, for which their English friends and the more radical representatives of the movement in America had opened the way, led to a great commotion. Channing, who was an Arian, and a believer in a certain sense in the atonement, came into the field, within a month of the "Panoplist's" review, with a protest against "the Aspersions contained in a late number of the 'Panoplist,'" in the form of a letter to Rev. S. C. Thacher, a brother Boston minister. In this letter he described the method of the "Panoplist" as a "criminal instance of unfairness," and declared that the statement that "the great body of Liberal Christians are Unitarians, in Mr. Belsham's sense of that word . . . is false." "The word Unitarian, taken in . . . its true sense, . . . includes all who believe that there is no distinction of persons in God." In that sense, Channing averred, "My worship and sentiments have been Unitarian;" but his Unitarianism and that of most of his brethren held, he affirmed, "that Jesus Christ is more than man, that he existed before the world, that he literally came from heaven to save our race, that he sustains other offices than those of a teacher and witness to the truth, and that he still acts for our benefit, and is our intercessor with the Father." To this letter, Rev. Dr. Samuel Worcester, who had been dismissed from his Fitchburg charge for his evangelical sentiments in 1802 and who was now settled at Salem, Mass., made vigorous reply. Channing in turn answered, and a sharp exchange of pamphlets followed. But the fact was that though the Liberals might protest against "a system of exclusion," the separation between them and the evangelical party was a reality, and a definite name for the new denomination was a great convenience. So convenient was it that Channing and the other Liberal leaders began at once to use the term "Unitarian" to describe their own party, though of course in the since popular New England signification of a denier of the Trinity, without defining the exact quality of that denial.

The Unitarians were now to all intents a distinct denomination, though this distinction became more manifest and the evangelical withdrawal from fellowship with them more pronounced after 1819. On May 5th of that year Channing preached his famous sermon at the ordination of Rev. Jared Sparks at Baltimore, Md.,—a sermon which was a careful setting forth not only of the doctrine of the nature of God, but of the whole system of God's dealings with men, as the preacher conceived them. Though not representing the prevalent type of modern Unitarianism, it has been regarded as a Unitarian classic. To this discourse Prof. Moses Stuart of Andover gave a strong reply during the same year, to which Prof. Andrews Norton of Harvard, Channing's friend, made answer defending the Unitarian position. Channing's Baltimore sermon was also the occasion of the vigorous "Letters to Unitarians" put forth in 1820 by Prof. Leonard Woods, Stuart's colleague at Andover, which drew forth the "Letters to Trinitarians and Calvinists" from Prof. Henry Ware of Harvard. This discussion and the rejoinders which followed on both sides covered the whole range of doctrines in debate, but it may be questioned whether the separation between the evangelical Congregationalists and the Unitarians had not become so complete as to make these elaborate publications productive of little actual result.

The year 1815 may therefore be assigned for convenience as the time of the Unitarian separation,—though exactness in date is difficult where the marks of division were exhibited, as they were in this case, by local action, by refusals to exchange, and withdrawals of fellowship, rather than the widely visible schisms which rend more centralized ecclesiastical associations. The real division,—the division of spirit,—was of course much earlier. From 1817 to 1840 the separation of local churches went on vigorously, and of these local drawings apart the most famous, by reason of the legal decision to which it gave rise, was that at Dedham, Mass., in 1818. In that town the majority of the church-members being evangelical, the society, i.e., the legal voters of the First Parish of Dedham, who were preponderatingly Unitarian, took the initiative and, in spite of the protests of two thirds of the church, called Rev. Alvan Lamson as their minister and invited a council of Unitarians to ordain him. The council, which included Channing, Ware, President Kirkland of Harvard, and other men of prominence, showed its partisan spirit by voting, in spite of a protest from the majority of the church, that "whereas cases may exist in which a majority of a church do not concur with the religious society in the call of a minister, . . . such cases may still be so urgent as to authorize an ecclesiastical council to proceed to the ordination." Naturally the council felt that such an astounding departure from Congregational usage demanded an explanation, and they therefore adopted a long justificatory declaration in which they affirmed that "the council regard the well-known usage, according to which, the first step in electing a pastor is taken by the church, as in the main wise and beneficial"; but also claimed "that circumstances may exist in which a minister may be ordained over a parish without the concurrence of the church connected with it"; and that "greater good is to be expected to this society and to the church in general" from this ordination than from its refusal. But it is not surprising that this "greater good" was not apparent to the evangelical majority of the church, which now withdrew from the Unitarian minority. The legal question now arose as to which faction of the ancient church was the First Church of Dedham, and entitled to use the meeting-house and property of the society; and this case was carried to the Massachusetts Supreme Court, where after arguments by Daniel Webster and Theron Metcalf on the various merits of the dispute, it was decided in 1820 that a church exists only in connection with a society, and in case of division in the church only that faction which is recognized by the society has a right to the name and the use of the property.

Under the operation of this Dedham decision the prevailing Unitarianism of the societies in many of the ancient towns of eastern Massachusetts led to the enrollment of the titles of a considerable proportion of the earliest Congregational churches of New England in the list of Unitarian churches. A careful report prepared by a committee of the Massachusetts General Association in 1836 enumerates 81 cases of ecclesiastical division, in which 3900 evangelical members withdrew, leaving property to the value of more than $600,000 for the use of 1282 Unitarian fellow-members who remained. But while the excision of Unitarianism was a cause of division in many churches, it is but just to say that a considerable number of ancient Puritan churches found themselves without serious controversy on the Unitarian side. This was noticeably the case in Boston, where of the fourteen churches of the Congregational order existing in 1800 within the large territory now embraced by the city limits, all but two, the Old South of Boston and the First Church of Charlestown, became Unitarian, and for the most part without internal commotion. It has been ascertained by a careful student of Massachusetts ecclesiastical history,—Rev. Dr. Joseph S. Clark,—that 96 churches in all were lost from the Congregational rolls, though in a large portion of these cases the evangelical members who withdrew formed new organizations to take their places. But many of the names thus lost were venerable for their historic associations, and the ability, wealth, and social or political distinction of those who withdrew to the early Unitarians was such as to make the loss a severe one from a worldly point of view.

The Unitarian movement was almost strictly local. Outside of eastern Massachusetts, the adjacent portions of New Hampshire, and one or two of the older towns of Maine, it has gained little footing. No Connecticut church has ever become Unitarian, except that of Brooklyn, and there the evangelical portion has kept the name and maintained the field in large measure. Connecticut soil has proved unfavorable for the planting of Unitarianism. A few Unitarian churches have found root in western Massachusetts and Vermont; but in general the regions where Edwardeanism had become powerful before 1800 have given scanty welcome to Unitarian speculations. Nor has Unitarianism itself escaped the control of an ever-increasing radicalism. The Arian and supernatural type of the separation gave place largely to the "transcendental" school before the middle of the century was reached, and while Unitarianism includes all shades of belief from a conservatism that is almost orthodox to a radicalism ready to dispense with the Christian name altogether, its general tendency has carried it farther and farther away from the now seemingly moderate liberalism of a Channing or a Norton.

The Unitarian excision is the only separation of importance in the history of American Congregationalism. Unitarianism was a movement of slow growth, a gradual change in attitude toward the main truths of the gospel, and was to some extent due to the introduction of a different type of culture from that which had characterized New England. In no invidious sense it may be said that a high degree of moral rectitude of conduct, a general diffusion of material comfort, and a comparatively unemotional type of religious experience, had idealized human nature in the thought of many, so that a vivid perception of the power of sin and of the greatness of the redemption necessary to overcome its effects had been lost. The same conditions of general comfort and social well-being tended to develop in the class to which Unitarianism powerfully appealed that keen appreciation of literary form which makes the roll of New England men of letters so largely a record of Unitarian names. And there was in the movement also a deep and unselfish humanitarian feeling and a high sense of duty, not due to material conditions but to the finer ethical effects of that Puritan training which Unitarians and Evangelicals alike inherit, which made many of the Unitarians conspicuous as leaders of social and political reform. It was a movement which exemplified many noble and desirable qualities in its more conspicuous representatives; but it was, from a spiritual point of view, none the less a movement which lost touch with those needs and feelings that the church universal has always recognized as deepest in mankind. Its loudest strife in its later stage was over the doctrine of the Trinity; but its most vital point was after all the practical question of the nature of man and the way of salvation. Channing declared in his reply to the "Panoplist" in 1815 that "we consider the errours which relate to Christ's person as of little or no importance compared with the errour of those who teach, that God brings us into life wholly depraved and wholly helpless." And one of the chief of living exponents of Unitarianism, Rev. Dr. George E. Ellis, thus defined its essential features nearly forty years ago, when the movement still preserved much of its original force and character: "Unitarianism stands in direct and positive opposition to Orthodoxy on three great doctrines, which Orthodoxy teaches, with emphasis, as vital to its system; namely, that the nature of human beings has been vitiated, corrupted, and disabled, in consequence of the sin of Adam, for which God has in judgment doomed our race to suffering and woe; that Jesus Christ is God, and therefore an object of religious homage and prayer; and that the death of Christ is made effectual to human salvation by reconciling God to man, and satisfying the claims of an insulted and outraged law. Unitarianism denies that these are doctrines of the Gospel, and offers very different doctrines, sustained by Scripture, in their place." In making this denial Unitarianism broke with the consciousness of the church universal, and made a separation between itself and evangelical Congregationalism not only inevitable but desirable.

The third important result of the awakened religious zeal of the churches was the introduction into New England of a new system of theological education. The main design for which Harvard and Yale had been founded was to train up a learned ministry, and they had fulfilled their purpose, judged by the low educational standards of the colonial era. It is difficult to imagine what New England would have become had it not been for their noble work. But that work was limited. The original courses of instruction at these colleges presupposed that the graduates would chiefly enter the ministry, and laid emphasis on theology, Greek, and Hebrew, as well as on dialectics; but the youth of the students and the elementary character of the curriculum gave the graduates what would now be considered an exceedingly scanty technical training. It was the custom, however, from early times for occasional students to return to college after graduation for a few months, or perhaps a year or two, of reading under the direction of the president and with the advantages of the library. The deficiencies of the system were recognized in the eighteenth century and led to the foundation of the Hollis Professorship of Divinity at Harvard by the gift of a generous Baptist merchant of London, Thomas Hollis, in 1721. In 1746 the beginnings of a professorship of divinity were made at Yale, though the chair was not filled till 1755. But though these appointments secured more or less regular lectures on doctrinal, historical, and exegetical topics for the undergraduates, they were not a very efficient or very popular means of instruction. It became increasingly the custom, especially after the middle of the eighteenth century, for ministerial candidates to take a few months of study with some prominent minister,—and though many of the New England clergy thus received students into their households, the Edwardean leaders most extensively engaged in this labor of education. Such intimate connection of pupil and teacher had much value in initiating the candidate into methods of pastoral labor, and familiarizing him with questions of practical parish administration, and beyond that he obtained an intimate acquaintance with the system of polemic divinity of which his teacher was the exponent. The method propagated schools of theology most effectively. But it is almost needless to point out that this system of education gave no broad view of church history, no careful study of linguistics or exegesis, and no extensive acquaintance with the development of Christian doctrine as a whole. A busy New England pastor of the last century had neither the time, nor the books, nor the technical education to give instruction along such lines.

The quickening of the churches under the new revival spirit led to a feeling among many that a better system of ministerial training should be introduced; but this feeling was transformed into action only after the loss of Harvard College to the Liberals by the election of Ware to the Hollis Professorship had impressed on the evangelical party the fact that such public facilities as then existed for ministerial training in Massachusetts had passed out of conservative hands. It has already been seen that the evangelical party of eastern Massachusetts included at least two elements,—an extreme Edwardean section, the Hopkinsians, or "Consistent Calvinists"; and an Old Calvinist section of varying degrees of strenuousness. The Hopkinsians had founded the "Massachusetts Missionary Society," and its "Magazine"; the hand of the Old Calvinists was more conspicuous in the beginnings of the Massachusetts General Association and the "Panoplist." Both parties were being brought into union by their common opposition to Liberalism, but during the opening years of the century they still felt considerable jealousy of each other. Now, on the defection of Harvard, representatives both of the Old Calvinists and Hopkinsians in Essex County, Mass., began in 1806 to lay their plans, each party at first entirely without knowledge of the others purposes, for the planting of a theological seminary.

The Old Calvinist movement had its center at Andover, where Samuel and John Phillips had founded the most famous of New England academies in 1778. The Phillipses were men of great political and social prominence, of sterling character, and of Old Calvinist principles, and they had given to their academy a strongly religious bent, had directed that the main doctrines of the gospel should be taught in it, and had even contemplated the eventual establishment in the academy of a professorship of divinity similar to the chairs at Harvard and Yale. John Phillips had also left funds in charge of the trustees of the academy to assist students "in the study of divinity under the direction of some eminent Calvinistic minister,"—funds from which students were aided from 1797 to 1808 in their training under one of the Andover pastors. It was natural, therefore, that the thoughts of the Old Calvinists regarding a theological seminary should group themselves about the academy at Andover; especially since the most prominent of the projectors of the plan was Prof. Eliphalet Pearson, who had been the first principal of the academy, and had continued one of its trustees during his incumbency of the chair of Hebrew at Harvard from 1785 to 1806. Now, in 1806, Pearson resigned his professorship and returned to Andover, convinced that the loss of Harvard to the Liberals demanded energetic counter-action. With Pearson there were associated in forming the plan for the seminary Rev. Dr. Morse, of Charlestown, theologically an Edwardean of the type of Dwight, but broadly sympathetic with the Old Calvinists, a man whose activity as an opponent of rising Unitarianism has already been noted, and Samuel Farrar, an Andover lawyer. Above all there were the "Founders," who eventually contributed the necessary funds, Samuel Abbot, Madam Phœbe Phillips, the widowed daughter-in-law of Samuel Phillips, the benefactor of the academy, and her son John Phillips, Jr., of Andover. In July, 1806, a "Voluntary Association," embracing Pearson, Morse, Farrar, Abbot, and one or two others, met at the Phillips residence and began to lay definite plans for realizing their purpose. During the following autumn a constitution for the proposed "Theological Institution" was prepared; and by June, 1807, the scheme had so far crystallized that an act was obtained from the Massachusetts legislature authorizing the trustees of Phillips Academy to hold funds for a theological seminary.

While the Old Calvinists at Andover had been engaged in the earlier portion of this undertaking, a few Hopkinsians about Newburyport had, without their knowledge, also been laying plans for a seminary. The leader in this movement was Rev. Dr. Samuel Spring, a pupil of Bellamy, Hopkins, and West, and an intimate friend of Emmons, who had been filling a distinguished pastorate at Newburyport since 1777, and who was reckoned with reason as, next to Emmons, the chief Hopkinsian in New England,

With Dr. Spring was associated his much younger friend, Rev. Leonard Woods, pastor from 1798 at West Newbury, a man who was classed with the Hopkinsians in early life, but whose catholic and judicious spirit, wide friendships, and sympathy with all types of New England Calvinism admirably fitted him to conciliate all the elements of the evangelical party. Under the influence of Spring and Woods three laymen of wealth and character, William Bartlett and Moses Brown of Newburyport, and John Norris of Salem, became interested by the beginning of 1807 in the foundation of a seminary, which they thought might be located at West Newbury and have Woods for its teacher of theology. None of these laymen were church-members at this time, and Brown alone became so, but they were men of the old New England type, much interested in religion, and solicitous for the advancement of the churches. These three laymen, whose contributions did much to make Andover Seminary a strong institution, were to be known in its history as the "Associate Founders."

The intentions of the two parties became known to each other through the intimacy of Woods and Morse growing out of their association in the publication of the "Panoplist," and to both of these friends it seemed desirable that the Old Calvinists and Hopkinsians should combine their forces in one strong seminary. Professor Pearson soon warmly espoused the same cause, and to his untiring efforts the ultimate accomplishment of the union was chiefly due. But Spring was suspicious of the full orthodoxy of the Old Calvinists, and disinclined to compromise, and Emmons threw his great influence in the same direction. It looked as if two hostile institutions would be erected almost side by side; and believing that union was unattainable, the "Founders" signed the constitution of their proposed seminary on August 31, 1807, and committed it to the trustees of Phillips Academy, who accepted the trust two days later. The theological standard now laid down by the "Founders" for the test of professorial orthodoxy was the requirement that each instructor should "be a man of sound and orthodox principles in Divinity according to that form of sound words or system of evangelical doctrines, drawn from the Scriptures, and denominated the Westminster Assembly's Shorter Catechism."

But through the persistence of Pearson and Woods the plan of union was revived; and at last mutual concessions, in which the chief generosity was exhibited by the Old Calvinists, brought about the desired result. To the Hopkinsians the Westminster Shorter Catechism, which was a satisfactory creed test in the estimate of the Old Calvinists at Andover, did not seem sufficient. Moreover, it appeared unsafe to the Hopkinsians that the choice of professors should be committed unreservedly to the trustees of Phillips Academy. But at last, on December 1, 1807, a union was fully determined, and in May, 1808, it was completed. During the early summer of 1807 Spring and Woods had prepared a decidedly Edwardean, and moderately Hopkinsian, creed for the use of the possible seminary at West Newbury. This creed had met with the approval of the "Associate Founders." The visitatorial system, of which a mild example existed in the Board of Overseers at Harvard, also commended itself to the "Associate Founders" as a possible means of controlling the action of the trustees of Phillips Academy. As a result, the "Associate Founders" and the "Founders" agreed that each professor should assent to the creed which the Hopkinsians had prepared, as a symbol in which those doctrines are "more particularly expressed" which are "summarily expressed in the Westminster Assembly's Shorter Catechism." Each incumbent of a chair endowed by the "Associate Founders" was required, in addition, to be a "consistent Calvinist." A self-perpetuating "Board of Visitors" was also named, charged to see that the provisions of the trust were duly executed by trustees and professors, from whose decision an appeal might be taken to the Supreme Court of Massachusetts. This complicated system of government, the only basis on which the two parties would unite in founding a single institution, was accepted by the trustees of Phillips Academy on May 10, 1808, and thus became the constitution of Andover Seminary. In the same spirit of conciliation, Samuel Abbot, the Old Calvinist "Founder," who had retained the right to appoint the first professor to the chair of Christian Theology which he had endowed, chose Leonard Woods; and the "Associate Founders," Hopkinsians though they were, chose Eliphalet Pearson to their professorship of Natural Theology. And so the seminary was opened for students on September 28, 1808, with an attendance of thirty-six.

The inauguration of Andover Seminary was an event of prime importance in the history of Congregationalism. It was the beginning of a new era of theologic education, it was the most formidable barrier erected against the spread of Unitarianism, it was a focus of missionary zeal, and its successful foundation marked the union between Old Calvinism and Edwardeanism in eastern Massachusetts, a union which averted a very serious division in the evangelical forces at a time when all their strength was needed. The seminary had from the first the confidence of the churches,—a confidence which was amply justified by the character and ability of its early professors. Under the guidance of Leonard Woods in the chair of Theology from 1808 to 1846; of Moses Stuart, who came from the First Church in New Haven, Conn., to succeed Pearson in 1810, and whose occupancy of the professorship of Sacred Literature continued till 1848; and of Ebenezer Porter, who was professor of Sacred Rhetoric from 1812 to 1832, not only were ministerial candidates trained as they never had been in America, but a far-reaching impulse was given to theological studies on this side of the Atlantic. Systematic theology, in the technical sense of that term, was esteemed a relatively more important branch of a seminary curriculum then than now, and the careful, clear, and thorough instruction of Professor Woods was of course of prime importance. His work was of the utmost value, standing as he did in his theology in broad sympathy with Old Calvinists and Edwardeans, in completing that union of the evangelical forces which his election to the Andover professorship had foreshadowed. But Professor Stuart did a service of scarcely less value by his enthusiastic leadership in Oriental Literature, a field then almost untrodden by Americans, and by his introduction of the study of contemporary German theology. Nor was the power of the seminary lessened, but rather increased, when Prof. Edwards A. Park, who had occupied the chair of Sacred Rhetoric since 1836, took, in 1847, the professorship of Christian Theology that had been held by Professor Woods, and remained its incumbent till 1881. Under Professor Park the Edwardean elements in the creed of the seminary were made more prominent than they had been under Professor Woods, and his conception of the "New England Theology" became part of the mental furnishing of more theological students than any other Congregationalist has ever personally taught.

The new system of theologic instruction inaugurated at Andover was immediately popular. The entering students in that institution during its first thirty years averaged sixty-two annually. Such results naturally encouraged the foundation of similar seminaries in other parts of the Congregational field. The first to follow Andover was that incorporated by the Massachusetts legislature in February, 1814, and which opened in October, 1816, at Hampden in what is now the State of Maine, but was then a district attached to Massachusetts. In 1819 its location was changed to Bangor, Me., where it has since continued and from which place the seminary takes its name. It was originally intended, as it still endeavors, to give special facilities to those who have not had the advantages of a college training, though this aim has not interfered with the maintenance of a high scholarly reputation; but it has always been one of the smaller of the Congregational seminaries. Through the labors of Rev. Dr. Enoch Pond,—a pupil of Emmons,—whose connection with it extended from 1832 to 1870, Bangor Seminary attained a strong position of influence in the region of which it is the center.

These advances in theologic instruction were naturally regarded with interest by the authorities of Harvard College, and the result was the enlargement of the old professorship of Divinity into a Divinity School,—of Unitarian sympathies,—in 1815.

A similar enlargement soon after took place at Yale College. It had been a cherished plan of President Dwight that a separate department for post-graduate theologic teaching should be established, but he was not permitted to see the desire carried into execution. In 1822, however, fifteen students of the academic class then graduating petitioned that they might be organized into a class in theology. The request met with the hearty approval of the college authorities, a fund of $20,000 was raised, and a Divinity School established as a separate collegiate department, having as its professor of Sacred Literature Rev. Eleazar T. Fitch, who had held the chair of Divinity in the college since 1817; and as its professor of Systematic Theology, Rev. Nathaniel W. Taylor, of whose life and work there will be occasion to speak at some length. Both were men of remarkable mental powers, and of very unusual pulpit abilities, but they were unlike in disposition, Professor Fitch being timid and retiring, while Professor Taylor was well fitted by nature to sustain the burden of theologic conflict. The Yale Divinity School soon became a power in the churches through the influences that flowed forth from his lecture-room.

Nathaniel W. Taylor was born at New Milford, Conn., in 1786, and after graduation at Yale in the class of 1807, he studied theology with President Dwight, whom he served as an amanuensis and by whom he was much beloved. In 1811, after Moses Stuart had accepted a professorship at Andover, he became Stuart's successor in the pastorate of the First Church of New Haven, and from that office he was called to the post in the Divinity School which he retained till his death, in 1858.

As has been pointed out in the preceding chapter, the Edwardean school by the beginning of the nineteenth century had divided into two wings,—an ultra-Edwardean or Hopkinsian section, and a conciliatory and moderate section of which Dwight was the leader. It was the tendency of this latter branch that Taylor developed in his own system. The elder Edwards had asserted human responsibility with positiveness, and this doctrine had been put in the fore-front by all the Edwardeans, though coupled by them all with the most strenuous assertions of the divine sovereignty. It was to this problem of human responsibility that Taylor turned his attention, and he endeavored to explain it in what he deemed a more positive and less objectionable way than the Edwardeans had thus far done. Man is not a creature, Taylor asserted, whose acts are necessitated in accordance with an unqualified law of cause and effect; yet every man's choices are so connected with man's antecedent conditions of soul and his situation that, to God's perception, it is certain what they will be, though man has full power of contrary choice at all times. This "certainty with power to the contrary" makes it possible for God to be sovereign and man dependent, while man is also perfectly unforced in his actions. The natural ability to choose aright is a real power, which can be exercised by the sinner, if he is aroused to action by appeal to the proper faculties of his mind. This appeal can be made to the sensibilities,—for Taylor divided the mental powers into the intellect, sensibilities, and will, unlike the older Edwardeans who had made the twofold distinction of will and understanding. The feeling to which an appeal can be made is self-love,—a statement startling enough to a Hopkinsian,—but Taylor held that the highest form of this self-love, the pursuit of the highest happiness, could never be inconsistent with that choice of the best good of the universe which is benevolence. Yet while man has entire natural power to change his character so as to love God supremely, it is certain that he will not so change his ruling purpose unless the divine Spirit so moves upon his sensibilities as to induce his will to act, yet to act without coercion.

Sin, Taylor maintained, is a voluntary disobedience to known law; it consists in sinning, it flows out of a bias to sin which will occasion the active transgression wherein sin consists whenever the circumstances are such as to be favorable to sinful action, but this bias or disposition is not in itself sinful. Taylor also denied that sin is the necessary means of the greatest good, as the older Edwardeans had asserted. He held that a system in which the free action of the creature is permitted may be one from which God is unable to exclude sin. Such a system of freedom may be preferable to a system of constraint in which God forcibly prevents sin by allowing no freedom to the creature. It may be the best system. But though the possibility of sin may not be preventable by God in a system of freedom, sin may be prevented consistently with the purposes of such a system by man's resistance to temptation, and such resistance would be preferable to any yielding to sin, not only for the interests of the individual but for those of the universe as a whole.

The opinions of Professor Taylor won the general approval of his colleagues, and they soon became known as the "New Haven theology." The first public statements that attracted any considerable attention to these theories, aside from rumors of class-room teachings, were "Two Discourses on the Nature of Sin; Delivered before the Students of Yale College, July 30, 1826," by Professor Fitch. In these sermons Fitch defended the proposition "that sin, in every form and instance, is reducible to the act of a moral agent in which he violates a known rule of duty." Two years later, September 10, 1828, Professor Taylor delivered the annual *Concio ad Clerum* before those of the ministers of Connecticut who had assembled at the Yale commencement, and set forth fully his theory of sin and of its non-preventability by divine power. This discourse aroused a keen discussion at once. Many of the more conservative Edwardeans of Connecticut had looked upon Professor Taylor with suspicion ever since his entrance on the duties of his chair; and it now seemed to them that he had made a serious departure from New England Calvinism in an Arminian direction and had denied the full sovereignty of God, by his theories regarding the nature and preventability of sin, and especially regarding self-love as a motive in conversion. Publications in criticism and in defense of the New Haven views followed in rapid succession, and with much warmth of feeling.

Taylor's sermon was answered speedily by Rev. Joseph Harvey of Westchester parish, in Colchester, Conn., and by Professor Woods of Andover Seminary; but a more energetic antagonist than either speedily came into the field. During 1829 Taylor reviewed, in a New Haven religious magazine, the "Quarterly Christian Spectator," an essay published in 1827 by Rev. Dr. Gardiner Spring, of New York, on the "Means of Regeneration," and in his reviews the New Haven divine once more made evident his interpretation of religious truth. That summer Rev. Dr. Bennet Tyler, then pastor of the Second Church of Portland, Me., "visited Connecticut and collected all the pamphlets which had been published" relative to the New Haven theology. The result of a "careful examination of this literature," he records, "was a full conviction that the New Haven brethren had adopted opinions which were erroneous and of dangerous tendency." And as a consequence of this conclusion he attacked Taylor's views with vigor in December, 1829, in his "Strictures on the Review of Dr. Spring's Dissertation." So thoroughly did Tyler become, from now onward, the champion on the conservative Edwardean side, in spite of the fact that the party included a number of other men of vigor, that the discussion was popularly known as the "Taylor and Tyler Controversy."

Like Professor Taylor, Bennet Tyler was a native of Connecticut, having been born in Middlebury, in 1783; and like Taylor he was a graduate of Yale, his class being that of 1804. After a pastorate at South Britain in his native State, he became president of Dartmouth College in 1822; and in 1828 entered on his charge at Portland, Me.

He was a vigorous writer, a natural leader, a man of sincere piety, of great positiveness of conviction, and a full sympathizer with the older Edwardeanism.

The next two or three years were filled with discussion, negotiation, and publication, and resulted in the formation of two clearly defined parties in Connecticut. Probably this conclusion was aided by the contemporary discussions in the Presbyterian Church which resulted in the division of that body into the "Old School" and "New School" factions in 1837. Certainly the Connecticut discussions were a factor in that separation. The first step in organized opposition to the New Haven views appears to have been taken on October 12, 1831, when a few ministers of Connecticut met at Norwich and organized a "Doctrinal Tract Society." The movement grew, and late in 1832, at the suggestion of Rev. Dr. Nathan Perkins of West Hartford, and of Rev. Joseph Harvey, an invitation was sent out to all the associations of the State and to a few of those of western Massachusetts asking them to send two pastors each to a meeting to be held at Hartford, January 8, 1833, "to consult on measures which it may be proper and necessary to adopt, in the present posture of our theological concerns." The response was by no means general; only about twenty ministers appeared at the meeting. But at the invitation of a committee chosen at this Hartford gathering a convention of thirty-six Connecticut ministers of conservative sympathies assembled on September 10, 1833, in a little schoolhouse in what is now South Windsor, but was then East Windsor, Conn. Among those present in this meeting were Rev. Drs. Samuel Spring of Hartford, Asahel Nettleton the evangelist, Nathaniel Hewit of Bridgeport, Daniel Dow of Thompson, George A. Calhoun of North Coventry, Joseph Harvey, and Rev. Messrs. Timothy P. Gillett of Branford, Frederick Marsh of Winchester, and Cyrus Yale of New Hartford. The result of two days of deliberation was the formation of a voluntary association of ministers, the "Connecticut Pastoral Union," with a conservatively Edwardean but not extreme creed, based on a draught which had already been submitted to the meeting at Hartford in the previous January and in which the New Haven peculiarities were distinctly opposed. This "Pastoral Union," into which the meeting at East Windsor had resolved itself, now took steps toward founding a new theological seminary, having its creed as the doctrinal test. Rev. Dr. Tyler was soon chosen professor of Christian Theology, and a fund of $20,000 was raised by January, 1834. The contributions of one of the larger donors determined the location of the new seminary at East Windsor Hill, and this determination was strengthened by the desire that the students should gain physical exercise, then just beginning to be recognized as of importance in educational institutions, by work upon a farm. The new seminary, known as the "Theological Institute of Connecticut," was formally opened on May 13, 1834, with Dr. Tyler, and Rev. Dr. Jonathan Cogswell of New Britain, as its professors. In the following October, Rev. William Thompson, a native of Goshen, Conn., and just entering on a pastorate at what is now Brockton, Mass., became professor of Biblical Literature. His connection with the seminary lasted till his death, in 1889, and to his wisdom, patience, self-denial, and teaching skill, whatever success the institution has had is chiefly due. Professor Tyler's connection continued till 1857, and in 1858, the same year that witnessed the demise of Professor Taylor, he died. Public interest in the particular questions in debate between the two institutions had been declining, and can scarcely be said to have survived the departure of the two champions. Fruitless efforts were made just before the deaths of Taylor and Tyler and again in 1864 to unite the two Connecticut seminaries. The isolated location at East Windsor Hill proved unfavorable to the younger institution, and it therefore removed in 1865 to Hartford, where after a few years of domicile in its new location and a very marked growth in strength, its name was altered to that of "Hartford Theological Seminary." It has always borne the somewhat conservative impress given to it by its founders.

Contemporary with the establishment of a second theological seminary in Connecticut, a very remarkable movement led to the undertaking of a great educational and missionary enterprise in Ohio, out of which, through a chain of circumstances of much interest, a theological seminary speedily grew. Oberlin College had its beginnings in the thought of Rev. John J. Shipherd, the young pastor of the Presbyterian Church at Elyria, O., a native of Granville, N. Y., who had had his theological training under the hymn-writer, Rev. Dr. Josiah Hopkins, long a Vermont minister, and settled at Auburn, N. Y., in 1830. Shipherd had as his associate in his plans Rev. Philo P. Stewart, a native of Sherman, Conn., who had been a missionary of the American Board among the Choctaw Indians, but was now living in Shipherd's household. In 1832 they conceived the idea of a Christian college, open to men and women alike, furnishing an education to all who wished at a moderateness of cost which should put it within the reach of the most needy, and ultimately offering preparatory, normal, collegiate, and theologic instruction. This institution they proposed to surround with a self-denying Christian community, pledged to common effort for the advancement of the Redeemer's kingdom. This far-reaching undertaking was begun almost as soon as it had been determined upon. A large tract of uncleared forest land in the Western Reserve was obtained, and in April, 1833, the Oberlin colony,—a band of people all of whom could trace back their family origin to New England,—settled upon it and erected a college building. Instruction was begun that year, and in 1834 the school was regularly organized. In September, 1834, the Oberlin church, an institution vitally connected with the college, was formed. This church was originally on the "Plan of Union"; but in 1836 it became wholly and actively Congregational, and since that time Oberlin has been a thoroughly Congregational community and college. No institution has been more useful to our churches than this educational center; its life has been one of intense spiritual activity, of deep consecration, of high, self-denying achievement, and Congregationalism to-day has few agencies for which it has more profound reason to be thankful than for Oberlin College.

It was the intention of the projectors of Oberlin that the foundation should ultimately include a theological department,—the actual establishment of that seminary came about unexpectedly, however, in 1835. Lane Seminary, a Presbyterian institution of "New School" sympathies, had been founded at Cincinnati, O., in 1829, and had opened its doors for theological students in 1832, with two of its three professors men of New England birth who had been prominent in Congregational circles, Rev. Drs. Lyman Beecher and Calvin E. Stowe. Soon after its opening the Abolition movement began to make a stir in the land, and the students of Lane Seminary, being located just on the border of slavery, entered with eagerness into the discussion and largely adopted antislavery sentiments. Alarmed lest the agitation should injure the seminary, its trustees in 1834, without consulting the faculty as a whole, adopted a rule forbidding the students to discuss slavery in public or in private. Four fifths of the students speedily left the institution in a body, and after some negotiation proposed to go to Oberlin provided Rev. Charles G. Finney could be secured as a theological instructor. At the same time Shipherd urged the Oberlin trustees to throw open their doors to colored students,—a step of then unheard-of boldness. The proposition was keenly opposed, but was finally carried by the casting vote of the presiding officer of the board, and it placed Oberlin permanently on the basis of the Christian equality of all men, white or black. At the same meeting the trustees elected Finney professor of Theology; and in the spring of 1835, a few weeks after this action of the trustees, the Lane students came, and Oberlin Theological Seminary was established.

Rev. Charles G. Finney, whose coming as professor of theology had been so earnestly desired in 1835, and whose connection with the college at Oberlin as teacher and as president was to continue till his death in 1875, was a man of remarkable gifts and marked peculiarities. He was born in Warren, Conn., in 1792, but his early training was in western New York. Here he grew up with meager opportunities for study, and intending to devote himself to the law, till he experienced a profound religious awakening in 1821. Licensed to preach in 1824, he became one of the most laborious of American evangelists, extending his efforts all through the New England and Middle States, and being characterized by a type of preaching and a method of revivalistic work which, though extremely effective, seemed to many to be extravagant, and led to some opposition even from evangelists like Lyman Beecher and Asahel Nettleton. Many incidents are yet related of his direct public prayers for individuals by name, and various other eccentricities of manner by which he was always marked. Finney settled in New York in 1832, and in 1834 became pastor of the Broadway Tabernacle Congregational Church of that city, from which post he went to Oberlin.

In his theology Finney belonged in a general way to the Edwardean school, but he gave to his system some features that were certainly far removed from the older "New England Divinity." He laid even more stress on the natural ability of the sinner to repent than the later Edwardeans had done. To his thinking, as to that of some of the New England Edwardeans, holiness and sin attach only to voluntary actions; but he drew a conclusion that was his own, holding that since these qualities are diametrically opposed they cannot coexist in man. Holiness is entire obedience to God; all sin is as positive and complete disobedience. When a Christian sins, his obedience is wholly interrupted for the time. But it is possible, by the aid of the Spirit of God, to live in continuous obedience even in this world, and every Christian should labor and should expect to make this abiding obedience the permanent condition of his life on earth. These doctrines seemed to many of Finney's contemporaries to savor of Arminianism, as they certainly did of Perfectionism,—a feeling that was not lessened when in 1836, partly through its desire to welcome Christians of all shades to its fellowship, the Oberlin church, which embraced the leaders of the college and community, dropped the doctrines of election and perseverance from its creed. The more strongly Calvinistic Congregational churches of the West, and New England generally, looked upon the orthodoxy of Oberlin with doubt, and this doubt strengthened the suspicions regarding western Congregationalism, which did so much to maintain the "Plan of Union" in operation in its later years, and which were not wholly removed till after the

Albany Convention of 1852. But the spiritual power and consecrated purpose of Oberlin in time won it great respect, though Finney's interpretation of Christian truth has never found large acceptance in the Congregational churches.

This brief sketch of the religious forces which molded Congregationalism in the period of awaking religious life and rapid transition in methods that forms the theme of this chapter would not be complete without the mention of a theologian who represented in large measure a breaking away from the Edwardean type of thought which had gradually come to dominate Congregationalism,—Horace Bushnell. Bushnell was a native of Litchfield, Conn., where he was born in 1802, and a graduate of Yale in the class of 1827. For the next four years he was a teacher, a journalist, and then a student of law and a tutor at his *alma mater*. A religious experience in 1831 turned his thoughts to the ministry, and he entered Yale Divinity School, where Professor Taylor was then in the height of his fame, graduating in 1833. The same year he began his only pastorate, that of the North (now Park) Congregational Church at Hartford, in whose service he remained till ill-health compelled his resignation in 1859. He died February 17, 1876. Never a man of vigorous constitution, he was an untiring worker, and a most public-spirited citizen, leaving the impress of his marked personality in many ways on the community where he lived.

Bushnell's first important publication was his "Discourses on Christian Nurture," issued in 1847. In this book he broke with the conception emphasized by the whole Edwardean school, which had looked upon entrance into the kingdom of God as by a "conversion," usually involving a conscious submission to God. This experience, while not denied to children, is characteristic of adult years;

and the tendency of the Edwardean reaction from the abuses of the Half-Way Covenant was to cause those who were the baptized children of the church to be regarded as little more in the way of salvation, as long as they were unconverted, than any other children. In this book Bushnell returned in large measure to the pre-Edwardean New England view; though he presented it in a very modern way. Membership in a Christian family and baptism ought, he held, to render the child presumptively one of the household of faith. The "true idea of Christian education," Bushnell declared, is "that the child is to grow up a Christian, and never know himself as being otherwise." For such a child a "great change of experience" is not necessary. "He ought not to be the subject of any such change; and if he is properly trained, will not be."

This presentation of the possibilities of Christian nurture, as Bushnell conceived them, aroused opposition from many earnest Edwardeans to whom his doctrines seemed to imply that a man became a Christian by education rather than by the direct change of his heart by a sovereign act of God. Professor Tyler of the Theological Institute of Connecticut was one of these. In a "Letter to Dr. Bushnell," printed in 1847, Tyler maintained: "That the child should grow up a Christian, it is necessary that he should become a Christian. . . . Those to whom the privilege is given to become the sons of God . . . are not Christians by natural descent. Grace is not hereditary. . . . They are not converted by any efforts of their own, made in an unrenewed state. . . . They are not converted by moral suasion, or by any efforts of man. They are not made Christians by education. . . . It is God's prerogative to change the heart."

Two years later, in 1849, Bushnell published a yet more debate-stirring series of discourses,—his "God in Christ."

In this work he presented a semi-Sabellian theory of the divine existence, and a view of the atonement which placed its entire emphasis on its man-ward aspects. To Bushnell's thinking, the Trinity is a truth of Christian experience: "I do not undertake to fathom the interior being of God, and tell how it is composed. That is a matter too high for me, and, I think, for us all. I only insist that, assuming the strictest unity and even simplicity of God's nature, he could not be efficiently or sufficiently revealed to us, without evolving a trinity of persons, such as we meet in the Scriptures." But "whatever may be true of the Father, Son, and Holy Ghost, it certainly is not true that they are three distinct consciousnesses, wills, and understandings. Or, speaking in a way more positive, they are instrumentally three,—three simply as related to our finite apprehension, and the communication of God's incommunicable nature."

In his judgment, likewise, the atonement is "the Life of God . . . manifested in Jesus Christ, to quicken the world in love and truth, and reunite it to himself." "My doctrine is summarily this; that, excluding all thoughts of a penal quality in the life and death of Christ, or of any divine abhorrence to sin, exhibited by sufferings laid upon his person; also, dismissing, as an assumption too high for us, the opinion that the death of Christ is designed for some governmental effect on the moral empire of God in other worlds,—excluding points like these, and regarding everything done by him as done for expression before us, and thus for effect in us, he does produce an impression in our minds of the essential sanctity of God's law and character, which it was needful to produce, and without which any proclamation of pardon would be dangerous, any attempt to subdue and reconcile us to God, ineffectual."

These opinions set forth in Bushnell's "God in Christ"

were at once attacked in the New York "Evangelist," the "Christian Observatory" of Boston, the "Princeton Review," the "Religious Herald" of Hartford, and elsewhere. A few months after the publication of the book, the Hartford Central Association, of which Bushnell was a member, took up the case, but decided eventually against action. Against this course, the Association of Fairfield West remonstrated in January, 1850; and in 1850 and 1852 the case was laid before the General Association of Connecticut, but that body did not interfere. Bushnell's church as a whole decidedly sympathized with its pastor, and since the case could still be brought before the local consociation for trial if three members of his church should make complaint, the church, on June 27, 1852, withdrew from the Hartford North Consociation,—a step which the general break-down of the consociational system that was to result in the suspension of the Hartford Consociation itself in 1871 rendered not very difficult.

These theories, and Bushnell's later works which in some measure enforced and developed them, notably his "Nature and the Supernatural" of 1858, "The Vicarious Sacrifice" of 1866, and "Forgiveness and Law" of 1874, not only created discussion, but two of the three views which have been described have secured an abiding following. The New England mind has in it little of the old Greek desire to speculate for speculation's sake; and Bushnell's thoughts regarding the Trinity, though pitched upon most prominently by his opponents, have had scant currency and have excited little real interest. But his "moral theory" of the atonement has gained considerable following, though its adherents are still a decided minority among Congregational ministers; and his conception of the importance of Christian nurture and of the consequences which may be expected from it has awakened even wider response, though it, too, is by no means unquestioned. Bushnell well represents a type of departure from some of the older New England ways of thinking, especially from the views of the Edwardean school which dominated the first half of the nineteenth century, that has become increasingly common during the last thirty years.

CHAPTER X.

THE DENOMINATIONAL AWAKENING—MODERN CONGREGATIONALISM.

THE general indifference regarding the extension of Congregational polity which had marked the epoch of doctrinal discussion introduced by the Great Awakening continued well toward the middle of the nineteenth century. It has already been pointed out that the three oldest national missionary societies of Congregationalism were interdenominational organizations in their earlier years. Under the "Plan of Union" a multitude of churches grew up in the older West neither purely Presbyterian nor wholly Congregational. Theological seminaries in their instruction laid little or no emphasis on Congregational polity. Ministers passing from regions where Congregationalism was prevalent to sections permeated by Presbyterianism changed their church affiliations as readily as they changed their residences, and Presbyterians coming to New England were as cordially received. The descendants of those who had crossed the ocean to establish what they believed to be the only polity warranted by the Word of God now seemed to hold that polity was a matter of geography rather than of principle,—that a church westward of the Hudson ought to be Presbyterian as surely as one east of that dividing stream should be Congregational.

But at last, soon after the beginning of the fourth decade of the present century, Congregationalism began to show signs of awaking to a sense of its own mission and its right to be. These evidences were first apparent in the regions where Congregationalism was brought into active comparison with other polities, as in the older and more recent West. State Associations began to arise in territories where missionary labors had been carried on under the "Plan of Union"; and afforded distinct evidence of the dawning self-recognition of the Congregational churches. The first of these then esteemed Western bodies to come into being was that of New York, formed at Clinton on May 21, 1834. The establishment of Oberlin College in 1832–34 was a step of the utmost importance for the history of Congregationalism in Ohio; and was followed on October 29, 1834, by the creation of the "Independent Congregational Union of the Western Reserve." In September, 1836, the churches and ministers of the Reserve were united into a General Association at Oberlin, designed "to afford such of them as choose, the free exercise of their Congregational rights." The Reserve was only a section of a State, but its character was so individual that the formation of its Association was an event of great importance. It showed that the Congregational elements were beginning to crystallize out of the general solution into which they had been cast by the "Plan of Union." But consolidation came slowly in Ohio, largely by reason of doctrinal divergences between the Oberlin theology and the older Calvinism; and a General Association for the whole State was not brought into being till June 24, 1852, when far-off Oregon had already had a State Association for four years. The General Association of Iowa was organized at Denmark on November 6, 1840; and that of Michigan at Jackson on October 11, 1842. Next came the State body of Illinois on June 21, 1844; that of Kansas in 1855, California in 1857, Indiana in 1858, and those of the newer Western States in rapid succession.

A glance at the sequence of these events reveals at once the fact that by 1840 the home-missionary pioneers of the Congregational body upon the frontier were making more strenuous efforts to advance Congregational polity than they had thus far done. Hence it was that Iowa had a General Association four years before the much older State of Illinois, and two years before Michigan. This increased emphasis on church government was not due to any prescriptions of the missionary societies or of the contributors to the missionary treasuries. It was owing to the awakening denominational consciousness of the Congregational body itself,—an awakening which first became evident in the West, and which at last aroused New England after it had fully demonstrated that Congregationalism was as well able to bring forth its characteristic fruits in the forming communities of the new States as it had been in the New England of two hundred years before.

This development of denominational spirit is well illustrated in the introduction of Congregationalism into the adjacent States of Illinois and Iowa. Illinois belonged to the "Old Northwest" which was organized into a free territory by the celebrated Ordinance of 1787. Iowa was a portion of the Louisiana purchase of 1803. The first connection of Illinois with Congregational missionary enterprise was in 1812, when Samuel J. Mills, the friend of foreign missions, made report regarding the region to the Connecticut Missionary Society. He found the Methodists and Baptists already at work on the field. But though Congregational missionary societies were actively at work in Illinois by 1814, their labors were at first wholly along the lines of the "Plan of Union." It was not till 1831 that there was a distinctly Congregational church in the State,—that of Princeton, which had been organized at Northampton, Mass., and had emigrated in a body. Till the arrival of that church in its Illinois home, the churches gathered by New England missionaries, and often composed of New England material, had become Presbyterian in their affiliations. After 1833, when four Congregational churches were formed, the polity slowly spread; and by 1843 the Congregational churches of Illinois numbered sixty-one. Yet so thoroughly had the consequences of the "Plan of Union" controlled the religious concerns of the State, and so widespread was the doubt whether Congregationalism could flourish outside of New England, that it was not till May 22, 1851, that the first Congregational church in Chicago was organized,—a city which now contains fifty-one churches of this order. Not a little of the early growth of Congregationalism in Illinois and the slow reversal of the prejudice against the polity as unadapted to frontier communities was due to President Julian M. Sturtevant, whose connection with Illinois College at Jacksonville,—the first Congregational college of the State,—lasted from its opening, in 1830, to his death, in 1886.

In marked contrast to these tardy beginnings in Illinois was the rapid introduction of Congregationalism into Iowa, —a region where settlements were beginning just about the time that the revived interest in polity first clearly appeared. The credit for having preached the first Protestant sermon in Iowa belongs to a Methodist, who visited that new Territory in 1834. But the "American Home Missionary Society" was in the field by 1835, and the Presbyterians and Congregationalists both organized their first churches in the spring of 1838. That of Denmark, which bears the distinction not only of being the first church of the Congregational order in Iowa, but the first beyond the Mississippi, was founded on May 5, 1838, in a New England settlement begun nearly two years before, and had for its minister Rev. Asa Turner, to whose energy and enthusiasm the Congregationalism not only of Iowa but of the whole West is conspicuously indebted. This work, so vigorously begun, was taken up by nine students from Andover Seminary, who had associated themselves for missionary labor while at that seat of learning, and who now, on their graduation in 1843, came to Iowa. Though they did not make the planting of denominationalism chief, they believed that Congregationalism was adapted to the West. The members of this "Iowa Band" were ordained at Denmark, November 5, 1843, and at once threw themselves into the work of upbuilding Christian institutions on the Congregational model. Through their influence and that of Turner, Congregationalism thus took deep root in Iowa while the State was still in the gristle. And Congregationalism manifested here the same interest in education which has always been one of its distinguishing marks. In 1843 an academy was opened at Denmark; and in 1847 the earliest college in the State—Iowa College—was established at Davenport, though since 1860 the location of this wide-awake Congregational school of learning has been at Grinnell.

Contemporary with these events in Iowa, the foundations of Congregationalism were being laid in Wisconsin. The earliest church of this order there was, indeed, that among the Stockbridge Indians,—a tribe that had been gradually driven westward from the Massachusetts home where they had enjoyed the services of John Sergeant and Jonathan Edwards, till they settled in Wisconsin in 1821. Here, as in Illinois, the Methodists and Baptists were early in the field laboring among the white immigrants, establishing themselves in Wisconsin in 1835–38. But by July, 1835, the "American Home Missionary Society" had entered the region. The first Congregational church of Wisconsin was gathered at Waukesha on January 20, 1838, and was followed in the same year by others at Kenosha and at Beloit. Here at Beloit, nine years later, and largely through Congregational efforts, one of the most valued of Western educational institutions—Beloit College—came into full being. In Wisconsin Presbyterians and Congregationalists seem to have thought from the first that the "Plan of Union" should be laid aside, and that churches should be formed distinctly of one order or the other; but this wise determination did not prevent cordial relations between the two denominations, which united in October, 1840, in the "Presbyterian and Congregational Convention of Wisconsin." This agreement made no provision for composite churches, such as had been characteristic of the older union. From this convention most of the Presbyterian churches withdrew within a few years, leaving it essentially Congregational.

Minnesota, the State immediately northwestward of Wisconsin, was originally foreign missionary ground. In 1835 the American Board began labor among the Dakota Indians about Fort Snelling; but the few churches which they gathered, some of which contained white persons, were affiliated with Presbyterianism. In 1849 the "American Home Missionary Society" entered the field; and as its first missionaries thither were Presbyterians, the churches gathered in 1849 at St. Paul and at Stillwater, as well as that formed in 1850 at St. Anthony, were of that order. But in 1850 Rev. Charles Seccombe and Rev. Richard Hall, missionaries of the same society and of Congregational sentiments, reached Minnesota. The day for founding mixed churches had about gone by; and though Seccombe had been commissioned by the society to St. Anthony, the little Minnesota Presbytery, which had just been organized, refused to install him over the Presbyterian church at that place unless he would join the Presbytery.

This just demand was met on Seccombe's part by an equally justifiable refusal to give up his Congregationalism, and he therefore gathered the first Congregational church of Minnesota at St. Anthony on November 16, 1851,—the body now known as the First Church of Minneapolis. Attempts on the part of the "Home Missionary Society" to unite the two churches in St. Anthony resulted in the ultimate junction of both in a Congregational body. In February, 1852, Hall founded the second Congregational church in Minnesota, at Point Douglas. Four years later the State Association came into being; and by 1858 the Congregational churches in the region numbered thirty, largely owing to the efforts of Seccombe and Hall. The impulse thus early imparted has given Congregationalism a strong hold on this State.

Contemporary with the establishment of Congregationalism in Minnesota the permanent introduction of this polity into Missouri was effected. The missionary spirit of New England had early gone out toward Missouri. In 1812 and 1814 Samuel J. Mills had investigated its religious needs in behalf of the Connecticut and Massachusetts Missionary Societies; by 1815 these bodies had begun sending laborers thither, and the work was taken up with vigor by the "American Home Missionary Society" at its organization. But partly owing to the doubt which existed in the minds of New England men during the early years of the century as to whether Congregationalism could flourish in the West, and partly by reason of the slight sympathy for New England institutions felt by the slave-holding and largely Southern population of the State, Presbyterianism rather than Congregationalism was introduced by these missionaries. With the exception of an abortive attempt to establish a Congregational church commenced at Arcadia in 1841, the beginnings of this denomination were at St. Louis on March 14, 1852, when the First Congregational Church was formed through the efforts of a man to whom Western Congregationalism was profoundly indebted,—Rev. Truman M. Post. This earnest Congregationalist was born in Middlebury, Vt., in 1810, and after service at Jacksonville, Ill., from 1833 to 1847 as professor in Illinois College and then as pastor of the Congregational church, he entered the ministry of the Third Presbyterian Church at St. Louis in 1847 on an engagement for four years. Here his views on polity were well known, though not advanced in any underhanded way, and this knowledge led to the establishment of a Congregational church under his pastoral care soon after his engagement with the Presbyterian body had terminated. Of this new church he continued the spiritual guide till his death, in 1886; but his influence was widely felt in denominational affairs and was a force far beyond the bounds of the State of his residence.

Congregationalism had reached the Pacific Ocean even before the events which have last been noticed. Oregon, the only region claimed by the United States which touched that ocean till the Mexican War had resulted in the conquest of California, was the first scene of its operations, and was at first regarded as foreign missionary ground. The American Board entered upon attempts at the Christianization of the Indians in 1835, sending out Marcus Whitman, a missionary physician, and Rev. Henry H. Spalding, with their wives. In 1836 these pioneers reached the land of their pilgrimage by the then perilous overland route. By 1838 their labors were reinforced by those of Rev. Cushing Eells, and other workmen followed. Oregon was still in dispute between the United States and Great Britain, and to Whitman's energy and skill its preservation to the United States was due. A journey to the national capital in the winter of 1842–43, at great personal hazard, prevented the possible abandonment of this valuable region to Great Britain as not worth the keeping. Whitman died a martyr at Indian hands in 1847; while Eells lived till 1893, and interwove his long and useful life in the history of the religious and educational institutions of the States of Oregon and Washington. The early missionaries labored of course among the Indian natives, but with the incoming of white settlers religious institutions were planted among them,—the first permanent Congregational church in Oregon being that at Oregon City, organized in 1844. On July 13, 1848, the Congregational ministers and churches of Oregon formed a General Association; and the same year the first laborer of the "American Home Missionary Society," Rev. Dr. George H. Atkinson, began his long career of service to the Congregational churches of the State. The Congregational love of education was exhibited by the founding, largely through the efforts of these missionaries, of Tualatin Academy in 1848, and its higher department, Pacific University, in 1853, at Forest Grove.

The discovery of gold in California in 1848 was followed by the great rush of emigrants thither in 1849, and with them came some who were interested in the souls of their fellow-men. Rev. Timothy D. Hunt, probably the first Protestant minister in California, reached San Francisco in November, 1848; and the next year there came Rev. Joseph A. Benton, like Hunt a graduate of Yale, and destined not only to be a leader in Congregational ecclesiastical affairs on the Pacific Slope, but later to be identified with Pacific Theological Seminary, at Oakland, from its foundation, in 1869, to his death, in 1892. The "Old School" wing of the Presbyterians was slightly in advance in obtaining definite ecclesiastical organization in California, gathering a church in May, 1849, but the Congregationalists were not far behind. The First Church, San Francisco, came into being on July 29, 1849, and Rev. Mr. Hunt, who had been the first minister on the ground, was speedily installed as its pastor. Two months later, the second church in California—that of Sacramento—was formed, with Benton as its minister. In 1857 a General Association was organized.

It is thus evident that soon after 1830 the denominational consciousness, largely though not wholly dormant in the early part of the century, began to awake, and Congregationalism all through the Western States began to take a more self-reliant and aggressive attitude. Though union efforts still continued, Congregationalists felt increasingly that their polity had claims which could not be ignored.

While this development was in progress in the West, a few men in the East were slowly arousing the older churches to a sense of their heritage in polity. Conspicuous among these leaders of Congregational thought was Rev. Dr. Leonard Bacon,—the son of a missionary sent forth by the Connecticut society, and actively pastor of the First Church, New Haven, from 1825 to 1866,—a relation which he did not wholly sever till his death, in 1881. Dr. Bacon was a man of commanding power as a speaker, of warm interest in the antislavery movement, of marked taste for historical study, and a natural leader of men. From his boyhood he was fascinated by the story of the struggles and successes of the New England forefathers. One of the earliest of the literary productions of his maturer years was the volume of "Thirteen Historical Discourses," of 1839, in which he told in graphic fashion the experiences for two centuries of the church of which he was the pastor; one of the latest of his writings was his "Genesis of the New England Churches," which he put forth in 1874. He was largely instrumental in founding the "New Englander" at New Haven in 1843, and the New York "Independent" in 1848; and was a powerful opponent of slavery. He was ardently a Congregationalist of a broad and catholic type, leaning a little to the side of Independency. Living in a State where the consociational modification of the Congregational system was strongly intrenched, his influence largely contributed to the abandonment of its more Presbyterianizing peculiarities. It was Dr. Bacon's good fortune to be able to communicate this hearty love for the Congregational polity to others, so as to kindle an interest in its investigation and development; and in his later life he came justly to be looked up to with reverence in ecclesiastical gatherings as an authority in all matters of Congregational usage.

Another leader to whom Congregationalism was conspicuously indebted in this period was Rev. Dr. Joseph P. Thompson, like Bacon a graduate of Yale, who held the pastorate of the Broadway Tabernacle Church in New York City from 1845 to 1871. With Bacon he was associated in the establishment of the "New Englander" and the "Independent"; and though he never came to be the authority on Congregational concerns that Bacon did, his labors for the advancement of the denomination were very considerable.

In Rev. Dr. Joseph S. Clark, of Massachusetts, a third minister largely influential in the revived appreciation of the New England polity appeared. A graduate of Amherst College in 1827, and of Andover Seminary in 1831, he had a brief pastorate at Sturbridge, Mass., but his chief activity was spent as secretary of the "Massachusetts Missionary Society" from 1839 to 1857. His last days till his death, in 1861, were devoted to the service of the "Congregational Library" and of the "Congregational

Quarterly," of which there will be occasion later to speak. No man knew the story of the Massachusetts churches better than he, and none was more convinced that Congregationalism had a mission. He had little patience with the readiness to subordinate polity to plans of union manifested so often by the Congregationalists of the first third of this century. "We have been well called 'the Lord's silly people,'" he declared; and his opposition to such unwisdom increased with his advancing years.

The efforts of these men, and of others whom they aroused or who labored with them, were greatly aided by the ever-increasing study of the life and ideals of early New England,—a study in which all scholarly New England has joined, and which has made the work and aims of the founders more familiarly and definitely known with each passing year since the early part of the present century.

The first impulse emanating from an official source looking toward greater recognition of the unity of Congregationalism, East and West, the removal of doctrinal prejudice, and a more aggressive assertion of Congregational claims, appears to have come from the then newly formed General Association of Michigan. In 1845 Rev. L. Smith Hobart, a Yale graduate of 1837, then pastor of the church at Union City, Mich., and secretary of the Michigan Association, proposed a "General Convention of Western Congregationalists" to deliberate concerning denominational advancement; and, as a result of an approval of this recommendation by the body of which Hobart was secretary, such a "Convention" brought together representatives of the churches of the Northwestern States and a few men from the East at Michigan City, Ind., in July, 1846. That body declared the adherence of the Western churches to the historic theology of New England, and discussed the feasibility of abrogating the "Plan of Union."

This impulse which went out from Michigan was taken up by the oldest of the General Associations on what had been Western home missionary ground,—that of New York,—and largely through the efforts of Rev. Dr. J. P. Thompson, of whom mention has already been made. As a result of an invitation issued by that body, asking every Congregational church in the United States that felt so disposed to send its pastor and a delegate, there gathered at Albany, N. Y., on October 5, 1852, the first council or synod representative of American Congregationalism as a whole that had met since the Cambridge Synod of 1646–48. In this "Albany Convention" four hundred and sixty-three pastors and messengers from the churches of seventeen States gathered. It was a body illustrative of the best spirit and embracing the leaders of the Congregational churches of East and West. And it proceeded at once to examine the denominational situation with fullness. Its Business Committee, under the guidance of Rev. Dr. Bacon, of New Haven, speedily announced its work to be to discuss: "1. The construction and practical operation of the 'Plan of Union.' . . . 2. The building of Church Edifices at the West. 3. The system and operations of the 'American Home Missionary Society.' 4. The intercourse between the Congregationalists of New England and those of other States. 5. The local work and responsibility of a Congregational Church. 6. The bringing forward of Candidates for the Ministry. 7. The re-publication of the Works of our standard Theological writers."

The labors of the "Albany Convention," thus vigorously mapped out, were carried out with equal energy. After a thorough debate, the "Plan of Union" was abandoned by a unanimous vote; the "American Home Missionary Society" was approved as impartial in its administration and the "American Education Society" was commended; intercourse between the Congregationalists of the East and the West was urged, and "insinuations and charges of heresy in doctrine and of disorder in practice" of a vague and sweeping nature "made against Congregationalists at the West" were discountenanced; the reprinting and circulation of the works of the fathers and theologians of New England was advocated; and the growing opposition of Congregationalism toward slavery was manifested in a unanimous vote that the missionary societies ought to support only such ministers in slave States as would "so preach the gospel . . . that, with the blessing of God, it shall have its full effect in awakening and enlightening the moral sense in regard to slavery, and in bringing to pass the speedy abolition of that stupendous wrong." But the most efficient aid given by the "Albany Convention" to denominational extension was its call for $50,000 to aid in erecting meeting-houses in Ohio, Michigan, Wisconsin, Iowa, Indiana, Illinois, Missouri, and Minnesota. The response from the churches to this appeal was immediate and hearty, and their gifts reached the sum of $61,891. A more permanent reply was the organization at New York in May, 1853, of the body then called the "American Congregational Union,"—an indefinite title which was exchanged in 1892 for the descriptive name "Congregational Church Building Society." This association was broadly planned "to collect, preserve, and publish authentic information concerning the history, condition, and continual progress of the Congregational churches in all parts of this country," and "to promote, —by tracts and books, by devising and recommending to the public plans of coöperation in building meeting-houses and parsonages,— . . . the progress and well-working of the Congregational Church polity." In this effort it began in 1854 the publication of the "Year Book" of denominational statistics, which passed later to the pages of the "Congregational Quarterly," and is now issued under the editorial superintendence of Rev. Dr. Henry A. Hazen, by the Publishing Committee of the National Council, through the "Congregational Sunday-school and Publishing Society." The main work of the "American Congregational Union" has been, however, the payment of "last bills" after needy churches have done all in their power to provide themselves with buildings; and by this work the society has been a conspicuous factor in Congregational advancement. At the close of its first forty years of existence (1893) it had completed 2340 houses of worship and 309 parsonages, and had given permanency to many a struggling church which would otherwise have perished.

A further consequence of the "Albany Convention," more local in its effects, but nevertheless of general importance to American Congregationalism, was the reorganization at Boston of the "Congregational Library Association" in the same month that saw the beginnings of the "American Congregational Union." The germ of such an undertaking originated as early as 1838 in the thought of Professors Bela B. Edwards and Edwards A. Park, of Andover Seminary, and in 1847 Professor Edwards publicly advocated such an undertaking. A beginning was made in a comparatively feeble way, and a society drawing its membership from the immediate vicinity of Boston was founded in February, 1851. This body was now remodeled and its membership greatly extended on May 25, 1853, when its largely efficient life really began. The library thus instituted has become the chief single storehouse of Congregational literature on the continent, and now contains 32,000 volumes, besides nearly 60,000 pamphlets. But as its work went on the thoughts of the "Congregational Library Association" began to turn toward the possession of a "Congregational House," which might furnish accommodation for such of the benevolent societies of this order as had their offices in Boston and serve as denominational headquarters. An old residence was purchased in the spring of 1857; and with a view to these enlarging functions the name of the body was altered in 1864 to "American Congregational Association,"—a title which it still retains. It was not till 1871, however, that the present well-located but ill-arranged "Congregational House" was obtained. It is the ambition of the society to replace the ancient structure speedily with a building more worthy of the denomination; but there can be no doubt that the possession of a "House" at all, as well as the magnificent library, is in no small measure owing to the impulse that went out from the "Albany Convention." Not a little of the success of this Association and its library is due to the untiring labors of Rev. Dr. Joseph S. Clark, its corresponding secretary and librarian from 1853 to his death, in 1861, and of his successor till 1887, Rev. Dr. Isaac P. Langworthy.

While this movement for the preservation of Congregational literature and the housing of the Congregational missionary societies was in its beginnings, there was entering upon a pastorate at Boston a man to whom Congregationalism is as much indebted as to any who may be named among its founders or expounders,—Rev. Henry Martyn Dexter. Dr. Dexter was of Pilgrim blood, a native of Plympton, Mass., a township which has been carved out of old Plymouth. Born in 1821, his education was at Brown University and at Yale College, and after his graduation at the latter institution in 1840, his theological instruction was received at Andover. A pastorate at Manchester, N. H., lasted from 1844 to 1849, when he was settled over what is now Berkeley Temple, Boston,—a relation which he continued till 1867. Dr. Dexter's inclination toward religious journalism was marked, and in 1851 he became the editor of the "Congregationalist," which had commenced its career in 1849. Under his hand it prospered, and in 1867 it was united with the pioneer of the American weekly religious press, the "Boston Recorder," which dated its origin from 1816. Of this joint publication, generally known simply as the "Congregationalist," Dr. Dexter remained till his death, in 1890, the editor-in-chief and one of the proprietors; and he made it the most influential journal of Congregationalism.

Dr. Dexter was a man of painstaking scholarly accuracy and of indefatigable industry, and all his enthusiasm was drawn out by the story of Congregationalism and especially of its beginnings. In the pursuit of the obscure facts of the rise of the denomination he ransacked the libraries and archives of England and Holland, while his own library, now in the possession of Yale University, is the best collection of Congregational sources ever brought together by a single student. It was with him a collection for use, and the employment he made of it is revealed in his elaborate contributions to Congregational history. Twenty-five publications from his pen are enumerated, besides his constant editorial writings. His "Congregationalism: What it Is, Whence it Is, and How it Works," printed in 1865, is the ablest and most thorough modern exposition of the claims and methods of this polity. His monumental work, "The Congregationalism of the Last Three Hundred Years," put forth in 1880, is not only a treasure-house of facts regarding the early history of the body, gathered from the most obscure sources oftentimes and combined with remarkable skill, it is indispensable to the student of Congregationalism by reason of its enormous bibliographical apparatus. His

"As to Roger Williams" of 1876 and "The True Story of John Smyth" of 1881 are careful siftings of the evidence regarding disputed passages of Congregational story; while his "Handbook of Congregationalism," published in 1880, is the most extensively used compendium of the polity which it treats in outline. But Dr. Dexter was much more than a mere student, he was an active man of affairs. No voice was more influential than his in his later life in Congregational assemblies. He was a large-hearted, generous, clear-sighted, and honorable leader. His Congregationalism was so intense as to reach the *jure divino* height seldom attained by modern Congregationalists, though characteristic of the first century of the history of the denomination; but he held his views in no spirit of uncharitableness. He opposed all Presbyterianizing tendencies; but he welcomed attempts at the expression of denominational unity by deliberative assemblies on a national scale and by missionary societies rendered actually representative of and responsible to the churches. He, certainly more than any other man, pointed out the line of development in polity actually taken by American Congregationalism from 1865 to the present day; and he deserves a high rank among those who are reckoned the formulators and developers of the Congregational system.

With Dr. Dexter there was closely associated in his more public labors for denominational advancement a still active minister, Rev. Dr. Alonzo H. Quint, perhaps the ablest ecclesiastical parliamentarian that modern Congregationalism has produced, and a thorough student of its polity. From 1853 to 1863 Dr. Quint was Dexter's near ministerial neighbor, as pastor of the Central Church at Jamaica Plain, Mass., and though Dr. Quint's later pastoral labors and other activities have sometimes carried him farther away from Boston, his connection with all Congregational developments that have flowed out from eastern Massachusetts has been intimate.

It was in November, 1858, that Rev. Drs. Dexter, Quint, and Joseph S. Clark joined in the projection of a magazine of Congregational history, biography, statistical investigation, and exposition of polity, which should do a more positive work for the memory of the past of Congregationalism and its present advancement than any existing periodical. The plan, which originated with Dr. Dexter, was laid before the "Congregational Library Association" in November, 1858, and the result was the issue of the first number of the "Congregational Quarterly" in January, 1859, under the editorship of the three ministers whose names have been mentioned, and with the sanction of the Association. With its second issue it also obtained the official approval of the "American Congregational Union" of New York, and the secretary of that society, Rev. Isaac P. Langworthy, was added to its editorial force. The usual vicissitudes of religious journalism produced various editorial changes during the twenty years of life which the "Quarterly" enjoyed; but though the magazine never received the support from the churches which it deserved, it was one of the most important educational agencies of Congregationalism during the period of development from its inception to the establishment of the triennial National Council in 1871.

While this development of Congregational activity was in progress in the East, the revived denominational spirit which had led to the "Albany Convention" was producing no less important results in the West. Chief of these consequences was the foundation of a new Congregational theological seminary at Chicago. The thought of this institution for ministerial education seems to have come to its first expression by an organized ecclesiastical body in the wide-awake General Association of Michigan, which had already led the way in securing united action favorable to denomination extension by Western Congregationalists. At its meeting at Ann Arbor, May 31, 1853, Rev. L. Smith Hobart, already conspicuous in Michigan Congregational affairs, presented "a plan for Theological education," which the Association referred to a committee for report the following year. A carefully prepared "Plan for a Theological Seminary" was accordingly prepared; and having been duly approved by the Michigan General Association in 1854, was laid by it before the other Associations of the Northwestern States. Iowa was the first to respond favorably, on June 7, 1854, and the other bodies gradually fell into line. The result was that, after some preliminary negotiation, a convention of clerical and lay delegates, representing the churches of Michigan, Iowa, Indiana, Illinois, Wisconsin, and Missouri, met at Chicago on September 26 and 27, 1854, and organized the Chicago Seminary,—the first theological seminary of any denomination in Chicago,—appointing boards of directors and examiners, or "visitors." The seminary thus constituted was opened for students on October 6, 1858. The founders were far-sighted and ingenious, and they had the advantage of living in a time when confidence in the power of the Congregational polity to care for institutions representative of large bodies of our churches was much greater than when the New England seminaries were instituted. Instead, therefore, of committing their foundation to the charge of a self-perpetuating board of trustees, whose action was supervised by an equally self-perpetuating board of visitors, and the orthodoxy of whose professional appointments was tested by an unalterable creed, as at Andover; or making their foundation simply a department of a university responsible to the general corporation which governs the whole educational institution, as at Yale; or placing its control in the hands of a board of trustees elected by a self-perpetuating ministerial club, as at Hartford,—they adopted the much more Congregational plan of making the seminary depend ultimately on the churches, its directors and visitors being chosen by a convention of the churches of the States west of Ohio and east of the Rocky Mountains, meeting triennially at Chicago, and in which every one of those churches has a right to be represented by its minister and a delegate. To this convention, and through it to the churches, Chicago Seminary is responsible for its teaching and its administration. The seminary, which commenced its work in 1858 with two professors and twenty-nine students, has grown marvelously, and now has in attendance two hundred and two young men, while its faculty, its buildings, and its endowment give it high rank among Congregational institutions for ministerial training.

Something of the new strength of Congregationalism in Chicago was due to the entrance on a pastorate over the First Church in that city in 1857, the year before the seminary opened its doors, of an earnest and influential upholder of Congregational ideals,—Rev. Dr. William W. Patton. Dr. Patton was a native of New York City, born in 1821, who had served churches in Boston and Hartford, and who now for twenty years was connected with Congregational interests in Chicago. His last years, from 1877 to his death, in 1889, were spent as president of that noble institution for the education of colored youth at Washington, D. C., Howard University. On September 5, 1867, the first number of the "Advance" was issued at Chicago, and Dr. Patton remained the editor of this widely influential Congregational weekly till 1872.

Meanwhile Congregationalism was pushing rapidly into

the newer West. October 9, 1854, saw the formation of the first church of this order in Kansas, at Lawrence; and a General Association followed in August, 1855. Nebraska's first Congregational church, that of Omaha, came into being on May 4, 1856, and the Association followed on August 8, 1857. Colorado received Congregationalism in 1863,—a church being gathered at Central City on August 23d, and being followed by churches at Denver and Boulder in 1864, and by an Association on March 10, 1868. What is now South Dakota was reached in 1868, and a church organized at Yankton on April 8th, of which Rev. Dr. Joseph Ward, one of the most useful of the more recent Congregational ministry, was pastor from 1869 to 1883, when he entered upon the presidency of Yankton College, which he had helped to found in 1881,—a post that he held till his untimely death, in 1889. Still existing churches were formed in the State of Washington, at Seattle, in 1870; in Nevada, at Reno, in 1871; in Utah, at Salt Lake City, in 1874; in Indian Territory, in 1876; in Arizona, at Prescott, in 1880; and the same year in New Mexico, at Albuquerque; in North Dakota, at Fargo and elsewhere, in 1881. Idaho and Montana saw the establishment of permanent churches in 1882; and Oklahoma in 1889.

This extension was marked, as elsewhere in the story of Congregationalism, by the desire to establish institutions of Christian learning. Among the colleges which now came into being, chiefly through Congregational efforts, are: Washburn, at Topeka, Kan., in 1865; Carleton, at Northfield, Minn., in 1867; Doane, at Crete, Neb., in 1872; Drury, at Springfield, Mo., in 1873; Colorado, at Colorado Springs, Col., in 1874; Yankton, as has been noted, in 1881; Whitman, at Walla Walla, Ore., in 1883 (on the basis of an academy founded by Rev. Cushing

Eells in 1859 and opened in 1866); and Fargo, at Fargo, N. D., in 1887.

A more distinctly ecclesiastical undertaking was the organization by the Congregationalists of California in 1866 of a "Theological Seminary Association," which opened in June, 1869, the youngest of our denominational schools of ministerial instruction, Pacific Theological Seminary, at Oakland.

One name cannot be omitted from this story of increasing denominational strength, though it belongs to the latter part of the period just held in review,—that of Rev. Dr. A. Hastings Ross, the most original contributor to the discussion of Congregational polity that the West has developed. Dr. Ross was a native of Winchendon, Mass., in 1831, a graduate of Oberlin College and of Andover Seminary, who after a pastorate at Boylston in the State of his birth from 1861 to 1866, served successively the churches of Springfield and Columbus, Ohio; and then from 1876 to his death, in 1893, the church of Port Huron, Mich. Dr. Ross early became a student of the Congregational system of government, publishing much in its illustration and historical exposition. His best known and most useful works were his "Pocket Manual of Congregationalism," which he put forth in 1883, and his elaborate treatise, "The Church-Kingdom," of 1887. His thinking, though strictly Congregational, linked itself less definitely with the historic presentations of the polity than did that of Dr. Dexter. He was more of an innovator, and more of an asserter of the powers of ecclesiastical associations. His most marked and probably his most permanently influential view,—that regarding the basis of ministerial standing,—was, however, largely the outgrowth of what must be considered a positive improvement in Congregational usage which had come about at the West. As instituted in Massachusetts and Connecticut at the close of the seventeenth and beginning of the eighteenth centuries, the local Associations were simply assemblies of ministers, and such they largely continue to be in the New England States. It has already been seen that these Associations had for one of their duties the recommendation of candidates to vacant churches, and the custom of licensure thus established has persisted in New England to the present day. The chief infelicity of this arrangement is that it makes a preacher's approbation to the churches the work of a ministerial body and not that of the churches themselves. The increasing desire on the part of the churches for consultation and local helpfulness has led to the general introduction into New England, in addition to the Associations, during the present century, of district and State meetings for discussion, composed of representatives of the churches and of the ministers, usually under the name of "Conferences." These "Conferences" do not take the place of councils, they do not advise in the formation or discontinuance of pastoral relationships, or in the establishment of new churches, nor do they attempt to solve church quarrels, as a council does; they are meetings for friendly discussion, and for the choice of representatives to State and national assemblies. In the West, however, the "Associations" were early and generally composed of representatives of churches as well as of ministers; and they have continued to exercise the functions both of the New England Associations and Conferences, thus causing ministerial licensure to inhere in bodies truly representative of the churches,—a method undoubtedly more consistent with Congregational principles than that usual in New England.

It was this Western development of the Association that Dr. Ross proposed to make the basis of churchly and ministerial standing. In the Congregationalism of the "Cambridge Platform" a minister remains such only while actually in ministerial relations to a definite church; but this theory, though ably defended by expounders of polity like Dr. Dexter, was early practically disregarded, and a man once set apart for ministerial service by ordination came popularly to be looked upon as in some sense always a minister, whether in a pastorate or not. This abiding ministerial character raised the question of "ministerial standing" and responsibility. How should the good character of a minister not in the service of a local church be assured to others, and to whom should he be responsible for his delinquencies? The question became more pressing as the country grew larger and ministerial changes more frequent. For this difficulty Dr. Ross proposed a remedy in placing "accountable ministerial standing in District Associations, with the right of appeal in case of injustice to a council of churches." In a like manner Dr. Ross would give churches standing and accountability in Associations. Probably the old consociational system of Connecticut gave to Dr. Ross some hints as to his plan; but it was chiefly due to his own systematizing of elements already appearing in Western Congregational development. It would be too much to affirm that Dr. Ross's suggestions have become generally recognized Congregational usage. His theory of churchly standing certainly has not; but his view as to ministerial standing bids fair to become so, the National Council having voted at its session of 1886 "that the State organizations and local organizations of churches be recommended to consider such modification of their constitution as will enable them to become responsible for the ministerial standing of ministers within their bounds, in harmony with the principle that the churches of any locality decide upon their own fellowship."

While this Western development of Congregationalism had been in progress, the great Civil War had convulsed the United States and brought its burden of responsibility and opportunity upon the Congregational as upon the other Christian bodies of the land. Unlike some American denominations, the Congregational body was not rent by the struggle. Although a few churches of this order existed at the South before the war, the denomination never obtained any footing which made it a factor in the religious life of that region so long as slavery continued. The attitude toward human bondage assumed by the "Albany Convention" in 1852 has already been noticed, and Congregationalism both in New England and the West was strongly antislavery for many years before the rebellion began. But if the Civil War did not bring to the denomination a problem of division and reorganization, it did open to denominational effort a section of country which had never generally accepted Congregationalism by removing that which the Northern churches of this order believed was the greatest hindrance to their southward spread,—slavery; and it presented a problem in the emancipated negro that appealed powerfully to the missionary spirit of these churches. So desirable was coöperation in meeting the opportunites of the hour felt to be, that at least a year before the conclusion of hostilities an extensive movement was in progress looking toward a general council of the representatives of American Congregationalism.

The impulse toward this gathering went forth, it is interesting to note, from that "Convention of the Congregational Churches of the Northwest," which met once in three years at Chicago to choose the directors and visitors of the Chicago Seminary, and to consider the interests of the great region from which the members of the Convention were gathered. That body, under the leadership of Rev. Dr. T. M. Post, of St. Louis, voted that, in its opinion, "the crisis demands general consultation, coöperation, and concert among our churches, and to these ends, requires extensive correspondence among our ecclesiastical associations, or the assembling of a National Congregational Convention." A month later the proposals of the Chicago Convention were laid before the General Association of Illinois, and by that assembly a proposition for a "National Convention," like that which met at Albany in 1852, was sent to the other State Associations; and, before the summer of 1864 was over, received the approval successively of the representatives of the churches of Indiana, Michigan, Iowa, Ohio, Rhode Island, Maine, Connecticut, Vermont, Massachusetts, New York, and Minnesota. The churches of New Hampshire were divided, and there the State body disfavored the proposal. By the several approving State Associations committees were appointed, by whose joint action the plan of the national gathering should be perfected; and, as a result of their negotiations in a "Preliminary Conference" at New York on November 16, 1864, a "National Council" was called to meet at Boston on June 14, 1865, having as its members clerical and lay representatives of the churches, chosen by the local conferences or associations in the proportion of two for each ten churches, or fraction of ten in excess of one half, united in each such local body. At the same time a number of topics for discussion were agreed upon, covering a wide range of denominational interests, and committees were designated by which these themes should be suitably presented to the Council.

On the day appointed, the "National Council" gathered together in the Old South Meeting-house at Boston a membership of five hundred and two representatives of the churches. It was the most important convention that had met since the Cambridge Synod, and it was much more widely representative than its immediate predecessor, the

"Albany Convention." It was a Council well worthy of the churches, both in the distinguished character of its membership and the thoroughness with which the topics presented to its consideration were discussed. The significance of the opportunities opening before the Congregational body were thoroughly appreciated, and an earnest advance to meet them was urged; but probably the most memorable of the events of this Council were the discussions regarding a Declaration of Faith and a Statement of Polity. In Congregationalism each local church draws up its own articles of belief in any language which it may deem proper, under the limitation, of course, that a grossly erroneous or heretical statement would subject the church adopting it to withdrawal of fellowship by its sister churches. But though Congregationalism thus asserts the autonomy of the local congregation, its councils or synods have never hesitated to formulate its general doctrinal position, not as a test to be imposed on particular churches by external authority, but as a testimony as to what the belief of those churches is. It was natural, therefore, that one of the tasks to which the attention of the Council had been directed by the preliminary committees was the adoption of a statement of the faith of the churches whose creation it was. Such a declaration was reported to the Council, therefore, by a committee which the Preliminary Conference had designated for the purpose, and consisting of Rev. Dr. Joseph P. Thompson, Prof. Edward A. Lawrence of what is now Hartford Seminary, and Prof. George P. Fisher of Yale Divinity School. This suggested form was referred by the Council itself to a new committee, which elaborated it, and, in particular, introduced a paragraph in which it declared that the faith of the Congregational churches was "the system of truths which is commonly known among us as Calvinism."

There can be no doubt that the prevailing doctrinal positions of Congregationalism were then and still are essentially Calvinistic. But the sympathies of the denomination had broadened since the opening of the century, and many who were earnest Calvinists themselves felt that it would be a mistake to tie Congregational fellowship to any party shibboleth, even to one so venerated and historically so descriptive of Congregational beliefs as the name of the great Genevan theologian. The result was that the proposed paragraph of definition was earnestly debated, till it became evident that, if pushed to a vote, it would be adopted by a decided majority of the Council, and as evident that this affirmation that Congregational doctrine is Calvinism would seem unduly divisive and sectarian to a respectable minority. Such was the state of affairs in the Council when the day came which had been set apart for an excursion to the historic scenes of Plymouth. To a few of the body it seemed that a reunion on a spot so fragrant with the memory of the struggles and sufferings by which Congregationalism was planted on American soil would furnish a fitting occasion for the presentation of a modification of the declaration under discussion, from which the disputed phrase might be omitted. Such a form was hastily prepared by Rev. A. H. Quint, chairman of the Business Committee of the Council,—its last sentences being written, with a hat as a tablet, on the train that bore the Council to Plymouth. The new draught was chiefly taken from the forms already before the Council; but with the addition of a new opening paragraph, a new expression of the essential unity of the whole Church of Christ, and the omission, of course, of the phrase "Calvinism." Presented to the Council assembled on Burial Hill at Plymouth, it was accepted, subject to slight verbal revision, and after the return of the Council to Boston was adopted by a rising vote without opposition on June 23, 1865.

The "Burial Hill Declaration," which thus came into existence, is the only statement of faith formally approved by a council representative of American Congregationalism as a whole since the Cambridge Synod of 1648. It expresses "our adherence to the faith and order of the apostolic and primitive churches held by our fathers, and substantially as embodied in the confessions and platforms which our synods of 1648 and 1680 set forth or reaffirmed." It emphasizes the excellences of the Congregational polity; but at the same time it declares that "knowing that we are but one branch of Christ's people, while adhering to our own peculiar faith and order, we extend to all believers the hand of Christian fellowship, upon the basis of those great fundamental truths in which all Christians should agree." It recognizes clearly the obligation to missionary service incumbent upon the Church of Christ. Its chief defects are its indefiniteness as to the extent to which the seventeenth-century symbols whereto it makes reference are to be considered as standards of present faith, its merely general treatment of such doctrines as it specifically mentions, and its rhetorical form,—a form better suited to an address on an historic occasion than to a creed for local and permanent use. But that a declaration of faith should be issued at all by a voluntary body speaking in the name of the Congregational churches of America was a fact of great significance, and one which showed how much the sense of unity in the denomination had been growing since the period of indifference to polity which had characterized the early part of the century.

The "National Council" of 1865 was also charged with the formulation of a statement of polity; and, at the instance of the Preliminary Conference, Rev. Dr. Leonard

Bacon and Rev. A. H. Quint had prepared an elaborate treatise on church government, similar in size and arrangement to the "Cambridge Platform," and a concise epitome; both of which were duly laid before the National Council. Here the proposed formulæ encountered considerable discussion; and the result was that the Council itself adopted a brief statement of principles, drawn up by Professor Park of Andover, which constitutes so succinct and so admirable an epitome of modern Congregationalism that it may well be quoted in full:

Resolved, That this Council recognizes as distinctive of the Congregational polity—

First, The principle that the local or Congregational church derives its power and authority directly from Christ, and is not subject to any ecclesiastical government exterior or superior to itself.

Second, That every local or Congregational church is bound to observe the duties of mutual respect and charity which are included in the communion of churches one with another; and that every church which refuses to give an account of its proceedings, when kindly and orderly desired to do so by neighboring churches, violates the law of Christ.

Third, That the ministry of the gospel by members of the churches who have been duly called and set apart to that work implies in itself no power of government, and that ministers of the gospel not elected to office in any church are not a hierarchy, nor are they invested with any official power in or over the churches.

The Council also referred the elaborate statements of polity that had been laid before it to a committee of twenty-nine, widely representative of Congregationalism geographically, to serve as a basis for the preparation of a more lengthy treatise on polity, which the committee might report directly to the churches. The result was the publication in 1872 of the so-called "Boston Platform,"—a careful exposition of modern Congregational usage, in length somewhat resembling the "Cambridge Platform" of 1648. But though it bore the approving signatures of the twenty-six surviving members of the committee, and was in every way worthy of them, its very length and elaborateness have prevented it from coming into any extensive use.

The Council also discussed with much thoroughness the work of evangelization in the West and South, church-building, ministerial education, and other problems of the advancement of the kingdom of God. It is needless to say that it had no authority to bind the action of individual churches, and that it was not a judicial body; but its influence was none the less widely felt, and it contributed none the less positively to Congregational advancement.

The missionary work at the South, which was one of the objects of consideration at this National Council of 1865, and for which the emancipation of the slaves and the collapse of the rebellion had opened a door, had been carried on for a number of years under great difficulties by a Congregational society which was now coming into prominence and much enlarged activity,—the "American Missionary Association." This association grew out of several little missionary bodies of antislavery sympathies, which had felt that the older missionary societies were not sufficiently outspoken in their denunciation of human bondage. The oldest of these centers of impulse was the "Amistad Committee,"—an association formed in New York to provide legal defense and religious instruction for the captured cargo of the slave-schooner "Amistad," seized in August, 1839, and brought to New London, Conn. As a result of the labors of this committee the "Amistad" captives were declared free by the United States Supreme Court, were given religious teaching at Farmington, Conn., and were sent to Kaw Mendi, near Sierra Leone, in Africa. In order to perpetuate and extend the religious impression made upon these poor Africans, a little association was organized at Hartford, Conn.,—the "Union Missionary

Society,"—under the auspices of which three missionaries were sent out with the returning captives, who carried on work with some success in western Africa. A third little center for aid to the negro race was the "Committee for West India Missions," formed in 1844 to provide the support of Rev. David S. Ingraham, an Oberlin graduate, and those who were associated with him in missionary labors among the freedmen of Jamaica. Still another of these minor organizations was the "Western Evangelical Missionary Society,"—a body formed by the association of the churches in the Western Reserve of Ohio in 1843, for work among the Indians.

The existence of these unions led to the thought of a larger organization, of similar antislavery tendencies, which could do a like work on an extended scale. The result was the formation of the "American Missionary Association" at Albany on September 3, 1846, into which the older minor organizations speedily merged themselves or their work. The "American Missionary Association" was at first almost as much a foreign as a home missionary society. By 1854 it had 71 missionaries at various stations in Africa, Jamaica, the Hawaiian Islands, Siam, and Egypt, as well as among the American Indians and the negro fugitives who had found a refuge in Canada. At the same time it entered heartily into the work of upbuilding antislavery churches at home, employing by 1860 as many as 112 home missionaries, chiefly in Ohio, Indiana, Michigan, Illinois, Wisconsin, Minnesota, Iowa, and Kansas. A few of its missionaries were laboring among the whites of the slave States, especially in Kentucky, where they laid the foundations of Berea College, and in North Carolina, encountering everywhere much popular opposition; but as long as slavery continued the negroes of the South were practically inaccessible, and the impression made by the

"American Missionary Association" upon that region was almost inappreciable.

With the outbreak of the war, however, the whole situation was changed; and the Congregational churches found in the "American Missionary Association" the agency through which to labor for the newly emancipated colored population. With the entrance of the Union armies into the South the society began, on September 17, 1861, at Hampton, Va., the first day-school for the freedmen; and as the war went on other schools were planted at Norfolk, Va., Washington, D. C., Cario, Ill., Newbern, N. C., and in many other places, the teachers and missionaries following closely in the wake of the armies. By 1864 the society had 250 laborers among the negroes. At the close of the war the whole Southern field was thrown open to its operations, and the "American Missionary Association" received the hearty commendation of the National Council of 1865, which advised the churches to raise $250,000 for immediate work among the colored population. As a result, the income of the society, which had amounted to $47,062 in the year ending in 1862, rose to $253,045 in that closing in 1866. By 1867 the society had 528 missionaries and teachers in its employ.

The need of the negro seemed to be general training of mind and body almost as imperatively as religious instruction, and the "American Missionary Association" therefore, from its commencement of labor among the freedmen, aimed at the establishment of permanent educational institutions open to students without distinction of race. Largely through the efforts of this society, the Hampton Normal and Agricultural Institute, at Hampton, Va., was opened in 1868,—a training-school which has done a noble work for the freedmen and the Indians, under the leadership of General S. C. Armstrong, its principal from its beginning to his death, in 1893. Atlanta University, at Atlanta, Ga., incorporated in 1867 and opened two years later, is another educational center in which Congregationalists, and their "American Missionary Association," have had a large share. A similar interest has been felt in Howard University, founded at Washington, D.C., in 1867, where the Theological Department is still under the care of this society. These institutions are controlled as a whole by their own trustees. More directly under the charge of this agency of the Congregational churches are: Fisk University at Nashville, Tenn., opened as a school in 1866 and incorporated as an institution for higher education in 1867; Talladega College, situated in the town of the same name in Alabama, opened in 1867 and chartered two years later; Tougaloo University, named from the Mississippi village of its location, and begun in 1869, still rather of the grade of a normal school than what its title shows that it aims to be; Straight University, begun at New Orleans in 1869; and Tillotson Collegiate and Normal Institute at Austin, Texas, chartered in 1876. In these institutions manual and industrial instruction accompanies a thorough intellectual training. Theological courses are also given in Fisk, Talladega, and Straight, as well as at Howard, Universities. And besides these institutions of a higher grade, the "American Missionary Association" has founded numerous schools of primary and secondary education, so that the schools of all grades now under its charge in the South number seventy-eight.

While the "American Missionary Association" was thus busily engaged in the work of education at the South, it by no means neglected the planting of churches. Its first church among the colored people was organized at Charleston, S. C., on April 14, 1867; and the second followed at Atlanta, Ga., in May of the same year. Besides a considerable number of congregations that have become self-supporting, the society now maintains 152 churches in the South, and by its aid Congregationalism is now represented in every Southern State. These Congregational workers have cared more for character than numbers, and it may be that the negro can best be reached in large masses by polities demanding less individual intelligence than that of New England; but though these Southern churches of the Congregational fellowship are still comparatively few, they represent much self-denying labor, they are a credit to the Congregational name, and they and the educational institutions which Congregationalism has planted are of great value in holding up a high ideal before the colored people and in offering them the means for its attainment. They have sent out spiritual quickening far beyond the bounds of their nominal fellowship. They have stood with uncompromising firmness for the principle that no distinctions of race or color should be made in educational privileges or ecclesiastical fellowship. At the same time it is just to remark that so thoroughly has the "American Missionary Association" been the historic representative of the antislavery spirit of the North that the "Congregational Home Missionary Society" has found it advantageous, without abandoning the principle that no man should be denied fellowship in a Congregational church on account of color or race, to introduce its laborers, and to a limited extent to establish churches, in the Southern field.

The "American Missionary Association" was founded to labor among the Indians and in the foreign field as well as for the negro race. Its Indian missions were for a time intermitted during the exacting period of rapid increase in its Southern work consequent upon the war; but they were resumed in 1870, and these labors were much increased when the American Board transferred its missions among the Indians to this society as a result of negotiations begun in 1874 and completed in 1882. These missions are still maintained, and have been extended to the Eskimos of Alaska. They now report 92 laborers, 12 churches, and 12 schools. As part of the same agreement with the American Board, the "American Missionary Association" assigned its foreign work to the care of the older society.

Two other missionary efforts have marked the endeavors of the "American Missionary Association" to reach the neglected races of the United States,—its work among the Chinese and among the mountain whites. Attempts at the Christianization of Chinese immigrants in California were begun by this society as early as 1852, but it was not till 1870 that they were entered upon with system or on an extended scale. The society now employs 40 missionaries in this labor, and with results which show that the effort has been fairly successful. The work among the neglected white inhabitants of the mountains of Kentucky, Tennessee, and North Carolina was begun in a very feeble way as early as 1857; but in 1882 it was taken up in earnest by the society, and has proved one of the most interesting fields of missionary activity to which the attention of Congregationalists has been directed.

An illustration of the missionary spirit of the Congregational churches, though not peculiar to them, is the growing tendency toward the organization of Christian women for the general advancement of missionary enterprises, and especially for reaching their heathen sisters with the gospel through laborers of their own sex. In January, 1868, as a result of some previous negotiation, about forty women of the vicinity of Boston organized the "Woman's Board of Missions," which speedily became auxiliary to the American Board, its purpose, as expressed in its charter granted by the Massachusetts legislature in 1869, being "to collect, receive, and hold money . . . to be exclusively expended in sending out and supporting such unmarried females as the Prudential Committee of the American Board . . . shall, under the recommendation of the Board of Directors of this corporation, designate and appoint as assistant missionaries for the Christianization of women in foreign lands; and for the support of such other female helpers in the missionary work, as may be selected by the Board of Directors, with the approbation of the said Prudential Committee."

The example of this society led to the organization at Chicago, in October, 1868, of the "Woman's Board of Missions of the Interior," and of the "Woman's Board of Missions for the Pacific," at Santa Cruz, Cal., in 1873, to do a similar work in the regions of which they are the natural centers. These societies have planted auxiliaries throughout all the portion of the United States occupied in force by the Congregational churches, and the result has been not only a notable increase in missionary labors and contributions, but the extensive banding together of the young people of these churches for missionary instruction and effort. So successful has the movement been that similar organizations of women have been formed in forty-one States and Territories in aid of the several home missionary societies of Congregationalism, though these State bodies are not gathered in any national association.

The youngest of Congregational missionary organizations is the "New West Education Commission,"—a society formed at Chicago and incorporated in 1879, having as its aim "the promotion of Christian civilization in Utah and adjacent States and Territories, by the education of the children and youth under Christian teachers, and by the use of such other kindred agencies as may at any time be deemed wise." By 1892 this commission had 28 schools under its charge, employing 68 teachers, and instructing 2812 pupils; but its separate existence ceased in 1893, as has already been mentioned, though its work continues, it having been merged at that time in the "American Education Society."

The evident advantages which had flowed from the National Council of 1865, the impulse which it had given to Congregational advance, and the general wisdom of its actions, led to the widespread feeling throughout the Congregational body that such an assembly, without judicial authority but representative of the denomination as a whole and able therefore to voice its sentiments and discuss its needs, should be a permanent instead of an occasional feature of Congregational religious life. To a few, such a regularly recurring assembly seemed a possible menace to ecclesiastical independence; but the majority of the denomination were prepared to see in a permanent National Council only a fuller expression of that fellowship of the churches which Congregationalism has always regarded as one of the peculiar merits of its polity, and which the voluntary system of the nineteenth century has proved itself as well able to foster as the State supervision of the seventeenth century. This feeling found a voice through a convention to which the approach of the two hundred and fiftieth anniversary of the landing of the "Mayflower" Pilgrims at Plymouth gave occasion.

In order to devise a proper celebration of that important event in Congregational history, the Church of the Pilgrimage at Plymouth asked its sister-churches to send delegates to New York to consult regarding the method of commemoration. As a result of this invitation a meeting was held on March 2, 1870, and a committee to take suitable action was appointed, including such champions of Congregationalism as Rev. Drs. Dexter, Quint, and Patton. At their instance, a "Pilgrim Memorial Convention," to which representatives of all Congregational churches in the United States were bidden, assembled at Chicago on the 27th of the following April. In this convention the impulse toward a permanent National Council was strongly manifested, and it therefore voted to "recommend to the Congregational State Conferences and Associations, and to other local bodies, to unite in measures for instituting on the principle of fellowship, excluding ecclesiastical authority, a permanent National Conference."

Thus invited, the General Conference of Ohio appointed a committee, with Rev. Dr. A. H. Ross as its chairman, to correspond with other State bodies and perfect the plan. The suggestion met with general approval,—the steps were the same which had led to the National Council of 1865, —the various State organizations appointed committees, which, at the suggestion of the General Association of New York, met as a preliminary convention at Boston on December 21, 1870. To this preliminary convention it appeared "clearly to be the voice of the churches, that a National Council of the Congregational churches of the United States be organized." It therefore invited them to meet by delegates chosen substantially like the representatives to the Council of 1865, and intrusted the drafting of a constitution for submission to the Council-to-be, together with the designation of the time and place of meeting, to a committee of which Rev. Dr. Quint was chairman.

As a result of all these proceedings, a National Council assembled at Oberlin, O., on November 15, 1871, with an attendance of 276 delegates representative of the Congregational churches of twenty-five States and Territories, and adopted a constitution organizing a permanent triennial body. The more important sections of this document are as follows:

The Congregational churches of the United States, by elders and messengers assembled, do now associate themselves in National Council:

To express and foster their substantial unity in doctrine, polity, and work; and

To consult upon the common interests of all the churches, their duties in the work of evangelization, the united development of their resources, and their relations to all parts of the kingdom of Christ.

They agree in belief that the Holy Scriptures are the sufficient and only infallible rule of religious faith and practice; their interpretation thereof being in substantial accordance with the great doctrines of the Christian faith, commonly called evangelical, held in our churches from the early times, and sufficiently set forth by former General Councils.

They agree in the belief that the right of government resides in local churches, or congregations of believers, who are responsible directly to the Lord Jesus Christ, the One Head of the church universal and of all particular churches; but that all churches, being in communion one with another as parts of Christ's catholic church, have mutual duties subsisting in the obligations of fellowship.

The churches, therefore, while establishing this National Council for the furtherance of the common interests and work of all the churches, do maintain the Scriptural and inalienable right of each church to self-government and administration; and this National Council shall never exercise legislative or judicial authority, nor consent to act as a council of reference.

And for the convenience of orderly consultation, they establish the following Rules:

I. *Sessions.*—The churches will meet in National Council every third year. They shall also be convened in special session whenever any five of the general State organizations shall so request.

II. *Representation.*—The churches shall be represented, at each session, by delegates, either ministers or laymen, appointed in number and manner as follows:

1. The churches, assembled in their local organizations, appoint one delegate for every ten churches in their respective organizations, and one for a fraction of ten greater than one half, it being understood that whenever the churches of any State are directly united in a general organization, they may, at their option, appoint the delegates in such a body, instead of in local organizations, but in the above ratio of churches so united.

2. In addition to the above, the churches united in State organization appoint by such body one delegate, and one for each ten thousand communicants in their fellowship, and one for a major fraction thereof:—

3. It being recommended that the number of delegates be, in all cases, divided between ministers and laymen, as nearly equally as is practicable.

4. Such Congregational general societies for Christian work, and the faculties of such theological seminaries, as may be recognized by this Council, may be represented by one delegate each, such representatives having the right of discussion only.

At the same time the National Council formally expressed the desire of the Congregational churches to promote the unity of the whole Church of Christ, affirming that:

To us, as to our brethren, "There is one body and one spirit, even as we are called in one hope of our calling."

As little as did our fathers in their day, do we in ours, make a pretension to be the only churches of Christ. We find ourselves consulting and acting together under the distinctive name of Congregationalists, because, in the present condition of our common Christianity, we have felt ourselves called to ascertain and do our own appropriate part of the work of Christ's church among men.

We especially desire, in prosecuting the common work of evangelizing our own land and the world, to observe the common and sacred law, that in the wide field of the world's evangelization, we do our work in friendly coöperation with all those who love and serve our common Lord.

Possibly the doctrinal statements of the constitution are more important for what is there left unsaid than for what is distinctly affirmed. The expression "commonly called evangelical," taken in connection with the broad offer of coöperation with those who are engaged in the service of the common Master, was understood at the Council, and has since generally been held, to extend a welcome to those of Arminian beliefs, and to be but a further illustration of the widening sympathy which led to the omission of the word "Calvinism" from the Declaration of Faith adopted in 1865.

The National Council has enjoyed the good-will of the Congregational churches as a whole since its beginning. Attempts to prevent its regular recurrence and to limit its expression of opinion by vote were indeed made by the General Associations of New York and New Jersey through fear lest it become dangerous to Congregational liberty; but no such anxieties have been entertained by the churches in general, nor have the protesting Associations taken any permanent attitude of opposition. It has gained the hearty support of the whole Congregational body; and, to Congregational thinking, it has solved the problem of securing the advantages of discussion, coöperation, and expression of opinion, on a national scale, without the interference with local liberty, the imposition of tests by majority vote, and the sacrifice of the rights of the individual church, inevitable in any system of judicial assemblies. No church, or body of churches, is bound to follow the recommendations of the National Council; but its discussions and opinions have always commanded respect and have had constantly increasing influence over the churches and the missionary societies through which their benevolences are administered. The National Council has led to more perfect adjustment of the relations of the various Congregational missionary organizations; it has relieved friction in their work; it has set in motion impulses which have made some of them more directly representative of the churches in their management, and which have brought about at least the beginnings of consolidation; it has systematized the statistics of the churches; and has undertaken the relief of disabled ministers, and of the destitute widows and orphans of those who die in the service of the churches. It has been efficient in promoting that hearty sympathy and cordial good-fellowship between the Congregational churches of all sections of the country which has been a growing feature of their life since the Albany Convention of 1852.

Probably the most noteworthy single effort of the National Council, however, has been the gift to the Congregational churches of a new Confession of Faith, expressive of the present theologic position of the denomination. Though generally approved by Congregationalists as a fitting presentation of the sentiments of the time and place and of the broad principles of which the denomination is the representative, the "Burial Hill Declaration" was too rhetorical in form and too indefinite in statement as to particular doctrines, as well as too sweeping in its approval of seventeenth-century formulations of belief, to be satisfactory as a creed for local churches or as an exposition of the faith of the Congregational body as a whole. The desire for a new and simple expression of faith was manifested at the National Council in 1871; but the impulse that led directly to its preparation went out from the Ohio Association, which, having considered the matter at its sessions of 1879 and 1880, laid before the Council in the latter year the question of the issue of a "formula that shall not be mainly a reaffirmation of former confessions, but that shall state in precise terms in our living tongue the doctrines that we hold to-day." At the same session of the National Council, similar requests were presented from the General Conference of Minnesota, and a Conference in Tennessee. Thus approached, the National Council on November 15, 1880, appointed a committee of seven to select twenty-five Commissioners, "representing different shades of thought," and widely distributed geographically, to prepare a creed. The Council left the members of this Commission free to adopt their own methods of proceeding, only stipulating, "that the result of their labors, when complete, be reported—not to this Council, but to the churches and to the world through the public press—to carry such weight of authority as the character of the Commission and the intrinsic merit of their exposition of truth may command."

The Commission thus selected was probably as thoroughly

representative of Congregationalism as any twenty-five ministers and theological instructors who could have been named; and the result of their careful deliberations was the publication, on December 19, 1883, of what has been usually called the "Creed of 1883." The confession bore the approving signatures of twenty-two of the twenty-five commissioners. Three refused their names; two of them deeming the symbol an inadequate expression of their views, and the third on account of absence from the meetings of the Commission. But though the "Creed of 1883" still has its occasional critics, it is, what the Commission was directed to make it, a simple, compact statement, in modern language, of the present beliefs of the Congregational churches. It is not binding on the churches any further than they choose to adopt it as a local expression of faith; but its use has been steadily increasing; and it gives the denomination, what no other considerable religious body in America possesses,—a widely recognized creed, of modern composition, and expressing a fair consensus of the present belief of the communion whose faith it sets forth.

The story of modern American Congregationalism is thus one of increasing denominational strength, of growing conviction of its own mission, and of more manifest fellowship and coöperation between its churches. At the same time this development has been accompanied by a hearty spirit of brotherhood toward other bodies which bear the Christian name and hold similar evangelical doctrines.

The past ten or fifteen years have brought the Congregational churches, as they have all other American religious bodies, face to face with much that is novel in doctrine and method; and the new tendencies of theologic discussion and of the practical application of the gospel to men have been viewed with as much interest by Congregationalists as by any class of American Christians. While the presentations of Christian truth which were characteristic of the first three quarters of this century have not been abandoned, the emphasis in doctrinal discussion of late years has shifted from questions of the atonement, of ability, and of sin, such as held a chief place in the debates of that period, to problems of the nature of inspiration, of Old Testament criticism, and of the future state. In a similar way the burden of discussion in regard to methods of Christian activity has to some extent come to rest on what are called the larger interests of the kingdom of Christ, the broad application of the gospel to the social condition of mankind, and much interest has been developed in "Christian Sociology." This alteration of emphasis is not peculiar to Congregationalism, it is characteristic of the age.

Naturally this change in the topics of debate, especially in regard to doctrine, while not substantially altering the views or the teachings of the denomination as a whole, has been productive of considerable controversy and has given rise in places to marked divergencies of opinion, without seriously threatening the interruption of Congregational fellowship, or the organic unity of the denomination. While the great body of the Congregational churches have not entered into the debate, two wings have developed, especially in eastern Massachusetts, which for want of better titles may be designated as progressive and conservative. The most marked exhibition of this divergence has been in regard to Andover Seminary,—an institution which has been more affected by the change of interest in the topics of doctrinal discussion and more responsive to the thought of European theologians than any other Congregational seat of learning. As has already been pointed out, the orthodoxy of its teachers is tested by a creed prepared by the "Associate Founders" and approved by the "Founders" before the opening of the Seminary; and the application of this test lies in the hands of the Board of Visitors. Though substantial departure from their creed was denied by the Andover faculty, it seemed to certain of the alumni of the institution that such essential modification of the historic standard had actually taken place; and at a meeting on December 28, 1885, they resolved to make complaint to the Board of Visitors against the published views of several of the professors. The result was a formal trial of charges involving five instructors before the Visitors at Boston, beginning just a year later, and the declaration by the Visitors on June 16, 1887, that Prof. E. C. Smyth, the president of the faculty, was removed from his chair of instruction. From this decision appeal was taken, as permitted by the terms of the Andover foundation, to the Massachusetts Supreme Court. After elaborate and complicated judicial proceedings, that tribunal, on October 28, 1891, set aside the finding of the Visitors on technical grounds, without passing on the questions involved in the controversy. Motion for a new trial before the Visitors having been made, and a further hearing of the parties involved having been held, that Board, on September 6, 1892, dismissed the complaint, now nearly seven years old, holding that further procedure on charges of such antiquity was not likely to be productive of good, but "without thereby expressing any opinion upon the merits of the case."

Nearly parallel with this discussion, but somewhat different in the questions involved and to some extent unlike in the parties to the controversy, a debate concerning the policy of the American Board in making missionary appointments has run its course. The doctrinal ferment, out of which the Andover trials were to grow, had been felt for several years previous to the presentation of the complaints against the Andover faculty; and certain features of what was called by its friends the "new theology" excited alarm among the more conservative thinkers of the Congregational body. Probably the view most popularly deemed characteristic of that theology was a speculation as to a possible contact with the Saviour and his forgiving grace in the future life for those who, like the heathen, had no opportunity for knowledge of the historic Christ in this world,—a view commonly called "future probation."

These speculations were first brought into the arena of discussion in the American Board at its annual meeting at Portland, Me., in 1882, where Rev. Dr. E. P. Goodwin, of Chicago, and Professor Park, then an *emeritus* member of the Andover faculty, denounced them as fatal to the missionary spirit. There was no general debate, however, at this meeting; and for the next three years the topic did not prominently enter into the discussions of the annual gatherings of the Board. But meanwhile the Home Secretary of the Board, by whom correspondence with intended missionaries was conducted, had pressed inquiry into the possible belief of candidates in these speculations; and the Prudential Committee, which has the power of appointment, had, it was alleged, rejected several because of lack of definiteness of conviction on the points involved, or full acceptance of the questioned theories. As a result, the matter came up with great earnestness of debate at the annual meeting of the Board at Des Moines, Ia., in 1886; and eventuated there in a vote declaring that the body was "constrained to look with grave apprehension upon certain tendencies of the doctrine of a probation after death" as "divisive and perversive and dangerous to the churches at home and abroad," and approving the action of the Prudential Committee. At the same time the Board instructed the Prudential Committee to consider the wisdom of inviting a council of the churches for advice in perplexing questions as to the views of missionary candidates.

The decision at Des Moines was not, however, felt to be final. Though it undoubtedly represented the desires of a majority of the churches at the time, a large and increasing party, who had no sympathy with the disputed theories, felt that the emphasis laid on doctrinal examination by the Prudential Committee and the Home Secretary was undue, and that a Board which carried on the foreign mission work of all the churches should be ready to welcome candidates to its fields of labor whom ecclesiastical councils were willing to install in home pulpits. But a yet larger party felt that any toleration of doubt regarding the truths of the debated speculations was dangerous. One or two cases of rejection by the Committee after the Des Moines meeting, notably that of Mr. William H. Noyes, increased rather than diminished the warmth of feeling; and the meeting of the Board at Springfield, Mass., in 1887, was a scene of even more animated discussion than that at Des Moines. The majority secured the reaffirmation of the Des Moines resolutions and the approval of the action of the Prudential Committee by a vote of more than two to one; and at the same time a report of that Committee disapproving of the reference to councils of cases of doubtful orthodoxy in missionary candidates was adopted. The Board at this meeting chose Rev. Dr. R. S. Storrs its president; and a few days later he signified his acceptance in a letter approving in the main the results reached at Des Moines and Springfield, but intimating that the Committee ought "to discriminate between the want of an opinion and the presence of one which implies or favors the objectionable theory; between even a vague hope, acknowledged to be unsupported by the Scripture, only personal to one's self, held in silent submission to subsequent correction, and a distinct dogmatic tendency or a formulated conviction."

For the next two years comparatively little of importance occurred. Mr. Noyes, who seemed to many to come within President Storrs's permissible category, was once more rejected by the Prudential Committee, and was sent to Japan as an independent laborer by the Berkeley Temple Church of Boston. Feeling grew, and when the Board met at New York in 1889 a heated discussion ensued, which resulted, however, in the unanimous acceptance of President Storrs's letter as a basis for action, and in the appointment of a committee of nine, under the chairmanship of Rev. Dr. G. L. Walker, of Hartford, to examine into the methods of administration pursued by the officers of the Board in relation to candidates. This committee made its report at the meeting at Minneapolis, Minn., in 1890, and unanimously recommended that the secretaries of the Board, in dealing with applicants for appointment, should be limited to two prescribed doctrinal questions: "1. What are your views respecting each of the leading doctrines of Scripture commonly held by the churches sustaining this Board? In answering this question, you may use your own language or refer to any creeds of acknowledged weight. 2. Have you any views at variance with these doctrines or any views of church government which would prevent your cordial coöperation with the missionaries of this Board?" All further doctrinal examination, it was recommended, should be conducted by the Prudential Committee itself, in the presence of such members of the Board and personal friends of the candidate as desired to attend. These suggestions were duly adopted by the Board, with a modification permitting the Prudential Committee to substitute correspondence for a personal examination when such personal meeting seemed impracticable.

For some time after this action at Minneapolis it was generally believed that friction in the Board had been practically ended, and the meeting of 1891 passed without a word of criticism or doctrinal debate. But the feeling was manifested in some quarters that the Prudential Committee and the secretaries had failed fully to carry out the Minneapolis resolutions or to act entirely on the basis of President Storrs's letter, and though it was denied that such charges were well founded, the question was reopened at the meeting at Chicago in 1892. Here the Board refused to make void its vote passed at Des Moines in 1886; but the minority was strong enough to lead to the passage of a resolution instructing the Committee to interpret that vote with liberality as well as with faithfulness. At the same time the Board asked its Prudential Committee to canvass anew the appointment of Mr. Noyes, whose record as a missionary in Japan had proved most creditable. But, though the Committee reopened the case, though it was shown that the missionaries of the Board in Japan desired Mr. Noyes as an associate, and that he had never taught the questioned speculation on the mission field, the Committee rejected Mr. Noyes for a third time, on his statement that his views had undergone no substantial alteration. The opinion of the churches, however, was increasingly in favor of his appointment on the ground of his efficient service, and when the Board met at Worcester, Mass., in October, 1893, this feeling was plainly manifest. A widely representative committee of fifteen, under the chairmanship of Hon. H. D. Hyde, of Boston, unanimously recommended "that this Board, in response to the expressed wish of its missionaries in Japan, and in recognition of the successful labors of the Rev. William H. Noyes in that empire, requests the Prudential Committee to offer to him an appointment as a missionary of the Board. The Board declares that this action is not to be understood as in any way modifying its former utterances on the subject of future probation;" and the Board adopted the suggestion by a vote of 106 to 24. This action was followed by the presentation and acceptance of the resignations of the Home Secretary, Rev. Dr. E. K. Alden, and of two honored members of the Prudential Committee; but within a few weeks the appointment thus offered was accepted by Mr. Noyes.

This long discussion led to an increasing desire that the Board should be made in some way more directly representative of the churches in the choice of its membership, —a desire that found expression in the appointment by the National Council in 1889 of a committee to consider the relations of all the benevolent societies to the Congregational churches. And so general was the feeling that an efficient representation of the churches in the Board should be brought about that this committee was able to report to the Council in 1892 that, since its appointment, twenty-one State bodies, embracing nearly three fourths of the churches of the denomination, had taken action favoring such a change. Urged thus by many State organizations widely representative of Congregationalism, the Board, at its meeting at Chicago in 1892, voted to try for one year the experiment of filling three fourths of the vacancies occurring in the ranks of its now self-perpetuating corporation from nominations made by the State bodies, the understanding being that the number of appointments to be made from any State should be proportionate to the membership and gifts of its churches. At Worcester, in 1893, the Board resolved to continue the experiment for two years more, and to increase its membership at the rate of twenty-five a year till it numbered one hundred more than at present (i.e., to 350). This system, or some better device, will doubtless be permanently adopted; and will make the Board in future directly representative of the churches in membership, as it has been in spirit during most of its past history.

The past few years which have witnessed this shifting in the topics of doctrinal discussion in Congregational circles have also beheld the introduction to some extent of new methods of Christian activity. Congregationalism is always favorable to individual initiative. A Congregational church can try any new plan of labor or order of worship without seeking the permission of any superior body. It lends itself flexibly to experiments, possessing the merits of ready adaptability to environment as thoroughly as they are enjoyed by similar systems of local self-government in the political world. One such experiment, introduced by a Congregational pastor, has become a movement of almost world-wide extent. On February 2, 1881, Rev. F. E. Clark, then pastor of the Williston Church at Portland, Me., organized a number of his young people who were desirous of beginning the Christian life into an association pledged to regular attendance upon and participation in its meetings, and distinctly coöperant in the activities of the church. The "Young People's Society of Christian Endeavor," which thus came into being, has been adopted by many other Christian bodies besides the Congregational churches, and has had an amazing growth, numbering within twelve years of its origin nearly twenty-eight thousand societies, with 1,650,000 members.

Another novel method of Christian work with which some Congregational churches have experimented, as they believe with encouraging results, during the last few years, is what is rather infelicitously called the "institutional church." Such a church aims not merely to unite its members in worship, Christian nurture, and benevolence by the ordinary channels of endeavor, but to touch the surrounding community at many points, providing reading-rooms, gymnasiums, and bowling-alleys, clubs for boys and girls, healthful amusement and instruction for the tempted and the homeless, all designed to make the gospel more effective in the upbuilding of an upright, self-respecting, Christian manhood and womanhood. Such extension of their work has been undertaken within a recent period by churches in Boston, Worcester, Hartford, Jersey City, Cleveland, and elsewhere; and though the movement is still so far in its initial stage that it is impossible to estimate its permanent value, it is of interest as illustrating the ready employment by the Congregational churches of any worthy methods of effort which seem to promise the furtherance of their main aim—the upbuilding of the kingdom of God.

A similar ready response to the broader aspects of the application of the gospel to human needs is to be seen in the recent introduction of sociological instruction into Congregational theological seminaries, and the incorporation of practical experience in the workings of preventative, reformatory, charitable, and evangelistic agencies as exhibited in the cities, as a part of the prescribed ministerial training. Harvard University led the way by offering elective studies in social ethics to the students of its Divinity School in 1880, and like courses were opened for the choice of the students at Andover in 1887. Hartford Seminary in 1888 became the first American theological school to require some knowledge of sociological principles as essential to graduation; and similar instruction became part of the course at Chicago in 1890, where the study was first made a separate department of instruction. At Yale Divinity School Christian sociology was introduced as an elective in 1892, and in the autumn of 1894 will become a fully established department of seminary work. Student residence in portions of large cities where the problems of poverty and crime are most pressing has been provided for the young men of Andover Seminary by the "Andover House" in Boston, and for those of Chicago Seminary in connection with the "Hull House" of that city. Nor has this interest been confined to the seminaries. Iowa College,—the long-established Congregational center of education in the State from which it takes its title,—has recently founded a chair of Applied Christianity; and the "Northwestern Congregationalist" of Minneapolis has become the representative of this new movement under the altered title of "The Kingdom" since the beginning of the year 1894. Here, again, it is too soon to form an opinion as to the permanency or value of the tendency; but it evidences the quick response of the Congregational churches and their institutions to all that is stirring the thoughts of Christian men.

A further illustration of the same ready adaptability of Congregationalism to novel methods is to be seen in its increasing employment of women in the more public aspects of Christian work. The organization of the Woman's Boards of Missions has already been described, and through their impulse not only are the women of the churches largely banded together for the support of missionary endeavor, the number of women workers on the fields of missionary labor at home and abroad is great and constantly increasing. Thus far these women have been almost exclusively employed in teaching, the healing of the sick, and the less distinctively ministerial functions; but the

"Vermont Domestic Missionary Society" has during the last two or three summers employed Christian young women to go about two by two in the remoter and more sparsely settled districts of the State, to all practical purposes as evangelists. The "Year Book" for 1893 reports the names of not less than thirteen women as ministerial licentiates, mostly in States west of the Mississippi. But women have gone further than this primary permission to exercise the gift of preaching. In 1880 the church at Nantucket, Mass., came under a woman's charge, though she was not reported as ordained. In 1893, however, the "Year Book" enumerated nine fully ordained women, in various towns in New York, Ohio, Illinois, Wisconsin, Iowa, South Dakota, and Washington,—seven of whom were in pastoral charge of Congregational churches. Of these all except one had been ordained since 1889. On February 14, 1894, the first ordination of a woman over a Congregational church in New England occurred at Littleton, Mass.,—the first settlement of a person of her sex effected by a council in the history of American Congregationalism. In most of these cases the circumstances have been somewhat exceptional, and such ordinations cannot now be called good Congregational usage, whatever they may become in process of time.

This desire to train and to employ women in a wide range of Christian activities appears also in the opening of the doors of Hartford Seminary in 1889 to women on the same terms as to men. It was not, indeed, the intention of the seminary to encourage women to enter the ordained ministry, and none of its students of this sex have done so; but it desired to offer whatever advantages it had to give to those who might add strength to the Christian life of the time as scholars, teachers, laborers in philanthropic enterprises, pastors' assistants, or missionaries.

Congregationalism at the present day is active in many directions. It is not afraid to try experiments, to discuss doctrinal truths, and to test methods of work. But whatever of novelty in method or in thought it may here and there exhibit, it never was more true to the main principles of faith and practice which it has inherited than at present, or more conscious of a mission to a sinning and suffering world.

CHAPTER XI.

CONGREGATIONAL FACTS AND TRAITS.

CONGREGATIONALISM, as a form of polity, is much more widely extended in the United States than the communion which bears the Congregational name. Though differing from one another in the details of their administration of this type of organization, especially in the extent to which the principle of the fellowship, as distinguished from the self-government of the churches, is developed, the Congregational polity is that of a large portion of the religious bodies of America. As Dr. Carroll has pointed out in the first volume of this series, the Baptists, the Plymouth Brethren, the Christians, the Disciples of Christ, the Unitarians, as well as a number of minor religious bodies, are essentially Congregational in government. This is also true of certain sections of the Adventists, of the Lutherans, and all the Hebrew congregations, so that the same authority classifies no less than 62,373 religious organizations,—nearly 38 per cent. of all congregations in the United States,—as of this polity.

But while the Congregational system of church government is thus widely diffused, and while other polities not distinctly Congregational have in many instances been modified in the United States from their European originals by the introduction of some Congregational elements, the body known as the Congregational churches has a distinct unity and history. It represents something more than a form of church government. It is characterized by a high degree of unity in doctrinal development, by a marked desire for learning both in the ministry and in the laity, by similar modes of worship, and above all, by a visible oneness of fellowship manifested in advisory councils and in occasional or regularly recurring assemblies for consultation. The Congregational churches therefore constitute a distinct religious whole,—as marked in its characteristics as any religious denomination in America.

The Congregational churches have not increased as rapidly in numbers as some religious communions, but their growth has been continuous and sure. During the first two centuries of their existence on American soil they were practically confined to New England; they have since spread into all parts of the United States, but largely with the diffusion of the New England element of our population. Beginning with a single church in 1620, the fellowship numbered about 53 congregations by the time of the Cambridge Synod (1646–48). Though minutely accurate statistics are wanting, it is thought that by 1696 the number of churches had increased to at least 160, including the congregations among the Indians. In 1760 Rev. (and later President) Ezra Stiles numbered the churches at 530; by 1845 they had multiplied to 1471, with 1412 ordained ministers; 1860 saw 2583 churches, with 2634 ministers; in 1870 the churches numbered 3121, and the ministers, 3098; in 1880 there were 3745 churches, with 3577 ministers. The census of 1890 reported the number of the Congregational churches as 4868, their ministers, 5058, and their members as 512,771. At the beginning of 1894 these churches were 5236 in number, their ordained ministers 5138, their licentiates about 400, and their membership 561,641. In 1894 these churches enrolled 646,694 persons in their Sunday-schools.

The missionary labors of these churches are carried on

by six national societies,—the "American Board of Commissioners for Foreign Missions," which conducts the efforts of the churches for the upbuilding of the Redeemer's kingdom in other lands; the "American Education Society," having as its object the assistance of needy students for the ministry, the upbuilding of colleges, and the maintenance of schools, especially in the newer districts of the West; the "Congregational Home Missionary Society," conducting home missionary labors in all parts of the United States, but chiefly in the North and West; the "American Missionary Association," laboring for the most part in the South and among the Indians and Chinese; the "Congregational Church Building Society," aiming to supply needy congregations with meeting-houses and parsonages; and the "Congregational Sunday-school and Publishing Society," which not only prints Christian literature, but carries on as a separate department an extensive mission work in planting and supporting Sunday-schools, especially in the newer parts of the country. Besides these six societies, two other organizations have a claim on the churches as a whole,—the "American Congregational Association," in charge of the Congregational Library and House at Boston; and the "Ministerial Relief Fund," for the aid of disabled ministers, their widows and orphans. These societies are assisted by the Woman's Boards and Unions and numerous State and local auxiliaries; and almost every church of self-sustaining proportions has its "sewing-society," or some similar local organization for the furtherance of missionary activity. As a result, the benevolent contributions of the churches to these societies and through other channels for the year 1893 amounted to $2,401,896. During the same annual period the legacies reported as bequeathed to the same objects reached the sum of $947,311; and the home expenses of the churches were reported as $7,000,838.

Modern Congregationalism has few representatives who would claim, as did the early teachers of the polity which these churches inherit, that its system is of exclusive divine authority. There have been prominent expounders of its polity within recent years who have held a *jure divino* conception of its claims. But, unlike the founders, the great majority of modern Congregationalists fail to find in the New Testament any minute outline of what the church should be or any inflexible pattern to which it must in all particulars conform. They gladly recognize the true churchly character of organizations illustrating other types of church government than their own. As far as possible they hold fellowship with all believers in Christ, however constituted. But while they thus fail to discover any hard-and-fast prescription of polity in the New Testament, they do find there certain broad principles applicable to individual and to churchly life, which they believe are better illustrated under the Congregational polity than under any other. They believe that that polity, more naturally than any other, tends to make the Christian disciple what the gospel intended he should be, a full-rounded, self-reliant, free man in Christ. They are confident that it best trains the individual Christian to an independent, intelligent, and responsible spiritual life. They also deem it more accordant with the genius of the political institutions of a free republic like the United States than any other form of polity, and hence peculiarly adapted to all lands where high intelligence and local self-government are characteristic of the people.

But, in particular, a Congregational church that is at all true to its ideal illustrates certain traits which Congregationalists hold to be of prime importance. It aims, first of all, to be a pure church. The belief that the proper material of a church should be regenerate persons has been characteristic of Congregationalism from the beginning. Though modified in regard to one sacrament in the Half-Way Covenant which prevailed in New England for a century and a half, it has always been the view of Congregationalism that admission to the full churchly privileges of communion and of voting is only for those who can claim a Christian experience. And with the abandonment of the Half-Way Covenant the belief of modern Congregationalism, though it ascribes potential membership to the baptized children of the congregation, holds that personal followers of the Lord Jesus are the only proper active members of a church. It finds no other type of a Christian church in the New Testament, it conceives no other to be really desirable. Such a local company of believers it holds now, as Congregationalism has held from the beginning, becomes a church by entering into a covenant to serve God and to aid one another in the Christian life. At the same time it maintains that all believers throughout the world are spiritually, though not governmentally, one body,—the church universal,—of which, as of each local church, Christ is the immediate head.

A true Congregational church is a learned church. This also has been a trait of the denomination from the beginning. Congregationalism believes that a learned ministry is the only permanently successful ministry; but it deems the intelligence of the pews no less important for the well-being of the church than that of the pulpit. A spiritual democracy, like a political democracy, requires self-control and wisdom in its membership for its best usefulness. This sense of the essential character of these qualities has led Congregationalism to plant colleges and schools from the time of its first generation on New England soil to its latest missionary endeavors, side by side with its churches. Yet it is not of the opinion that these schools of learning should be controlled by any sectarian bias. It willingly fosters education by the State, but it believes that all education should be dominated by a broadly Christian spirit. It holds that scholastic advantages should be open to all, irrespective of color or race; and it regards the school as a missionary agency only secondary in value to the preaching of the gospel.

A Congregational church is also a missionary church. In this particular the story of Congregationalism is one of increasing strength. Its missionary spirit did indeed appear in its efforts for the Indians in the seventeenth and eighteenth centuries; but the opportunities for such labors were slight, and no portion of Protestant Christendom had yet awakened to a full sense of obligation to the heathen world. But Congregationalism has always had men of a missionary impulse, like Eliot, the Mayhews, Edwards, or Brainerd; and with the new revival epoch which began in the closing years of the last century, missionary zeal became one of the conspicuous traits of the Congregational body as a whole. No duty of the gospel is more clearly recognized by the churches of this denomination at the present day than that of carrying the gospel to foreign lands and to the destitute regions of our own country; and Congregational self-government has clearly demonstrated that the full control enjoyed by a local church over its own affairs does not impair a feeling of wide obligation or prevent union with other churches of the same fellowship in the support of highly organized missionary endeavor.

A Congregational church is likewise a democratic church. It believes that all its membership, whether in the pulpit or the pews, are brethren, and are equally concerned in its welfare and administration. But the Congregational churches have not always been as democratic as they now are. As has been pointed out in the course of this history, Browne's early democratic theories speedily gave place to the semi-aristocratic administrative conceptions of Barrowe; and these Barrowist ideals dominated all early New England practice. But it has also been seen that the American development of Congregationalism led to full democracy by the beginning of the present century. A Congregational church regards its pastor as the first among his brethren, the leader of its worship, the director of its labors, the moderator of its meetings; but with no power to command obedience. It is the church, not the pastor, that decides regarding admissions, dismissions, and excommunications, that formulates articles of faith and rules of procedure, that determines as to representation in councils, that appoints officers and committees. Doubtless the voice of the pastor is usually decisive when he makes his opinion known; but the decision rests in the hands of the church, not in his. And this decision is voiced by the votes of the membership. Till well into this century voting was a privilege only possessed by male members of adult years; but the general usage of the Congregational churches now extends it to all members of maturity, both men and women, without very strictly inquiring whether they have attained a legal majority. At the same time, like all democratic bodies, the Congregational churches make large use of committees to handle any specially difficult business and to report their results rather than their processes for the approval of the church. Most churches of size have a "Prudential Committee," which naturally includes the deacons, to aid the pastor and to conduct with him the examination of candidates for membership; but all such committees are viewed as possessed of power simply by delegation from the church to which they owe their being.

A Congregational church is, moreover, a free church. The self-governing constitution of each local church has been a cardinal principle of Congregational polity from its beginning. No Congregational church is under the dominance of any other ecclesiastical organization or person. This freedom enables such a church to choose its own officers. Though Congregational practice esteems it good order that a minister be placed in pastoral charge of a congregation by the advice of the representatives of neighboring churches gathered in council, the ultimate basis of the relationship, in modern as in early Congregationalism, is his election by the church, and his acceptance of the choice. So fundamental is this principle that modern Congregational usage esteems a man a pastor who is in the service of a church by its definite vote, even if no council has been called to advise on his installation,—though it deems such a relation less regular than when "settled by council." In the same way a church has entire freedom to elect its deacons, or add to them any other officers which it may desire, and in these cases modern Congregationalism recognizes no occasion for advice from the representatives of other churches gathered in council.

This freedom also enables a church to formulate its statement of doctrine in its own words. Congregationalism originated in the belief that the Bible is a sufficient and an authoritative exposition of polity as well as of doctrine, and it has at all times held that the conformity of its beliefs and practices to the Word of God is of prime importance; but it has allowed each church to express its conception of Christian truth in its own way. Such expressions become tests for membership in the local church which adopts them in so far as that church desires to use them for such a purpose. At the same time, as has already been pointed out, the Congregational churches in their representative gatherings have never hesitated to present their faith in public confessions, but such general confessions are not binding on any local church unless adopted by its own act. They are witnesses to the faith of the churches in general, not tests of ministerial fitness.

This freedom likewise enables a church to order its worship as seems most fitting to its members. The founders of the Congregational churches in the United States came out from the liturgical system of the Church of England into what they rightly deemed the liberty of unprescribed form and unfettered, or, as they said, "unstinted," prayer. They rejoiced in their freedom of access to God in public worship in words of supplication or thanksgiving suited to the actual experiences of the hour. Indeed, many of them doubted the rightfulness of the use of a rigid liturgy at all; and the Prayer-Book seems to have been one of the rarest of volumes in early New England libraries. Congregationalism, as a whole, has always found the liberty of a non-liturgical worship congenial to its taste and adapted to its spiritual profit. But no prescription prevents any church that finds beauty and appropriateness in appointed forms of supplication or common confessions of faith from employing these methods of worship if it sees fit; nor does any rule ordain the exact form or proportion of the various elements entering into public worship. Each church is free to adapt its methods to its own necessities. There has been throughout the recent history of the denomination a constant tendency to increase the variety of the services of the house of God by larger use of music, by responsive reading of portions of Holy Writ, by the employment of printed outlines and forms of worship; but these modifications have not deprived the sermon and the unwritten petition of the central place in Congregational worship which they have always occupied. There is also noticeable in many churches an increasing observance of the greater memorial days of the Christian year,—Christmas, Good Friday, and Easter,—days which the fathers carefully left unmarked. There is likewise a tendency in some quarters in the Congregational body, as in some other denominations, to introduce of late the recognition of certain special days not accepted by the church universal, like "Children's Sunday,"—a form of calendar for the Christian year much less to be desired than the observance of days which have been considered for ages commemorative of the earthly life of our Lord. But none of these movements have gone far enough to alter the general character of Congregational worship, which is still essentially non-liturgical, and still regards Sunday as the most sacred of all ecclesiastical days and the only one the observance of which is binding upon the Christian. Modern Congregationalism makes large use of the prayer-meeting, in which, besides the minister, the male members generally, and in some places their feminine associates, are encouraged to take part. But each Congregational church is free to choose the number and nature of its services, and to adapt them as best it can to its own wants and the necessities of the community where it is placed.

A Congregational church is, finally, bound together in mutually responsible fellowship with other churches of the same denomination. This feature of American Congregationalism is probably the trait least understood by the representatives of other communions; but it is that which most distinguishes the Congregationalists of the United States from the Independents of Great Britain, and from most of the other denominations of America which are essentially Congregational in polity. The Congregational churches of the United States developed the principle of fellowship in early colonial days, and they have ever regarded it as of the highest value. They believe that each local church has Christ as its immediate head, and stands in a sisterly relation to every other similar congregation. They believe that, like the members of an earthly household, while they have no right to sit in judgment one on another or to punish one another, they owe to one another counsel in difficulty, consultation in important action, and warning when in apparent error. They hold that, as brothers and sisters may be compelled to cease communication with a sinning member of a human family, so sister-churches, having failed to call back an erring church from its evil practices, may withdraw fellowship from it while it continues in its way. The expression of this fellowship is chiefly through advisory councils, consisting of the pastors and delegates of churches, and often, though rather by courtesy, of a few additional individuals, summoned to give their opinion in cases of ministerial settlement and dismission, ordinations, the organization of new churches, or difficulties arising in a congregation. A council may be called by a church, a party in a church in case of quarrel, or a company of persons desirous of being recognized as a church. It may consist of the representatives of any churches which may be invited and may choose to accept; but it is not considered good usage in modern Congregational practice to call the majority of its members from elsewhere than the immediate vicinage. No church or person not named in the invitation, or "letter-missive," may have a seat in a council, nor can any business be discussed that is not specified in the same warrant, nor has the council a proper quorum unless a majority of the possible members invited are present. Its advice is not a binding judicial decision, but a friendly counsel; yet instances where the opinion of a council is not followed are exceedingly rare.

Congregationalism further illustrates the fellowship of its churches by their union all over the United States in district conferences and associations, in State bodies, and finally in the National Council, for consultation at fixed periods. These various expressions of fellowship knit the Congregational churches into one body, while preserving to each local congregation the rights of self-government and individual initiative.

Congregationalism has had a history of over three hundred years since its beginnings in England. It has been more than two centuries and a half on American soil. It settled and molded New England; and through its influence on the political institutions of that region it has contributed far beyond any other polity to the fashioning of the political ideals of the United States. It has sought more than any other polity on American soil to promote education. It has been forward in missionary activity. It has maintained a high, strenuous ideal of the Christian life. It has been a prime force in the political, intellectual, and spiritual development of America. But while its adherents are thankful for the heritage of noble men and worthy deeds into which they have entered, they believe that it has a greater mission yet to perform than anything which it has done in the past. They believe that while the Congregational body may never become the largest of the tribes of our American Israel in its nominal communion, its principles of democracy, freedom, self-government, and responsible fellowship will increasingly penetrate and mold all American Christian life; and they are confident, also, that, under the guidance of the Divine Spirit, its story will be one of growing numerical strength, usefulness, and spiritual power as the years are added to its history.

INDEX.

The American Church History Series.

BY SUBSCRIPTION, ... IN THIRTEEN VOLUMES, AT $2.50 PER VOLUME

Vol. I.	The Religious Forces of the United States,	H. K. CARROLL, LL.D., Editor of The Independent, Supt. Church Statistics, U. S. Census, etc.
Vol. II.	Baptists, ...	REV. A. H. NEWMAN, D.D., LL.D., Professor of Church History, McMaster University of Toronto, Ont.
Vol. III.	Congregationalists, .	REV. WILLISTON WALKER, Ph.D., Professor of Modern Church History, Theological Seminary, Hartford, Conn.
Vol. IV.	Lutherans, .	REV. H. E. JACOBS, D.D., LL.D., Professor of Systematic Theology in the Ev. Lutheran Seminary, Phila., Pa.
Vol. V.	Methodists, . .	REV. J. M. BUCKLEY, D.D., LL.D., Editor of the New York Christian Advocate.
Vol. VI.	Presbyterians, . . .	REV. ROBERT ELLIS THOMPSON, D.D., Philadelphia, Pa.
Vol. VII.	Protestant Episcopal, .	REV. C. C. TIFFANY, D.D., New York.
Vol. VIII.	Reformed Church, Dutch,	REV. E. T. CORWIN, D.D., Rector Hertzog Hall, New Brunswick, N.J.
	Reformed Church, German,	REV. J. H. DUBBS, D.D., Professor of History, Franklyn and Marshall College, Lancaster, Pa.
	Moravian, ...	REV. J. T. HAMILTON, D.D., Professor of Church History, Theological Seminary, Bethlehem, Pa.
Vol. IX.	Roman Catholics, .	REV. T. O'GORMAN, D.D., Professor of Church History, Catholic University, Washington, D. C.
Vol. X.	Unitarians, . .	REV. J. H. ALLEN, D.D., Late Lecturer on Ecclesiastical History, Harvard University, Cambridge, Mass.
	Universalists, . .	REV. RICHARD EDDY, D.D., Providence, R. I.
Vol. XI.	M. E. Church, So.,	REV. GROSS ALEXANDER, D.D., Professor Greek and N. T. Exegesis, Nashville, Tenn.
	Presbyterians, So., . .	REV. THOMAS C. JOHNSON, D.D., Professor Ecclesiastical History and Polity, Hampden-Sidney, Va.
	United Presbyterians, .	REV. JAMES B. SCOULLER, D.D., Newville, Pa.
	Cumb. Presbyterians, .	REV. R. V. FOSTER, D.D., Professor Biblical Exegesis, Cumberland University, Lebanon, Tenn.
Vol. XII.	Disciples, . .	REV. R. B. TYLER, D.D., New York.
	Friends	Prof. A. C. THOMAS, M.A., Haverford College, Haverford, Pa. R. H. THOMAS, M.D., Baltimore, Md.
	United Brethren, . .	REV. D. BERGER, D.D., Dayton, Ohio
	Ev. Association, .	REV. S. P. SPRENG, Editor Evangelical Messenger, Cleveland, Ohio.
	Bibliography, . . .	REV. SAMUEL MACAULEY JACKSON, New York.
Vol. XIII.	History of American Christianity, . . .	REV. LEONARD WOOLSEY BACON, D.D.

www.ingramcontent.com/pod-product-compliance
Lightning Source LLC
Chambersburg PA
CBHW031821270326
41932CB00008B/501
* 9 7 8 3 3 3 7 7 6 6 9 6 2 *